PENGUIN BOOKS

HOW TO BE A VICTORIAN

Ruth Goodman is a historian who specializes in the social and domestic life of Britain. She works with a wide range of museums and other academic institutions, exploring the past of ordinary people and their activities. She has presented a number of BBC television series, including *Victorian Farm*, *Victorian Pharmacy*, *Edwardian Farm* and *Wartime Farm*. In each of these programmes, she spent a year recreating life from a different period. As well as her involvement with the *Farm* series, Ruth makes frequent appearances on *The One Show* and *Coast*.

How to be a Victorian

RUTH GOODMAN

PENGUIN BOOKS

To all those who persuaded me to step forward into the nineteenth century

PENGUIN BOOKS

Published by the Penguin Group
Penguin Books Ltd, 80 Strand, London WC2R ORL, England
Penguin Group (USA) Inc., 375 Hudson Street, New York, New York 10014, USA
Penguin Group (Canada), 90 Eglinton Avenue East, Suite 700, Toronto, Ontario, Canada M4P 2Y3
(a division of Pearson Penguin Canada Inc.)
Penguin Ireland, 25 St Stephen's Green, Dublin 2, Ireland
(a division of Penguin Books Ltd)
Penguin Group (Australia), 707 Collins Street, Melbourne, Victoria 3008, Australia
(a division of Pearson Australia Group Pty Ltd)
Penguin Books India Pvt Ltd, 11 Community Centre,
Panchsheel Park, New Delhi – 110 017, India
Penguin Group (NZ), 67 Apollo Drive, Rosedale, Auckland 0632, New Zealand
(a division of Pearson New Zealand Ltd)
Penguin Books (South Africa) (Pty) Ltd, Block D, Rosebank Office Park,
181 Jan Smuts Avenue, Parktown North, Gauteng 2193, South Africa

Penguin Books Ltd, Registered Offices: 80 Strand, London WC2R ORL, England

www.penguin.com

First published by Viking 2013
Published in Penguin Books 2014
005

Set in Bembo Book MT Std
Typeset by Palimpsest Book Production Limited, Falkirk, Stirlingshire
Printed in Great Britain by Clays Ltd, St Ives plc

ISBN: 978-0-670-92136-2

www.greenpenguin.co.uk

Contents

Preface

I want to explore a more intimate, personal and physical sort of history, a history from the inside out: one that celebrates the ordinary and charts the lives of the common man, woman and child as they interact with the practicalities of their world. I want to look into the minds of our ancestors and witness their hopes, fears and assumptions, no matter how apparently minor. In short, I am in search of a history of those things that make up the day-to-day reality of life. What was it really like to be alive in a different time and place?

History came to life for me as a hobby, but once that spark was lit it quickly became a passion and, finally, a profession. From the very start, an element of practical experimentation has been key to the way I try to understand the past. I like to put time and effort into studying the objects and tools that people made and used, and I like to try methods and approaches out for myself.

Take, for example, a dark wool coat lying in a drawer at a small museum in West Sussex. Heavily worn and lined with a patchwork of fabrics, it belonged to a farm labourer and dates back to the 1880s. The coat reminds us that here was a man who sweated and left stains on his clothes, who physically felt the cold and whose wife spent hours carefully and neatly sewing up the tear still just visible on the right-hand side, next to the buttons. When I look at that careful repair, I'm reminded of the sewing textbooks in use in Victorian schools for working-class children. A trawl through the bookshelves leads to a set of instructions, accompanied by beautifully drawn diagrams. With needle and thread in hand, I can attempt to follow these instructions on a tear in one of my own garments. His wife was evidently well trained (particularly if my own struggles are to be noted). Questions spring forth. How widespread was such needlework education, and was it likely to have been women who carried out such repairs? If it takes me over an hour to do the work, would my Victorian forebears have been quicker? When would they have fitted such a chore into their day?

Such intimate details of a life bring a feeling of connection with the people of the past and also provide a route into the greater themes of history. As a tear in a man's coat can lead one to question the nature of mass education, or to look into the global nature of the textile industry, so too the great sweeps of political and economic life bring us back to the personal. The international campaign against slavery and the American Civil War would, in combination, have devastated the trade in cotton, driving weavers back into hunger. This would have pushed up the price of the labourer's coat, making that repair more necessary.

Queen Victoria's reign spanned more than sixty years and encompassed vast social, political and economic changes. Industries rose and fell and scientific revolutions overturned the old understanding of how the world worked. People's ideas of right and wrong were challenged, and legislation was dragged along in the wake. With all these different things going on, how, then, can one talk about what it was like to be a Victorian?

This book is my attempt. It is a personal exploration, following my own fascinations, questions and interests. There is much that I have missed, and there are many excellent books that relate in more detail the political, economic and institutional shifts of the period. I aim to peer into the everyday corners of Victoria's British subjects and lead you where I have wandered in search of the people of her age.

I have chosen to move through the rhythm of the day, beginning with waking in the morning and finishing with the activities of the bedroom, when the door finally closes. Where I can, I have tried to start with the thoughts and feelings of individuals who were there, taken from diaries, letters and autobiographies and expanding out into the magazines and newspapers, adverts and advice manuals that sought to inform and shape public opinion. Glimpses of daily life can be found in items that people left behind, from clothes to shaving brushes, toys, bus tickets and saucepans. More formal rules and regulations give a shape to the experience of living, from the adoption of white lines to mark out a football pitch to the setting of a standard of achievement for school leavers.

In this hunt for the ordinary and the routine I have tried to experience elements of the life myself. Many of these experiences came when I spent a year on a Victorian farm, and later some time at a pharmacist's shop, over several television series. Others have come as part of my own ongoing explorations: testing recipes, making clothes, following hygiene regimes, whittling toy soldiers. All these experiences have been useful, if not always successful, and have helped me frame questions and think more critically about what the evidence is telling us. Ultimately, there is also a degree of empathy and imagination involved. Let us begin then, with imagining ourselves waking up at the end of a Victorian night.

1. Getting Up

It began with a shiver. Rich or poor, in city dwelling or farm labourer's cottage, the first step out of bed was likely to leave you cold. The wealthier classes often had coal fireplaces and iron grates in their bedrooms, but these were rarely lit. Jane Carlyle, the wife of Scottish essayist Thomas Carlyle, lived in a fashionable London town house in the 1850s (see Plate 8). Despite her family's income, fires were only prepared upstairs at desperate times, when bedrooms were used by the sick. Once, when a fire was indeed lit for her at a wealthy friend's home, she described it as a 'wanton luxury', one that made her feel quite guilty about her own robust good health.

For Jane Carlyle, the day began at around 7.30 a.m., but her servant would have been up much earlier than that. Mrs Beeton's *Book of Household Management* recommends that a housemaid should begin her work at 6 a.m. in the summer and 6.30 or 7 a.m. in the winter, reflecting the amount of available daylight. Hannah Cullwick was a woman who worked in domestic service her entire life. For many years, she kept a diary recording her daily working routine. In her neat blue handwriting she writes that she usually woke at six, although if there was extra work to be done it could be much earlier. Spring cleaning, as the days lengthened, generally entailed a 5 a.m. start, but there was also the occasional lie-in. On Christmas Day in 1863 she stayed in bed until a luxurious eight o'clock. Each morning, she would light the fires, shake out the carpet, polish the dining-room furniture, eat her own breakfast, clean a pair of boots and scrub the front steps before her employer's family woke up.

Dawn was the signal for most working people to rise, but many men had more fixed hours of waking. For those who had to keep very early hours and be punctual, such as factory workers, the services of a 'knocker-upper' were invaluable. Armed with a long cane and a lantern, a knocker-upper wandered the streets at all hours, tapping on the windowpanes of his clients. One of the reasons for his unusual profession was that clocks and watches were expensive items and few working-class people could afford their own. For the knocker-upper, however, a capital investment in a timepiece could provide the basis of a meagre livelihood. He worked through the night and into the early morning, each of his numerous customers paying a penny a month for his services. Such men could be found in industrial towns and cities across Britain from Portsmouth to Inverness, even extending to smaller market towns such as Baldock in Hertfordshire, where one of the three local breweries employed a man to wake their draymen at 3 a.m. With a population of only two thousand, Baldock still had a sufficient number of early-morning workers on the railway, in the brewing industry and at a host of small workshops to keep a knocker-upper in employment.

Fig. 1. The knocker-upper with the tools of his trade, circa 1900.

Once you were up, to add warmth and comfort to an other-wise chilled start, at any hour, you would hope to step out on to a mat rather than the bare wooden floor. Aristocratic homes had handsome woven carpets in the best bedrooms, but even in the upper echelons of society the rooms of sons and daughters often had to make do with an old rug that had seen better service in a more prominent part of the house. Among the less wealthy, underfoot provision was scarce. If you were fortunate and lived in a textile-weaving district, such as parts of Yorkshire, rag rugs were a popular solution. These were very simple to produce but required a significant amount of material. Those living near a mill could afford some early-morning foot warmth due to the cheap supply of loom ends and spoilt goods available.

I have made a number of these rugs in different styles, following the two main techniques of the day, by using a metal hook to pull strips through a sacking backing, or by plaiting together strips of cloth into a single length that is then coiled into a spiral and sewn in place. A rug that is merely three foot long by two foot wide consumes the equivalent of three blankets in its construction. For most people during the period, without access to local offcuts, this would have been a luxury. Tiny foot-square rugs were therefore more of a possibility for working-class families, made from worn-out clothes and scraps of cloth left over from sewing projects. It is noticeable when compared with later examples from the Edwardian period and onwards that Victorian bedroom rugs are on the small side. But a simple square of cloth still made a great difference as the Victorian summoned up the courage to start the day.

In addition to an unlit fire and sparse carpeting, windows were often left open overnight in bedrooms, to allow cool currents of fresh air to circulate. This was largely a response to the regular warnings about stale and stifling homes that arose in the work of Dr Arnott, a respected scientist and member of the Royal Institution who was interested in a range of atmospheric phenomena and 'sanitary' matters. Somewhat garbled reports in the popular press of one of his experiments fuelled a Victorian paranoia about lack of oxygen in the home. One recorded that 'a canary bird suspended near the top of a curtained bedstead on which people are sleeping [would] generally be found dead in the morning.'

Dr Arnott and others were concerned about the build-up of carbon dioxide – then usually referred to as carbonic acid – in poorly ventilated spaces. Of course it is true that people can asphyxiate in a sealed environment if there is insufficient oxygen present. But it was feared that there was a danger to human respiration in ordinary domestic environments equipped with coal fires and gas lamps, if not of actual suffocation, then of poisoning and ill health due to breathing too high a concentration of carbon dioxide. Bedrooms were especially worrisome, as people spent so long in them. Dr Pye Henry Chevasse, a physician who wrote health manuals for the layperson in the Victorian era, was willing to go so far as to state that it was 'madness to sleep in a room without ventilation – it is inhaling poison; for the carbonic acid gas, the refuse of perspiration, which the lungs are constantly throwing off, is . . . deadly'. This was a powerful argument, and no medical authority during the rest of the century was willing to challenge it with confidence. Some, such as Dr Chaumont, sought to quantify the problem by allotting required oxygen levels: he recommended 4,000 cubic feet an hour per person for healthy living. But since that was the volume contained by a room ten feet high, ten feet wide and forty feet long, the average Victorian bedroom could not possibly supply that amount of oxygen to its occupants. Twenty-first-century analysis would simply say that Chevasse and his peers grossly underestimated the movement of air in and out of rooms and buildings.

Today, our own homes are very much more effectively sealed than any Victorian interior and yet we rarely find ourselves with problems of carbon-dioxide poisoning. Despite sealed double-glazing and the absence of chimneys, modern estimates suggest that the air within a house changes completely every two to three hours. Victorian advice, however, was not only to keep chimneys open even when not in use, but to keep a sash window open both at the top and the bottom to allow for a free flow of air through the room, regardless of the weather outside. In homes where there was no chimney, ventilators could be installed over the door to create a through draught when the windows were opened.

If, as a Victorian, you could not bear to open the windows, you could hope to improve the indoor air quality with a bowl of water. The popular guidelines of the day were to 'set a pitcher of water in a room' and in 'a few hours' it would have absorbed all the respired gases and the air would 'become purer, and the water utterly filthy'. Another simple experiment to check how much carbonic acid was present was described in advice books and school textbooks. *The Science of Home Life*, a book designed for schoolgirls, instructed that 'if we pour some clear lime water into a shallow dish or saucer, and leave it exposed to the air for an hour or so, we shall find a whitish crust or scum on the surface of the liquid. This proves that carbonic acid is present in the air.' Sadly, neither of these experiments was remotely accurate, scientifically speaking. In the latter case, it was more likely that some of the water would evaporate and thus leave a scum of lime; in the former, the 'filthiness' of the water may have been an illusion of the mind. Either way, poor scientific method was being used to back up a popular idea.

Did people really leave their windows open all year round? Practice seems to have varied. According to some reports into the living conditions of the poor by a range of philanthropists, researchers and officials, clutches of children would huddle at night on bare mattresses beneath permanently open windows with only their day clothes and each other to keep them warm. Their parents were trying to do the right thing. They were frightened of poisoning their children, though by keeping the windows open they had no hope of providing warmth for them. Other reports, equally horrified, talk of large numbers of people sleeping packed together in rooms with the windows firmly sealed shut. For these people, the possibility of being warm influenced them more than talk of poisoned air. Henry Mayhew, a journalist for the *Morning Chronicle* newspaper, recalled in his interviews with the poor that 'their breaths in the dead of night and in the unventilated chamber rose in one foul choking steam of stench.'

For the vast majority, unheated rooms with open windows made for a bracing start to the day. On leaving bed, people would perch precariously upon whatever the household could conjure up in the way of a rug. Then would come the ordeal of the morning ablutions.

The Stand-up Wash

For most of the Victorian period, the stand-up wash was the main form of personal hygiene and the start of most people's daily routine. For men and upper- and middle-class women it happened as soon as they rose from their bed, still clothed in their long, voluminous nightshirt or nightdress. But the servants and those who had to clean out the grates, black the range and light the fires generally had to wait until they had finished the morning's dirty jobs before they had their wash. Hannah Cullwick fitted her morning wash in just before she cooked the family breakfast, often making use of the kitchen facilities. 'Wash'd me at the sink and laid the cloth for our breakfast,' she recorded on 11 August 1863. But most stand-up washes happened in the bedroom, where all the utensils would be ready and waiting.

All a person needed was a bowl, a slop pail, a flannel, some soap and a single jugful of hot water brought up from the kitchen (see Plate 2). Cold water was also an option, and many people used it, hoping to improve their circulation. This had the advantage of immediacy, too, as a jug could be brought up to the room the night before and stood alongside the bowls and towels in readiness. Unfortunately, however, Victorian soap simply did not work in cold water – it neither dissolved nor lathered – and a hot-water wash with soap was generally recommended once a week in order to remove grease, even if you took a cold-water wash daily.

The stand-up wash is still a very efficient and eco-friendly technique if you happen to be staying somewhere with spartan facilities. With a single jug of water it is perfectly easy to wash and rinse the whole body. A little water is poured into the bowl and the flannel is dipped in and then wrung out. Some soap is applied and the scrubbing of the body can begin. When this first bowl of water begins to look murky it is emptied into the slop pail and freshly filled from the jug. And so it goes on until you are clean all over. Rather like scrubbing a floor, body washing could be done in sections, one bit scrubbed, rinsed and dried before moving on to the next. This allowed a person to remain mostly dressed throughout the operation: each area was un-dressed, washed and re-dressed before the next was exposed. You could wash in this way without becoming severely chilled in a January bedroom, and with a great degree of modesty if you had to share accommodation (as most people did). It was even possible to wash parts of yourself beneath an extant layer of clothing. A loose nightgown or nightshirt could be worn throughout if necessary, while still allowing access to all parts of the body with a flannel. Once the last drop of clean water was used finally to rinse out the cloth and washing bowl, the slop pail of dirty water was taken downstairs and disposed of.

Fig. 2. Morning ablutions at the wash stand, 1850.

From an affluent lady living in a stately home with the finest-quality hand-painted-porcelain toilet set to the agricultural labourer's wife with her mismatched, cracked earthenware jug and bowl, the stand-up wash provided the quintessential Victorian hygiene experience for women. A woman would begin by heating a kettleful of water, or have a servant do this for her. For the wealthy, who would store plenty of coal in the cellar to fuel the fire, and perhaps employ a maid to carry the water, daily warm-water washing in a bowl was commonplace. For those with a houseful of children and no paid help, a kettleful of hot water each was pushing at the bounds of possibility, and washing came less often or was confined to a cold-water rinse. For the very poor, struggling in cramped, heavily overcrowded rooms and working punishingly long hours with little to eat, carrying jugs of water up and down stairways in a cold home was just one energy-sapping step too far.

Bathtubs were not the norm and, where they did exist, were normally used at the end of the day (we will examine them in detail towards the end of the book). They were largely used by men. Modesty played a large part in this. Men might have felt happy wandering along the corridor of a wealthy house in a bathrobe, but far fewer women did – they would have felt much too vulnerable and exposed. In the few working-class homes that employed a tin bath in front of the fire, men and children were its usual occupants. Even within a family setting, few women were willing to be naked in the kitchen, and even men preferred to bathe wearing a thin pair of cotton drawers in such semi-public surroundings.

Fig. 3. Advert of a girl with her wash bowl, a can of hot water and a bar of Sunlight soap, 1895.

The stand-up wash remained one of the most common forms of washing throughout the century, whether with hot or cold water, with or without soap. It provided a fast morning wash and could prepare a person for the day. That people washed with water at all, however, was a new development. Before the

Victorian period, it had been believed that the pores of the skin allowed disease to enter and penetrate the body. While healthy sweating allowed poisons and effluvia to exit through the pores, it had been thought important to protect the skin from too much exposure to sources of infection; water opened the pores and was therefore best avoided. Disease was believed to be carried in evil miasmas (vapours) in the air, thickest and most dangerous where smell and damp were most evident. Walk through the stinking mists rising from tanners' pits or stale dung heaps, past open sewers or the bleaching and dyeing works, and infection would be hanging in the air around you, threatening to enter your nose, mouth or skin. The sensible person would have avoided these areas when they could and carried scents to drive away the miasmas. They would also have kept their skin covered and sealed against such threats.

Victorian scientific developments concerning skin and its function introduced some radical theories. Experiments in sealing the pores were undertaken, famously with a horse. The poor animal was carefully varnished all over with several layers of shellac (the same solution that is used to varnish furniture) to ensure a complete seal, and died within hours. It was assumed that it had asphyxiated, thus 'proving' that the skin played an important role in respiration as well as perspiration. Twenty-first-century anatomical understanding would simply state that the sealing of the pores led to the animal overheating and dying of heatstroke, however, for most of the Victorian period, there was a serious, if erroneous, view that the pores of the skin were an important, though secondary, route for oxygen to enter the body. The older idea of poisons and waste products being expelled through the skin continued, yet at the same time Victorian science saw a pressing need to change the way people cared for their skin.

Previously, it had been good hygiene practice to keep the

body well wrapped up, with the layer next to the skin consisting either of cotton or linen, which could be easily and thoroughly laundered. Shirts, drawers and stockings for men, and chemises and stockings for women, covered the whole body apart from the head and hands. Nightwear, which consisted of long shirts for men and ankle-length, long-sleeved nightdresses for women, with bed socks and nightcaps in the winter, provided a similar all-over layer in bed. The clean and healthy person changed this underwear layer as often as possible. Daily was good – several times a day better – for those with the time and stock of clothes, while among the less wealthy members of the population many changed from separate nightwear to daywear, which helped in the process. Constant clean underwear absorbed the sweat and dirt of the body and, each time you changed, the accumulated dirt was taken away. Dry rubbing of the body with a clean linen towel also helped to remove dirt, grease and sweat from the skin and gave the added benefit of stimulating the circulation, thus promoting a healthy glow and a general tonic to the whole system. These rubbing or body cloths could be easily laundered, ensuring that your skin could be kept clean and healthy without the dangers of water, which could cause a chill or open the pores to infection.

It works. I know, because I have tried it for extended periods. Your skin remains in good health and any body odour is kept at bay. A quick daily rub-down with a dry body cloth or a 'flesh brush' (a pad of suede leather on the back of a wooden brush) leaves the skin exfoliated, clean and comfortable. The longest I have been without washing with water is four months – and nobody noticed. I much prefer the cloth to the brush for this method of cleaning oneself. Naturally, you need to pay special attention to your armpits and the cloths are most effective when they are older, softer and more absorbent. Many modern writers and historians like to revel in the opinion that people were dreadfully malodorous in the past, before modern washing with water took hold. My own experience makes me sceptical about their claims.

It is true, though, that the Victorian belief that one's skin could breathe led directly to the introduction of soap and warm water for washing. Medics were concerned that blocked pores were the danger and could lead to poisons building up within the body, causing debility, sluggishness and, ultimately, death. Water and soap could provide healthy, open-pored skin, which would, in theory, rush valuable oxygen to the blood, thus stimulating the whole body. It would also allow a free flow for toxins to exit the body, carrying away the harmful by-products of sickness and disease.

Victorian theories about washing and the skin led people to think carefully about their clothing and, particularly, their night clothing. The advice was to wear light, porous layers, and not to be bundled up too closely, even in the cold. Garments were marketed for their breathability, as were blankets. We have a few reminders of these items today in twenty-first-century fabrics such as Aertex for sportswear and cellular-weave cot blankets, which are light and warm but very permeable, to allow air to reach the skin. However, unlike these items, which equate breathability with comfort, many porous Victorian items of clothing were still very arduous to wear. The 'health' corsets of the late nineteenth century are a prime example. Marketed for their newly improved design, they were meant to assist with chest and breathing problems, but this did not mean freedom for the ribcage. No, the 'sanitary' and 'health' corsets of the 1890s were just as heavily boned and tightly laced as before; they just had additional holes in them, to allow the skin to 'breathe'.

Deodorants and Body Odour

The morning wash was transforming the Victorian idea of smell, although commercial deodorant would not be available until the next century. As increasing numbers of Victorians, at least among the middle classes, began their day with soap and warm water, body odour took on a new dimension, one that divided the nation. William Thackeray, in his 1850 novel *Pendennis*, coined the phrase 'the great unwashed'. It was quickly adopted to describe the working class and to distance their social betters from them. The middle and upper classes smelt quite differently – strongly of soap and, preferably, with not a trace of stale sweat. Based on animal fats and caustic soda, Victorian soap had its own unique, sharp smell which

Fig. 4. Disinfecting and medicated soaps carried a distinctive scent.

effectively masked most bodily odours. Later in the century, soaps perfumed with scents such as lavender, violet and rose became popular, and drew even more attention to an individual's washing habits. These floral scents, which never completely obscured their soapy ingredients, provided a nasal badge of honour, one that the washed population could wear with pride.

Despite undertaking more physical labour, which led to dirtier clothes and more pungent body odour, the working class were much more conservative about washing with water. They were not buying or reading the new health and home manuals that recommended the method. But, perhaps more importantly, both washing and laundry were much more of a challenge for them, as they had far fewer facilities for either activity.

Soap and hot water could be a substantial expense for those living on the poverty line, not to mention the cost of laundry equipment itself. At the outset of the Victorian period, a four-ounce bar of soap (roughly the same size as those currently sold in Britain) cost the same as a good joint of beef. A middle-class family following the new washing regime could use three or four such bars in a week, something that was well beyond the purse of many. Even at the end of the era, after a series of major technological advances had reduced the price several times, sufficient soap to wash the bodies and clothes of a working-class family still required 5 per cent of the weekly budget. And the additional cost meant that a built-in copper to boil water for laundry was by no means common in working-class houses. A wringer made a significant difference to the amount of labour involved in a large-scale clothes wash, but this, too, cost money and, even at the end of the century, the majority of the working classes had to manage without. It is hardly surprising then that the working classes had such a different smell to that of the wealthier.

Laundry, as we shall examine more closely later, formed a

major part of this olfactory division. Clothes that held on to sweat and other emissions of the body were, naturally, ideal breeding places for bacteria and smells. On the other hand, wool was best at allowing the sweat to evaporate freely and effectively. Members of the twenty-first-century hiking and climbing fraternity are beginning to re-learn this Victorian lesson. Pure wool is once again making its mark, with 'odourless' socks and merino-wool base layers. Hi-tech man-made fibres cannot compete with traditional wool on these terms.

In those areas of one's clothing that were tight, or where sweating was likely to be heaviest, it was advisable to have an extra layer of removable, easily washable clothing. For Victorian women, their tight-fitting bodices, sleeves and armpits were a particular problem. While vests and chemises could be cleaned, it was also wise to use dress protectors – small, detachable pads that were slipped into the armpits of the dress. These could be taken out and washed separately, and they prevented delicate or ornate garments from becoming ruined. You can still buy dress protectors in traditional haberdashery shops.

Dusting powders were another aid to achieve a desirable body smell. Based either upon starch or talcum powder, and with or without an added scent, these powders absorbed sweat and made it easier to remove. Such powders were a staple product on the shelves of apothecary's and chemist's shops. The most expensive came in round, ceramic pots, complete with a circle of sponge with which to apply the powder. Cheaper brands had a pierced lid that allowed the user to shake the powder directly on to the skin. For the truly cost-conscious customer, retailers sold plain powdered starch or talc by weight. A wipe under the arms and other 'parts prone to smell' with a cloth dipped in ammonia was a final routine for those who were still worried. Ammonia, which kills the bacteria that create body odour, was a very effective deodorant. Slightly less efficient was a wipe with vinegar.

This killed the bacteria less aggressively than the ammonia but had the advantage of being less irritating to those with sensitive skin.

The Importance of Cleanliness

Beyond preventing unsavoury smells, the Victorian personal-hygiene regime was about health. And health was undergoing perhaps its greatest revolution of all time.

The basic idea of germ theory had been circulating for a while, but the theory was not fully proven until Louis Pasteur demonstrated at the start of the 1860s that decay was caused by living organisms present in the air. His experiment was a simple one, with one sample exposed to the air and the other in a vacuum. The sample in the vacuum did not rot until air was admitted to the vessel. There could be no doubt thereafter that the tiny organisms visible under the microscope were the source of the decomposition. Decay and putrefaction were not the product of spontaneous generation, as had been previously thought, but a result of the action of living creatures. And living creatures could be killed – ideally, with an agent that would eradicate the 'germs' without harming the patient. Pasteur's next breakthrough was in identifying carbolic acid as a substance that could be used to do just that.

As other people began to take up these ideas, more and more information about the micro-organisms they were discovering emerged. Perhaps the most celebrated advance from this new rush of research came from the work of Dr John Snow (one of the founding members of the Epidemiological Society of London), who identified the source of a cholera outbreak in 1854, successfully realizing that every case could be traced directly to a single infected water pump in Broad Street, Soho. The removal of the handle of the pump almost certainly saved hundreds of lives.

Miasma theory had held that bad air was the cause of all and any disease, but how that disease was expressed by the body could depend upon the person rather than the source of infection. According to the old theory, the same evil miasma could be expressed in one individual as a lung disease and in another as a stomach complaint, depending upon their constitution and circumstances. It was not until 1879, however, that the German physician Robert Koch was able to prove that specific bacteria caused specific diseases. By 1884, the bacterias responsible for typhoid, leprosy, diphtheria, tuberculosis, cholera, dysentery, gonorrhoea, malaria, pneumonia and tetanus had been isolated. This was a truly revolutionary shift in understanding, which had a huge impact upon the investigation and treatment of disease. From a cleanliness point of view, however, it changed both everything and nothing.

If germs were everywhere – in the air and the water and upon every surface – then cleanliness was more important than ever. The removal of dirt had always been seen as a way to protect your family from disease. But whereas, before, you were removing the causes of the evil miasma, now you were removing the germs themselves. All the old cleanliness routines were still entirely relevant and useful. Germ theory, like the older thinking, emphasized the usefulness of cleaning the privy, regularly emptying cesspits, sweeping the house, laundering clothes, scrubbing kitchens, washing up, and so forth. Housework was valuable in preserving health whichever theory you ascribed to. So, too, was community cleanliness: germs could be fought as effectively as miasmas by good town management of waste, by regular street cleaning, by prosecuting those who dumped waste in public areas. Personal hygiene also had value with both germ and miasma theories of disease. A clean body neither generated bad airs nor harboured germs.

If Hannah Cullwick's morning wash still took place at the

sink in the kitchen, after the widespread acceptance of germ theory she would have no longer worried about opening her pores with hot water and she would have been keen not just to wash her hands but to disinfect them. Carbolic acid remained one of the most popular disinfectants. Sold in liquid and powdered form at pharmacist's shops, but also pre-mixed with soap, it offered a way of cleaning that went beyond looking and smelling pleasant. Its own sharp smell came to mean 'clean' in the new, sterile sense of the word. A maidservant who smelt of carbolic soap came to be one whom mistresses had faith in, one whom they were much more likely to employ. (Today, a very similar 'coal tar' soap is on sale if you want to get a measure of Victorian cleanliness, although the active ingredient now is tea-tree oil. Manufacturers do, however, make sure that the soap still has the smell of carbolic acid, which even now carries cultural overtones of sterile safety.)

Teeth-cleaning

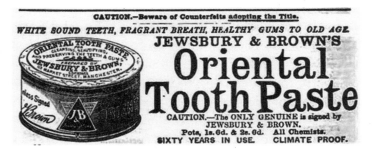

Fig. 5. Toothpaste advert, 1897.

With the body clean and sweet-smelling, many people were keen to move on to dental hygiene. Toothbrushes looked, in shape, much like those we are accustomed to today, although their handles were made of bone or wood and the bristles generally of horse- or pony-hair. The usual word for what we would call toothpaste was 'dentifrice'. Many such pastes were prepared at home, the simplest no more than a little soot or salt. Commercial forms could be bought over the counter, however. Most dentifrices, whether home-made or bought at the chemist's or pharmacist's, were simply flavoured and often coloured abrasives – polishes, in effect. Here are three recipes taken from early editions of the *Englishwoman's Domestic Magazine*:

> Camphorated dentifrice. Prepared chalk, one pound; camphor one or two drachms. The camphor must be finely powdered by moistening it with a little spirit of wine, and then intimately mixing it with the chalk.
>
> Myrrh dentifrice. Powdered cuttlefish, one pound; powdered myrrh, two ounces.
>
> American tooth powder. Coral, cuttlefish bone, dragons blood, of each eight drachms; burnt alum and red sanders, of each four drachms; orris root eight drachms; cloves and cinnamon of each half a drachm; rose pink, eight drachms. All to be powdered and mixed.

The powdered chalk and cuttlefish provided the polish, gently abrading the teeth. These are the two most common ingredients in all dentifrices, followed by soot and charcoal, which were equally effective but couldn't be made up into such attractive pastes. Camphor (derived from a tree of the laurel family), myrrh and burnt alum (a naturally occurring mineral used in water purification, dyeing and deodorant) gave recipes a more 'medicated' taste. These would all have lingered in the mouth; the camphor and alum may well also have had a small antibacterial effect. The American tooth powder would have been a very strongly coloured product. The powdered coral, the dragon's blood and the rose pink were all colouring agents complemented with spices to add flavour and to scent the breath.

The ingredients to make up these recipes were widely and easily available from pharmacist's and chemist's. All were traditional substances of long standing and most people were familiar with them. The chalk really was just chalk rock finely ground to a powder – the very same material that many people used to scrub out sinks and baths and which still to this day forms the abrasive base of many well-known brands of kitchen and bathroom cleaner. Powdered cuttlefish was made from the hard plate inside the fish's body, sometimes found washed up on beaches. It is perhaps best known in Britain today as a dietary additive for budgerigars. Ground to a powder, it is both finer and softer than chalk. Powdered charcoal has about the same softness as cuttlefish but has the added benefit of acting as a deodorant: a breath freshener. Soot, however, is my personal favourite, the one that I would recommend as an alternative to modern toothpaste formulas. Despite its colour, soot is the softest of all the abrasives, helping to shift plaque and tartar without irritating or damaging either teeth or gums. It is safe to consume in occasional small quantities and, of course, it rinses cleanly and completely away.

Some of the other ingredients should be approached with more caution. Burnt alum is a caustic substance and even small amounts can cause soreness and irritation when used in such a sensitive environment as the mouth. It was well known in Victorian times as a cleaning and bleaching agent. Camphor was best known both then and now, domestically, in its role in deterring clothes moths. It's a smell that, once smelt, is never forgotten. It's not necessarily unpleasant, but it is distinctive. Rather like the overpowering 'minty freshness' of many brands of modern toothpaste, the smell of camphor provided a form of personal advertising, telling the world at large that you had brushed today. Dragon's blood, despite its exotic-sounding name, was one of the less worrying ingredients, being simply the root of a plant that yields a bright-red dye still sometimes used as a food colourant. The presence of so many pink and red colouring agents is perhaps the most surprising element of the recipes, when the modern preference is for white toothpastes. Victorian taste required toothpaste to mimic the colour of healthy gums rather than the desired colour of teeth.

I am wary of trying Victorian medical recipes unless I have a full understanding of all the various ingredients, and I would suggest that you should be too. I have never used the American tooth powder quoted above, but my experiments with plain soot and cuttlefish powder have been happy ones. Small amounts of either ingredient dabbed on to a damp toothbrush seem to do a good job, and if, like me, you don't much enjoy a toothpaste that fills your mouth with strong-tasting froth, it can offer a pleasant alternative.

Sanitary Towels

Fig. 6. One of the earliest adverts for sanitary towels, 1898.

For women of childbearing age there was one further element to the morning hygiene ritual. At the end of the century it was possible to walk into a shop and purchase sanitary towels over the counter. For those too embarrassed to do so, a mail-order service promised to deliver them in plain brown packets. Adverts for these products began to appear discreetly in magazines, relying heavily on medical imagery. Cheery nurses in crisp, starched uniforms held understated parcels as if they were wound dressings. In one of the needlework magazines at the turn of the century, an early advert bears the words 'Southwell's Sanitary Towels' emblazoned on an unobtrusively held packet. However, in a later edition of the magazine, the same advert has been quietly altered so that a hand obscures much of the lettering, leaving only 'Southwell's S— Towels' visible: even the word 'sanitary' was deemed too intimate for most people's sensibilities. Commercially available products such as sanitary towels were a great innovation; no one before could have imagined that something so personal could be sourced outside the home. Printed information and instruction on the subject, however, was still scarce. Such things were not much spoken about, even among women, and certainly even less written about. One of the best practical descriptions was recorded at the very end of the century by an American writer, Dr Mary Allan. She suggested that a sanitary napkin should be suspended from the shoulders with a pair of braces. It would then be joined together at the front and at the back with a button sewn on to its ends. The napkin or pad therefore had buttonholes to allow it to be attached to the support straps. It should be made, she advised her readers, from a square of cotton nappy material sixteen inches square:

> About three inches from one end, make on each side an incision four inches long. Fold this strip in the middle lengthwise, and sew together up to the incisions. This makes a band with a sort of pocket in the middle. Hem the cut edges. Fold the napkin over, four inches on each side, that is, as deep as the incisions. Then fold crosswise until you can enclose the whole in the

pocket in the band. This makes a thick centre and thin ends by which to attach the napkin to the suspender.

The idea of suspending the sanitary pads from the shoulders seems to have been an unusual one. For, while literary references to their form are rare, there are numerous surviving Victorian sanitary towels and belts. Folded away in trousseaus and at the bottom of drawers, they have remained as a quiet reminder of the practicalities of femininity. These were usually suspended from a belt that went around the waist. Some of these belts were no more than a piece of tape; others were much more substantial, and shaped. Probably the most comfortable to wear were those that resembled the yoke portion of waist petticoats, similar to modern suspender belts, except that there were two straps front and back to support a single towel, rather than four to hold up a pair of stockings.

I have never seen any examples of Dr Allan's cleverly folded napkins – thick in the middle and thin at the ends – although they do sound like an ingenious idea. Most of the surviving examples take the form of slim cotton bags, open at one end so that they can be stuffed with an absorbent material. They generally have a tape loop at each end to attach them to the belt. This cotton bag was laundered after use, but the absorbent material it contained need not have been. Anything could have been used for this. For many, it would have been a rag of some sort, which may have been thrown away after use, or, when resources were scarcer, laundered. Others may have been able to employ natural materials such as moss. Dr Mary Allan's napkins have no bag at all; it is the napkin itself that is attached to the suspender, diagonally, by its corners, the rest of the material folded around to create the bulk. It is possible that this was common American practice, while those surviving examples that I have seen were used commonly in England.

I have used the belt-and-bag method myself. In terms of comfort and effectiveness, it is not much different from modern sanitary protection. Yes, Victorian sanitary towels can leak – but then so do the modern ones. Yes, they can feel wet and uncomfortable if you don't change them often enough – but, again, so can the modern ones. However, they do differ from today's equivalents in two obvious ways. Firstly, they are suspended. Knicker-wearing was a new phenomenon for women, gradually spreading throughout the population as the century progressed, but, even by 1900, when most, if not yet quite all, women had taken to them, they were not suitable for holding sanitary towels in place. The knickers of 1900 were a large pair of loosely fitting bloomers. They were not elasticated and had to be large and loose to permit movement, which meant that they could not hold anything against the body. Pre-1880 knickers had been even less suitable as a support for sanitary wear, as they were split-crotched, consisting of two legs joined only at the waistband. Sanitary pads required the belt to hold them in place. This method didn't go out of use until the late 1970s.

The second main difference to today's sanitary towels is the Victorian sanitary napkin's recyclability. From my own experience, this is an unusual idea to adjust to. We are now so used to the concept of disposable sanitary protection that it can seem very unsavoury to be laundering such items. But they are certainly no less unpleasant to deal with than nappies. As with nappies, it is best to clean them in a bucket of cold, salty water with a lid. Just drop the soiled cotton and linen in a bucket and leave to soak. Most of the unwanted matter will wash off in the soak. All that is then left to do is to pour away the dirty water and rinse. They will be most of the way to being clean before you even have to touch them.

With basic hygiene attended to, it was time to put on some clothes.

2. Getting Dressed

Men's Clothes

Underwear

Standing in his cold bedroom, Victorian man would have pulled off his nightclothes and quickly donned a vest and a pair of drawers. Vests could be sleeveless, but most covered the entire arm, all the way down to the wrist. Warmth was the most sought-after attribute in a vest; as vests were never intended to be seen by anyone but the family or the occasional laundress, fashion had little impact. The drawers, too, were intended to provide protection from the cold. They were ankle-length and fastened at both the waist and the bottom of the leg to keep out draughts. Some were fastened with buttons; others with tape ties. Together with a good pair of socks, these provided the base layer over which the other clothes sat.

Tony Widger was a fisherman in Seaton, South Devon, at the turn of the century. One misty morning, his lodger recorded him 'pattering about the kitchen in his stockings (odd ones), his pants and his light check shirt' before delivering a cup of tea up to his wife. Completely covered by his underwear, apart from his hands and face, Tony Widger was not embarrassed to be seen by his lodger friend or by his loved ones in a state of half-dress, although he would not have dared set foot outside attired in this manner. Male underwear carried far fewer sexual associations than that of women. This total coverage also served another function. A Victorian man would have been disgusted by the idea of wearing nothing between his legs and his trousers; he would have thought it very unhygienic; and underwear could be washed far more frequently than outer-wear.

Britain's climate made the idea of wearing warm, woolly underwear very attractive most of the year. Flannel was the fabric of choice; it was one of the cheapest woollen cloths and had a soft, open weave that was naturally insulating without being heavy or stiff. From the latter half of the 1840s, however, there was another form of woolly underwear available, if you could afford it. There was a substantial display of machine-knitted undergarments at the Great Exhibition in 1856, compan-ies vying with each other over the fit, fineness and washability of their goods. The most expensive brands took care to use long, staple-combed wools so that their products didn't irritate the skin, and the garments were shaped to follow the contours of the body in order to offer warmth without bulk or folding. They were expensive, however: something for the wealthier middle-class man.

The general comfort or discomfort of underwear varied according to the style and material of the vest. Flannel was warm, but some people found it itchy. Swansdown, a cotton fabric, was a less abrasive alternative, and was cheaper. How-ever, it offered little stretch or 'give' and, as a result, such vests were known to restrict movement. Perhaps the best solution to wool's itchiness could be achieved with a series of small 'facing strips'. Wool was most irritating in the areas that rubbed around the collar and cuff, so sewing a wide cotton tape inside the collar and beneath the cuffs did generally solve the problem. The same technique could be employed upon knitted woollen vests. These were by far the stretchiest of the alternatives, giving complete freedom of movement with no additional bulk of fabric at the waist.

Drawers (or, as Tony Widger's lodger called them, 'pants') were also available in cotton, flannel or knitted wool. With these garments, it was the waist that was most likely to cause discomfort. An elasticated waist was unusual. Elastic fastenings for clothes were patented in 1820, but for most of the century their use was restricted to gloves and boots. This left two options: the drawstring waist or the simple cloth waistband fastened with a button. Drawstrings caused a bulky ridge at the waist which was uncomfortable, so most pairs of drawers had a fitted cloth waistband, faced on the inside with cotton. A deep band of cotton would also generally line the bottom of the drawer legs so they wouldn't rub or irritate when fastened.

Socks, or 'stockings', in Tony's case, could occasionally be made of silk, but almost all were wool. Frame knitting machines commercially produced good-quality, reasonably priced socks, but home-produced hand-made examples could still be found at all levels of society. Regardless of process, they were all hand-darned at some point in their life cycle. A good darn was nearly invisible and was as comfortable as the original fabric. A bad darn was a torment to wear; hard and lumpy, it could lead to blisters as surely as a badly fitting shoe.

Towards the end of the century, a hybrid piece of clothing began to make an appearance: the combination. Vest and drawers were combined into a single, all-encompassing garment with a fly at the front and a drop-down flap at the back. This is the underwear familiar from films about the Wild West. The style seems to have been especially popular in turn-of-the-century America. Just like the separate vest and drawers, it provided coverage for warmth and put a layer of washable fabric between the body and the outer clothes. In Britain it remained a stylistic choice rather than taking over from the popular vest and drawers.

Fig. 7. 'Combinations' became increasingly popular as the new century began.

Shirts, which went over the vest, were both 'under-' and 'outer-' wear in some senses, as the social etiquette of the time dictated that waistcoats and jackets were to be worn at all times. While, in modern Britain, the shirt is a perfectly respectable garment that is regularly on display, even in quite formal situations, this was not the way the Victorians thought of it. Collars and cuffs were visible – but often entirely separate garments to the shirt, to which they were fastened in place with buttons and studs. Shirtfronts could be seen beneath the jacket and waistcoat, but to remove the jacket and expose the shirtsleeves was something done in only the most casual and informal of circumstances. Images of Victorian life, be they photographs, paintings or engravings in newspapers and magazines, rarely showed men without their jackets on. When they did, it was usually to make a point. Men at home with their families at the end of the day in front of the fire might remove their jackets, especially if they were working class. Men involved in sport or brawling were often jacketless, as were those working at some of the rougher manual trades.

Although they were mostly hidden from view, shirts were fashionable items and available in a surprising number of colours and patterns. Checked, striped and spotted shirts were common in the early years among the wealthy elite, but over time, at the more moneyed end of society, they began to be replaced by white. Crisp, perfect whites became the mark of a gentleman. Meanwhile, the working man moved in the opposite direction. His shirts had been white – or at least cream or pale in colour – at the beginning of Victoria's reign, but as the rich began to discard their more fanciful threads in the 1870s and 1880s, the working man embraced them. A striped or checked shirt proved much easier to keep looking fresh than a pure white one, and lent variation to his faded wardrobe. At the end of the century, the checked shirt became a badge of the manual labourer, including fishermen like Tony Widger.

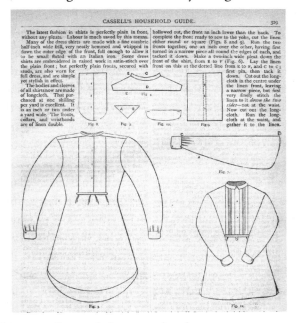

Fig. 8. Shirts were frequently home-produced.

More visible than the shirt, the collar, cuffs and necktie often formed the focus for male attire. The mere presence of a collar carried clues to one's class, while its exact form, state of cleanliness and the quantity of starch used to whiten and stiffen it spoke of a man's position within the social hierarchy. Labourers, both agricultural and industrial, generally wore collarless shirts, with a cloth tied loosely around the neck in place of a tie. Wearing a collar of any sort set a man apart from this group, except on Sundays, when even labourers often went to the extra trouble and expense.

Turned-down collars, much as are worn with shirts in the twenty-first century, were considered to be informal dress and were worn only by the wealthier classes when engaged in leisure pursuits. Heavily starched stand-up (detachable) collars, on the other hand, were the formal choice of the day and were essential for any sort of business or office work. In the 1840s, men wore their formal collars higher at the front than at the back, with the starched points lying on their cheeks, just above the jawline. Later fashion dictated that the points be folded down away from the face in a style similar to the modern wing collar that still appears on formal shirts worn with a bow tie. The height of the collar then subsided for several decades, before becoming taller and taller in the final few years of the 1890s.

The amount of starch it had become customary to use was staggering. The resultant collars were rigid and sharp enough even to use as a pastry cutter. Producing a collar that was this heavily starched meant ironing it into its final shape. But a flat, ironed collar that one tried to bend around into a circle to go around the neck was in danger of cracking. Starching to this extent at home was almost impossible. Most people sent their collars out to a professional laundry, where there were circular steam irons over which the collars were slipped and pressed into shape. Even at the bottom end of the clerical classes, where finances were so tight the majority of the washing was done at home, it was usually better to send collars out to the laundry.

In addition to the shape and colour of the Victorian man's undergarments, the woolliness of his underwear was a widely discussed topic in Britain at the time, as well as in the far-flung places of British endeavour. Whether he was navigating the upper reaches of the Orinoco River or ice-climbing in Tibet, a man was advised to wear plenty of wool next to his skin. In the last two decades of the century, Dr Jaeger became the leading proponent and proselytizer of the cause. As he proudly advertised, his company had supplied woollen underwear to Stanley on his famous expedition to equatorial Africa in 1887 in search of Dr Livingstone. It was his company, too, that supplied almost every expedition to both the Arctic and the Antarctic, up to, and including, both Ernest Shackleton's 1907–9 adventure and Captain Scott's ill-fated attempt to reach the South Pole.

OUTFITS FOR ABROAD.

The JAEGER COMPANY make a special feature of outfits for Abroad—Arctic, Tropical and Sub-Tropical. Every Expedition of importance for the last twenty-five years has carried " JAEGER," including :—

Sir H. M. STANLEY,
　Equatorial Africa, 1887.
Dr. NANSEN,
　Arctic, 1893.
JACKSON-
　　HARMSWORTH,
　Polar, 1894.
WELLMAN,
　Polar, 1898.
DUKE OF ABRUZZI,
　Arctic, 1899.
ZIEGLER-BALDWIN,
　Arctic, 1901.
NATIONAL ANTARCTIC
　(" Discovery "), 1901.
NATIONAL ANTARCTIC
　Relief, 1902.
ZIEGLER-FIALA,
　Polar, 1903.

ARGENTINE,
　Antarctic, 1903.
BERNIER'S CANADIAN
　Polar, 1904.
ZIEGLER Polar
　Relief, 1905.
WELLMAN,
　Polar, 1907.
BRITISH ANTARCTIC
　(Sir E. SHACKLETON),
　　1907-1909.
Ex-President ROOSEVELT,
　Mid-Africa, 1909-10.
DUKE OF CONNAUGHT,
　Mid-Africa, 1910.
BRITISH ANTARCTIC
　(Captain SCOTT, R N.), 1910.
AUSTRALASIAN
　Antarctic Expedition, 1911.
　(Dr DOUGLAS MAWSON).

Fig. 9. A list of Dr Jaeger's most adventurous clients.

However, the idea went back to before the days of Victoria. In 1823, Captain Murray of the HMS *Valorous* returned to Britain after a two-year tour of duty amid the icebergs along the North Labradorean coast, a place where one would expect every seaman to be grateful for each additional stitch of clothing. The ship and her crew were in port for only a matter of weeks before putting to sea again, this time bound for the West Indies and a climate radically different from that they had experienced in the previous two years. But, during those few weeks, the captain, being a firm believer in the efficacy of woollen underwear, ordered two flannel shirts and two pairs of flannel drawers for every man on board and instituted a regime of daily inspections to ensure that all the men wore them. He proudly reported upon his eventual return to Britain that, despite the great change in climate, he had not lost a man. This was a health record, and one that he ascribed to the wearing of wool in all climates, including the tropical.

The basic argument in favour of woollen underwear was its insulating properties. These were obvious in cold climates, but most Victorian advice-givers liked to extend this insulative capacity to become a way of keeping heat out as well as keeping it in. There is some truth in this. If, for example, you work in front of a hot fire or a furnace, any sort of clothing will act as a barrier, but wool is very much better for this purpose than cotton or linen. Wool insulates your body from the blast of the heat, and sparks simply smoulder and go out on it. Heat that comes from the direct rays of the sun can, similarly, be mitigated by wool. (Desert people generally find that covering up is the best way to deal with the dry heat and powerful rays of the sun. Again, many find that wool is better for this purpose than cotton.)

However, heat that comes with high humidity or with a general heating of the air rather than from a direct source cannot be

guarded against by insulation. In these conditions, the proponents of woolly underwear called upon another of wool's
properties: its porous nature. Wool drew sweat away from the
skin, allowing a gentle cooling that reduced the danger of sudden chills. Sudden chills were a general Victorian fear, and it was
widely accepted that neither great heat nor great cold was as
dangerous to health as the rapid change from one to the other.
Contrary to twenty-first-century understanding, Victorians
believed that it was these changes of temperature that caused
people to 'catch cold'.

Back in Britain, benefiting from this new popularity, Dr Jaeger
established his Sanitary Clothing Company, which expanded the
perceived advantages of woolly-underwear wearing to include a
detoxification and slimming function. He believed that wool-clad
skin would be stimulated in its natural functions, exhaling more
toxins and watery fats than skin that was merely covered in cotton:
'The tissues may be automatically drained and kept drained, of
the excess of fat and water.' This, he said, was far more efficacious
as a means of losing weight than mere diet or exercise. However,

Fig. 10. Portrait of Dr Jaeger, wool's leading advocate, 1911.

in order to work fully and properly, woolly underwear, he maintained, was not enough. Underwear, outerwear and bedding must be exclusively wool, with not a thread of cotton in sight, not even for sheets or shirts (or even, in the case of women, corsets). It was a complete 'sanitary' system of clothing.

In his zeal, Dr Jaeger wrote and published articles and pamphlets, designed clothing (including socks with five separate toes) as well as bedding, and opened first one shop and then a chain of outlets for his approved goods. One chain of fashion shops still bears the Jaeger name in Britain today, although, sadly, now they are unlikely to stock a single woolly vest on the shelves.

Town and Country Clothes

Carefully preserved by the Rural History Centre at Reading is an agricultural labourer's jacket, a garment that speaks eloquently of a particular Victorian lifestyle. The jacket is stiff, solid and very hard-wearing; its colour can be best described as 'whitey-brown' and it is stained by heavy use. All the edges are firmly bound in cotton tape to compensate for the extra wear that would develop with time around the cuffs, pockets and hems. The inside of the collar is greasy and marked with sweat, while the arms of the jacket have faded in a pattern that can only have occurred if the rigid material they are made of had wrinkled up with wear and stayed in that wrinkled position for years of sun and rain. The outermost areas of the arms have faded, while the parts trapped in the depths of the permanent folds have darkened. More grease has stained the front of the jacket, perhaps from it rubbing up against horses, while the shoulders, which took the brunt of the weather, are the most faded areas of all.

When Tony Widger, a member of a similar class, got dressed for a day's work, he wore a pair of trousers and a Guernsey jumper. The jumper represented the closest thing there was to a uniform among fishermen, and marked out the members of his profession as a distinctive social group within Victorian society. Elsewhere at the start of the period, the clothes of those who lived and worked in towns and cities were noticeably different from those in the countryside. Countrymen wore heavy, hard-wearing cotton fabrics that were mostly pale and undyed. Townsmen wore dark-coloured wool.

Out in the countryside, over the top of their waistcoats and trousers (clothes worn by men of all classes), men sometimes wore not a coat but a smock. These too were made of taut, strong, undyed cottons. They were pulled on over the head like a tunic and protected the underclothes beneath. Most distinctive was the stitching, which held the pleats perfectly in place at the neck and shoulders.

Fig. 11. Two working-class men, 1876. The nearest (*left*) wears a rural smock.

Unlike a coat or a jacket, a smock required no skill in cutting out. Simple, large rectangles were pulled into shape by the stitches, which, although they could be beautifully done, were, it has to be said, relatively simple to execute. Smocks could therefore be made at home by those without tailoring training and were cheap and practical. However, by the 1840s, smocks were fading away from the fields of Britain. Older men in more conservative parts of the country hung on to wearing them for a short period, but the young soon wore jackets like the one preserved today in the Reading Rural History Centre.

Heavy canvas-style fabrics provided good-value trousers for working men in the countryside. They tended to be made with a twill weave to give more flexibility, and they were available in a number of subtly different styles. The style we are most familiar with today is the weave known as jean, which was especially popular among workers in America, where the climate was warmer. Jeans, like flannel trousers or corduroys, soon became known by the name of the fabric alone. American workers preferred jean, or the even cheaper denim fabric (jeans made from denim rather than true jean fabric have now inherited the name 'jeans'), but most British workers wanted more warmth from their cotton trousers. For this reason, moleskin became the most popular choice by the end of the nineteenth century. Moleskin was, again, just a single weave of pure cotton fabric which had a raised and brushed nap. This meant that the outer side of the fabric had a soft and felted feel; you could only see the weave on the inside of the cloth. It was significantly more insulating than jean, being wind-proof because of the raised nap, and was just as long-lasting. And, although all cotton fabrics got wet easily, they also dried quickly.

It is still easy to buy moleskin and corduroy trousers in Britain today, but the main difference between these and those worn by nineteenth-century workers is that the modern versions finish at the hips. Victorian trousers, despite many fashion variations over the years, always carried on up towards the ribcage, keeping the lower back covered and warm, no matter how much digging or stooping one had to do in the course of physical labour outside.

To protect his legs and trousers, the countryman added a pair of gaiters to his outfit. In their simplest form, gaiters were a rectangle of sacking wrapped around the lower leg. They were tied with one piece of string just below the knee and another around the ankle. Had the countryman walked into town, he would definitely have stood out. Thomas Hardy nostalgically recalled the early-nineteenth-century fashion of the countryside and the fading away of its distinctive style as town clothes began to take its place. He most pithily summed up these differences in 'The Dorsetshire Labourer', an essay written in 1883. He said that 'twenty or thirty years ago revealed a crowd whose general colour was whitey brown flecked with white . . . now the crowd is as dark as a London crowd.' Indeed, by the 1880s, when Hardy was writing his essay, most countrymen had swapped over to black moleskin jackets and trousers, second-hand broadcloth and tweed.

By this time, agricultural workers looked much the same as industrial workers in their dress, at least superficially. Some older rural clothes often remain in period images, but one must be careful: they are rarely the snapshot of real life we might hope for. Most, even the more casual scenes, were in fact carefully posed, with people who were deliberately asked to bring and wear certain clothes by the artist or photographer, who was often in search of his own idea of the rural idyll. Incidences of smock frocks and sun bonnets were frequently part of the agenda.

But if the countryman of the 1830s and 1840s was most likely to be dressed in an array of pale-coloured but durable cottons, the townsman was much more likely to be dressed in wool clothes of one quality or another and, more particularly, of one age or another. Despite enormous technical advances in spinning, weaving and dyeing, the actual sewing of clothes in the 1830s was still done entirely by hand, which of course had an impact upon the prices and qualities available. If everything had to be hand-sewn, and the costs of that borne, there was little benefit in using poor-quality fabrics. It made much more economic sense for the poorer sort of townsperson to purchase second-hand clothes of good quality. This is what most men did until the second half of the century. A fine suit made by a tailor would last for a very long time, and long after it had gone out of fashion. Such suits formed the usual clothes of the working townsman.

I have handled many pieces of Victorian clothing for men. They don't feel at all like the clothes and fabrics we are all so used to wearing now. When we look at images of people in Victorian dress, what we tend to notice mostly is the changes that have occurred in fashion. The fabrics the garments are made of go largely unnoticed.

If you pick up a man's coat from either 1834 or 1901, you will immediately see that certain characteristics of the fabric and construction will be the same, regardless of the change in fashion between those two dates. The wool will be heavily fulled (or felted) and you will not be able to see the weave. Rather like a felt hat, the cloth will be dense and at least a millimetre thick. It will have a tendency almost to stand up by itself, the weaving is so tight. The fabric does not bend and flex so readily as the woollen fabrics that we, in the twenty-first century, are accustomed to, and it will be heavy. The garments are sturdy, solid and windproof, and only the very heaviest of downpours will get them wet. Water usually stands on the surface, drying off in the wind before it has a chance to seep into the fabric. Such materials and such coats continued into the twentieth century. If you have ever felt a Second World War greatcoat, you will have a good idea of the Victorian coat. Policemen and nurses continued to be issued with cloaks and capes in similar qualities of fabric until the 1960s. Wool was designed to protect a person from the great outdoors, in days well before there were any Gore-tex, polar fleece or other high-tech, polycarbon-based textiles available.

Throughout the period, indoor and outdoor temperatures in Victorian Britain were not so far apart. Most people, including the wealthy, lived in much colder rooms than we do now. The weight and fineness of a twentieth-century wool suit, which is lighter and less substantial, would have been considered suitable only for colonial service in the Victorian mind – something to be worn in the tropics. Which, when you consider that most of us now spend our days in offices and buildings heated to around 18–24°C, is what we essentially use them for: we now have tropical temperatures in our daily lives. The Victorian office, however, was likely to be around 10°C, if heated at all, in winter. Many reports exist of the ink freezing in the inkwells of workplaces, as well as schools. Victorian suits therefore needed to offer much more warmth than their modern counterparts.

Fashion and Technology

Fashion and changes in textile technology affected all Victorian men. Although their overall appearance did not fluctuate as dramatically as that of women, nonetheless, even the poorest factory worker of 1901 looked markedly different from his 1837 grandfather, and his clothes were produced and sold in an entirely different manner.

PARIS FASHIONS FOR MARCH.

Fig. 12. A frock coat, 1850.

For the wealthy man, fashionable outerwear at the very start of the period consisted of trousers – which had just taken over from breeches as male leg-wear – a waistcoat and a frock coat. The frock coat was almost always made of good-quality broadcloth. This was a fabric with a very long history in Britain and one that tailors were well used to working with. Beau Brummell, and other fashion leaders of the late eighteenth and early nineteenth century, had made the immaculate, superbly cut and perfectly fitting broadcloth coat the epitome of good taste. The young Benjamin Disraeli, before he embarked upon his political career, was well known as an especially well-dressed young man, his frock coat nipped in at the waist using a newly developed system of darts to create a flawlessly smooth finish at its very slim waistline. Many young men at this date wore corsets to achieve the tiny waist then so fashionable for men. Whether Disraeli did or not is a matter for conjecture: in an 1826 cigarette card of him when he was twenty-two years old he looks as if he may have done so. He certainly opted for flamboyant colour, sporting on that occasion a bright-orange waistcoat, red trousers, a shortened frock coat and a cane (see Plate 19). The more solid citizen's frock coat was warm, well-tailored, with a waist seam (though not as shaped as some), and came down to just above his knees (see Plate 14).

Trousers in this early style were tight-fitting down to just above the knee, without a crease down the front. Without turn-ups, they flared out from the ankle, down over the shoe, and only the toe peeped out. They did, however, come with a strap which buttoned up beneath the shoe. This pulled the fabric down taut, preventing it from flapping about around the ankle or from riding up and spoiling the sharp look. Many different fabrics and colours were acceptable when it came to trousers in

Fig. 13. The height of fashion in 1850: a young man sports a tall top hat, a jacket that is unfitted to the waist and a pair of slightly wider checked trousers that flare over the shoe.

the 1830s. Cream and buff were felt to be especially young and daring, but stripes and checks were also common, with darker colours generally favoured by those who had to make their clothes last longer. Unlike the working countryman, the wealthy and the townsman's trousers were usually woollen. Flannel was a very popular choice, as was serge. These fabrics were much lighter and more flexible than the broadcloth used for the frock coats, but still substantial by today's standards.

Waistcoats were where a man could really indulge himself (see Plate 12). Embroidered examples were expensive, but the new technological developments in dyeing, fabric printing and weaving made some very striking fabrics affordable. One didn't need a large amount of cloth to make a waistcoat, as even the grandest designs had plain cotton backs to them. A little money could therefore make a big impact. A woollen waistcoat added insulation to an outfit, whereas a silk one spoke of luxury and sophistication. Different still, a printed cotton waistcoat was an inexpensive way of indulging in some extravagant graphic design. Sporting images were very popular, especially those from horse racing: galloping steeds and vibrantly clothed jockeys. Jousting knights and heraldic motifs gallivant over the surface of a woven wool waistcoat currently in the Victoria and Albert Museum. A tartan, velvet waistcoat in the same collection would have been both practical and expensive, as well as dazzling in its punchy colours. Floral designs were also popular, with many of the patterns in pink. The riot of colour and decoration was unending. Nothing was too bright or too garish for a waistcoat, nor too feminine.

With the arrival of the sewing machine, the making and selling of men's clothes underwent a fundamental change – one that had a huge impact on what most Victorian men wore. First invented in 1845 by American Elias Howe, the sewing machine was developed by another of his countrymen, Isaac Merritt

Singer, into something that could be mass-manufactured and mass-marketed. He opened a series of shops in Britain in 1856 and, almost overnight, the price of men's clothes plummeted.

Fig. 14. By 1876, the coat and trousers had become straight, almost tube-like in their fit.

The wealthy continued to visit their tailor, who made clothes to fit their individual measurements. The sewing machine made very little difference to these businesses, as the intricate work involved in the creation of close-fitting clothes remained easier to perform by hand. But, for everyone else, the sewing machine opened up an entirely new shopping experience and access to very different sorts of clothes.

A small, 'ready-to-wear' clothes industry had been in existence for centuries, making loose-fitting, simply shaped garments. As well as underwear, it had been producing cheap trousers and coats in hard-wearing fabrics in a 'three sizes fits everyone' approach. Although considerably cheaper than the 'made-to-measure' work of conventional tailors, their hand-sewn clothes were still beyond the financial reach of many working-class people. Until the 1860s, most working-class Victorians had looked extensively to the second-hand markets for their clothing.

A Liverpool factory worker in 1850 would have visited 'Paddy's Market', where a large two-storey building housed the best in second-hand clothes. The place was packed with stalls. Some specialized in individual garments, and others offered entire outfits. There were qualities to fit all purses, from the very best cast-offs of a shipping magnate with only the slightest of wear on the seat of the trousers to the threadbare rags of a Lancashire weaver. Some of the clothes had seemingly come straight off their previous owner's back, but most had been laundered, mended and pressed. The pace of business was brisk, and the goods – if worn – were generally of high-quality cloth. Other cities had similar markets. In Manchester, it was Knot Mill Fair; Belfast had its Open Courts; Birmingham boasted Brummagem Market; and in London it was Petticoat Lane.

By 1870, however, our Liverpudlian worker could turn his back on other people's cast-offs, because the ready-to-wear market had exploded. Huge clothing emporiums had opened all over the country selling machine-sewn clothes in the simplest of shapes and fabrics. New clothes were now affordable even to factory workers, as long as they remained in work. Alongside these new, cheaper clothes came innovative and aggressive marketing. 'Ikey cords, cut up slap with the artful dodge and fakement down the sides, 10 bob' were the words emblazoned on the façade of one East End London establishment. This, roughly translated, meant a pair of fashionably cut corduroy trousers with a stripe down the side for about 40 per cent of the price you would pay if you went to a tailor for the same garment. The stripe down the side was the latest fashion touch, although, in truth, no genuine gentleman going to his tailor would have asked for a pair made of corduroy.

For a man with employment in the rapidly expanding clerical sector, the new shops meant that he could own more clothes that followed the current trends. E. Moses & Son and H. J. & D. Nicholls were two of the most well-known chains catering for this market. They fitted their shops to the very highest standards, mimicking those of the fashionable elite, with large expanses of mirrors, glass and highly polished wooden counters. The clothes on offer may have cost less than half of what a tailor would charge, yet the choice was wide and the shops were careful to follow what was happening among the fashionable upper classes closely. This was a shopping experience that gave very humble men a taste of the sartorial high life.

At the same time as sewing-machine technology was transforming male dress, chemical technology was undergoing a revolution. The new chemical dyes of the 1860s were stronger and more light-resistant than any that had gone before. While women's clothes would become almost dayglo, for men, this meant black. Black had previously been a difficult colour to produce, and one that faded fast. Victorian town dwellers, however, had a pressing reason for choosing it. Coal smuts from domestic fires and industry swirled continually in the air, settling on everything and turning it a sticky black. Pale colours quickly became unsightly in this atmosphere, and even the wealthy saw good reason to choose colours that didn't show the 'blacks' too readily. The new, non-fading black was an immediate success, and townsmen began to dress predominantly in dark colours.

Towards the end of the period, the fashionable shape that the generally black, ready-made clothes had first mimicked from the 1860s had now lost its accentuated waist. Coats were now straight from the shoulders, with little or no definition at the waistline; many were cut without a waist seam at all, and hung in one piece down to the lower thigh. The frock coat was receding into formal wear, while new, looser-fitting coats with wide, baggy sleeves became more common. Trousers, too, were going through a baggy phase. They no longer had the strap beneath the boot to hold them in place but were allowed to move about. This was, of course, a much easier style for the ready-made market to imitate than a tightly fitted design. It was also a much more comfortable style to wear; informality was in vogue and male fashionistas of this date were usually portrayed in relaxed poses. Tartan trousers also seem to have been popular for a few years among the more daring.

Fig. 15. 1884 was a time of baggy trousers and loose-fit coats for mature men while the modern lounge suit was emerging as the fashion of the young.

By 1890, as Hardy had bemoaned, the countryside had also turned black. In part, this was due to the invention of light-fast dyes, but, more decisively, it could be traced to the cultural pull of the cities, and of London in particular. The old cotton/wool divide between the town and country had broken down, with black moleskin fabric now covering as many factory workers as farm labourers, and cheap woollen trousers and jackets appearing in the countryside as much as in the towns. There were still, however, a few subtle differences. Gaiters, for example, were worn throughout the century by men in the countryside keen to keep the mud off their trousers; townsmen had far less need of them. Scarves were rarely seen on countrymen, even in the depths of winter, but townsmen liked to be well guarded around the neck for much of the year. There were thus still discernible clues as to a man's urban or rural background, but each could blend with the other in a crowd.

The wealthy man of the 1890s was approaching a look we would all recognize today as the formal suit of our own era. The lounge suit became the dominant style, sidelining the frock, tail and morning coat into dress for special occasions. (There remains to this day a roaring trade in morning coats for weddings.)

With both wealthy and working men now wearing the same sorts of clothes, it wasn't just the urban/rural divide that was blurring. To the casual eye, or in, say, a photograph, a working man in his Sunday best could be hard to distinguish from a much wealthier gentleman of leisure. In reality, you could tell the difference at twenty paces. The tailor-made suit fitted snugly and evened out any oddities of body shape; it hung smooth and wrinkle-free. The off-the-peg, ready-made suit was much looser on the body. Its fit was only ever approximate, and the fabric had a tendency to look worn within a few weeks of purchase.

Today, while it is relatively easy to see surviving fashionable Victorian clothing in museums, it is much harder to find the clothes that would have been worn by those at the bottom of

Victorian society; they rarely endure the rigours of time. There are, though, some photographs that give an accurate picture of what such clothes were like. Take, for example, those taken of prisoners from 1871 onwards. Unlike in most other Victorian images, the subjects and their photographers did not have a chance to change their clothes or dress especially for the camera. These pictures represent what each individual was wearing at the moment of their arrest – generally, their everyday work-wear, not their Sunday best or a specially selected costume. They depict, almost exclusively, working-class people, and usually the poorest end of this class. The clothes on display are worn in layers and show wear and the worst of fit: everything appears either three sizes too big or three sizes too small. Shirt, waistcoat and jacket are usually visible; vests often show at the neck, and in many of the pictures there is more than one waist-

Fig. 16. Portrait of a criminal. Charles Mason, shortly after arrest, 1871.

coat or jacket being worn on top of another, some done up and some left open. Rather than wearing high-quality, warm fabrics, these people were simply layering up with whatever extra garments they could find. All the garments have rips, repairs and patches, and they mostly look filthy.

Take Charles Mason. A labourer and a shoemaker, he was thirty years old when he was arrested for stealing an overcoat. The coat he is wearing in the photograph is dark, woollen, battered and worn. All the buttons are missing and the lining has come away. Beneath the coat is a dark jacket that is at least two sizes too small. Under the jacket is a collarless white shirt that can just be seen with a large, striped scarf wrapped around Mason's neck and tucked down into his trousers. With neither the coat nor the jacket fastening properly, the scarf was his only way of keeping his chest and stomach warm. Yet the general shapes closely echo fashionable wear. He is dressed emphatically – if poorly – as a man of the 1870s, not as a man of the 1830s or even the 1850s. These clothes would have been acquired when and where possible, in the best affordable state of repair. Yet while people were willing to wear whatever came to hand in order to keep out the cold, it didn't mean such men were not interested in looking good or fitting in with those around them.

Hats

Like jackets, hats were rarely removed in public. Britain was a hat-wearing society and, among men, hats were taken off only momentarily, in order to show deference or respect. While they clearly had the function of keeping men's heads warm and dry, they also engendered a strong cultural feeling of independence and self-respect. A man put on a hat when he went out to face the world; it was part of his personal armour, much like make-up can be for some women.

The style of an individual's hat varied, depending on fashion and their social position, as well as their profession or chosen activity. There were top hats and straw hats, bowlers and flat caps, deerstalkers and trilbies, sports caps and berets.

Fig. 17. The 1850s topper was shorter than the 1839 equivalent, but still around two inches taller than the modern top hat.

The most prestigious hat throughout Victoria's entire reign was the top hat. Originally, the top hat was extraordinarily large – fourteen inches high for the most flamboyant of rich, young men. But within ten years it had settled down to the ten inches in height that looks familiar to modern eyes. There was a range of top hats on the market, of varying qualities; the practised eye could discern which marked out the businessman, which the lord. Yet the top hat was never truly affordable. A basic one could be bought by a factory worker for around two weeks' wages. At the other end of the scale, the very best silk topper, with its own special leather box for storage and transportation, would cost a factory worker the equivalent of three months' wages. These were hats that spoke of wealth. Their long currency as upper-class headwear also came to give them an aura of respectability beyond the vagaries of fleeting fashion. Young and dandy in 1837, they were sober and formal sixty years later. The opera hat, however, managed to cling on to its original insouciance. A collapsible top hat, generally lined in a bright-red silk, it continued to speak of playful, even salacious, rich lifestyles.

Country parsons held on to an older style of hat with a four-inch-high crown and a very wide brim. Being outside fashion lent it a serious demeanour, one which became more and more closely associated with piety as time went on.

Fig. 18. Hat for a curate.

The bowler hat began life in 1849 when William Coke, a customer of shopkeeper brothers William and Thomas Bowler, asked them to design a hat that would be robust and easy to keep on. William (or his relative Edward Coke; there is some contention over the issue) had specifically wanted a hat for his gamekeepers to wear. Their top hats were forever being knocked off by low-hanging branches when they were out in the grounds. He wanted something strong enough to withstand the outdoor life without expensive damage but also something smart that would give his men protection. William and Thomas produced a prototype for his approval. Mr Coke is reputed to have taken the hat outside and stamped on it twice to test its durability.

Fig. 19. Bowler hat.

Within only a few years, bowler hats were being widely worn by the gentlemen of shooting parties, as well as by gamekeepers. Cheaper than a top hat, and much longer-lasting, they gradually became the preferred headwear of bankers and clerks, eventually making an appearance on the heads of ordinary agricultural labourers. The one group of heads on which the bowler did not appear was factory workers. When clerks, bankers and managers adopted the bowler as their customary headwear, it became a symbol of middle-class status within the towns and cities. Working-class townsmen who had the temerity to adopt the same hat as their middle-class 'betters' would have received short shrift – and were likely to find themselves jobless. Wearing a bowler out in the countryside, however, carried a different set of cultural allusions, allied with country sports and pointing to a commonality between the upper- and working-class wearer.

Straw hats were another option for men, but were not suitable for town wear; agricultural labourers used them to cover their heads and shade their necks when working out in the fields and the upper classes wore them for holiday, leisure and sporting pursuits along the river, at the seaside or when attending a cricket match. A straw boater was an exceedingly solid item, capable of being bowled down the street. The straw plaiting and hatting industry located around Luton in Bedfordshire made an array of styles for both men and women, and several of my own female ancestors were recorded as working as 'straw plaiters'. The boater, however, was by far the dominant style for men. It was formed of long strips of plaited wheat straw sewn into a spiral. Unlike many other straw hats, boaters were made of several layers of this plait and, once finished, were entirely rigid. A good boater could last a person the majority of their lifetime. For most of the century they were a luxury product, but, around 1880, straw plait began to be imported from China, hugely undercutting the domestically produced plait and pushing my ancestors into serious poverty. Suddenly, with cheaper hats available, humble clerks could join their wealthier brethren in owning special holiday headwear for afternoons in the park or weekends away.

Fig. 20. Straw boater.

If straw boaters were for boating, as well as for general countryside leisure, other sports came also to acquire their own associated headwear. Small pillbox hats graced the heads of those partaking in athletics or gymnastics, and early cycling clubs also adopted the pillbox as part of their uniform. Small and light, and resembling the shallow, round boxes that pills were sold in, the pillbox hat sat happily on the head even when a man was engaged in vigorous exercise. Made of soft cloth, it was also ideal for emblems and badges to be sewn upon. By the end of the century, commercial companies were using the style for active delivery staff. To this day, American bellboys wear pillbox hats.

Fig. 21. The sporting cap.

Peaked caps have had a very long history as sporting headgear. Eighteenth-century jockeys wore brightly coloured caps, as did the competitive long-distance walkers or 'pedestrians' who were the crowd-pulling sporting sensation of the first two decades of the nineteenth century. Rugby School began giving out free peaked caps to its rugby players in 1837. Cricketers moved over to peaked caps in around 1850, and footballers generally sported the same style. It may well have been this long sporting tradition that made the cloth peaked cap gain such widespread popularity among working-class men at the end of the century. Up until the 1880s, working men of both town and country would have been much more likely to wear a felt hat. Round-crowned and round-brimmed, such hats quickly became softened and shapeless in the rain, although their floppy appearance didn't stop them being effective in keeping sun, wind and rain off a man's head. By 1901, however, the urban working-class man had moved over, en masse, to the flat cap. While his country cousin had a range of options, the flat cap became the townsman's most iconic garment.

Fig. 22. Shapeless round hats were worn by working men until the 1880s, when the flat cap gained popularity.

Women's Clothes

Underwear

Victorian pornography varied from giving charmingly naive glimpses of a woman's ankles, via titillating shots of a seductress resplendent in corset and drawers, to some very graphic compositions in which the models were most definitely not wearing any drawers at all. Usually, however, the first garment a woman would put on in the morning rarely featured in the world of adult entertainment. A woman's chemise, rather than being a risqué item of *un*dress, carried cultural overtones of purity. At the end of the Victorian period, a soap advert could consist of a young woman dressed in only her chemise, with her hair flowing loosely over her shoulders, and it was still thought to be chaste.

The chemise was almost always made of cotton, and although there were subtle changes to its style over the years, it remained essentially a simple tube-like garment with short, capped sleeves. It left a woman with bare arms, a plunging neckline and exposed lower legs. Nightdresses conforming to this shape are still widely available in high-street shops in Britain today (although a Victorian woman's nightdress was more substantial, covering her arms and falling as far as her ankles).

Standing in her chilly bedroom, the Victorian woman would then pull on her drawers. The drawers, or knickers, we wear today are largely a Victorian innovation: there is only occasional evidence of their existence in Britain prior to the Victorian era, but by the end of the reign they had become de rigueur. They began as two separate knee-length legs drawn together with a waistband. Obviously, this left a gap between the legs that was entirely exposed.

Initially, such garments were greeted with hostility. Drawers, so the thinking went, were nothing but an imitation of men's underclothing and as such an assault on feminine virtue and respectability – the biblical injunction against women dressing as men (and, indeed, men wearing women's clothing) had long held sway. It had also been traditional for prostitutes to wear, and then remove, the garment as an extra layer of titillation for their clients. The fact that drawers were commonly worn in some other European countries, such as France, only added to the resistance against them. But there were some practical reasons, too, for the hostility.

An additional layer was simply a nuisance. A pair of knickers would have been worn under a long skirt and several petticoats, each of which already covered the body from waist to ankle. Wearing knickers as well made it difficult to change quickly, particularly if a woman needed to relieve herself. I have, unfortunately, experienced this problem myself when wearing Victorian clothes. Removing one's undergarments to answer a call of nature is not an easy task, and can leave you in an uncomfortable tangle.

The introduction of the crinoline as a fashion garment, however, would act as a spur to knicker-wearing. Crinolines, or hooped skirts, were frames made of steel and cotton tape that held a woman's skirt away from her body. With the outer dress now raised, there was no difficulty when using the privy. However, new problems arose. Every incautious movement, or a sudden gust of wind, could tilt the crinoline and skirt up to an angle that exposed the legs to view. A pair of drawers promised added warmth, now that the skirts were so far away from the body, as well as a welcome degree of modest coverage should the crinoline be caught by the wind.

Over time, drawers, or knickers, became more widely acceptable. Queen Victoria was a keen adopter, and collections of historic clothing throughout Britain today contain pair after pair of plain cotton drawers, exquisitely hemmed and discreetly monogrammed with her initials. Surviving examples show that she was happy to wear knickers that were partially joined between the two legs, a common feature at one stage in the development of knicker design up to the 1880s, but that she chose not to follow knicker fashion thereafter, eschewing the fully sewn-together drawers that began to appear at the end of the century.

One of the most interesting surviving pairs of knickers I have examined dates from the late 1860s. They were worn by a working-class woman, are fashioned in blue cotton and are firmly and expertly sewn with an open crotch. They are slightly longer than many later pairs and fasten below the knee with a small button, which gives maximum coverage and prevents them from riding up the leg. They are well washed and soft with wear, but they have also been repaired by their one-time owner. Patches have been carefully sewn over the knees, testament perhaps to the number of hours the woman would have spent scrubbing floors and cleaning grates.

The intimate nature of these garments meant that they were among the most commonly home-produced clothes of the period. The ready-to-wear market knew better than to advertise drawers too prominently, even though they were simple to mass-produce and required very little to be adjusted to different sizes. The simplicity of the cut of Victorian drawers is symptomatic of this home production. People wanted the simplest of shapes so they could repeat them to accommodate the whole family. A basic diagram could provide all the information a woman needed to make a pair, whereas something more complicated, such as a shirt, might require a full-sized pattern. Lace of varying grades was often added to later Victorian drawers, but, in the main, they were plain and functional; the fanciful and silky confections that can sometimes be found in antiques shops are usually Edwardian rather than Victorian.

With the chemise and drawers covering most of the woman's body, it was left to the stockings to complete a full 'base' layer. Made of cotton, wool or silk, they were machine-knitted by 1837 and available in a range of colours. White was fashionable at the start of the century, but from the 1850s onwards brightly dyed and patterned stockings were being worn by the young and daring. Green, lilac, tartan, paisley, striped, spotted and

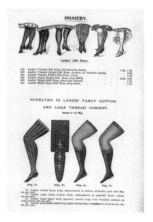

Fig. 23. Ladies' 'fancy' stockings.

checked were just a few of the choices; such a range paid dividends when an ankle was occasionally flashed at a young suitor.

More conservative black stockings became widespread in the latter years, and were especially advised for pre-teen girls, whose short skirts revealed more of their calves. Wool was the warmest and most reasonably priced option, as well as being considered the healthiest, due to its insulating qualities. Silk stockings were a luxury product affordable only by the few. They also required careful attention and laborious darning if they laddered.

From the 1880s, women began to use suspenders to keep their stockings up, initially held by a separate suspender belt and later from suspenders sewn on to the bottom of the corset. But, until that point, the Victorian stocking was held in place by garters fastened around the leg just above the knee. Varicose veins could become a serious problem if garters were too tight and thus impeded circulation. However, failure to secure them tightly enough could lead to acute embarrassment: the stockings could fall to the ground, along with the garter, and be dragged around the shoe. This was doubly shaming, as both stockings and garters were considered to be extremely intimate and sexual garments. Still, I am sure that many men enjoyed the spectacle!

It was intended that the chemise, drawers and stockings be regularly changed, due to their close proximity to the skin. Daily was ideal. There was a garment, however, that could not be washed at all, and this made the cleanliness of the first layer all the more important.

Corsets were worn throughout Victoria's reign by women of all classes (see Plate 9). Even records from prisons, asylums and workhouses contain corset provisions for female inmates. They offered fashion, naturally, but to the Victorian mind they also offered self-respect, sexual attractiveness, social conformity and a range of health benefits.

Fig.24. A typical corset, 1869.

The belief that a woman's internal organs required support was a strong and persistent one. Men, it was thought, were much tougher and less in need of this assistance, and yet even for them it arose as a concern, with the popularity of 'flannel body belts' widely reported. Dr Jaeger fretted about the need for men to 'gird their loins' (the loins being not the thighs but the muscles that run down either side of the spine). To 'gird' did not mean to tense but to cover these muscles. For women – the weaker vessel – the need was seen as all the greater. In Victorian thought, the womb and other reproductive organs made female midriffs more delicate and problematic. Ironically, this may well have come to be the case, as a corseted woman, especially one who had been corseted from childhood, did lose muscle tone. With a corset to perform many of the supportive functions of the back and stomach muscles, these muscles went largely unused and therefore became, to some degree, weak and atrophied. If such a woman left her corsets off for a day or so, she would probably find the lack of them disconcerting and tiring, and would struggle with the floppiness of her middle regions. She was likely to return to her corsets with a sense of relief, confirmed in her opinion that they were a necessary garment.

Periodicals such as *Female Beauty* stated that 'women who wear very tight stays complain that they cannot sit upright without them, nay are compelled to wear night stays when in bed.' The erect posture that was required of both men and women gave this feeling added potency. Unlike the stigma-free, laid-back culture of the twenty-first century, relaxed posture, for the Victorians, went hand in hand with slovenly behaviour and loose morals. The good-looking, the successful, the fashionable and the strong were those who stood or sat erect.

Standing and sitting up straight is much easier in a corset than without. From my own experience, you can slouch as much as you like and still look impeccably upright. If you are sitting in a chair, it helps if you perch on the front edge so that you can settle the edge of your corset at the right angle. In this way, you can stay, with no effort at all, beautifully poised for hours on end.

In addition to the benefits of support, it was thought that a corset provided the warmth a woman's vulnerable insides required, and that allowing the kidneys and other organs to become chilled was foolish and dangerous and could lead to a range of illnesses and disorders. In wearing corsets, women were protecting themselves from the vagaries of the British weather. Corsets were particularly valued for being a windproof layer. Many medical men praised women for wearing them, contrasting their healthy behaviour with the propensity of some men to leave themselves exposed. Doctors, in general, were very supportive of female corset-wearing. Their only reservations concerned not the corsets themselves but the practice of 'tight lacing' – of using corsets to change the shape of the female body dramatically. Mainstream medical thinking was that an uncorseted woman was as foolish as one who was tightly laced. A properly fitted and properly worn corset, on the other hand, could prevent the straining of the ligaments supporting the womb. It was also good for a healthy bladder, averted back injuries, helped in the recovery from childbirth, facilitated healthy diges-. tion and generally assisted a woman in leading an active life. Or so it was thought.

A neat, corseted figure was, ultimately, what society expected of a woman. Wearing one meant that she was daily proving to herself, and to her neighbours, that she had standards and, more importantly, self-respect. An uncorseted woman was thought to lack self-control and would have faced public disapproval and crude assumptions about her lifestyle. Only those who were prepared to be social outcasts went without.

The corsets of the 1840s and early 1850s were often home-made and were no more complicated to make than the bodice of a dress. Patterns and instructions were to be found in many women's magazines up until the 1860s. One of the best and easi- est to follow appeared in the *Workwoman's Guide* of 1838. The corsets shown consist of four cotton panels sewn together, with the addition of gussets: two for the breasts and, sometimes, two more to go over the hips. The boning in many of these hand- made corsets was often minimal, just a couple of pieces either side of the lacing holes to prevent the lacing from rucking up when fastened and a single rigid 'busk' resembling a ruler slipped into a pocket in the cotton at the front of the corset. This central busk would form the primary stiffening, and could be of wood, whalebone, horn or metal. The rest of the shaping was achieved by cording, the threading of lengths of cord or string through closely sewn channels. The corset was then laced together at the back.

A lightly boned, corded corset like this is a very easy thing to wear, more comfortable, in my opinion, than the under- wired bras of the twenty-first century. A corset moulds the body into an elegant shape, supporting the bust and smoothing out the lumps and bumps. It is warm to wear, and not too constricting. Even with enthusiastic tugging on the lacing, it is hard to achieve more compression than is produced by the shapewear currently on sale in today's high-street shops. A corset is perhaps too hot to wear in the height of summer, and the busk length must be just right so that it does not dig in (contrary to popular expectation, longer is better: ending somewhere on the pubic bone seems to be most comfortable), but it provides a smooth, compact solidity to the torso that looks attractive through the outer clothing of the day, holding everything firmly in place and providing a fashionably high bust-line.

Professionally made corsets and more fashionable corsets of this date usually contained more panels, eight being a common number. In addition to a central busk, bones were fitted front and back and also followed the curves of all the seams holding the eight panels of material together. With these corsets, a much tighter lacing was possible, and was practised. Wooden busks were replaced with the more flexible whalebone or steel, which meant they could be pulled in against the stomach as the laces were tightened.

As the 1850s slipped into the 1860s, the pressure to show oneself possessed of a small waist continued to build. The old home-made corsets began to dwindle away as more people turned to professionally made equivalents that could enable them to attain a more fashionable shape. This was the age of the corset horror story. There is one frequently quoted letter to a women's magazine that sums up the worst excesses of the practice, written by a woman who had not only gone through the experience but was perfectly happy to have done so: 'I was placed at the age of fifteen at a fashionable school in London, and there it was the custom for the waists of pupils to be reduced one inch per month until they were what the lady principal considered small enough. When I left school at seventeen, my waist measured only thirteen inches, it formerly having been twenty-three inches in circumference.' That this is no exaggeration is proved by the survival of a few of these tiny-waisted corsets. To put this into perspective, the waist measurement of the average toddler is about twenty inches. Such drastic reductions in waist size could be achieved only by a woman wearing, over a period of time, a series of smaller and smaller garments and corsets, both day and night, and eating a very regulated diet with a number of tiny meals replacing the three main meals of the day.

Fig. 25. Tight lacing, 1863. Notice how the shoulder blades are drawn together.

In other reports of the practice at fashionable schools, it was stated that the corsets were removed for only one hour a week, in order for the girl to wash. Several accounts talk of the 'pain' of tight lacing, but also say that it passed if you could just bear it for a while. Girls would compete with each other for the smallest waist and, amid the admissions that they sometimes fainted and suffered from headaches, they also remain positive about the experience. It seems, for some young women, to have given them a 'high'. As with painful initiation ceremonies and rites of passage, a small group of young women found in tight lacing an excitement, a pride and a sense of belonging. But it *was* a small group of young women at this extreme end of corset-wearing. The vast majority of surviving Victorian corsets and outer clothes of this period are nothing like so small in the waist. Nineteen to twenty-four inches is the common range for fashionable young women's clothing, with clothing for older women usually rising by several inches. By twenty-first-century standards, these are still very small waists. A size ten dress is currently averaging twenty-seven inches at the waist. By Victorian measures, my own figure would be described as 'corpulent', requiring the larger pattern sizes stocked by the paper-pattern shops. Adverts promising to contain and control the 'stout' and 'matronly' figure would, confronted with a thirty-six-inch chest and twenty-nine-inch waist, only just do it. And yet, according to current statistics, I am still very slightly slimmer than the average British woman of today. All the evidence suggests that most Victorian women were – be they rich or poor – slim.

As a 'corpulent' woman with a 'matronly' figure, I have worn several styles of Victorian corset for extended periods of time. When I reduce my waist by two inches, I adjust very quickly and suffer no real problems. I, of course, do have some excess body fat that can be compressed; a slim woman with less spare flesh would find it harder. However, when I take four inches off my waist, things do start to become more difficult.

Allowing the body time to adjust is important when wearing a corset. Most people, including practised corset-wearers, find them tight to put on at first but, after a couple of hours, they can manage with them much tighter than initially. When making a bigger change, there is a much longer adjustment period and you have to be willing to be patient, and not get upset or anxious. If you are not used to corsets it is very easy to feel constricted and to imagine that you are having trouble breathing. The panic can make it difficult to breathe and the situation can escalate. I arrived at Victorian corset-wearing as someone who already had plenty of Tudor corset-wearing experience, so although the two experiences proved to be very different, I was at least aware that I needed to give myself time. The body does adjust. After a few days I found that I was able to be as vigorous in my corset and with my waist reduced by four inches as ever I was. I was soon charging around after escaped pigs and scrubbing floors, just as before.

The problems I did experience with wearing such corsets were not the ones I had expected. The most immediate was trouble with my skin. Twenty-first-century underwear can leave me sore in the areas where shoulder straps and other bits of elastic press. The corset caused the same problems as the elastic, but all over my upper body. It was worst when I had been hot and then cooled down, as the sweat left salt on my skin, which then rubbed. This could be agony. After an eighteen-hour day working hard in my corsets, my skin would be an angry red mass and the itchiness almost unbearable. In my experience, corset itch rivals chickenpox.

The other problem I encountered took slightly longer to manifest itself. I was experiencing some problems with my voice and eventually went to see a speech therapist, who noticed that I was breathing almost entirely with my upper chest and hardly using my diaphragm at all. It seemed that I really had adjusted and adapted to the corseted life. With my lower ribcage compressed, I had learned to get the oxygen I needed without troubling my diaphragm. It certainly made sense of some Victorian health advice I had previously found rather quaint. Dr Pye Chevasse in his *Advice for Ladies* extols at some length the virtues of singing as good exercise. Now I knew why: plenty of strong, diaphragmatic singing was just what I needed.

Many people, when they think about the compression caused by corsets and hear about waist sizes, are under the impression that it is the soft area above the hips and below the ribcage that is affected. This is only partly true. The lower sections of the ribcage, as Victorian medical treatises made clear, were also very much involved in the squeezing. If you look at an image of a tightly corseted Victorian woman, you see that the waist decreases in size smoothly down from the bust, but there is no sudden angle where the ribs stop. When you wear a corset, you become very aware of this. It is the compression of the ribcage that interferes with the breathing, and I certainly found that it was this area that was most uncomfortable. The soft tissue around the waist didn't give me much trouble at all. As a corset is tightened, the lower ribs are pushed down and inwards. At the same time, the whole torso is remoulded from being, overall, oval to becoming round. It is this change in shape that gives those first two inches of compression much of their visual impact. It is an optical effect, for the same volume presented as a cylinder appears much smaller.

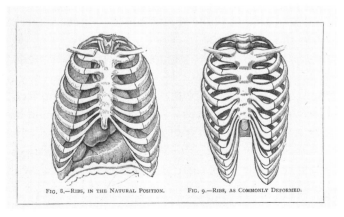

FIG. 8.—RIBS, IN THE NATURAL POSITION.   FIG. 9.—RIBS, AS COMMONLY DEFORMED.

Fig. 26. A woman's ribcage, before and after corsetry.

At the end of the day, when I took off my corset, there was always a strange moment – an odd sensation when everything tried to return to its natural shape. I felt my ribcage re-inflating, which took a rather disconcerting five or six seconds.

My experiences of corsets have come after a lifetime mostly lived without them, so will always be different to those of people who have worn them since childhood. I cannot expect really to know how Victorian women felt in their corsets. They were entirely used to them; their stomach and back muscles had developed – or not – to take account of them; and they had grown up with ways of moving that suited what they were wearing.

The Victorians themselves did have a raft of concerns about corsets and waists. Various authors warned women that tight lacing would cause problems with the chest, with digestion and reproduction, would deform the skeleton and (this is the one that was often presented as a clinching argument when seeking to persuade women to stop) give rise to a red nose due to poor circulation. The problem, however, came in defining 'tight lacing'. Where did health-giving support and moral control give way to health-impeding tight lacing? An inch or two off the natural circumference of the waist was clearly not a major health hazard in the eyes of the majority of the population. People were accustomed to the idea and used to seeing their mothers so girded.

Trying to ascertain what was healthy and natural for women could be problematic. If corsetry was near-universal and waists really did reduce in size as a result, it could be hard to find a model or exemplar. Most writers turned to Greek and Roman statuary as a socially acceptable way of talking about female bodies. Classical statuary showed the naked female form in a respectable manner and combined that respectable nakedness with a useful lack of corsetry. The Venus de Medici was much discussed as a model for women to emulate, for here was an avowed beauty, life-size and with a twenty-six-inch waist.

Fig. 4.—Figure with Waist of Natural Size.

Fig. 5.—Figure with Waist Deformed by Artificial Compression.

Fig. 27/28. Silhouette of a 'natural waist' and a corseted female figure, 1869.

In addition to mainstream fashion corsets came 'health' corsets. We might well imagine that these garments – the commercial result of the strong and frequently published worries about corset wearing – would be less constricting. However, a quick glance at both adverts and surviving examples confirms that they were generally as stiffly boned as the fashionable corsets. Their claims to health rested instead upon features such as air holes to allow the skin to breathe, which, following my own experience of skin problems when corset wearing, I would be happy to try out.

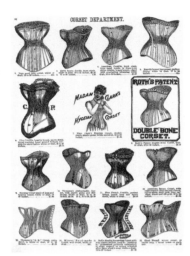

Fig. 29.
An advert for
'health corsets'.

Once the corset was in place, the remainder of a woman's underwear could be put on. Petticoats were the next consideration. These came in a number of shapes and varieties. The basic set consisted of one flannel petticoat and one cotton petticoat, although more could be added. The white cotton petticoat went on first, as this could be easily washed. Accidents during menstruation made this a very sensible arrangement, and the practical nature and function of the garment meant that it was usually simple in shape and without decoration. The flannel petticoat was to provide warmth and, again, was generally simple in shape, though it often had some small embellishment. It was also short – just below the knee in length. Like many of these petticoats, an original example that I own has a cotton waistband in order not to add any bulk or spoil the effect of the corset. These two were the basic, practical petticoats worn by all classes of women throughout Victoria's reign. Those seeking to emulate the fashions of the day, however, required additional underwear.

The corded petticoat was the simplest and cheapest method of adding shape, and consisted of a white cotton petticoat with a series of lines of stitching running around the hem with string or cord threaded into the spaces between the stitching. It stiffened the fabric, making the petticoat stand out, but could still be washed. Fashion in the 1840s and 1850s called for ever bigger skirts, supported by more and more petticoats. One such petticoat was often made of a fabric woven from horsehair. Called 'crin au lin', the horsehair was woven into a fabric that was supremely stiff, springy, light and abrasive. By gathering up this fabric, a woman achieved a frill that was strong enough to resist being crushed or flattened by the weight of the skirt over it. However, in 1856, a lightweight steel crinoline was invented that made these petticoats redundant. Hoops of steel wire were threaded into tapes arranged in concentric circles around a new, single petticoat (see Plate 10). These cage-like structures allowed women to discard the many heavy layers of petticoating they had worn previously. Crinolines could be bought in numerous shapes and combinations, according to the dictates of fashion – and they were almost always bought rather than home-made, as they were not especially expensive garments, retailing generally at a third of the price of a dress of similar quality. Later in the century, when fashionable skirts were slim at the front and sides

Fig. 30. One of *Punch* magazine's many cartoons about crinolines, 1856.

but enormous at the rear, bustle pads (like feather-filled cushions) and steel and cotton crinolettes (frameworks worn under the rear of the skirt) took over. The pads, at least, could be home-made, with one account of a mistress discovering that her maid simply used a number of dusters tied on beneath her skirt to create the effect.

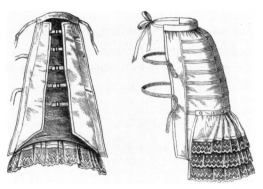

Fig. 31. Crinolettes.

One of the reasons all these support garments were so popular was that they could be used to transform the style of an existing dress. If a woman got the general silhouette right, a fashionable look could often be achieved economically, with little amendment to the outer garment itself. They all, of course, presented their own challenges to wear. Most critically, you had to know how large you were, so that you could accurately negotiate tight spaces. Sitting could be quite an art in some of these petticoats. Anything that stuck out predominantly at the back required a diagonal approach to chairs. Images of the fashionable lady of the 1870s show that she perched on the very front of the chair at an angle of approximately forty-five degrees, leaning slightly forward. It is a very elegant look, but also an eminently sensible one when wearing a bustle or crinolette. In about 1885, the fashionable woman had to relearn how to walk as well as sit, because petticoats and skirts became narrower and narrower. The difficulty in walking was in part the point: it prevented such fashions being easily emulated by women who had to work. The trick, I have found, is to adopt a slightly circular gait. At each step, it pays to move the foot outwards, describing a semicircle, rather than just stepping forwards. This ensures that the fabric has no chance to form any folds or tucks that would further constrict movement, keeping it at all times taut. In addition, such a gait gives a swaying motion to the hips, which the tight skirt is very good at showing off. A woman wearing such clothes and walking in this manner could look alluring, even if she could not go anywhere quickly.

Fig. 32. Ladies perched on the edge of their chairs, 1889.

The final layers of female underwear were the various vests, camisoles, corset covers and chest preservers that went on over the corset. Some were for warmth and some to soften the visible corset line across the chest. Many Victorian cotton camisoles and corset covers survive, and are still frequent finds in antique shops, along with nightgowns and baby clothes. They are beautiful garments, in the main, with embroidery, lace and ribbons. The more prosaic day-to-day versions, which were designed primarily for warmth, were much more common, but few survive today. Finer clothes have a much greater historical survival rate than more functional items.

The Great Exhibition of 1851 featured the wares of more than ten manufacturers of knitted vests. These knitted vests were more expensive than their flannel counterparts, which could be easily made at home. For those who were really struggling financially, and for whom even a flannel vest was beyond the budget, a simple chest preserver was a welcome help. These were flat pieces of flannel, leather or hare skin that could be laid across the chest and held in place, rather like a baby's bib, with a tape around the neck, and another at the waist to prevent it from riding up. Some wealthier, more fashion-conscious women also opted for chest preservers – of the hare-skin variety – as they provided warmth without bulk, thus preserving not only their chests but also the ultra-slim look of their bodices. For the very poorest, several sheets of newspaper could be used in a similar way to keep out the wind. The overgarments for less wealthy women were generally shawls of some type, and because there were many jobs that were difficult to manage with a shawl, the newspaper between bodice and corset was often essential. Having had days when I have had to work outdoors in the depths of winter in Victorian clothing, I can attest that this is an invaluable addition.

Outerwear

The dress the young Queen Victoria wore on her first day as Queen was not absolutely in the *latest* fashion, incorporating as it did elements that had appeared in fashion plates over the previous year. Originally made up in plain black silk, it has now faded to a rich brown. A pair of vertical fringes runs down the skirt to one side, and the sleeves concertina along the arm, held in tight, miniature pleats at the shoulder and controlled by a series of bands the length of the arm. It was not a difficult dress to copy, and if you switched to printed cotton rather than silk, it was one that was within the reach of not only most middle-class girls but even some servants. The fashion plate that allowed a competent seamstress or dressmaker to keep up to date with the latest trends was becoming much more widespread, and was a great help if you were based well away from London but still wished to stay in sartorial touch. Local dressmakers produced most of the country's dresses, which were made to measure for individual clients. Being able to reproduce

Fig. 33. Fashion plate, *The Ladies' Cabinet*, 1839.

fashionable garments was a big selling point for such business-women. Some women at home did have the skills to produce whole outfits, but most stuck to manufacturing the many underclothes needed by the family. Making a mistake with the more complicated outer clothes would be an expensive mishap – better by far to leave it to the professionals. You may have to pay their fee, but at least you averted the risk of ruining the only piece of fabric you could afford to buy that year.

Another option, halfway between home and professional production, was to use a travelling dressmaker. She came to the house and did all the cutting out and fitting, while you and your daughters did most of the sewing, under her supervision. This worked very well financially if you made up a series of garments all in one go, perhaps a dress for each of the women of the family. Alternatively, you could unpick an old dress and use it as a template to cut a new one. It was an economical way around the difficulties of fit; it did, however, leave you woefully out of date.

If you could afford none of these options, then you turned to the thriving second-hand-clothing market. If a young woman worked in service, she would often be given clothes by her mistress, and this was a major route for clothes to move between classes. Some families provided a uniform for their servants, which helped considerably, but it was also common practice for mistresses to give maids their cast-offs. Since many families objected to servant girls looking too fashionable – like their 'betters' – many of these clothing gifts were sold or passed on. Such movement of clothes was so common that people were accustomed to seeing poorer members of society dressed in slightly worn clothes and in fashions that were a few years out of date. This in itself formed a spur to fashion: if you failed to keep up with it, you were in danger of looking like a servant.

Regional fashions were easily discernible in the 1830s and 1840s among working-class people. In the fishing villages of the north-east, some women wore quilted petticoats that had been fashionable wear in the 1760s. Women in most other parts of the country had long abandoned these garments, but they were still popular, and widely made by the fishermen's wives along this stretch of coast, because the locals had come to think of them not as old-fashioned garments but as part of a style unique to themselves. Welsh women, too, often had a regional identity and were well known for their tall black hats and red shawls, and also for their preference for using the local striped wool cloth to make their skirts. Irish women, different still, were often characterized by bare feet and short, knee-length skirts. The fast-growing fashions of London coexisted with traditional dress in all these communities, but local considerations still endured. A woman in the Rhondda Valley might well have found that the cheap printed cottons so abundant in Cheshire and Hertfordshire were not so readily available to her as the coarsely striped local wools. Tradition also played its part, and there were provincial fashion leaders who held sway in small areas. To wear the clothes of one's community could make a person feel closer to their home; looking like an English outsider sometimes held little appeal. As the railways pushed their way into every corner of Britain, some of these local considerations began to have less influence. Materials became more evenly available, and people moved around more often. In 1861, the tax on paper was repealed, and this, along with a series of technological leaps forward in the printing industry, made books, magazines, flyers, catalogues and posters significantly cheaper and more prolific. Fashion information was one of the boom areas of print, and served to standardize aspirations across the country. The beautiful, hand-coloured fashion plates of the 1839 magazine *The Ladies' Cabinet* would have reached the eyes of several thousand women at best, but those included in the Beetons' publication, *The Englishwoman's Domestic Magazine*, of 1862 were seen by ten times that number. The first full-size paper patterns had been available in Britain in the 1830s. By 1858, there were at least ten different pattern shops in London, selling both over the counter and by mail order. In 1860, the Beetons began to include full-size paper patterns from a leading French fashion house in their magazines, alongside the fashion plates. In 1876, the American company Butterick opened a shop in Regent Street, joining the throng. Their patterns began at three pence and went up to two shillings, with between forty and sixty designs arriving each month. The industry proved enormously successful, and paper patterns became an essential part of magazines aimed at women.

Fig. 34. Fashion plate, *The Englishwoman's Domestic Magazine*, 1862.

By 1860, the fashionable shape, which was supported by both the corset and the crinoline, was tiny-waisted and enormously skirted. A woman slipping on her dress over a steel crinoline had a lot of fabric to arrange carefully over the surface. Most of the accounts we have from women who wore them, including a girl in her mid-teens at around the time of their introduction, are positive in tone: 'Oh it was delightful; I've never been so comfortable since they went out. It kept your petticoats away from your legs, and made walking so light and easy.' But there were disadvantages. Managing such vast and bouncy skirtage could be tricky. Sitting down had to be re-learned if you were not to expose too much of yourself. A discreet lift of the back of the skirt worked; this could be achieved with a flick of the hips that made the crinoline bounce up. If that was too difficult, you could reach back and find the uppermost hoop through the layers of skirt and lift it a few inches. Narrow doorways were more of a problem, involving an ungainly squashing process. And then there was the ever-present danger of a sudden gust of high wind, which could leave you scrambling to hold your skirt down. The cartoonists loved crinolines, and

UNDER THE MISTLETOE.

Fig. 35. *Punch* cartoon of a crinoline causing consternation under the mistletoe.

huge numbers of satirical prints poured from their pens. *Punch* left no joke untold – and, besides, it gave a respectable gloss to publishing pictures of ladies' underwear. There were images of women sitting in omnibuses, their skirts pushing men out of the windows, of picnic parties with women sitting upon the grass, exposing themselves as their crinolines ballooned upwards, of women stuck in doorways, and of lovers vainly trying to embrace while kept apart by the woman's skirts.

Personally, I am very fond of crinolines; they are a huge amount of fun to wear. I enjoy the way they sway and bounce around. Some Victorians, though, found this most *un*attractive, complaining about the eye-jarring nature of the jiggling and jerky movements caused. Women, such people felt, should be smooth and graceful at all times. It is of course possible to move gracefully in a crinoline, but not everyone is a natural dancer. The one complaint I have about them is the draught, and this was also a common grievance among Victorian women. When you were accustomed to having your lower body swathed in layer upon layer of cloth, to then be reduced to wearing just a pair of cotton pantalettes between you and the great outdoors was none too comfortable.

By 1862, between 130 and 150 tons of steel were being consumed each week by the crinoline trade. This was a thriving business, and constituted one seventh of Sheffield's entire output of steel. It was not just restricted to the fashionable elite but became an element of dress encompassed by a surprising number of working women. There were many jobs a woman could not do while wearing a crinoline, such as pushing a coal wagon underground or any form of field work. But other tasks, such as sewing and dressmaking, were possible. Many women adopted a middle stance, in that they wore a crinoline on Sundays, but not during the working week. Many of the pit lasses photographed in the 1860s wearing their trousered workgear were also photographed in their Sunday – crinolined – best. The journalist Henry Mayhew once opined that every woman in Britain must have had two sets in her wardrobe to account for the volume of sales.

Those trousers the pit girls wore were attracting a lot of attention in the 1860s. They were not so much regional costume as occupational clothing. Many photographs showed these women wearing men's trousers, but in a peculiarly female fashion. Underground, women had traditionally moved the coal to the surface after the men had dug it out. This meant pushing or pulling laden trucks along low-ceilinged tunnels. The most efficient way of doing this for most women was to lean forward at a considerable angle, using their body weight to do some of the work. Skirts worn at the customary length would have tripped them up in this position, so they were required to be either very short – around mid-thigh – or tucked up to a similar height. The latter made far more sense, since the skirt could be unrolled for warmth and respectability above ground. However, bare legs meant that knees could get scraped as the women laboured, and there was also the issue of decency: often they were working alongside men. Pantalettes, or drawers down to the ankles, were already worn by small children beneath their shorter skirts, and it is thought that these were initially in use by the pit lasses. But the work and environment was dirty and harsh, and substituting men's hard-wearing trousers for the drawers was, ultimately, an obvious choice. Their trousers became famous, and were worn beneath skirts that were tucked right up to mid-thigh height at work. It was a distinctive look, but not a masculine one; it became an occupational uniform, a badge of status and position in its own way.

Throughout Victorian Britain, people were marked out by their mode of dress, recognizable instantly by occupation. Fishwives working along the east coast of Scotland and the north-east coast of England generally wore several striped woollen skirts, one on top of the other, tucked up to leave the feet and legs bare from the knees down. They complimented these with a shawl tightly crossed over the chest and tied behind. Many took a huge amount of care when they tucked, to ensure that the different patterned stripes were folded in such a way as to create a pleasing appearance. Dressed like this, these women worked on the rocks and the beaches, helping men to launch and haul in the boats, emptying out the catch and preparing it for sale. Up on the quayside, their skirts now untucked, they wrapped large oilskin aprons around themselves when it came time to gut and salt the fish. It was a very practical adaptation of dress, and one that was so distinctive it attracted the attention of gentlemen photographers, illustrators and even the retailer Debenham & Freebody, who in 1876 sold a range of children's outfits based on the women's designs and style.

Fig. 36. A fisherwoman, 1875.

The colour of clothes underwent its own revolution in the middle of the Victorian period, and this coincided with the height of the crinoline phase. In 1856, William Perkins discovered a new form of dye which could be manufactured from coal tar, at that time a waste product. Mauve was the name he gave to this novel shade – and it was extremely bright. Emerald-green, magenta, solferino and azuline followed, each one vivid and garish, particularly when used for the purpose of dyeing silks. Fashion in the 1860s held nothing back; forget subtle and tasteful, this was the age of pizzazz. Combined with crinolines and a penchant for fringing, many of the dresses that survive from this period would put the most exuberant of lampshades to shame (see Plate 11).

Fig. 37. An exuberant moment in women's fashion: enormous skirts and bold trimmings.

The introduction of the sewing machine led to an elaboration of extra frills and trimmings at the top tier of the fashion pyramid, as the same amount of work could now produce more effect. Lower down the scale, it led to a quiet rise in the number of garments people owned. Outworkers, sweatshops and factories were able to lower their prices, as the sewing machine speeded up the manufacturing process, and stimulated demand. In the short term, it put a terrible strain on the poorer women who took in piece work. Desperately poorly paid, they could not afford to purchase, or even hire, a machine, which left them trying to compete by hand with the wealthier sewing-machine owners. The adjustment period was a harsh one, and it went on for quite some time. I bought, many years ago, a Victorian nightdress. Later, I discovered it featured in an 1889 mail-order catalogue. This meant it was a standardized garment made more than thirty years after the introduction of the sewing machine, and produced on a commercial scale. Yet it is entirely hand-sewn, presumably on a piece-rate basis, by just such a worker.

As the 1860s drew to a close, the fashionable skirt shrank at the front and sides, leaving the fabric of the skirt to be swept back, and up and over the large rear. Luckily for many cash-strapped fashion followers, this was a style change which could be accommodated by the simple purchase of a new crinoline (or crinolette), with already owned skirts being arranged in folds and tucks over it. Gradually, these new crinolines became no more than bustles, with the general silhouette of the figure becoming slimmer and slimmer, and the bodice becoming longer and sleeker.

By the end of the 1880s, the ready-to-wear market for women began to catch up with that for men. While bodices still largely defied mass production, requiring far too much fit for nineteenth-century factory methods, the range of garments that were for sale ready-made was rising. Underwear and nightwear had previously been manufactured at home by women, but by this decade vast quantities were being produced commercially. Sewing machines and machine-made lace had made the production of chemises, combinations and nightdresses much quicker, and the product more attractive. Such items were very popular with women lower down the social ladder, who were only too glad to shift the burden of such sewing on to other shoulders. Petticoats and skirts were now also available ready-made, as was a range of cloaks, coats and other overgarments.

For those for whom even the ready-to-wear market was just too expensive, and for whom occupational or regional dress had little meaning, clothes still carried one important cultural message. Were you a member of the 'respectable poor', or were you one of the desperate? As long as you could keep up appearances, there was hope, but sink below the acceptable level of clothing standards and doors would be slammed in your face, opportunities closed off to you. With a presentable set of clothes, you were employable, but few would take on someone whose clothes had gone beyond that almost intangible boundary. Cleanliness was part of it – worn clothes that were obviously cared for were much more acceptable than dirty or unkempt ones – but you also needed a certain coverage, the full quota of garments. Even among beggars this mattered. Henry Mayhew's interviews with members of the London poor highlighted this on several occasions. A beggar who looked like a working person with worn but 'decent' clothes generally took far more money than one who was dressed in rags and tatters. People understood and sympathized with someone temporarily down on their luck, but for a beggar without respectable clothing there was no respect.

Often, the same dress could carry one set of meanings when worn by one person, and a completely different set of connotations when worn by another. If, say, a desperately poor person was given a very finely made and fashionable dress as an act of charity, and they wore it despite having no shoes or stockings to go with it, few would regard them as passing muster in terms of respectability. Such an outfit would have engendered thoughts of prostitution in the Victorian mind, and the recipient of the dress would be far more sensible to sell the good dress on and buy a cheap but more complete outfit with the proceeds. In this outfit, a job could be successfully sought or lodgings secured.

Worse still, in the eyes of many, were workhouse clothes. These provided some warmth but were laden with shame. Each workhouse union was free to choose its own uniform. Most remained roughly in line with the general styles of working-class clothing of the period, erring towards the old-fashioned. Liverpool Union in 1843 recommended that the adult women be issued with two unbleached calico chemises, one flannel petticoat, a grey linsey skirt, two jackets (described as bedgowns, an antiquated phrase even during the period) of stout blue-and-white-spotted printed calico with a calico shawl of purple and white, two aprons, two pairs of black wool stockings and a pair of shoes. With everyone the same, the uniform would have been instantly recognizable to the population at large. The fabrics were among the very cheapest of the day and, with only cotton fabrics covering the upper body, would not have been very warm. Having two chemises, two jackets and two pairs of stockings, the women could maintain a reasonable level of cleanliness with one set on and the other in the wash. But there was no provision for changes in the seasons, let alone for individuality. Women's clothes within a workhouse were usually made up by the women themselves, which might suggest that they were allowed at least to make sure they fitted, but in practice this was usually frowned on by the management, who preferred to set sizes so the clothes were interchangeable. A woman would therefore wear whichever garment was handed to her from the week's wash, rather than having her 'own'. Some of these uniforms were scarcely updated throughout the entire history of the workhouse, which made workhouse clothing increasingly anachronistic and even more noticeable to those outside. A photograph of St Pancras workhouse in London taken at dinner time in 1900 shows hundreds of forlorn women sitting in rows dressed in a baggy version of 1850s dress.

The Feel of Clothes

I have made and worn a variety of Victorian women's clothes; suffered through numerous corsets and sworn at several sewing machines; hand-sewn whole outfits in styles up to the mid-1850s; and persevered with hand-turned and treadle-driven (powered by the worker's feet) machines when making later clothes from the period. I have learned the techniques for 'fanning' a corset, for handling horsehair, and I have spent hours drawing threads for handkerchief edgings. It has been enjoyable, time consuming and extremely interesting. There is no single resource that can make you better understand and appreciate the written accounts of the time. And if the making has taught me a great deal, so too has the wearing.

This would not have been true if I had worn mock-ups or theatrical costumes produced in modern times and with modern materials and techniques. Costumes available from prop houses – even the finest in the world – are made with the needs of film, theatre and actors in mind. Some are beautifully made to period patterns; most are rough approximations. Some are made from fabrics that closely mimic those of the period, yet others are often made out of something cheap and available. The need for speedy changes of costume in the theatre often means that these costumes come with zips and Velcro, regardless of the nominal date of the costume. Most costumes are made to go over modern underwear. There is, of course, nothing wrong with any of this. But it does mean that most theatrical costumes are very different to wear than the original clothing would have been, and that they are of little value as research tools. If you want to know what it truly felt like to wear Victorian clothes, you have to commit yourself fully, and that means sourcing the right fabrics, cutting out the pieces using the right pattern-cutting techniques for the date (they changed a lot), using the right sewing thread, the right tools for the job, the right techniques (ways of doing things also changed regularly). It also means wearing all the layers, not just the few that show. It is difficult, but the experience is quite different and very revealing.

Every set of accurate period clothing I have ever worn – and there have been a few of them, not just Victorian – has influenced the way I move. Each outfit changes your general posture, whether sitting, standing or walking. It also changes how you do things; each era's clothes make some movements easy and comfortable and others awkward and unnatural. I find myself using completely different techniques and approaches to do the same job or activity, depending on which type of clothing I am wearing. Take using a sickle, for example. I have cut a field of corn with a sickle in dress of the 1620s, edged a field (the new-fangled horse-drawn reaper-binder machine couldn't manage the areas next to the hedges) wearing clothes of the 1870s and cut down an overgrown allotment with a sickle in the 2010s. In the earliest of these sets of clothes I found that the best way to do the job was to stand with one foot in front of the other with the front knee well bent. I then leant my left elbow upon that knee, supporting my weight and saving my back. I advanced up the field with the sickle in my right hand, first loosely gathering a bunch of stems in the curved blade, then grabbing the tops of the stalks with my supported left hand and sharply cutting with a snatched, jerking movement with the sickle. The 1870s set of clothes pinched and dug in when I tried to repeat the same motion wearing them, but I found that if I kept my weight more central and settled into the corset I could bend forwards and work more squarely on, with my back muscles relaxed, as the springy steels of the corset were supplying the support. The

2010 clothes required another adjustment; in the end I gave up trying to stand at all and shuffled along on my knees. Every activity and movement is influenced in this way. We don't often give much thought to these matters, as styles tend to change slowly and we all adapt as we go along, rarely noticing the changes in our behaviour that fashions bring.

The Victorian experience of wearing clothes of course changed as styles altered in the course of the sixty-plus years of Victoria's reign. It also varied enormously depending on the social class of the wearer. No one surviving in the workhouse had much of an idea what it was like to wear a ballgown; nor did many middle-class women have much of an idea what it was to be a trouser-wearing pit lass.

The most noticeable and universal point to make about Victorian women's clothes is the layering. Rich or poor, 1839 or 1901, Victorian women wore a vast number of individual items of clothes. And most of these layers were cotton-based. Silk dresses were made up on cotton backing, as were most woollen dresses. Dresses, chemises, drawers, corsets, corset covers, stockings and petticoats could all be cotton. There were a host of other fabrics that were used, but cotton was undoubtedly the dominant fibre in most women's wardrobes. Even with the addition of a flannel petticoat or two – the most common way for wool to enter a woman's wardrobe – washable cottons were important. The many layers added warmth without bulk and put a fully washable layer between the skin and the unwashable corset.

This held true throughout the period. Cotton was a cheap fabric – generally about a third of the cost of good wools, and nearer a tenth of the cost of silks – though, unsurprisingly, there was much discrepancy in price. Linen could be used instead of cotton but, again, it was much more expensive. As well as its cheapness, cotton also offered colour, variety and pattern. Fabric printing with engraved metal rollers had arrived in the late eighteenth century, allowing bright colours and varied designs, including a great many floral patterns, to fall within the reach of very ordinary people. Patterns of cloth could fade in and out of fashion quickly and easily, but even members of the working class could have attempted to follow them. Choice was one very important thing that cotton offered many Victorian women. The range of colour and pattern available to those on very strict budgets was large and appealing.

Another common theme was the skin-tight fit of bodices. Sleeves and skirts changed dramatically in size and shape over the years, but the upper part of women's garments remained very snugly held against the body, even over the parts that were not corseted. These garments did not stretch and had very little 'give' in them. A range of movements could make the fabric pull and dig in at the armpits and around the neck. As a result – and from my own experience – you quickly learn to stop twisting to do tasks, and reaching up above your head is rarely comfortable. The cut of Victorian bodices encouraged you to fetch a stool to reach that top shelf, or to get up and turn around rather than turning around in your chair.

Big skirts were very much a Victorian theme and, while their actual size rose and fell, as did the overall shape, at all times there was plenty of material sweeping about. Victorian homes, especially later on in the era, were notorious for clutter, but were you able to look a little closer, you would notice that the clutter was confined to items and objects at and above waist level. Anything left lying around below that height would soon get knocked over. There were no low coffee tables in Victorian Britain; occasional tables and stands were tall and brought most household goods out of the danger zone.

With figure-hugging bodices and large skirts, another common experience was being warm from the waist down and freezing from the waist up; it was no coincidence that many women clutched their shawls so tightly. The tailor-made business suits at the very end of the 1890s were the only real exception, when jackets produced along the lines of men's clothing in tweeds and other wools were worn over the bodice or blouse. Having worn some surviving suits myself, I can certainly understand why these became so popular with those who could afford them; they are just so much warmer.

Although they may be bulky and awkward in twenty-first-century environments, I have nevertheless found Victorian clothes to be perfectly practical in a Victorian setting. With no central heating and no clutter below waist level, many of the problems of Victorian clothes in a modern locale simply fall away. If I stick to Victorian activities, such as hauling buckets of coal or singling a field of turnips, I find myself being glad of the many layers of clothing and grateful for the back support the corset provides. When I think now of a Victorian woman lacing up her corset, tying her garters and buttoning her dress, I think of a woman dressing sensibly for the hard day of work ahead.

3. A Trip to the Privy

When the practical business of washing and dressing was complete, a trip to the privy was often the next part of the morning routine.

The Privy

Most privies were sited at the far end of the garden or yard, as far away as possible from the house, so a trip to it was generally made after you had taken the trouble to get dressed.

Traditionally, a privy consisted of a hole, a repository for, effectively, a compost heap of waste, over which was erected some form of lightweight shelter, comprising wooden walls, a sloped roof and a door. The door had a gap of a few inches at the top and bottom to allow a gentle draught of air to circulate; this meant that most privies were well ventilated. If an outhouse was too tightly sealed, the smell could quickly become unpleasant.

Inside was a wooden seat, rather like a shelf, raised above the ground. It was relatively comfortable to sit upon even in the frostiest of weather (a modern plastic seat would have been far colder). The best kept of such outhouses had their walls and ceilings whitewashed regularly, their floors and seats sternly scrubbed daily, and were stocked with a good supply of toilet paper, or newspaper squares, and a vase of fresh flowers.

Most privies were hygienic and functioned well, as long as there was enough time and space for the waste to decompose naturally, away from people and their water supplies. It helped, of course, if the waste was managed in the same way a compost heap would be, with an equal measure of fibrous, absorbent materials such as straw, leaf litter, wood shavings, scrunched paper and dry earth added to the waste. In some areas of the country, the pigsty was situated next to the privy, so pig manure and soiled straw could be added to break the waste down more quickly.

Away from the cities, the privy continued to be in use well into the twentieth century, because it was clean and cheap. For the rural Victorian, therefore, it remained almost completely unchallenged.

However, as soon as the number of people using a privy increased above the decomposition rate, it would quickly fill up. If there was more land at your disposal, this was not a problem. A new hole could be dug a little further away and the shelter moved to a new location. A thick layer of soil dug from the new hole could be used to seal off the old pit, which could continue to decompose undisturbed. The real problems occurred when people started living in more densely populated areas, without access to long gardens that kept the privies away from homes and water supplies.

In London, the authorities tried to solve the problem by insisting that people regularly scoured out the holes beneath the privies (otherwise known as cesspits). When privies filled up, the waste was dug out and removed from the city to great compost heaps in the countryside, before being spread on to the fields once it was safe to do so. At least, that was the theory. Each parish in the city had its own street scavengers and official jakesmen to clean out the public facilities; their carts trundled the streets at night, when they would cause the least nuisance. Local laws required that private householders hire these men regularly to clean out their own homes and carry the waste away. Sadly, not everyone was as conscientious as they should have been, and prosecutions for overflowing privies causing offence to the neighbours were frequent.

As towns and cities became larger and ever more populated, the problems grew. Pools and puddles of filth from overflowing and inadequate privies became increasingly common in the poorer districts, where people could ill afford to have them cleaned. Similarly, unscrupulous landlords were loath to spend money on their slum properties. The sharing of facilities only exacerbated the problem. One survey carried out in Sunderland in the 1840s recorded one privy for every seventy-six people, while, in Worcester, one privy was recorded as being shared between fifteen families. The journalist Henry Mayhew frequently wrote about the living conditions of the poor of London. His reporting was a call to action to his contemporaries, and his observations were reflected in towns and cities the length and breadth of Britain. One evening he accompanied the night-soil men as they went about their business emptying out the cesspits in much the same way their predecessors had been doing for the last three hundred years. A special long-handled shovel was their main tool, used to haul the excrement into large wooden buckets, which were then slung on to a pole, or the handles of the shovels, and carried between the men out to a cart in the street. Mayhew described the smell as 'literally sickening'. If the privy being cleaned was located in a well-kept courtyard with direct access to the street, then the operation could be carried out without too much inconvenience to the householders. However, particularly in the poorer and more crowded districts, the excrement had to be carried through people's homes, often in the middle of the night. In the Victorian period, the jakesmen charged around one shilling per privy: a poor living for them but still a major expense for working-class households. The cesspits they were emptying were usually small. Mayhew records that most city cesspits were brick-lined and held about a cubic yard of sewage. Many, however, were unlined or had no mortar between the bricks. Some people left the base unlined to allow liquid matter to drain away into the soil: it was only the more solid waste that was hauled away by the night-soil men; the rest would leach into the soil. Basement dwellers were known to find it oozing in through their walls.

Fig. 38. Jakesmen at work, 1861.

In the largest cities, and London in particular, the subsoil was becoming saturated with human detritus, and it began seeping through the earth to pollute the groundwater that fed the wells. Even for people who believed in the miasma theory of disease, this was considered to be highly unpleasant, but the direct link between polluted groundwater and illness was only just being discovered in the 1830s and 1840s. After all, the water from these wells both looked and smelled clean. It would be the pioneers of epidemiology and germ theory who would first see the danger signs.

In 1849, an inspection of over fifteen thousand houses was made in the City of London. Some of the results were disturbing.

Twenty-one houses used their cellar as a cesspool; thirty had cesspools that were overflowing; and two hundred and twenty-three cesspools were classed as 'full'. Around five thousand more were classified as 'offensive' or 'unhealthy'. Of the houses inspected, this represents approximately a third having major problems with human refuse.

Reliable supplies of piped water offered a solution. It was believed that the flushing away of waste from people's homes and places of work would create a much healthier and more convivial environment. But while private enterprise in early Victorian towns and cities was rapidly – if in piecemeal fashion – bringing piped water to town dwellers, there were few people who were willing to pay for the large-scale investment needed to install drains and a sewage system to take it away. With private enterprise failing so visibly, in 1848, pressure mounted for the government to act, and it became illegal to build houses without a drain connected to a public sewer. At this date, 'public sewers' usually meant local rivers. Sir John Simon, then Medical Officer of Health to the City of London, concluded in a report that was to be influential in bringing about this new legislation, that 'part of the City might be described as having a cesspool city excavated under it.' As a believer in miasma theory at this point in time, he was concerned to get the waste away from people's homes, but he had little thought for it thereafter. His great drainage push was initially successful in forcing the problem out of the individual house and into the Thames. This alleviated the soil contamination of the previous decade, but at the expense of the waterways. It took the Great Stink of 1858, when sacking soaked in chloride of lime had to be hung at the windows of parliament to combat the nauseating smell rising from the river, before the politicians were sufficiently convinced that a solution to the problem had to be found.

Fig. 39. The 'Great Stink' of 1858, as depicted in *Punch*.

The vast engineering feat undertaken over the next few decades to combat sewage was one that not only worked, largely eliminating cholera and typhoid from London and then, as they followed suit, the other main towns and cities of Britain, but is still the backbone of the system in place today. An enormous network of brick-lined drains and sewers collected waste and channelled it not out into the streams and rivers but to large treatment works where it could be filtered and purified before the clean water was returned to the river system.

The Water Closet

In 1851, seven years before the Great Stink, water closets, or WCs, had attracted the public's attention. The first public water closets opened that year in Fleet Street. They were also displayed in several washrooms at that year's Great Exhibition at Crystal Palace, which would have been most people's first chance to see them. However, they were not exactly a new invention in 1851. The first diagram of a water-flushing toilet (complete with a small fish swimming in the cistern) was Elizabethan. Invented by the writer Sir John Harrington in the 1590s, or so he claimed, this first incarnation of the modern toilet was a development on from the old monastic habit of siting the latrine over a small stream of flowing water. Several sixteenth- and seventeenth-century houses in London are described in inventories as having privies that were regularly flushed by rainwater collected in tanks and then channelled away by guttering. In the late eighteenth century, a number of technical improvements began to take place. Different types of valve and shapes of toilet bowl and rim were introduced to direct the flow of water. Development continued throughout the nineteenth century with many competing designs arriving upon the market simultaneously. These not only differed in terms of engineering, but were also designed to accommodate particular social groups. A range of simple closets in cheaper materials, for example, was produced for servants and inmates of institutions, who were thought to be incapable of operating the more expensive mechanical-valve models.

Fig. 40. The two main styles of water closet: the 'wash-down' and the 'valve'.

For all the advantages of rapid waste removal, the early adopters of water closets still had their problems. Many simply piped the waste into their old cesspits, some even directing it to the gutters in the street. Another problem was the initial lack of an 'S-bend' pipe. In early water closets, the contents were tipped out from the basin by means of one of a number of differing valves or pans, and a flow of water then cleared the bowl and pan into the waste pipe, which ran straight from the toilet to the sewers. Without a one-way S-bend pipe, any smell or fumes from the sewer could easily waft back up the pipe and into the homes of the wealthy. With the miasma theory of disease so prevalent, this caused untold worry, as well as nasal discomfort. The new water closets were therefore thought to be much less hygienic than the old privy at the bottom of the garden, which, however foul and overflowing, was at least situated outside in the fresh air, and not in the home, exhaling its dangerous fumes day and night.

I regularly use one of these early models of Victorian WC when I am working in Haddon Hall in Derbyshire. Even with an S-bend to prevent the smell of the drain wafting back up, the WC still retains an odour, no matter how carefully you try to keep it clean. Victorians experienced the same problem, as was pointed out by S. S. Hellyer in 1877 in his book *The Plumber and Sanitary Houses*: there was no way of cleaning the underside of the pan. The water from the flush simply did not reach, and in order to clean the toilet manually it was necessary to dismantle the whole appliance. Victorian WCs in general require much more regular attention to keep clean than their modern-day equivalents.

Flushing systems gradually improved, delivering much more forceful streams of water which *were* capable of dispersing waste more reliably, and the hinged pans came to be replaced with the full 'wash-down' system that remains the twenty-first-century standard: water is forced out under the rim, washing the whole surface of the toilet bowl, and the force of that water is the mechanism that pushes the waste down the pipe. From the 1870s onwards, the water closet was on the march. Once the initial problems were overcome, in towns, they became the must-have convenience of the day. As part of a marketing drive, the new railway companies even advertised their availability at train stations. In many districts, train stations were the first public buildings to install WCs. They were a facility that not only impressed the customers but drew locals to inspect the novel sanitary ware.

Dry Closets and Pail Closets

Outside major towns and cities, however, these new-fangled toilets remained few in number. Piped water, for country dwellers, was a luxury, and one that most of them would have to wait until well into the twentieth century to experience. Rural water closets were possible if you could find a way of filling a tank, and, though some large country houses went to elaborate lengths to achieve this, they were the rare exception. But the century's great interest in sanitary matters did not pass the country dweller by, for they had seen another development: the earth closet. This was a form of dry composting that was devised to reduce the smell and render the waste much safer. The system was designed to utilize topsoil, which is naturally rich in bacteria, to break down human faeces quickly into compost. If the two materials were well mixed, given plenty of ventilation and kept dry, composting was so complete that the same earth could be reused several times over without any problems. The patentee, in 1860, for this system, which was based to a large degree on traditional privy management, was the Reverend Henry Moule. Earth had long been added to privies as an aid to composting and smell reduction, but Moule's novel intervention was to keep it dry so it could be reused. He, along with several other companies, also set about making earth closets that would be easy to use. The most popular and longest-lived proved to be the self-contained portable unit. Shaped like an old commode box with a hole in the seat that led to a bucket, this held a tank on its back. When you pulled the lever, a certain amount of earth fell from the tank into the bucket on top of the faeces in the bucket. The bucket was regularly emptied into an area reminiscent of a woodshed, where the composting would occur. For country dwellers, this was a useful improvement on the plain privy.

Fig. 41. An earth closet.

In towns, or in large institutions, it was difficult to obtain sufficient earth. Household ash offered an alternative. With almost every home burning coal, most Victorians had a plentiful supply of cinders. Urban schemes in Manchester, Rochdale, Burnley and a host of Midlands towns adopted this technology for their 'pail closets', which were very similar to the country toilets. The buckets were regularly collected, and in some areas were disinfected before being returned, or returned with a layer of dry, absorbent material to improve their efficiency. The areas in which they were used in organized and well-regulated public initiatives reported a huge impact upon health statistics. In Rochdale alone, the death rate dropped from 27 per cent in 1870 to 21 per cent by 1878.

Toilet Paper

Just as water closets were newly common in Victorian Britain rather than being an entirely new invention, so too was toilet paper. Cheap seventeenth-century publications were termed 'fit only for "bum fodder"', indicating that people were recycling printed material as toilet paper. For most of the Victorian era, it was indeed newspaper that provided most people with the means of cleaning themselves. Advertisements, paper bags and old envelopes were also pressed into service. Cut into squares with a hole in one corner through which they could be threaded on to a piece of string, the toilet paper used by most Victorians was a home-produced affair. The idea of spending good money on something that you were going to throw down the privy or WC was one that seemed ridiculous to most of the population. However, as news of germs began to spread, it seemed sensible that the material you used to wipe away disease-carrying faeces from your body should be impregnated with some germ-killing agent. The earliest commercially produced toilet paper was thus 'medicated', and so the industry began.

America was the leader in this field, with the first brand being launched in 1857. The British Perforated Paper Company began production in England in 1880; its products could be bought in packs of one hundred or five hundred sheets. Emphasizing the medical nature of the product, rather than its comfort or convenience, the manufacturers sought to make it a necessity of healthy life.

The medicating process left the paper hard and shiny, much like tracing paper. Indeed, the medicated toilet paper that was still the norm in schools of the 1970s and even 1980s was often pressed into service as tracing paper in the classroom – as long as it was a new, clean pack, of course. Soft, absorbent toilet tissue is very much a late-twentieth-century phenomenon.

4. Personal Grooming

Back in the bedroom, and still before breakfast, the morning routine continued as men and women prepared their hair, beards, face and hands for the day ahead. This could be a fifteen-second appointment with a comb or the start of an elaborate personal-grooming ritual. For women, in particular, it could be a lengthy process, and a wide array of tools, lotions and potions took centre stage in the bedroom.

Women: Hands and Fingernails

Hands and fingernails had a special place in the lexicon of female beauty. Most women were engaged in hard, heavy work, both in the home and elsewhere, which tended to leave an indelible mark upon their palms and fingers. Blacking ranges, scrubbing privies and hand-washing mountains of laundry left calluses, chipped nails and deep stains ground into the skin. The continual use of cold water reddened the complexion, and arthritis would often set in, swelling joints and deforming fingers. Most people's hands were filthy, elbow deep, as they were, in dirt or messy tasks for much of the day. A pair of soft, lily-white hands with perfectly manicured nails was often a badge of idleness. (Of course, there are exceptions: I am sometimes accused of not working hard because my nails are too long for someone who does stuff with their hands. Sorry, folks, that's just the luck of the genetic draw. The rest of me might be nothing special, but I just happen to have super nails, incredibly strong and healthy.)

By the same token, soft, pale skin and slim fingers free of all blemishes and scars could mark you as a lady. However, in order to be able to function as outward signs of wealth, the hands needed to be scrupulously clean, free of any dryness or eczema, and the nails unbitten.

Fig. 42. Scrubbing floors was not conducive to perfect hands.

There were of course fashions in fingernails, as there are in every-thing, and a lady would need to know exactly how her hands should be presented, what shape to trim her nails to, whether she should polish them, and so forth. *The Lady's Every-day Book* helps with some of these conundrums: 'They should be of an oval figure, transparent, without specks or ridges of any kind; the semi-lunar fold, or white half circle, should be fully devel-oped, and the cuticle which forms the configuration around the root of the nails thin and well defined, and when properly arranged, should represent as nearly as possible the shape of a half filbert.' A lady was encouraged to sit down at her dressing table with a small pair of nail scissors, a bowl of warm water, half a lemon, a nail file and a leather nail-buffer. First, she would dip her nails in warm water for several minutes to soften them, then use the lemon to help clean and bleach the nails. After a few minutes of scrubbing with the lemon, she would soak her nails once again. Next, she would trim her nails into perfect ovals, not too long, in order that they did not harbour dirt, but not too short either, as that made for ugly, stubby-looking fingers. The nail file followed, not only to round off the cut edges, but also to file down the ridges on the face of the nail. The end of the file was used to loosen the semicircle of skin at the base of the nail, and any unsightly tags of skin were removed. Then came polishing with the leather buffer: five minutes buffing the nails of each hand each day was considered to give the best results. Some ladies at this point rubbed a very small amount of hand cream into their nails, but others felt that they got much better results if they rubbed them against their own scalp for a few seconds, using the natural oils of the head to condition them. Nail-biting was widely condemned for making them ugly; and white marks were felt to be unsightly and could be polished and bleached out with repeated compresses of spirits of wine and camphor.

The hands could themselves be improved with a variety of skin bleaches and creams. Lemons were a lady's first line of defence against freckles, red marks and moles. Daily scrubbing of the face and hands, as well as the nails, with a slice of lemon was thought to be an essential part of the morning beauty regime. This was usually followed by washes made of almonds and rosewater to make the hands soft and supple. If you were in the unfortunate position of having to do some work around the house before assuming the mantle of a lady in the afternoon (which, occasionally, some of the women's magazines were willing to admit might be the case for some of their readers), then creams concocted from rosewater, oatmeal and lard were especially helpful, soothing and moisturizing skin that had been subjected to too much harsh soap and water.

For the majority of women all this was, of course, out of the question. Hands dug potatoes, singled turnips, picked coal and washed out other people's chamber pots. Lard, if you could get it, helped to heal chilblains and broken skin – but that was the best you could hope for.

Women: Hair

In 1837, when Victoria ascended the throne, fashionable young women tended to part their hair in the centre, and crosswise from ear to ear over the top of the head. Smooth and straight, all the hair at the back was drawn into a high, tight bun. The hair at the front, divided into two, fell down smoothly on either side of the face, in front of the ears. It was then looped back so that the ends joined the bun. Alternatively, ringlets were worn and allowed simply to hang down one's cheeks.

The bonnet was a big influence upon this hairstyle. Bonnets were worn whenever a woman ventured outdoors; a hairstyle that was forever being crushed and disarranged by the putting on and taking off of a bonnet was simply not practical, so the

Fig. 43. Hairstyle, 1839. Smoothly parted from front to back, ear to ear, with a bun high on the back of the head. The style also called for elaborate detail around the ears.

back of the head remained simple and tightly contained in its bun. The hair at the side of the face, however, was showcased by the bonnet. It could be braided, worn loose or encased in nets, and was curled, straightened or worn in ringlets. The braids varied in thickness and number; they could be wound around the head or folded flat against themselves.

It was no accident that in an 1839 edition of the magazine *The Ladies' Cabinet* the twenty or so fashion plates included only one in which the model was not wearing a bonnet or headdress. The lone exception managed to enliven the usually sober style reserved for the hair at the back of the head (normally covered by the bonnet), by allowing a couple of ringlets to hang from the bun, as well as the more usual ear-loop detail at the side of the face. Fashion plates of 1839 also reveal a short-lived variation, in which the centre parting was replaced by two separate partings expanding back from the centre of the forehead in a V shape.

For those who were too busy earning a living to bother with elaborate hairdressing, the simple centre parting and high bun

THE TULIP BONNET.

Fig. 44. Bonnet of 1850.

worn under the bonnet was fashionable enough; one put one's effort into the bonnet rather than the hair. I have dressed my hair in a number of Victorian styles, reflecting the different historical dates I've explored, and this is one of the very easiest to achieve, and one of the securest, rarely falling down or requiring adjustment during the daytime.

Gradually, over the next fifteen years, the preoccupation with hair framing a woman's face subsided. By 1852, the bun was worn in the centre of the back of the head and the hair divided by a single centre parting. All the hair was drawn smoothly and loosely back over the ears into the bun. The key word had become 'smooth'. Those with naturally curly hair would have had a very difficult time. The occasional ringlet could still be worn about the ears at parties (ears themselves were definitely out; all the styles covered them completely). Bonnets are not so strongly in evidence by the early 1850s as they had been, and those that are evident are a little smaller and sit further back from the face. This was the style Queen Victoria would stick with throughout her life, eschewing all the changes in fashion of those around her.

Five years later, all this had changed again. The bun has now slipped right down the back of the head to the nape of the neck, and curls are back. It's all about a deep, lush abundance of thick, curly hair loosely caught back in soft, rounded shapes. Now it was the turn of the straight- and fine-haired woman to despair. Nothing but hours of curling tongs and pots of hair product could produce the look for her. Bonnets fell a little further from view. This was a style that was to dominate for the next twelve or so years. The nets and snoods used to contain the bun from around 1860 onwards made it a relatively quick style to achieve for those with good, thick hair and helped poorer women adopt a similar fashion to that worn by their more wealthy sisters. Hannah Cullwick, the woman in domestic service mentioned earlier, is wearing her hair in this way, complete with netted snood, in several photographs taken of her in the 1860s. I, too, have done a lot of housework with my hair swept back over my ears to the nape of my neck. I wore the style with a small cap rather than a snood and also found it to be a practical style. There was a tendency for strands to work loose and fall down the sides of my face, but that could largely be controlled with judicious use of 'bandoline' – of which, more, later.

Fig. 45. 1863. The bun has slipped down to the nape of the neck.

In around 1870, the bun is on the rise again, and ears come out of purdah. Swept up and back, without any sort of parting, the hair is piled into a bun on the back of the head in such a way as to maximize the bun's volume. The bigger the hair, the better: huge, coiling tresses wrapped loosely round and round, held with decorative combs and stuck with flowers. The idea was to create a great edifice at the back of the head, leaving the neck completely clear and visible. Rather like the famous statue of the Egyptian Queen Nefertiti, the long, exposed neck was to be emphasized by the huge profusion of hair balanced at the back of the head. It was a difficult look to maintain while doing any sort of useful work; it was likely to collapse if you moved around too vigorously. Working-class women were therefore shut out from this style, which may well have been part of the point. It also required a good head of hair. Lots of wealthy women had to turn to hairpieces to stand any chance of achieving it. It was a style, too, that saw the end of the bonnet. Hats took over: they could simply perch on top of the confection without interfering with it too much. This was one aspect of the new style that more ordinary women could follow, and they did. Bonnets were so last year; hats were hot.

Fig. 46. 1875. Volume was key to the fashionable, swept-up style.

The bun continued its rise – by the 1880s many women were wearing it on the top of the head, though more towards the back than the front. Some cut a longish fringe, carefully curled and dressed at the front to give more volume and interest there, rather than everything being about the back of the head. Popping the bun on top of the head gave a much greater stability to the style, and in the late 1880s and 1890s you begin to see much more active women partaking in the fashion. Schoolmistresses and servant girls were able to rejoin the fashion parade. I personally enjoy wearing this style – it is quick to put up in the morning and much more stable than the big hair of the 1880s –

but I do have some difficulty keeping it looking tidy throughout a long day, particularly outdoors.

Hairpieces

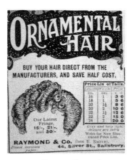

Fig. 47. Hairpiece advert, 1902. The trade in human hair flourished.

The large and elaborate hairstyles of the Victorian age, especially the latter half, created a strong demand for hairpieces. After all, very few women were naturally endowed with the amount of hair seen in adverts or on fashion plates. Hairpieces of all colours, sizes and shapes were available for those whose hair was too thin, too fine or even of normal thickness. Entire clip-on buns could be purchased that were tailored in the latest style; so were braids of hair to wrap around your own. Individual tresses were sewn on to small, discreetly coloured tapes that could be used like hair extensions, and there were preformed ringlets attached to hairgrips that could be clipped to any desirable spot. The hairpieces were often available in the very latest fashion, with manufacturers keeping a close eye on the trendsetters and offering 'looky-likey' copies within days of a new style appearing in public. Actresses were both large-scale consumers of such hairpieces and frequent instigators of new styles.

For the poor and destitute, selling your hair was an option. It could fetch a good price, particularly if it was of a fashionable shade. The makers of wigs and hairpieces were only interested in long hair, as the sorting and forming work invariably resulted in some loss of length. Blonde hair was in shortest supply, whereas red was not often in demand. Unscrupulous undertakers were known to sell hair from corpses – one of the reasons many working-class people preferred open-casket funerals. While the poor, willingly or otherwise, supplied a section of the hair market, they did not meet demand. As a result, there was a strong trade in human hair across the empire, especially in hair from India, which was thought to be a closer match to European varieties than that from other countries. Sources in India were no more ethically sound than home-grown ones, probably less so. Once the hair arrived in England, it was bleached and sorted before being sold on to a host of hair workers in small workshops, mostly based in London. Finally, it would appear on the head of a society lady.

Washing Your Hair

At the start of the nineteenth century, washing your hair was a daring task, and one that went against conventional health advice – you were supposed to brush and comb it thoroughly twice a day to dislodge any dirt. Brushing would also spread the natural oils and 'fluids' across the length of the hair, improving its condition. Most women began the operation by laying a cloth around their shoulders on which to spread their hair. This prevented the brush or comb from catching on any fastenings or trimmings on their clothes, and served to keep any dirt removed from falling on and dirtying their outfit. In addition, as they brushed, it gave them a clear idea of just what it was they were removing from their head and hair. (I recommend that you try this yourself after a day outside; even if you washed your hair the same morning, you may well be surprised at what emerges.) One of the benefits of this method was that, if you were unlucky enough to contract headlice, you would at least quickly know you had caught them and could act accordingly.

However, as the century, and new scientific thinking about the nature of skin and its breathing pores, developed, the habit of washing one's hair with water began to be promoted. The *Englishwoman's Domestic Magazine* of June 1853 noted that 'the belief that washing the head induces catarrh or headache, or injures the hair is erroneous, as the application of water to the skin is the most natural and effectual method of cleaning it, and of keeping open the pores, through which the perspiration must pass, in order to ensure its healthy condition.' It is likely that because of the length of their hair, women were keener to degrease it than men theirs, but the similarity of hair to textiles could also have prompted them to think of washing it in the same way as they would think of laundry.

From the 1840s, brushing one's hair was no longer considered to be effective as a method of cleaning it, but the old practice was still thought useful. Indeed, it had acquired a new function: it was said to help re-moisturize the hair after the washing had stripped it of its oils. Five full minutes of brushing morning and night was recommended in order to stimulate the natural production of oils and to move those oils along the strands of hair to 'furnish vigour and nourishment'.

A range of washes for the hair were widely recommended, most of which were relatively basic. Rosemary water was particularly popular. At its simplest, you would gather a small bunch of the herb together, lay it in a bowl and fill the bowl with boiling water. Once the water had cooled, the rosemary was strained out and the wash was ready to use. This was an ancient folk recipe that first appeared in sixteenth- and seventeenth-century books – indicating that some women at least had washed their hair occasionally throughout the non-bathing centuries. Rosemary water had the advantage over plain water of being slightly astringent, so it removed more grease.

The bowl of warm water was placed on the washstand (or the kitchen table, if you didn't have a separate washstand), and a towel was placed around the neck to stop water running down it and wetting the clothes. A woman then leant forward and dipped her head into the bowl, using a small jug to pour more water over the back of her head.

Using soap on the hair was a much newer idea and did bring with it some need for caution. The soaps available could be very harsh and alkali, and a strong soap could leave not only the hair dry and brittle but the scalp sore; the colour could also be bleached. Those with naturally greasy hair fared best; those with dry hair could find themselves in trouble. Many discovered that the bleaching effect of the soap did not so much lighten the colour of the hair as impart a greenish tinge to it. Rainwater did a better job, it was thought, than hard water, but the real point was to choose your soap with care and to use it sparingly. When washed, the hair would need additional help from a pomatum or hair oil to make it smooth and glossy once more, and finally a thorough brush was required to move the oils along the length of the hair, right down to its ends. 'In regard to the hair too frequent washing should be avoided; and daily washing of hair is too frequent, rendering it dry and brittle. Probably once a week is sufficient,' recommended Dr Robertson in what would remain standard advice for the next century.

Styling Your Hair

This was a private activity in Victorian Britain. Men might go to the barber's shop to have their hair and beard trimmed and shaped, but women dressed their hair themselves, or got their maid to do it for them in the privacy of their own homes.

Holding your chosen hairstyle in place was not easy. The sleek, shiny precision that was favoured throughout the period, with not a hair out of place, could not be achieved by the vast majority of women without additional help from a range of mixtures, potions and lotions. Even those most averse to anything that smacked of personal vanity felt the pressure to be at least neat and tidy. Dr Pye Chevasse in his *Advice to Wives* commented, 'It might be said that it is utterly impossible for a lady to keep her hair tidy, unless she use some application to it. If such be the case, either a little scented castor oil or cocoa nut oil, may, by means of an old toothbrush, be applied to smooth the hair.' For most of the Victorian period, such preparations were generally produced at home, and so various recipes were always present in magazines aimed at women. Bandoline was the name of such fixatives, and is the substance from which modern hairspray derives. (If you were to put a Victorian bandoline mixture into a twentieth-century spray bottle, you would be hard pressed to spot the difference.)

Hair fixatives were made from a range of ingredients, some using starch as the fixing agent, some a series of resins. They were then perfumed, coloured and a preservative added. Every one of these multifarious ingredients turns up in today's modern hairspray brands. In a typical recipe, *The Young Ladies' Journal* advises 'gum tragacanth [a resin also used when icing cakes], one drachm and a half; water, half a pint; proof spirit [made by mixing equal parts of rectified spirit and water], three ounces; and otto of roses [we would call this the 'essential oil of roses' today], ten drops'. If that did not suit, the magazine carried a similar recipe using gum arabic (a resin used in food today, as well as in hair products) instead of the tragacanth. I have made and used both types of gum and am hard pushed to say which one I prefer.

The gum arabic seems to give a stronger hold but is harder to brush out. The lasting effect they both provide – for most of the day, in my experience – is very similar to that of modern products that describe themselves as 'freeze hold'. Another bandoline recipe begins with rice starch being mixed with rectified spirit as a preservative, and then with one of a range of perfumes. I have tried this one as well, and it is very easy to make up and apply. The hold was not as strong as that of the gums, but it did brush out easily. While it was on my hair it was clear, but as soon as I brushed it out it fell away as a white dust. I was delighted to learn that this removed with it any dirt and grease from the hair. A really thorough brushing after using this bandoline leaves the hair in really good condition. Whereas the gum bandolines quickly build up in the hair and require a good warm-water wash to get rid of them, you can manage for a very long time without washing your hair if you use the starch bandoline. One of the more unusual recipes is based upon the gel-like substance that can be extracted from moss – the same stuff that makes it so good for bandages. Sphagnum moss is boiled in water for an hour or so until the water thickens, then the liquid is strained and mixed with a little alcohol, which acts as a preservative. I have not tried this one, but I see no reason why a clear sticky gel that washes out in water wouldn't work perfectly well.

Hair oils were something between a conditioner and a lotion for frizz control and were also very simple to produce. Most were based upon olive oil, with scent and, sometimes, colouring added. Pomatums, however, were closer to modern, shape-defining waxes; they melted in the fingers, making them easy to apply, then set to hold little curls and wispy bits in place. Essentially, they consisted of animal fats and waxes melted together then scented. As with fixatives, there are a huge variety of pomatum recipes: pomatums may be scented with lavender oil, lemon oil, bergamot, and rose oil in particular, but there are also spice mixtures with, for example, cinnamon and nutmeg, herb mixtures with, say, rosemary and thyme, and even expensive myrrh-scented concoctions. The fats could be anything from lard and suet to mutton or deer fat; the waxes were usually described simply as 'white' but could be made of beeswax, paraffin wax or stearin (from whales). Everyone had their favourite mixture: the one that tamed their hair the best, or was affordable, or smelt right. It is clear from all these recipes that how you wanted your hair to smell was as important and individual as how you wanted it to look. The pomatum wax I prefer is made from one of the simpler recipes, contains lard and beeswax and is scented with thyme. I use it very sparingly on short, unruly wisps of hair that are otherwise impossible to control.

Hair Dye and Removal

Colouring your hair was more problematic. Anyone looking to women's magazines for advice on this matter was likely to be met with a series of horror stories and tales of hair loss. Hair dye, even the most enthusiastic proponents would have admitted, was limited and unpredictable. In essence, you could only really dye your hair one colour – black – but you could attempt to bleach it too, if you were brave, with ammonia and alum. Throughout the century, there were specialist hairdressers who offered both these services. Their usual aim, as was the amateur's at home, was to cover up grey hair rather than change a shade. But the chemicals involved were corrosive, and accidents were common.

Sufficient interest in hair dye meant that a number of firms did produce commercial products for home-dyeing. A substance known as 'the unique powder' formed the basis of these products in the 1840s and 1850s. In reality, it was a mix of slaked lime and litharge (the natural mineral form of lead; something that is no longer permitted in hair-dye formulas), both of which could be cheaply purchased from any apothecary or pharmacist's shop.

'Unique powder', on the other hand, was expensive. Once you had acquired it, you mixed it with boiling water to form a paste as thick as mustard and carefully applied it to the hair, taking care not to get it on the skin. This was often done in the late evening, and the home-dyer would wrap her head up tightly in an old towel before going to bed. In the morning, she would wash and comb the powder out. If she was lucky, she found herself with a head of dark, glossy hair.

The next advance in hair-dye technology came in the 1860s and divided the process between two separate bottles of liquid. The first contained hydrosulphates of ammonia, a solution of potash and distilled water, which was carefully applied with a toothbrush and left for fifteen or twenty minutes. The second bottle held nitrate of silver and more distilled water and was brushed or combed into the hair. The results were generally held to be an improvement on the previous type of hair dye, but could look stark and unnaturally dark. And it was safer than the earlier lead-based dye but could still cause caustic burns on the scalp.

Another dangerous operation was the removal of unwanted hair. From the beginning of the century, a number of products were available on the market which claimed to destroy unwanted hair permanently, or to save you the time and pain of plucking. These were based upon a range of caustic substances, such as sodium hydroxide, that would dissolve the hair. The danger was that, if they touched the skin, they could cause serious burns. Pastes made of alum were also employed, and were just as dangerous. One unexpected outcome was that, if you were very careful, it was possible to achieve the modern equivalent of a chemical skin peel and hair removal all in one – but only if you got it just right. A little too much, and painful burns could

result. Other less worrisome mixtures were, basically, ineffective, although that didn't stop people parting with their money
in the hope that they would work. Even plucking could have its
drawbacks, as the pores were often left large and inflamed,
which could lead to infection. For most Victorian women, the
hair they were trying to remove was facial. Eyebrows were the
main target although, like today, some women also worried
about faint moustaches. Preparations that softened and bleached
the hairs were thus equally welcome. For the most part, these
involved lemon juice, rosewater and almonds worked into a
series of pastes and held on the face overnight with masks and
plasters.

In the last five years of Victoria's reign, a new treatment
became an option for the wealthy woman troubled by unwanted
hair – electrolysis. A fine needle was placed at the root of each
hair, into the follicle itself, and a small electric current passed
along the needle. Electrolysis remains a hair-removal treatment
to this day, but of course it was not something a Victorian
woman could do at home as part of her morning ritual. This was
a beauty treatment that required multiple trips to a professional
practitioner and was affordable only to the super-rich.

Women: Cosmetics

The next stage of a Victorian woman's morning routine required
her to decide whether to put on her make-up. Victorian cosmetics conveyed a complex mix of social messages. 'On no
subject connected with a lady's toilet does there exist so much
variety of opinion as on the use of artificial paints,' opined *The
Lady's Every-day Book*. That a woman was required to make an
effort to be attractive was accepted across society. Again and
again, the warning echoed that a woman should not 'let herself

go'. If she was to fulfil her God-given role as a homemaker, a woman must use physical attractiveness to encourage her husband to stay within the circle of home, family and fidelity. Paying attention to her own appearance ensured not only that her husband would not stray into immorality, it also raised the spirits and gladdened the hearts of all the men she came into contact with.

For those of a more strictly religious outlook, the pressure was no less great for being couched in terms of neat, simple purity. Magazines such as *The Quiver*, aimed at a strongly religious non-conformist audience, or publications such as *The Sunday at Home*, targeted at more of a Church of England audience, still carried essays about female appearance, and feminine beauty was called upon to breathe religiosity into once-resistant male hearts.

For some Victorians, feminine beauty and purity could rightfully stem only from natural remedies such as pure water, healthy living and inner contentment. Mrs Jaimeson was strongly of that opinion. In a letter of hers that was published in *The Girls' Own Paper* she wrote that 'in the morning [they must] use pure water as an ablution; after which they must abstain from all sudden gusts of passion, particularly envy, as that gives the skin a sallow paleness.' She also believed that pimples could be prevented by a light diet, that a daily walk provided all the colour cheeks needed, that getting up at dawn made the lips bright and red and that 'a desire of pleasing will add fire to [a woman's] eyes.' Meanwhile, there was a list of behaviours that could destroy a girl's looks, such as staying up late, playing cards, reading novels by candlelight and any outward display of surliness. Other Victorians were less vehement upon the subject but nonetheless agreed with Mrs Jaimeson in principle.

Another common concern about cosmetics was with the possibility of health risks. As one commentator put it, 'all kinds of paint spread upon the skin, it is obvious, must interfere with the perspiration.' The belief in the role of the skin as an organ of respiration and detoxification made anything that would block the pores a dangerous practice. While the water-washing campaign was in full steam, sealing the pores on the face seemed a very foolish thing to do. Florence Nightingale had talked of blocked pores causing a long, slow poisoning through the skin. The further belief that any matter trapped on the surface of the skin could be reabsorbed through the pores only made cosmetics seem even more hazardous.

The use of cosmetics could thus carry a number of negative connotations. Wearers were choosing to be unhealthy and unmodern and were clinging to outmoded behaviours. Poorer women could not afford any kind of cosmetics but, in a perverse way, this gave them an unexpected lift in social standing. A mill girl could just as easily wash her face and hands in cold water every day as a lady in a grand house, and she could feel just as confident in her facial looks. Rural working-class girls, in particular, were often held up as patterns of pure beauty in popular novels and stories. Engravings of young dairymaids or shepherdesses are dotted through many popular publications. The non-wearing of cosmetics was a very democratic strand in popular opinion.

Some women felt uneasy about the deceit wearing make-up could entail. There was a worry that trying to appear as something you were not lacked honesty. Such feelings were couched in terms of bad taste. One woman noted that:

> . . . we violate the laws of nature when we seek to repair the ravages of time on our complexion by paint; when we substitute false hair for that which age has blanched or thinned, or conceal, by dyeing, our own grey hair; when we pad our dress to conceal that one shoulder is higher than the other. To do either is not

only bad taste, but it is a positive breach of sincerity. It is bad taste because the means we have resorted to are contrary to the laws of nature.

The moral question was one that vexed many minds. Would this sort of physical deceit encourage other forms of dishonesty? Was a woman who painted herself to be trusted? It was widely assumed that prostitutes used a great deal of paint, although descriptions by journalists and other commentators often expressed surprise at how little was actually in evidence among them.

However, in the morning, a woman could use some cosmetic lotions that she herself thought more medicinal than aesthetic. Freckles were an unwanted discoloration of the skin in many people's minds: the archetype of a beautiful woman was one with clear, pale skin, and freckles were seen as blemishes, no better than spots and pimples. Most apothecaries and pharmacists mixed their own formulas to sell at the beginning of the century, but, by the end of the period, these locally made products were joined by a host of national brands. Most were cheaply priced, aimed at young women with small allowances. They were beyond the usual reach of servant girls, but a lower-middle-class girl, the daughter of a clerk perhaps, could purchase a face cream or two. Home-made versions were equally popular and usually employed exactly the same ingredients as those available from the pharmacist. A recipe from 1858 to cure a blotched face could include rosewater and sulphate of zinc; the resulting lotion was to be used to rinse the face before a moisturizing cold cream was applied. There are several products available for skin problems to this day that incorporate exactly these ingredients.

Hand and face creams could be viewed as medicinal, too, protecting the skin from the ravages of the weather, repairing damage from soap and water and heat from the fire. Both were available commercially throughout the period, and both could be made up at home. Traditional ingredients aroused less suspicion, so many of the recipes relied upon reworking ancient mixtures which women remembered their mothers and grandmothers making and using. Rosewater and almonds featured heavily, as did elderflower water, with its natural glycerine (still a major component in several brands of moisturizer). Elderflower water is the one I would recommend most heartily, particularly the home-made version. Pick a big bundle of fresh elderflower and put it into a bowl, pour a jug of hot water over the flowers and leave for a minute or two. Next, wash yourself in the water, using the flowers as a scrub. The natural glycerines give your skin a wonderful silky and soft feel. The rosewater and almond mixtures in all their forms are usually effective too. Sugar was another traditional ingredient in face creams, along with lavender, oatmeal and lemons. However, I am less keen on using the sugared varieties, which I have found leave the skin feeling tight.

Powder, Cold Cream and Colour

According to several Victorian advertisements, 'a lady's toilet table is not complete without this or some other absorbent powder. It not only dries the skin, but also tends to give a smooth surface and conceals pimples.' Most powder was simply scented and occasionally coloured starch – the very same substance that would have been used later in the day for the laundry, and similar to a fine talcum powder. Orris root (the tuber of a species of iris) was often present in order to hold the scent. The colour, when it existed, could come from one of a number of plant or beetle sources. This was not an expensive item to produce at home, so long as one chose an unscented mixture, and a woman could always raid her laundry starch and use it straight from the box.

Plain starch was used in powder for its white colour, which could make the complexion a shade lighter and help a woman to achieve the paleness that was so desired. Coloured powders were harder to produce at home but could be bought in a series of shades. Pinks were the most common, as they could be used like blusher. Some people did see powder as a cosmetic, but its very simplicity and cheapness tended to allow it to pass under the wire as 'medicine'. The main objection to powder centred upon its pore-blocking action, but it managed to escape any other form of censure. A coloured powder was therefore a way in which those looking for rosy cheeks could achieve them without admitting to themselves that they were 'painting'.

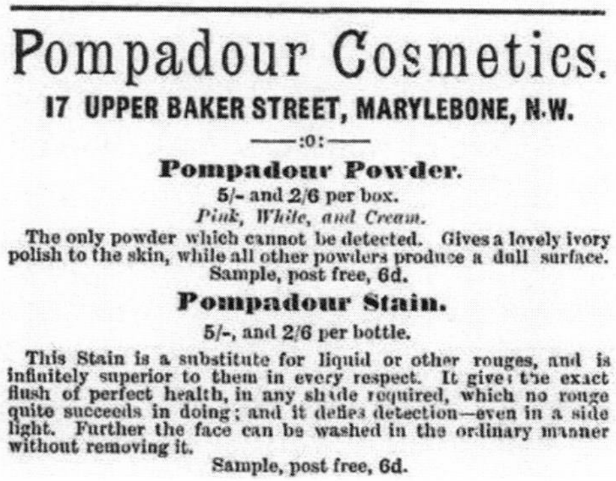

Pompadour Cosmetics.
17 UPPER BAKER STREET, MARYLEBONE, N.W.
——:0:——
Pompadour Powder.
5/- and 2/6 per box.
Pink, White, and Cream.
The only powder which cannot be detected. Gives a lovely ivory polish to the skin, while all other powders produce a dull surface.
Sample, post free, 6d.
Pompadour Stain.
5/-, and 2/6 per bottle.
This Stain is a substitute for liquid or other rouges, and is infinitely superior to them in every respect. It gives the exact flush of perfect health, in any shade required, which no rouge quite succeeds in doing; and it defies detection—even in a side light. Further the face can be washed in the ordinary manner without removing it.
Sample, post free, 6d.

Fig. 48. Cosmetics advert. Brands began to proliferate at the end of the Victorian age.

The term 'cold cream' has gone out of fashion in the twenty-first century, although many people still use the product today (Nivea and Ponds are two of the better-known modern brands). Almost any 'moisturizer' that comes in a pot rather than as a liquid can be called a cold cream; and the products we currently call 'foundation' are essentially cold creams mixed with a coloured face powder. A Victorian woman who applied cold cream to her face, followed by an even dusting of powder, would have presented a very similar appearance (although generally paler in colour) to a twenty-first-century woman wearing foundation or 'concealer'.

As for eye make-up, no Victorian wore eyeshadow – that would have to wait for the early silent films – but eyebrows could be darkened with charcoal, elderberries or burnt cloves. A solution of green vitriol was also recommended, and was applied by means of a brush after the eyebrows had been washed by a decoction of oak galls (the small, round growths that appear on oak trees in the areas where oak-gall wasps feed). They could also be plucked to shape without anyone shouting 'paint', and eyelashes were sometimes trimmed regularly with tiny scissors in the mistaken belief that it would make them grow more luxuriously.

If you were willing to risk being someone who 'painted', then there was another set of health risks you needed to know about, as *The Lady's Book* warned: 'The most deleterious sorts of paints are those in which mineral and metallic substances prevail. Great care ought, therefore, to be paid to the nature of such articles, especially when bought ready prepared; and nothing of this sort should be used without knowing the ingredients of which it is composed.' Much of the make-up on the market still contained red and white lead as the main colouring ingredient; some used mercury, just as they had done back during the reign of Queen Elizabeth I. These were very dangerous substances and could be absorbed through the skin – or worse, if used in lip colour, ingested by the wearer. There is no conclusive evidence that anyone died from cosmetics poisoning alone – the diagnostic technology of the day is unable to tell us – but such cosmetics can hardly have improved anyone's health. The poisonous nature of the ingredients was, however, well known in Victorian Britain, and home-made make-up was acknowledged to be a safer option, as you could be sure what was in it. A safer colour could be obtained from known plants which could then be made into the different forms of paint on the market. Brazil wood, alkanet (a native British plant that many people think of as a common weed) and beetroot were all recommended in different recipes, usually precipitated on to chalk. Crushed cochineal beetles (also used for food colouring until recently) provided another organic alternative. Having created a suitable and safe pigment, the home make-up producer could choose her preferred method of using it.

To produce a coloured powder, French chalk or talc would be reduced to a very fine dust. Ground cochineal beetles or very finely chopped alkanet roots would then be steeped in a small volume of water overnight, then the liquid strained off and poured over the chalk or talc powder. After thorough mixing, the resultant paste would be spread out thinly on sheets of paper and left to dry. Once it was completely dried out, the coloured chalk or talc would be carefully broken up again until it regained its powder form. Coloured powder like this could be applied by scooping a small amount into a fine cotton bag, tying it tightly and dabbing it upon the face.

If you preferred a coloured pomade – something, in texture, like modern lipstick – the carefully ground beetles could be mixed with animal fat and plenty of white wax. Cocoa butter could improve the absorption rate. Such pomades were applied with the fingers and rubbed into the cheeks and lips. This was undoubtedly the simplest form of 'paint' to produce at home.

Rouge en crepe was considered to be one of the easiest forms of colour to use, the one most likely to achieve a natural look. A strong liquor of colour was first made from beetles or plants, and added to water. Small squares of gauze material were then steeped in this liquor, before being dried out. Rubbing these pieces of gauze on the skin transferred the colour from the fabric on to the face.

I have produced a number of Victorian pomade-style paints, including a range of six different shades using alkanet root, cochineal beetles and Brazil wood as the colouring agents. I have also experimented with a range of fat and wax mixtures. They all worked to an extent: all imparted colour, all could be applied reasonably accurately and all had acceptable staying power.

Painting with these Victorian reparations was very much an art in itself; it was only too easy to misjudge the strength of the cosmetics and make a concoction that was either highly toxic or which, when applied, made your face resemble that of a clown. How many women used such 'paint' is not known. Few would admit to doing so, even when their friends and relations found it patently obvious. There are no sales figures as such, but there were a small number of brands available at pharmacist's or by mail order for those who were looking for more discretion, and the number of such brands seemed to be on the rise at the end of the century. Magazines and advice books continued to include information about them even when they advocated cosmetic abstinence.

Perfume: For Men and Women

The final touch before embarking on the day proper was the application of perfume.

Perfume was a fashion item. Just as today, scents went in and out of style with enormous rapidity. When Victoria ascended the throne, the dominant scent, or at least the one most advertised, was eau de cologne. Mr Rimmel's *Book of Perfumes* has as the base of eau de cologne the distilled flowers of the orange tree: a careful mixture of both the sweet and bitter varieties of orange blossom blended with the expressed oils of their rinds. It was a long-established scent, which had first been produced and made popular in the eighteenth century. The oils were mostly made in the south of France and in Italy, but the blend had been perfected in the German city of Cologne. As a perfume, it was originally favoured by men (both Beau Brummel and Beau Nash, two famous arbiters of male fashion, were reported to make extravagant use of it), but by the third decade of the nineteenth century it was used by both sexes in England. A sharp, clean scent that cut through other smells, it could be applied to handkerchiefs and gloves as well as the body.

Eau de cologne was also cheaper by volume than a true perfume. A true perfume contains only the essential oils that create its distinctive aroma. Eau de cologne, on the other hand, was diluted with distilled water. For this reason it was known as a toilet water (meaning scented water for use in personal hygiene). It was used throughout a man's toilet, from being dabbed behind the ears to being worn as aftershave. The diluted form of eau de cologne and its subsequent lower price meant that more people could afford to use the fragrance and that those with more money to spend could use it liberally. It was stocked by gentlemen's barbers as well as apothecary shops and was affordable – at a pinch – by wealthier tradesmen if they were sparing with its use. Since it is still produced today, it is easy to get a scent of the 1840s.

Bergamot and lemon oil, sometimes employed separately but more often used in combination, was the signature smell of the middle years of the century. Almost everything was scented with this mixture, from hand creams and hair pomades to pincushions. More often associated with women, it was rarely used by men, whose consumption of fragrance was in sharp decline from the 1850s onwards. One of the main attractions was its availability. Both oils were reasonably priced, as far as natural plant-extract oils went, and both were even cheaper when synthesized. They could be purchased in apothecaries, in chemists' and pharmacists' shops. The fashionable scent of the mid-century was within the grasp of more people than eau de cologne had ever been. Even a working-class home, as long as the adult male was in full-time employment, could boast a pot of lemon and bergamot in some form. It was also a smell that was easy to incorporate within home-made cosmetics. The oils combined well with the fats and greases in the ointments and pastes that women made up themselves.

Today, to appreciate what these smells were like, one need only take a short trip to the aromatherapy section of a health-food shop, where you can purchase both oils for yourself. Be careful not to overdo it; Victorian perfume was used sparingly.

By 1880, bergamot and lemon had started to lose their appeal. They seemed old-fashioned and crude compared to the heavier, more complex scents of the fashionable world. These were full of musk and ambergris, patchouli and spice oils, all of which were expensive. By the 1890s, high-fashion perfumes were never single scents, and were made not from one or two ingredients

Fig. 49. Perfume advert. Several brands of perfume were heavily marketed on both sides of the Atlantic.

but from eight or twelve different extracts. Sold in tiny amounts in long, slim, beautifully decorative glass vials, they were a total expression of wealth. Perfume had once again become the preserve of the rich.

Meanwhile, in the mass market, lavender oil came to dominate the cheaper products. The end of the century was a time of two smells, exotic and musky at one end, while the rest of society was awash in lavender oil, lavender water, lavender soap, lavender pot pourri and lavender bags. A new industry grew up to satisfy the demand, with dedicated lavender growers both here and in France supplying commercial producers. Most late-Victorian girls learned how to gather their own lavender from the garden and make up lavender bags: taking a small bunch of stems, tying them tightly together just below the flower head with sewing cotton, bending the stems back over the flower heads, weaving in and out of those stems with a length of ribbon, and finishing off with a bow. It is something I learned to do myself when I was a girl, and indeed taught my daughter in turn.

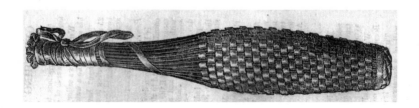

Fig. 50. Lavender bound with ribbon, *The Young Ladies' Journal*, 1866.

Some Victorians opined that, whatever its scent, perfume per se was out of favour. 'Costly perfumes, formerly employed as a mask to want of cleanliness, are less required now that soap has become a type of civilisation.' In truth, sales of perfume were rising dramatically, due to its widespread availability. Chemistry was transforming the world of smell. At the onset of the reign, the vast majority of perfume was derived from botanical sources, distilled from plants and, in a few cases, extracted from animals. These substances were expensive, as large volumes were required to produce the concentrated oils. But, as the century unfolded, chemists were synthesizing an increasing range of scents from the most unpromising sources. Coal tar and its various fractal derivatives were throwing up an amazing array of odours. Oil of pear, apple, almond and pineapple could all be produced from coal tar, as could the phenomenally popular lemon oil. These artificial scents were vastly cheaper to produce than the old botanicals. The new chemicals democratized perfume, spreading it further and further down the social scale until, by the 1870s, even servant girls were buying scented soap. In its own turn, it was this very democratization that drove the late-century fashion for the more complex, heavier and very much more expensive scents. Fashion turned to those smells that no one had been able to synthesize, distancing them from the servant girl once again.

Men: Hair and Beards

Men obviously did not have to address the vexed question of make-up as part of their morning routine, but they did need to pay attention to both their hair and their beard. Long hair was never fashionable for Victorian men, at least not at the back of the neck. Throughout the period, men's hair stopped at the collar; however, there was still a great amount of variety in grooming the hair, from smooth and oiled to thick and unruly.

Style of facial hair, equally, could range from clean-shaven to full, bushy beard.

In 1837, the fashionable young man retained something of the Napoleonic, with a dash of the Romantic poet about his hair. It was combed forwards from the crown of the head without any sort of parting. In this way, the hair framed the face not with a straight edge but in a series of gentle curls and individual locks, which many men needed additional assistance from hair products to achieve (we will examine these later in the chapter). These kept the hair in place, and were similar to today's hair gels.

At this time, the face was usually clean-shaven, apart from a small section of sideburn that ran down in front of the ears and stopped at the hinge of the jaw. It was a mannered look, and one that spoke of civilized society, but it still contained a hint of the wilds.

The next few years saw sideburns grow longer and lusher. The young Prince Albert, when he arrived to marry Victoria, sported just such sideburns. He was fortunate to possess naturally curling hair that gave a thick and luxurious appearance to his locks. The longer sideburns were adopted initially by those who wanted to look more serious. The eighteenth-century dandy had been a clean-shaven man. Facial hair was a visible sign of the Victorian rejection of effeminate frivolity associated with the past. Moustaches, too, began to make an appearance after many decades of absence.

Side partings came next, and transformed the look. Good male hair was now thick, dark and wavy. Parted at the side, it fell downwards rather than being swept forward. Curls were encouraged around the face and in some men extra length was allowed to the fringe and the hair on top of the head to create the desired soft volume. The royal family portraits of the 1850s show Albert with the very pattern of perfect male grooming, a pattern that had been the fashion for some years.

MR. JOHN SADLEIR, M.P. FOR CARLOW.

Fig. 51. Mutton-chop sideburns, 1850.

Trawl through further images of 1850s men, from all classes, and the one major variation you will see is the rim beard. The sideburns were allowed to extend down the face and join up across the chin. However, this was still not a full beard. The area below the bottom lip was shaved, leaving only a thin, horizontal strip of beard across the lower part of the chin. It was an iconic mid-Victorian style, and one with international appeal, and was adopted by both Isambard Kingdom Brunel and Abraham Lincoln. It could be combined successfully with a moustache, but only if the moustache was small and neatly trimmed. This was an appearance that boldly asserted a man's masculinity – he was vigorous and physically capable of growing a full beard – but it also showed that he was so civilized and well groomed that he could be carefully clean-shaven at the same time. Like all truly successful fashions, it had resolute staying power. In the 1850s and 1860s it dominated, but even when change came some men continued to wear the style, even to the end of the century – the last adherents being fishermen in the Edwardian period around sixty years later.

Fig. 52. The rim beard, 1850.

The late 1860s saw more men opting for a clean-shaven appearance, often with a small moustache. These were the youngest men, particularly the unmarried, and they were wholly unconcerned with appearing 'capable' or important. If the wearers of the rim beard were the policy makers and the reserved gentlemen of the day, the clean-shaven were the young lovers of the world.

In the 1870s, men could let themselves become hairier. From 1874 to 1875, there was a peak of the wild style, with a shaggy full beard, an enormous, untrimmed moustache and a plentiful, curly and slightly unkempt head of hair. Not everyone opted for this particular look; this was the era of the greatest hair variety. Moustaches, rim beards, sideburns and clean-shaven styles were all present at once. But the decade belonged to the big and the bushy, which was a new trend. While the rim beard was evidence that its bearer had clung on to the discipline of shaving, this fuller beard aimed for a completely grizzled expression of masculinity. It was popular among intellectuals as well as some manual labourers, each of whom had their own, very different, reasons for wishing to project an aura of machismo.

Charles Darwin sported a fine example of a big, bushy beard, perhaps wishing to highlight his credentials as an explorer.

(From Photograph by Mr. H. T. Reed.)

Fig. 53. The big 'bushy' beard, 1870.

Towards the end of the century, the fiery appearance of Darwin and others like him was reined in. Many a man still had a full beard, but now it was likely to be short and elegantly trimmed in the style of Prince Edward (the future Edward VII). Indeed, the strongest of all styles was now a cleanly shaven face with a small, carefully shaped moustache. Hair, too, was now noticeably shorter than it had been all century, and much straighter. The luxurious curls and waves had faded. Edwardian man was to have far less hair in general than his generations of Victorian forebears.

Baldness

Baldness, as today, was the bane of many a man's later life. Its cause and treatment was a popular subject. Theories abounded as to why some men lost their hair and others did not; why for most men it was later in life but for a few it could occur even in their teens.

Few scientists had turned their attention to the study of baldness, which meant that those seeking information often had to
fall back on older works upon the subject. Of these, the most
influential and widely quoted was Alexander Rawlinson's 1816
'Practical and Philosophical Treatise upon the Hair' and his
'Essay upon the Hair', which was published a few years earlier.
His explanation of baldness was perspiration: one reason, in his
mind, why baldness affected men so much more than women.
'It generally arises from violent exercise, from whence arises
perspiration . . . It relaxes the roots, the acidity prevents the
fluid acting on the hair, which occasions it to waste.' His remedy was the regular use of a fine Macassar oil applied to the hair
to replenish its 'fluids', along with a regime of regular cutting.
Rawlinson believed that a trim once a fortnight would invigorate the individual hairs. Shaving, he felt, merely coarsened them
and should therefore never be employed on the head. Careful
regular cutting, on the other hand, would speed growth while
not affecting texture. By the middle of the century, investigations into the nature of the skin and hair follicles had of course
proved this to be impossible, due to the fact that all the growing
occurs deep in the follicle. But the confusion remained and continued well into the twentieth century; my own mother would
recommend the practice to me as a child.

The use of oil on the head continued to be standard advice
for almost every problem with hair throughout the century,
including baldness. While Rawlinson advocated a light oil, one
that he manufactured and sold himself, other recipes could be
much heavier and were based upon lard or beef-marrow fat.
Most were mildly coloured and perfumed. I have followed a
simple hair-oil recipe from the period myself. I took some olive
oil, added some thinly sliced alkanet root and brought the mixture up to the boil: it turned a rich red. I strained out the roots
and, finally, scented the oil with a few drops of bergamot oil. A

small amount on the fingertips massages well into the hair, making it shiny and easier to style. Use too much, and the hair quickly feels greasy. The trick with a hair-oil regime rather than a shampoo regime is in the brushing and combing. But if it was baldness that a man was worried about, then he would have tried to coat the hairs, especially at the roots, with a thin film of oil in order to protect them from his own perspiration.

Heavier preparations were generally easier to massage into the scalp. This recipe is typical, including, as it does, a 'magic ingredient' known as tincture of cantharide: 'Pomade against baldness. Beef marrow, soaked in several waters, melted and strained, half a pound; tincture of cantharides (made by soaking for a week one drachm of powdered cantharides in one ounce of proof spirit), one ounce; oil of bergamot, twelve drops.'

The man responsible for the popularity of the magic ingredient was Erasmus Wilson. Otherwise called 'Spanish fly', the cantharide is an emerald-green beetle that was widely used medicinally to remove warts, counter irritation and as an aphrodisiac. Wilson was a purveyor of baldness cures, and his publication of recipes for home production as well as his role as a supplier of commercial products ensured a wide distribution of his ideas, even if he was often not credited. His applications were 'to be used once or twice a day for a considerable time'; but if the scalp became sore, they were 'to be discontinued for a time, or used at longer intervals.' Other brands such as Dupuytren and Cazenaze followed suit, and their pomades were also cantharide-based. As a well-known medical ingredient used in a variety of soothing ointments, it must have seemed a very plausible baldness cure to many men. It was certainly popular, and featured in a lucrative line of products.

Sometime around 1850, a rival explanation of baldness began to emerge: baldness could be caused due to a loss of blood supply to the hair follicles. This new explanation gained traction and, by 1901, it had become the most widely written about and medically endorsed assessment. Treatments, based upon the premise that stimulating blood flow in the scalp would aid hair growth, involved regular bouts of friction, wearing looser-fitting hats, taking cold-water baths and changing to a meaty diet and undertaking vigorous exercise. Rubbing in oily hair preparations was anathema to those who followed this theory, and public attacks upon the claims of other commercial baldness cures abounded. However, the new explanation never entirely drove out the older idea of baldness caused by perspiration. The anti-perspiration lobby continued, and despite also recommending looser-fitting hats and cold-water applications, it looked to treatments including lighter diets, moderate exercise and less mental exertion – along with the use of a good hair oil or pomade.

Another theory that arose towards the end of the century was that hair loss was the result of 'germs' that persisted on the scalp. The medical profession distanced itself from this notion, but it had an immediate appeal to many members of the public. For if almost every other ill in life was rapidly being proven to be caused by 'germs', why not baldness as well? Believers in this cause advocated their own products laced with various disinfectants, along with close-fitting caps, new hairbrushes and shampoos.

Hair Care

Men in 1816 didn't wash their hair with water. 'Cleanliness is requisite, with respect to the hair as to any part of the body,' Rawlinson affirmed. But just as washing with water was not part of the full body-cleansing regime so early in the century, nor was hair washing. Rawlinson expected men to clean their hair with a comb and brush. He instructed them to be particularly thorough with the comb if they used any form of powder in their hair, which many older gentlemen still did in the first decade or so of the nineteenth century. His Macassar oil was also part of the cleansing routine; he asserted that it would prevent tangling, aid the brushing and nourish the roots.

Managing your hair without water and shampoo is something that I and several of my friends have tried. The experience does seem to vary, from those who have no trouble at all maintaining the regime to those who quickly slip back to the use of twentieth-century products. It appears that repeatedly stripping the oils out of the hair does stimulate the scalp into producing oils more quickly, and that the more often you use shampoo or soap, the quicker the hair becomes greasy again. As soon as you stop using shampoos and soaps, the hair gradually settles down. If you do nothing, however, it turns into pungent 'dreads'; the odour can be horrendous. Brushing and combing, when done thoroughly and frequently, makes all the difference. It also helps if the brush is a natural-bristle one, and it must be cleaned daily as part of the routine.

Dust, dirt and grease are mechanically removed during the combing and brushing process, and, perhaps counter-intuitively, adding fresh oil to the hair daily actually helps. The additional lubrication enables everything to move along so that dandruff, dirt and human grease are transported along the length of the hair and away. Well-brushed but unwashed, hair doesn't get smelly, and it certainly doesn't become brittle, frizzy, flyaway or split. Ultimately, how greasy it gets seems to vary from person to person. I have finally settled on a halfway house that seems to suit me, wherein I do give my hair a shampoo every few weeks and a simple water rinse once a week. Combing and brushing do the rest. But I would also point out that Victorian hairstyles work much better with slightly greasy hair, so when I am spending any length of time living with Victorian hair I am quite happy to abandon the shampoo altogether.

By the 1840s, occasional washing of men's hair with water was creeping in, led by women, who had adopted the process first. For most, of course, it meant a swill around in cold water to dislodge the dust and dirt. Some were willing to risk soap, although it did tend to leave the scalp sore in some cases.

Having washed their hair, however, most men liked to apply fresh hair oil to create a glossy, rich sheen and to prevent it from becoming brittle. Lighter oil preparations were worked into the roots until they were absorbed by the scalp. A small amount was used at each application as the intention was to condition the hair, not make it greasy. The heavier pomatums were designed more as styling agents. This recipe for one such hair-styling product existed at the more exotic end of the market: 'Mix two ounces of bear's grease, half an ounce of honey, one drachm of laudanum, three drachms of the powder of southernwood, three drachms of the balsam of Peru, one and a half drachms of the ashes of the roots of bulrushes, and a small quantity of the oil of sweet almonds.'

Once made up, this recipe would have looked and indeed behaved much like modern hair products. I have never followed this recipe to the letter – bear's grease today is difficult to procure, not to mention unethical (they really did mean the fat of a bear) and no one will sell me laudanum either (an opiate mixed with alcohol). However, I have concocted a version using pig's grease and vodka. It formed a pale, gel-like ointment with a mildly flowery scent.

The directions instructed that a small portion of the product be taken on to the fingers and used like a tip wax to give definition to individual curls and to prevent flyaway ends. Moustaches were also frequently shaped and tended in this way. Some of these preparations were coloured; the 'Black Pomatum, in sticks, for the eyebrows, whiskers, etc' that was described in Harry Beasley's *Druggist's General Receipt Book* was applied so as to give definition to the shape of moustaches and eyebrows as well as to hide grey hairs. Mascara was the other name given to these coloured moustache waxes. Mascara is still widely available, of course, even though it is now used by women for their eyelashes, rather than by men.

Most pharmacists stocked a wide range of male hair products by the 1870s, carefully packaged to differentiate them from female varieties and varying in price for the rich and the poor. Gowland's Lotion was one of the longest lived. In 1816, at the time that Jane Austen was writing *Persuasion* and making her heroine's vain father, Sir Walter Elliot, recommend it by name, it was already an old-established product. It was still being heavily advertised in the *London Illustrated News* in 1850. Men were the primary market when hair products first became commercialized, and, as a result, the early product lines were heavily biased towards male use.

For town dwellers with more money at their disposal, a regular trip to the barber's dealt with all their hair-styling and shaving needs. A wealthy, fashion-conscious man might visit such an establishment twice a day to achieve the perfection of appearance he desired. The morning shave was generally thought to be the most efficacious, when the hairs of the beard were considered to be at their softest and most amenable. However, an evening shave allowed a man to look his immaculate best for dinner engagements. Barbers knew their customers well and were careful to stock a variety of the very latest male grooming products, from hair oil made of equal parts almond and olive oil and scented with bergamot and orange oil to make the hair glossy and easy to manage, to 'bay rum', an alcohol-based lotion scented with bay leaves, oil of lime and oil of cloves used as an aftershave (this is still available, most widely in America).

A trip to the barber's could be a ritualistic experience. The customer made himself comfortable in a chair while the barber laid out his array of hair oils, soaps, razors and strops (flexible strips of leather or canvas used for sharpening the razor). Towels were brought, unfolded with a practised flick and placed about the customer's person to protect his clothing. Next appeared a bowl of steaming-hot water. There were those who claimed that cold water was best for shaving, but the majority of barbers used hot water, and most customers expected it. At more expensive barbers', a gentleman's face was then thoroughly washed in the water with soft soap before being just as thoroughly rinsed and dried. A fresh bowl of hot water was brought and the barber proceeded to work a special shaving soap into a lather. This was mixed in a lather box using a badger-hair brush. A light oil was massaged into the face both to protect the skin from the caustic action of more soap and to improve the lather upon the face. The lather was then transferred from the lather box on to the

Fig. 54. At the barber's, 1900.

face with the brush and worked generously all over the area to be shaved. Now the barber turned to his razor and prepared it for use.

The leather strop was taken from its sheath and one end hooked to the wall. The barber checked that his strop was free from cuts or nicks and that his strop paste (a mixture of an abrasive powder and grease) was smoothly and evenly spread upon it. He began to work the razor carefully and skilfully along the strop to bring the edge of the blade into perfect sharpness. This was a moment of professional pride; the movements were large, flowing and theatrical. For many a barber, the final touch was always several passes not along his strop but across the palm of his hand, which many considered to give the very finest edge of all. The razor was of the 'cut-throat' variety and made of steel (not stainless steel). The very best razors had ivory handles, either in their natural pale colour or stained black. Cheaper razors commonly had bone handles, or, occasionally, tortoiseshell. Most barbers began the shave with the awkward area under the nose and around the upper lip – unless, of course, the gentleman sported a moustache. He held the razor between his thumb and first two fingers with the blade lying parallel to the length of his thumb. His other hand gently stretched the skin to be shaved so that it was taut against the blade. A skilled barber completed the actual act of shaving in about thirty seconds, before rinsing and drying his customer's face. A range of post-shaving products, such as eau de cologne or bay rum, was then offered to the customer, designed to close the pores, soothe any irritation and fragrance the skin. The cost of a full shave, including all the products and treatments, in a good-quality establishment could set a gentleman back sixpence. A daily trip to the barber's could therefore be an extravagance for even a middle-class customer. A more basic service, in a humbler shop, with nothing more than a simple shaving soap, could cost a penny. But, even at this price, a trip to the barber's was still something of a treat for most working-class men.

A common sight in cost-conscious homes would have been a man standing shaving every morning in his bedroom at his wash stand, or in the kitchen. He would have had with him his cut-throat razor, a shaving brush, a bar of special soap, a bowl of cold water and a mirror propped up in front of him. Some hot water made the ritual both easier and more pleasant, helping the soap to lather and the hairs to soften, just as a splash of after-shave bought from the apothecary or chemist's brought fashion into the daily regime for those who could afford it. Trimming a beard could be a much simpler option than shaving, but, throughout the Victorian era, there were plenty of working-class men who were willing to brave the cold water and cut-throat razor in search of the appearance they personally favoured.

Fig. 55. Inexpensive products for the working man.

5. Morning Exercise

By the middle of the century, gymnastics had become a regular part of many men's morning routine. Knee bends, stretches, arm waving, shadow-boxing and running on the spot for ten to twenty minutes every morning was considered a good way to start the day, promoting as it did a good and vigorous circulation of the blood around the body and the brain. In the larger cities, gymnasiums with a full range of apparatus and instruction were available for those keen to do even more. Most were aimed at wealthy young men but, as the century progressed, gymnastic facilities became increasingly available to those with less to spend. As early as 1868, Lambeth Public Baths in London was draining its main pools in the winter to convert them into gymnasiums (see Plate 23). These were available for the public to use at much the same rates as they had been charged to swim in the plunge pools. By 1881, the baths' posters advertised 'every appliance for healthful and manly exercise of all kinds, and a good track for running, walking, etc.'

It offered parallel bars, a boxing ring, a high bar, trapeze-like swings, dumb-bells and fencing, as well as a running track. Entrance fees were 3d a session: low enough to admit the wealthier members of the working class and high enough to carry a promise of strict supervision to prevent the middle classes being put off by fears of raucous behaviour.

Outdoor gymnasiums, first at Primrose Hill in London and Peel Park in Salford, pointed the way for more inclusive provision. In 1858, vaulting bars, parallel bars, seesaws and swings were installed on a patch of spare land on Smithdown Road in

Liverpool, completely free of charge to the community for adult-male gymnastic use. Over the next five years, three further free 'playgrounds' opened in Liverpool. The male body beautiful was becoming more muscular.

Exercise for girls was a much more worrying subject. A girl's developing body was thought to be easily upset and at risk of permanent damage if involved in even the lightest of energetic pursuits. It was feared she could be left unable to fulfil her primary function in life: the bearing of children. This was a long-standing, traditional belief fuelled by the Ancient Greek theory that the womb was mobile within the torso. Despite nineteenth-century anatomical studies, which definitively informed the early Victorian doctor that the womb was, in fact, firmly anchored by a series of ligaments, medical opinion was still concerned about undue movement. Miscarriages were widely ascribed to falls and jolting movements, and the stable formation and growth of the womb, as well as related organs, was believed to be in danger if a young girl was vigorously 'throwing herself about'. Most parents firmly believed that allowing their daughters to jump out of trees or to cartwheel in the street was unforgivable and irresponsible parenting; they would be failing to secure their daughter's long-term health. This was of the utmost importance when a girl was approaching and in puberty, when the reproductive organs were settling into an adult pattern and form.

Once out of toddlerhood, young girls were traditionally encouraged to sit still and play nicely, to be absorbed by needlework, books and other physically non-strenuous activities. Their brothers could be encouraged to charge around with sticks, climb trees and jump into ponds, but the girls were always called indoors when things became too boisterous. Parents made a special effort to provide suitable games and pastimes for daughters, separate from those they provided for their sons. Boys were required to be vigorous if they were to grow up to be strong and manly, but girls ran the danger of unsexing themselves if they did the same. Obviously, such a separate and fastidious upbringing was easier for middle-class parents to achieve than working-class families (whether in their own homes, or someone else's, most working-class girls had a great deal of the heavier sorts of housework to do, and it was difficult to treat them differently from the boys), but, despite this, most families still made provisions to keep a watchful eye on the activities of their daughters.

However, at the same time as these traditional worries were influencing girls' lives, there was another set of new anxieties that led people to suggest that girls ought to be moving around more often – that they needed *more* exercise, not less. Many people observing the population were horrified by how many weak and feeble women they saw; others were concerned about the large number – as they believed – of women who remained childless, despite being married. British womanhood seemed to be unable to carry out its full range of duties. It was thought that too many young women were narrow-chested, overly thin, pale and sapped of energy. Just as there was concern about developing the male physique through gymnastic exercise and sport, girls, too, were soon encouraged to build healthier, stronger bodies. But they could not be expected to undertake the same exercise as men and boys, which, of course, was held to be far too dangerous. What was needed was the right sort of exercise: one that would maximize health, muscular development and vigour without endangering reproductive systems or spoiling feminine silhouettes.

In the 1860s, Dr Pye Chevasse, along with most mainstream members of the medical profession, recommended walking. *Lots* of walking. Not athletic hill-walking or anything else too strenuous, but daily, hour-long walks, especially to be taken in the morning, when the body was fresh. The walk was to begin gently and be vigorous enough to warm the body but not so vigorous as to produce perspiration. Regular walking outdoors in the fresh air, felt Dr Chevasse, would act as a general health tonic for the whole system without the risk of placing any undue strain upon the reproductive organs; he recommended a regime of walks and sitz baths (sitting in a few inches of cold water) as a cure for barrenness. Dr Chevasse was particularly concerned about figures from one survey, which recorded that one in eight married women remained childless. To him, this was the result of females living unhealthily, particularly young, unmarried females. He felt that it was quite wrong for a girl to marry unless she was in good and robust health, ready for the duties of procreation and motherhood. The right sort of gentle but regular exercise was, in his and many other physicians' minds, the way to ensure that happy state of health.

The value of walking was that it didn't jiggle the torso around too much. The chest would be expanded by all the good, fresh air while the limbs were exercised and the whole of the abdomen remained smoothly carried and undisturbed. It was also a free form of exercise requiring no special clothes, equipment or location. Anyone could walk around out in the open air, even the very poorest. Nor did walking in any way compromise respectability – indeed, if you carried a small basket or parcel, no one would even know you were taking exercise; they might simply assume you were performing an errand.

The wealthy middle-class girl could be taken out daily by her governess for a walk, and the few girls' schools that were in existence for the middle classes often made a point of advertising their afternoon walks to potential parents in their prospectus. Sunday-school teachers, enlightened employers and a host of other people who saw themselves as supporting girls from poorer backgrounds were equally vocal in advocating walking to the girls who came under their sway. Even workhouses and prisons advocated outdoor walking exercise for girls and women, albeit round and round a grim yard.

Callisthenics was to be the girl's equivalent of gymnastics. Swedish-style, systematic and scientific exercise for men, with its swinging on bars and leaping over vaulting horses, was considered particularly unsuitable for girls. Such exercises involved much too much movement of the body for feminine safety, and would not be possible in modest female clothing. But, by the 1880s, a modified form of these exercises was being promoted for use by girls. (It was fine for boys, too, but, while there were many types of exercise available for boys, for girls it was one of very few options). Callisthenics concentrated particularly upon moving the arms and shoulders, and generally left the torso immobile. *Cassell's Household Guide* offered a series of very well-illustrated sections detailing a whole course of physical exercise and development that could be conducted within the privacy of your own home. This guide, along with the magazine version of the same publication, offered many middle-class girls their first information about the drive for physical fitness, and their first chance to be involved.

Despite the very serious tone of the articles, callisthenics could really be described as prancing around in your underwear. The special clothing advocated involved a pair of ankle-length bloomers, some sort of loose shirt, no corset, a short skirt down to the knee – all in white cotton fabric – and a 'pretty coloured sash' tied around the waist. The attractive femininity of this outfit was heavily promoted in an attempt to overcome some girls' resistance to looking odd. Calling this collection of garments a special callisthenics outfit probably also helped. From a cost perspective, however, taking off your outer clothes and corset and tying a sash around your waist in the privacy of your own bedroom was a very cheap option (see Plate 20).

The exercises were particularly recommended for girls, as they were felt to 'expand the chest' – by which was largely meant the lungs. Poor nutrition, air pollution and interminable hours spent hunched over needlework all undermined a girl's respiratory system. As a result, exercises that seemed to open and expand the lungs, strengthening the muscles of the chest, became a priority. It was hoped that such callisthenic exercises could not only correct posture and counteract the sedentary nature of girlhood but could also, by strengthening the lungs, make girls more resilient in fighting off infectious lung diseases such as tuberculosis.

My daughter and I have attempted callisthenics, with mixed results. I, personally, found the exercise to be ridiculously simple. Standing still in a room while waving my arms about did not feel at all taxing or exercising. I hardly worked up a sweat. My daughter, however, had a rather different experience. Within a few minutes of the routine she was complaining that her arms and shoulders ached, and the next day she was visibly stiff and sore. The difference, I think, lies in scrubbing and digging. My life, particularly during my periods of Victorian living, contains much of both. I would not call myself fit; I know that I am woefully unfit, in fact, but I have undertaken a large amount of washing and gardening, all of which use my shoulder muscles and arms. My daughter hadn't: her life was, at that time, in many ways much closer to the life of a Victorian middle-class girl. Not in the hours at a needle perhaps – although I am proud to say that she does sew – but in comparable hours at a computer keyboard and with a pen in her hand. Modern life, for many of our young people, requires a lot of sitting still, hunched over something small and repetitive in the movements it demands you make. So perhaps I am wrong to poke fun at an exercise regime that promotes standing in your bedroom in your undies waving your arms around. Maybe the Victorian devisers of callisthenics for girls had a point: girls needed to be moving their arms and shoulders around more vigorously and freely. It relieves tension in the shoulders and neck; it strengthens muscles, making good, healthy posture easier, reduces the chances of developing RSI-style problems and, if you do enough of it, it is a perfectly good, if gentle, form of aerobic exercise that stimulates blood circulation and deeper breathing.

The ability to undertake callisthenics in private was a major boon. With so much concern about public modesty, a form of exercise that could be carried out totally in private made it possible and accessible to anyone who had somewhere private at their disposal. Middle-class girls who couldn't risk being seen taking part in any body-revealing activity could do callisthenics. The illustrated exercises were the forerunner of the work-out video.

Meanwhile, many working-class girls got plenty of callisthenic exercise whether they wanted it or not. The modesty and suitability of doing callisthenics was widely promoted by a number of health reformers, and their advice was rigorously enforced in the last two decades of the nineteenth century by the management and trustees of most institutions. Schools intended for the education of the poor were the most enthusiastic. Girls could be lined up in the yard and drilled in the callisthenic exercises with no additional outlay. This 'physical education' was intended to set them up for a healthy life, ensuring an even development of the whole body, but particularly of the lungs. Strong, healthy, working-class girls would, it was hoped, make proficient and agile factory workers for a few years. But, even more importantly, they would then become healthy mothers to future generations of healthy, working-class children. Some employers saw the financial benefits of callisthenics. The Bourneville factory on the outskirts of Birmingham had a policy of compulsory callisthenics for all female employees under eighteen years of age; a considerable proportion of its workforce consisted of young women between the ages of eleven and eighteen. A special outdoor exercise area was set aside for them, and each girl was required to do two half-hour classes a week during company time. Cold and boring it may have been, but it did have some health benefits, even if it wasn't quite the tuberculosis antidote its most enthusiastic proponents hoped.

6. Breakfast

Much as today, breakfast timings varied in the Victorian period according to the working pattern of the family. Most factory workers would begin their day's labour at seven or eight o'clock, eating a hasty meal before they left the house. If they worked within an easy walking distance, it was possible for the whole family to sit down to enjoy a shared hot breakfast together. Farmers and agricultural labourers, on the other hand, were out at dawn, and many returned to the kitchen only after several hours of hard toil. Domestic servants, too, were often required to defer breakfast, starting household chores and serving food to their masters and mistresses before they themselves could eat.

For the Widgers, a working-class family from the South Devon town of Seaton at the very end of the Victorian period, breakfast was always a busy affair. It was orchestrated, of course, by Mrs Widger, who prepared the food for her five children, her husband, who was a fisherman, and the gentleman lodger, who kept a record of their daily routine. The lodger described the kitchen as the family's main living space. It had a table, several wooden chairs (all broken in one way or another) and one armchair. All along one wall was a large wooden dresser that was cluttered with everything from pots of fish hooks to chipped china, postcards, balls of string, a lace butterfly mounted on a piece of card (Mrs Widger's mother was a lace-maker), a packet of biscuits on the top shelf, out of reach of the children, a tin of tea leaves and several pots of jam. Across the ceiling was strung a series of ropes that permanently supported a revolving selection of fisherman's jumpers, family underwear and the smaller fishing nets as they dried.

But Mrs Widger's kitchen and cookery represented some of the best facilities and provisions a Victorian working-class family could aspire to. In addition to her frying pan and baking tray, she had a large brown enamelled kettle and two medium-sized saucepans at her disposal. The assortment of crockery in the kitchen was rather idiosyncratic, acquired over many years. Much of it was chipped or even broken in two, but it was still pressed into service. One plate, broken almost perfectly in half, was particularly prized for its usefulness in mashing potatoes. The cooking range, which sat in the fireplace, was small and built into the chimney, with an oven on one side (but no water boiler on the other, unlike some more expensive models). Next to the chimney, in the alcove formed against the outside wall, was a built-in cupboard where Mrs Widger kept the coal. To save space, she would keep her frying pan balanced precariously on top of it.

A hunk of bread or a bowl of porridge accompanied by a cup of tea was by far the most common Victorian breakfast for those in working households. Porridge was more likely to be eaten in the north of England, where oats were a major crop, while bread was more commonplace in the south. Porridge or bread would, for many, have been served with a glass of beer. Beer was the traditional drink of Britain and, in a world of marginal survival, provided not only valuable calories but a range of minerals and vitamins that were otherwise lacking in most people's diets. However, tea gradually became the dominant morning drink as the Temperance Movement persuaded more and more people to turn their backs on alcohol. Coffee and cocoa, for similar reasons, also grew in popularity.

The advantage of a bread and beer breakfast was the lack of preparation required. Fires did not have to be lit, so one did not need to wake up early to tend them. For those with a very early start, who could not return home to eat later in the morning, it was the most sensible option. But if water needed to be boiled or something needed to be cooked, the range would have to be started.

There were two popular types of range, both coal-fuelled. Coal was already in widespread use in towns and cities, thanks to canals and railways transporting it cheaply across the country. Steam engines made the extraction of coal easier, providing the pumping systems that kept so many mines from flooding as well as winching both coal and men up to the surface. Up until the 1860s, and for many more years in large numbers of households, the older open cooking range dominated. This was an open coal fire held in an iron grate with one or more simple iron boxes at its side (see Plate 4). The smoke made its own way directly up the chimney. The newer, closed range, or kitchener, which began to grow in popularity around the time of the Great Exhibition, channelled the smoke around inside the range first to extract extra heat. Made of heavy cast-iron plates, the kitchener formed a solid, black presence in the room. At its heart was usually a single coal-burning firebox, around a foot deep. Widely spaced iron bars formed the floor of the box, allowing the ash and cinders to fall away into a tray that could be emptied. Fresh oxygen entered up through these bars, as well as from a grating at the front that could be opened and closed to change the oxygen flow to the fire within. Most domestic ranges had a single oven at one side of the firebox and a water-boiling tank at the other. On top of everything sat an iron cooking surface. Heat would pass directly through the cast-iron firebox to the oven. Heat was also circulated around the kitchener by flues, which would carry hot smoke and waste gases. The flues had one final purpose, which was to allow the gases to escape up a narrow, built-in chimney. Ideally, a good kitchener completely removed the smoke from the room (see Plate 5).

By the end of the century, the kitchener had taken over. This was also the model the Widgers used. I have cooked on both types of Victorian range. They both require time to get going, effort to keep clean, and care and attention to make them work at full efficiency. In some ways, the older open range has the advantage. It is simpler to use, and there is less to go wrong. You're often cooking directly on the fire itself, which means that it would have been much quicker to heat food in the morning. A kettle could go on the open fire within minutes of it being lit, and boiled in another five. If you wanted to cook for breakfast, then it would have been best to choose dishes that could be produced on the direct heat of the fire, so as not to have to wait for the whole range to come up to temperature. This may well have been a factor in the rise of the fried breakfast. Light poaching in small quantities was also possible at this early hour of the day, as was toasting. However, if you embarked on large-scale boiling or baking, you would be very hungry indeed before whatever it was had finally cooked. There was absolutely no point in trying to bake anything in the morning. Baking was an afternoon activity – a tradition that survives in many families – because, by then, the oven would be hot enough.

It is likely that, for servants cooking on an open range for their masters and mistresses, the first stage of breakfast involved raking out the cold ashes from the previous day, brushing the range down vigorously with a stiff brush to remove burnt-on food and ash from all its surfaces and black-leading (rubbing it all over with a greasy black graphite mixture) the whole thing. This was a filthy job, but if you didn't do it the filth would spread during the day to all the pots and pans, cloths and aprons. Next, the fire had to be laid and lit. Cooking on the closed-in kitchener was similar, but there were even more areas to be brushed down, including all the flues, which soon blocked up if you did not remove the soot regularly. Even a light coating of soot reduces the conduction of heat, so a dirty kitchener was even harder to use. Once all this was done, you could fill the kettle. But you would still be looking at forty-five minutes before it boiled, and another hour before you had brought the whole range up to cooking heat.

The Widger household routine was adapted to include one everyday luxury – the early-morning cuppa. As soon as the family woke, a screw of paper, a handful of twigs and a couple of lumps of coal were added to the still-warm cinders from the day before, and life was coaxed back into the fire. Most mornings this took no more than a minute or two of blowing gently on the coals, which would still be smouldering. But even if there was no life left in the cinders, the warmth made lighting the fire relatively simple. A kettle would be boiled and the adult members of the household would take a cup of tea and a biscuit back to bed for a few minutes. Only later in the morning, when the men had gone to work and the children had been packed off to school would Mrs Widger clean out the grate and brush out the flues. The kitchener was kept going all day, providing warmth and hot water, via the kettle, as well as cooking the day's food.

However, although among the urban population these two types of coal-fired iron ranges dominated Victorian cooking, there were still many people who were using neither. In remote rural districts, coal was not always the cheapest and most available fuel. In areas of Devon and Cornwall, wood remained in wide use. In South Wales, coal was cheap but, up in the hills of Snowdonia, wood, gorse and furze hung on, while Ireland and the Highlands of Scotland continued to use peat as their main domestic source. Each fuel required its own equipment and influenced what people could cook. Much of what we think of as regional speciality dishes have a link to these differences of fuel and technology. Porridge and oatcakes, for example, were both cooked over the low, smouldering heat produced by peat fires, thereby gaining a smoky, peaty flavour. A fierce, intense heat such as a straight coal fire produces would lead to burnt porridge pans and a pile of toasted oatmeal crumbs. It is perhaps a lucky coincidence that the areas of Britain where soils and climate favour the growing of oats, being too poor and harsh for other grains, are also those that produce peat.

A Victorian cook had to adjust to the practical aspects of the fuel she was using and the tools she had at her disposal – and it *was* usually 'she'; the number of professional male cooks was small even in larger establishments. As the century progressed and living standards rose, working-class breakfasts, thankfully, became more varied and wholesome. According to social reformer Seebohm Rowntree, in 1900, breakfast for a Yorkshire labourer's family of five children over the course of a week consisted of bread, bacon (just enough for the man of the house to have a slice each day) and coffee, with butter available as a treat once a week and dripping rationed over three days, due to its cost. Cocoa also occasionally joined the spread, and was widely, and rightly, held to be a healthy and energy-giving drink. If it was made with milk, it added significantly to the nutritional value of one's daily intake. For those with a little more money, such as a railway worker, whose wages were more than double those of a labourer, the choice of breakfast was wider still. Throughout the week he could look forward to eggs, sausages and cake, as well as a more plentiful supply of butter, but, again, the women and children of the house ate a smaller selection of food than the wage-earning man.

Hannah Cullwick records in her diary that bread, cocoa and tea constituted her usual breakfast, and she ate it after she had first cooked and cleaned for her employer's family. But the breakfast she made for them was far different from her own. As well as consisting of larger portions of everyday items such as bacon and eggs, it featured smoked haddock, toast, marmalade and small breakfast rolls that she would bake the night before.

Fig. 56. Cocoa was a popular breakfast drink.

Visitors to one of the statelier country houses could have looked forward to an even fuller breakfast menu. Ribs of beef, pickled oysters, shrimps, radishes, plovers, *oeufs cocottes*, a piece of salmon *au bleu*, a Bayonne ham, Russian caviar, croquettes of fish, grilled sheep's kidneys, patties of chicken, mayonnaise of turbot, raised pie of pigeon, blanquette of lamb and broiled fillets of mackerel were all on one suggested menu for a party of ten to twelve people in 1865. A menu like this certainly required a later dining hour. Even if the servants woke at 5 a.m. to clean and light the ranges, the kitchen staff would have needed to work incredibly hard to produce such a spread by 10 a.m.

However, despite these instances of plenty and routine, the most common Victorian experience relating to food was hunger. It was never very far away. Absolute starvation was rare, with some notable exceptions, but long-term malnutrition was rife. Large numbers of people woke up famished and spent their working days – and much of their working lives – in a state of semi-permanent wanting of food. It is recorded in fiction, in newspapers, in people's own accounts, in the investigations of the social reformers, in court records and in entry records at the workhouse. Unsurprisingly, it left its indelible mark upon the bodies of the people.

Let us pause for a moment in our Victorian routine to consider the scale of this hunger, and its causes. It dictated the course of one's day like nothing else.

Hunger

At the start of the Victorian period, food was in short supply all across Europe. The situation was magnified by the potato blight that swept through the continent, in wave after wave. In 1845, it was estimated that around a third of the potato crop was lost; in 1846, this figure rose to three quarters. Potatoes are rich in vitamin C and can provide more calories per acre than any other food crop, initially a great boost to the feeding of a population – but it can also be a trap. Ireland, in particular, had become a monoculture. Before the blight struck, it was estimated that a third of Ireland's population was dependent upon potatoes: they formed well over 80 per cent of the people's total diet, sometimes being eaten for breakfast, lunch and dinner. Exploitative forms of land holding had allowed smaller and smaller parcels of land to be rented out as 'farms', and huge numbers of families were surviving on one-and-a-half-acre plots, supplemented by contract labour. Nowhere else in Europe was as dependent on the crop, so, while the famine-related deaths elsewhere rose to peak figures of one hundred thousand, those in Ireland were, by most estimates, well over the one million mark.

When food had been in short supply before in Ireland, during the 1780s, the British government in Westminster had banned exports of foodstuffs to force supplies on to the market, thereby lowering prices. But in the 1840s, with hundreds of thousands starving to death, and hundreds of thousands more succumbing to disease in their weakened state, Irish produce continued to be sent across the sea, mostly to England. Horrifying reports arrived in London, but few of those in power were willing to give them credence: the reports were regarded as exaggerated, histrionic and sentimentalist. More and more voices were added to the cries for help, but attitudes only hardened. Belief in the free market and its ability to adjust to economic swings lay deep in the bones of the political classes. Interference, it was believed, would only worsen the situation: free 'hand-outs' of food were thought to engender dependence and undermine enterprise. Provision by the state actually fell at this time of desperation. Meanwhile, W. E. Forster described whole communities 'like walking skeletons, the men stamped with the livid mark of hunger, the children crying in pain, the women in some of the cabins, too weak to stand'. Whole families were found dead upon the floors of their bare homes. Men, women and children lay dead along the roadside. At workhouses and hospitals, desperately weak inmates died in droves as fever took hold.

Fig. 57. The potato famine in Ireland, 1847.

The Highlands of Scotland was also a potato economy but, fortunately, saw far fewer deaths. Misery and hunger did, however, still force 1.7 million Scots to emigrate. These two desperate exoduses, from regions far from the seat of power, permanently scarred the face of Britain. Yet if the horror of hunger in the 1840s was so unequally intensified in Ireland and the Highlands of Scotland, the rest of Britain did feel its breath as it passed.

The scarcity and variety of food depended on where in England you lived. In 1844, before the blight struck, Friedrich Engels, the Marxist industrialist, described the diet of labourers from northern manufacturing towns in England. 'We find [their] animal food reduced to a small bit of bacon cut up with the potatoes; lower still, even this disappears, and there remain only bread, cheese, porridge, and potatoes.' Another author, A. Combe, in his treatise upon digestion, asserted that the poor in northern towns lived entirely upon porridge and potatoes. While hardly a rich diet, the additional oats meant that those who had them proved more resilient to famine when the potatoes failed. Meanwhile, in the lowlands of Scotland and the most northerly points of England, milk joined oats as the basis of a diet that was also rich in root vegetables. Elsewhere, vegetables were a rarity for working-class groups, who were unable to afford them. Although almost totally lacking in meat or fish, the northern, working-class English diet offered a reasonable nutritional balance.

In the rural south of England, however, the diet of agricultural labourers was perhaps worse than anywhere else on the mainland. These were people who survived not on porridge and potatoes but on the far less nutritious staple of bread alone. For all its hardships, the diet of the northern factory worker made stronger, healthier bodies than that of the rural southerner, whose health was further undermined if they were unable to get the beer that traditionally accompanied the bread – and poverty and tea-drinking were forcing beer out of reach as part of the agricultural labourer's general consumption. As Victoria's reign began, southern rural families were surviving upon little more than a pound-weight loaf of bread each a day. This was a diet that made the Poor Law model diet for able-bodied men (on four days of the week) of one and a half pints of gruel, nineteen ounces of bread and three and a half ounces of cheese sound almost appealing. Long-term hunger was a common experience. In 1865, Joseph Terry wrote a memoir, looking back to his childhood in pre-Victorian days: 'It is utterly impossible for me, were I ever so wishful to do so, to describe what I suffered for want of proper nourishment . . . Sometimes scarcely would I taste anything for days together, at other times live entirely upon turnips taken from the fields or any kind of wild fruit or roots I could procure.' Such memories never left people.

By the 1860s, food prices had fallen and wages had risen marginally. Edward Smith, in 1864, recorded this improved state of affairs when he noted that most farm labourers enjoyed a relief from the diet of pure bread with one hot meal a week. Better still, he mentioned that Lancashire factory hands were eating oatmeal, bacon, butter (in small amounts), treacle, tea and coffee, as well as bread. It was not surprising, therefore, that so many families were leaving the country for life in the industrialized cities. No matter how dreadful the living conditions there, a full belly was a full belly. As Britain continued to industrialize, people were willing to endure almost anything, including sickness and early death, in order to eat more.

If the diet of most Britons was starting to improve, there were still some groups who were caught out by the economic turns of the age. Alice Foley's mother remembered the near-starvation of her childhood, when the American Civil War interrupted the supply of cotton and left Lancashire's handloom weavers without work. The pinching of her stomach and the humiliation of the soup kitchens remained vivid. Like many others, although she was desperate for food, she detested the free soup that was on

offer. From a glance at the recipes, prepared by middle-class philanthropists, it is easy to see why. Most consisted primarily of
water, with scarce amounts of actual food. Mrs Beeton's Useful
Soup for Benevolent Purposes calls for 4 pounds of beef trimmings, 4 pounds of pearl barley, about 8 pounds of onions and a
sprinkling of herbs to make ten gallons of soup.

Fig. 58. Soup kitchens, 1862.

By the 1890s, those families with an adult man in work could
expect to eat regularly. Yet whenever a family had trouble with
health, unemployment or bereavement, survival could still be
marginal at best. Jack Lannigan was living in Salford when his
father died. His mother tried to support him and his brother by
taking in laundry, but it was not enough; the boys both begged
for food so that the family could survive and stay together. Jack
recalled that 'the workers would file out into the street carrying
their wicker lunch baskets and when they heard our voices "'Ave

yer any bread left, mister?" they would hand anything they had left out to us.' Chip shops were another source of food: the boys would travel from shop to shop asking if any scrapings of batter from the vats could be spared.

Alice Foley, living in Bolton at about the same time, recorded a diet that was common for working-class families: 'mainly milk, porridge, potatoes and butties of bread and treacle with a little meat at weekends'. In comparison with the diet of working-class people in the 1840s, or even the 1860s, this was a big improvement; previously, such food would have been affordable only to the wealthier families of skilled workers. However, the milk that Alice Foley remembers was far from widespread and would have represented a determined attempt by her parents to improve her health: the benefits of milk for children's health were by then well established, although the full scientific reasons were largely unknown.

As Jack Lannigan's experiences remind us, hunger remained a part of Victorian life to the end of the period. One survey undertaken in 1892 in Bethnal Green, one of the poorest parishes in Britain, found that children were still living on a diet that consisted almost exclusively of bread. For over 80 per cent of these children, bread formed seventeen out of twenty-one meals in the week.

Effects on the Body

The effects on people of hunger, short rations and vitamin deficiencies are hard to overestimate. Hunger pangs are painful, stomachs bloat with wind and nausea sets in. Very few of us in modern British society have ever experienced more than a day of this; fainting from hunger is something we read about rather than undergo ourselves. Strict dieting may give us a small idea of the experience, but there is obviously an enormous psychological difference between going without food by choice and going without by necessity and without any hope of the situation improving. Developing cravings is something that can occur if we have to adjust, for example, to a fat-free diet. Our thoughts and conversation might return over and over to food, driving out other thoughts and desires. But for many Victorians, food was permanently and exclusively on their mind, and they could do nothing but watch the effects of hunger reap damage on their families, powerless to prevent it. Every gripe of the stomach would seem to last for ever, trying to sleep was difficult, and to concentrate even harder. To say that people got used to eating less in the Victorian period, or that they didn't know any different, is very misleading.

I try to hold these thoughts in my head whenever I think about the historical Victorian experience, because hunger is at the root of it. The skeletons of the people of Victorian Britain show us the marks of hunger. The average height of a man convicted of a crime in London between 1869 and 1872 was five foot five and a half inches. That is three and a half inches shorter than the average height of a twenty-first-century male Londoner. Similarly, the average height of a woman convicted of a crime in the same period was five foot one and a quarter – two and a half inches shorter than the twenty-first-century average. These heights were also shorter than those recorded in the skeletons of earlier Londoners: excavations have shown that medieval Londoners were two inches taller than their Victorian counterparts. The figures may be skewed by the fact that those who were convicted of crime in the Victorian period will mostly have been drawn from the poorest segment of society. But they do tell us that chronic lifelong nutritional stress must have been the day-to-day experience of many.

Victorian commentators themselves noticed a difference in height among the contemporary population, with many people noting how much smaller, at every age, working-class people were than the upper classes. Several newspaper and magazine articles point to a four-inch height difference between a twelve-year-old Etonian and a twelve-year-old lad from the East End of London. It takes a lot of hunger to do that to people.

Even with enough food to stave off the worst hunger pangs, the nature of the diet itself brought sickness and deformity. Scurvy (caused by a lack of vitamin C) and rickets (a vitamin D deficiency that leads to soft and deformed bones) were evident across the country. The potato famine of the 1840s brought a large rise in cases of the former among the poor – it was worst in Ireland, although bad, too, in the north of England. Only occasional fresh greenery (and the vitamin C it contains) is required to protect a person from scurvy, but those in towns and cities had no access to such food. They had no garden in which to grow their own vegetables, and greens were sold at much higher prices relative to starchy foods (which did a much better job of making a person feel full).

Wherever mixed agriculture survived, such as Wales, lowland Scotland and some parts of north and western England, it was still possible for land around a dwelling to be gardened for vegetables, which provided essential vitamins. But the corn-growing lands of the south-east and Midlands offered much less access to land for its workers. Almost every available plot, no matter how tiny, was taken up with the main agrarian business of the region.

Rickets was reported in the *Medical Gazette* of 1871 to be discernible in as many as one third of the population of the large manufacturing towns and cities. In a healthy lifestyle, sunlight and animal fats provide the main sources of vitamin D. Without them, bones soften and deform. The diet of the Victorian poor rarely included animal fats and, for those living in the industrial cities, heavy smog shut out much of the sunlight. Rural people were at least likely to get plenty of natural light, even if they may have eaten less animal fat than townspeople.

In 1889, Bland Sutton published his findings from a famous experiment he had conducted at London Zoo. The Zoological Society was having trouble rearing lion cubs; so far, all attempts had failed, the cubs developing severe rickets and dying. Some pioneering work had been carried out over the previous half-century which seemed to indicate that rickets was a dietary problem rather than an infectious disease, and that animal fats and calcium were involved. On Sutton's advice, the zoo expanded the diet of the lion cubs from lean meat alone to include crushed bone, milk and cod liver oil. In three months, all signs of rickets had vanished, and the cubs grew strong and healthy. The results were a sensation, and widely reported in the press. Cod liver oil quickly became the new cure-all, administered in schools, hospitals, workhouses and families to improve the health of children. It became the very first food supplement.

Fig. 59. London Zoo's healthy lion cubs, 1887.

While hunger was at its cruellest among the poor, it sent its tendrils winding around the lives of the more wealthy too. Mrs Gaskell, in her biography of Charlotte Brontë, discussed the state of perpetual hunger the Brontës were kept in as children. Requests for more food were met with pious lectures about carnal desires and pampering to greed. Keeping children on short rations, especially girls, is a theme that runs throughout Victorian child-rearing practice. The self-control and self-denial induced by hunger were thought to teach enduring habits of self-sacrifice and to aid in fashioning a more moral individual. Girls, in particular, were to subdue the appetite by an effort of will.

Many accounts of life at boarding schools, both for girls and boys, report that here, too, food was short. A. A. Milne, who attended Westminster College in the 1890s, recalled that 'one was left with an inordinate craving for food. I lay awake every night thinking about food; I fell asleep and dreamt about food. In all my years at Westminster I never ceased to be hungry.' A fear of 'animal passions' often induced middle- and upper-class parents to restrict the diets of their children. Sending children to bed without supper was not only a punishment for unacceptable behaviour but was also seen by some parents as a preventative measure, actively reducing a child's propensity for mischief. Mr Bumble, the workhouse master in Charles Dickens' *Oliver Twist*, is horrified at the idea of giving the workhouse children meat; he believes that such food would lead to violent, riotous rebellion. Prison governors throughout the Victorian period express the same concerns about the inmates in their charge.

The strength and persistence of advice to wealthier parents about suitable diets for children to focus on 'plain' food – by which the Victorians meant carbohydrates – tended to put middle- and upper-class children's diets much closer to that of their poorer compatriots than a consideration of money alone might lead one to think. Nursery food was eaten and prepared separately from adult meals, and could be controlled in content and quantity. Recommended food for children included large quantities of bread and jam, boiled puddings (such as spotted dick or jam roly-poly), milk and milk puddings (rice pudding, macaroni pudding, tapioca pudding and sago pudding were several varieties), along with some boiled meat and fish on occasion. Not too much fruit – indeed, fruit, as well as fats and vegetables, were notably lacking from most children's fare.

Oliver Twist, before his fateful request for 'more', had suffered with the other boys of the workhouse 'the tortures of slow starvation for three months'. The workhouses were public institutions that offered the destitute board and lodging in return for work, but the workhouse diets from this period (*Oliver Twist* was published in 1838) were dreadful and show that Dickens was not exaggerating. Ignorance of what the body required nutritionally, coupled with a strong desire for economy and the belief that those receiving welfare should be worse off than the independent poor, resulted in diets falling short of the minimum sustenance for basic survival. Twenty-first-century analysis of workhouse diets estimates that they offered 20 per cent less than the minimum calorific requirement today, and records that they were seriously deficient in a range of minerals and vitamins. Slow starvation seems to have been the lot of many prisoners too. Most Victorian prisoners lost significant amounts of weight, despite, for the most part, already being underfed when they were committed. People wasted away. A few pioneering voices attempted to claim that this was a dietary issue and called for better and more varied food to be provided, but the authorities in the 1840s seem to have believed that wasting away in prison was a product of confinement – a natural effect of imprisonment aside from diet. Also, if prisons were to get a name as places providing decent food, then people would surely commit more crime in an attempt to gain entry. Ultimately, both these institutional starvation diets came about because of the abysmal food of the poor.

7. The Main Business of the Day

Getting to Work

The working day, however long or short, was for more and more people during the Victorian period bordered by the business of getting there. Domestic servants were the only expanding group who carried no travel burden. In the 1830s, there were still substantial numbers of people whose work was based at home, but these numbers were in sharp decline. Small-scale family workshops were giving way to factory production, and fewer and fewer small-scale farms remained economical. Walking to work was becoming the norm both in the countryside and in the towns. Long and exhausting hours forced most families to live as close as possible to the workplace of the primary breadwinner: overcrowded and unsanitary homes were still preferable to an hour's walk at the end of a sixteen-hour shift. Some did, however, walk huge distances daily out of necessity, when work was too transitory to warrant moving home, or when rents, even for single-room slum dwellings, were too high. It was the very same juggling act of money, time, convenience, job opportunity and family pressure which guides the lives of twenty-first-century commuters.

The very wealthy had always been able to put some distance between themselves and their place of business if they so desired, by using horses and carriages, but it had hardly been convenient even for them. Novels of the late-eighteenth and early-nineteenth century, from Jane Austen to Charles Dickens and Anthony Trollope, make it clear that upper-class gents attended to business between the hours of ten in the morning and four in the afternoon. This did not mean that the clerks, lawyers and agents they were consulting worked only these hours – 8 a.m until 7 p.m. was considered a normal day for them – but that it was the only available business slot for gentlemen who were expected to travel into town from some distance. The prevalence of this pattern even dictated bank opening hours.

As Queen Victoria ascended the throne, the first murmurings of change had begun. The first railway lines and horse-drawn omnibuses offered regular commuting services to those who could afford them. Neither train nor bus, at this point in time, was interested in carrying working-class passengers; theirs was a service for the wealthy or middle-class person; the timetables and routes were tailored to their specific needs. Trains and omnibuses alike were in the business of delivering gentlemen to the City of London and to the business and commercial districts of all of the major towns and cities in time for a ten o'clock start.

Fig. 60. A horse-drawn omnibus, 1866.

Middle class these modes of transport may have been; comfortable they were not. Initially, neither trains nor omnibuses had heating or lighting, but then neither had their older competition: the horse-drawn carriage. Seats were small, and the lack of suspension made journeys painful.

A horse-drawn omnibus was, essentially, a glorified cart, or slow-moving stagecoach (see Plate 15). Though they varied in size and design, most were about twelve feet long and less than six feet wide, with a single bench seat along each side. They were roofed over, and, on the roof, a further two bench seats ran back to back along the centre; a low railing ran around the edge to prevent people falling out. Access to the roof was via a ladder at the rear of the vehicle. Most companies running such vehicles considered them capable of carrying twenty passengers inside and a further sixteen on top. One writer of the early 1850s, however, saw fit to caution would-be passengers, instructing:

> When you mount or dismount from the top of an omnibus, do it calmly and leisurely, first with the left foot, then with the right, then with the left again and so on; never displace one foot till the other is securely planted. When you are on the roof, or the box seat, hold on by the nearest rail; for if you do not do so, a sudden start of the horses, or a jerk over a rut, is liable to pitch you off into the road.

Such advice was much needed, as those early omnibuses were precarious in the extreme.

If you were looking for a transport thrill, a horse-drawn omnibus might have been just the thing. Even traffic jams were an adventure on the top of such a bus. Horses were prone to bolting and acting unpredictably in a crowd of vehicles; holding on tight was a sensible measure. But if climbing up and down a ladder (particularly difficult for women in long skirts and no knickers) or grimly hanging on to a railing was not to your particular taste, you could squeeze inside. This, too, required a degree of care, as the space was tiny, each passenger being allotted roughly half the space of a commuter train seat today:

> It is a sort of tacit understanding that the passenger last arriving should make his way towards the end of the vehicle, and your endeavouring to take an intermediate seat would be resented as an act of aggression. When you have the choice of seats, do not take the one nearest the driver, or that at the farthest end; in the former case your feet are likely to be trodden on by the passengers as they come in and go out; and in the latter situation you have a difficulty in making the conductor understand when you wish to alight.

Just as on the London Underground train today during rush hour, a failure to follow the etiquette of omnibus travel provoked hard stares and sharp comments. The conductor stood on a small running board outside at the back of the vehicle (there was no room to stand up inside), helping passengers on and off, taking the fares and shouting out the stops.

The trains had their own trials, tribulations and etiquette. Many of us today may have had an opportunity to travel by steam train on one of the many preserved railways. But as British Rail was still running steam trains in regular service in the 1950s and 1960s, the majority of surviving and restored engines and carriages are, unsurprisingly, from the latter end of the steam period rather than its beginnings. In general, modern trips by steam are powered by a locomotive engine and we as passengers are seated in carriages from the 1930s rather than the 1830s. Today, these preserved railways offer us, for the most part, an experience of steam travel that has benefited from over a hundred years of improvement and technological advance. The early-Victorian traveller, on the other hand, had a very different experience. The carriages in which they sat were short-wheel-based and fitted without suspension, which meant that they often bounced and jerked around violently. There was no corridor running the length of the carriage, so whichever door or compartment you boarded, you were trapped in it for the duration of the trip. If you wanted anything to eat or drink, or to use the toilet facilities, you had to get off the train at the next station, along with everyone else, in a frantic rush.

Fig. 61. The trains of 1850 could be very uncomfortable. Facilities were basic.

Station stops were long by modern standards, and it was perfectly possible to run along and jump on to a moving train. Yet a person still had to keep their wits about them; tea shops were common at train stations and it was known for passengers to miss trains because they were waiting for their hot drinks to arrive. The trains were also quite slow. Hundred-mile-an-hour trains were a dream of the future; for most of the nineteenth century, the average speed was nearer thirty.

Railway carriages themselves had a reputation for being filthy from the smuts and cinders that blew in through the ill-fitting windows. Second-class passengers were sometimes advised to bring with them an 'air cushion' to sit on for long journeys, as only first-class carriages had any sort of upholstery. When Benjamin Goodwin and his son Albert recalled their second-class journey to work in the 1890s, the two-mile walk at the end of it was, they remembered, a welcome relief.

Fig.62/63. The first- and second-class carriages of 1884. Coaches were becoming more pleasant.

Adding to the passengers' disorientation was the new invention of the timetable. In the twenty-first century, the concept of specified times for a service is accepted, as is the onus upon the passenger to be in the right place at the right time. But in the 1830s, 1840s and 1850s, this was uncharted territory for most people. The many guides and advice for travellers usually began with a reminder of this basic fact. 'The first thing which a person should do who is about to travel by rail is to ascertain certainly from the timetable the hour at which the train starts,' wrote one such advisor in 1854. The first nationwide book of timetables was printed only in 1839 and, with a plethora of independent rail companies running lines and with no interest in sending passengers on board their competitors' trains, confusion around these timetables abounded. By 1900, there were 160 separate railway companies in operation, and the *Bradshaw Guide* that listed all their timetables ran to over a thousand pages. Fares varied from one company to another, and were often inconsistent even along a single line. A Crouch End passenger writing to the local newspaper in 1884 (and signing himself only as 'one who was had') pointed out that if he made the six-minute journey to Mildmay Park on the North London Railway, he paid the same fare – 10d – as someone travelling to Broad Street, although that was double the distance. In addition, if he were to use the Great Northern Railway from Crouch End to Finsbury Park, a similar journey as that to Mildmay Park, it would cost him only 4d.

But, in spite of all of these problems, train journeys were cheaper, faster and generally more comfortable than anything that had gone before. Lower-middle-class clerks and office workers found a whole new freedom in them, able now, like their wealthier colleagues, to contemplate living somewhere well away from the place where they worked.

In 1868, Liverpool led the way in introducing horse-drawn

trams to its streets. The trams were much safer than omnibuses and could carry twice as many people at twice the speed. Other towns and cities rapidly followed Liverpool's example. The trams were more stable than the omnibuses, and much more substantial vehicles, able to incorporate a narrow staircase to the top deck rather than the ladder of old. In the 1890s, the horses gave way to electric power, and it was from this moment onwards that trams truly became affordable to the working classes. Lines were extended to include the poorer areas of towns, and special workmen's rates were introduced.

Meanwhile, in London, the world's first underground railway was born in 1863, in a flurry of publicity. Not all the publicity was positive. *The Times* was vociferously sceptical, predicting first technical failure, then commercial failure, as, surely, no one would wish to travel on a system that ran through tunnels 'inhabited by rats, soaked with sewer drippings and poisoned by the escape from gas mains'. *The Times*, however, had got it wrong: forty thousand people travelled on the newly opened Metropolitan Underground Railway in its first week, and passenger numbers continued to grow rapidly, with trains at fifteen-minute intervals from Paddington to Farringdon Street and back again via Euston and King's Cross.

Originally, the underground railway was envisaged as an 'atmospheric' railway powered by compressed air. But the impossibility of sealing all the leaks led this first underground experiment to fall back on the old steam technology. Underground trains, for the first twenty-five years of their operation, therefore provided a service swathed in smoke and steam, relieved only by the numerous ventilation shafts that dotted the city. Electrification of the underground followed the electrification of the trams by a few years, but when it did arrive, in 1890, it did so in company with an array of new and cheaper ways to construct deep underground lines, as well as some more cost-effective fares. In 1900, the Central line, with its circular tunnels and flat twopence fare – it was marketed as the 'Tuppenny Tube' – came into being and proved very popular. The London Tube system was moving very large numbers of middle- and working-class workers in and out of the central London districts. By 1882, nearly 25,700 workmen's tickets were also being issued daily for overground services in London. By the end of the century, the better-off and employed working classes, as well as middle-class people, were getting used to the joys and sorrows of commuting. Workers could search for employment over a wider area; they could have a degree of choice over their home location, which allowed some, if not all, to find more pleasant, healthier housing; and the shorter working day gave them slightly more time and energy to make those journeys. Shorter hours but longer journeys was a trade-off that sadly left many Victorians away from the family home for almost the same total time as before.

There remained a large body of workers whose wages were simply too low or too sporadic to permit them to take advantage of the new travel opportunities, but even for those who could and did, commuting could be a cold and crowded experience. Complaints about severe overcrowding on trains and on platforms, queues at ticket offices, inflated prices, cancelled trains and delays were loud and frequent.

Tickets had to be bought on the day of travel and were valid only for the trains of that particular railway company. Anyone wishing to change trains had to purchase separate tickets at their interchanges along the journey. The most comfortable seat was widely held to be the one in the corner with its back to the engine. This position minimized the amount of ash and smoke liable to blow into your face and also offered the best protection from the jerking and jolting of the ride. From the start, however, many commuters found themselves having to stand during their daily journey to work. An overflowing carriage brought a much higher profit margin to the train company, which saw little financial incentive to invest in more carriages.

In keeping with this austerity, to begin with, stations were devoid of even the most basic of facilities, such as shelter from the rain, lighting or any indication of where trains were going. It was up to the porters to announce as loudly and lucidly as they could the arrival of each train, its destination and stopping points. They were also to call out the name of the station the train had arrived at, as, for many years, the simple expedient of putting the name of the station on signs on the platform was not considered. In among the noise of the engine and the slamming of doors, it was no surprise that the man's voice carrying this vital information could easily get lost.

As the century progressed, improvements filtered through the network. More lines were built and more trains ran so that, by 1880, Britain had four times as many railway stations as it does today. A myriad small urban and suburban stations delivered workers to every major employment concentration, both serving and promoting vast new areas of housing. At first, the new districts were predominantly for the wealthier worker, reflecting the costs of commuting. But as fares fell at the end of the century, working-class suburbs also sprang up. Pricing was critical; for many workers, even the most marginal fare increase could price them off the network. In the more urban areas, trams and omnibuses could find that their passenger levels surged when the railways added half a pence to the fare.

During the 1870s and 1880s, fish-tailed gas burners, named because of the shape of the flame they produced, supplied station lighting. At first, these were very dim, but they were still better than total darkness. They were gradually replaced by electricity in the 1890s. For many people, their first encounter with both the electric light and the WC was at their local railway station, long before such amenities reached their homes. *The English Illustrated Magazine* gave a vivid description of the 1890s station which captures something of the mood: 'At night, standing under the bridge just where the steps come down from Bishop's Road station and looking outwards, the scene is most impressive and weird. High in the air gleam two great electric lights, the apexes of two ghostly pyramids of light, around swirls the steam of passing engines, beneath all is rush, swish, and darkness, and innumerable coloured lights twinkling and blurred.'

Air Pollution

As our worker stepped out into the streets to make their journey on foot, train, tram or omnibus, they found themselves battling with the atmosphere. Today, we take it for granted that most of the air we breathe will be good, but Victorian Britain suffered from immense air pollution. Millions of domestic coal fires were pumping smoke and smuts into the atmosphere, as were factory chimneys and passing steam trains. A huge number of industries were also expelling a range of other chemicals into the air to join all that smoke, much of it highly toxic. The pottery towns of Staffordshire were known to be especially bad, the air a discernible brown and yellow colour from the exhaust of the kilns. It was highly acidic, too, and on damp, foggy days people reported it burning the insides of their mouths and noses. Life expectancy in such places was noticeably shorter than elsewhere.

The 'pea-souper' smogs of London were an even greater problem. They had slowly been getting worse over the generations as coal fires had become more numerous. To some extent, people took them for granted; London was just like that, there was no point in causing undue fuss. But the effects were life-threatening. London sits in a natural basin, and the weather can act as an atmospheric lid, trapping the air and smoke of the city in place. Unable to dissipate, the air gets thicker and thicker, the pollutants more and more concentrated. On bad days, you could hold your hand out in front of you, wave it about and not be able to see it at all. You didn't see people coming, you heard them – coughing as they approached. Delivery men had to use a boy, who walked along the kerb with one hand on the horse and one foot – invisible to him – knocking against the kerb at each step. When they got to a junction, the pair would slow to a crawl as the boy felt his way across and tried to find the kerb on the other side. Similarly, navigation was practised by counting the junctions or lamp posts. The whole of the city slowed to a shuffle. Most people wrapped a scarf around their mouth and nose when they were out as a sort of crude filter; there was little else they could do. Despite medical advice that those with weak chests should stay indoors at such times, most people had to keep going, trying to earn a living as best they could. Street thieves and muggers could operate almost with impunity, disappearing entirely within feet of the crime scene, making the smogs even more dangerous.

For such an enormous problem, the smogs and solutions for how to cope with them were not widely discussed in public. The population, including the medical world, seems to have viewed the pollution as one of the inevitable aspects of life. There was nothing to be done but leave the towns – something that even many wealthy people could not afford to do. Many gardening books included more information about the impact of smog on life in the cities, and London in particular, than health manuals. This was because the air pollution was so extreme that huge numbers of species simply wouldn't grow in London. Whenever the air was damp or it rained, the water combined with the pollutants, creating a range of noxious compounds, including sulphuric acid. Other pollutants were simply washed out of the air, falling on to the plants and the soil, as well as on the people. This toxic cocktail could be withstood by only a handful of the hardiest species. London gardening was about finding the species which could survive. Plane trees and rhododendrons still dominate London plant life – a legacy of this semi-sterility. Just further out into the suburbs, where it wasn't quite so bad, roses flourished, the acid rain killing off the fungal diseases that plague them elsewhere.

People sometimes had to spend their whole lives in this plant-killing environment. Respiratory problems beset Victorian life: while tuberculosis killed hundreds of thousands until antibiotics arrived in the twentieth century, just as with pneumonia, bronchitis and asthma it was a disease that was exacerbated by the poor quality of the air. Even on a clear day, black smuts could sail through the air like black snow, settling on everything and leaving a sticky, greasy layer upon people's hair, their clothes, the buildings, the plants and, if they had their windows open, inside their homes too. Indoors produced its own quota of smuts, from the kitchen range and from any other fireplace in the building, but, in towns and cities, the air outside was even thicker than the air within.

Health and Safety in the Workplace

Having arrived at work, there was a whole new set of dangers to contend with. The Victorian workplace was renowned neither for its healthy environment nor for its safety record. This held true if you were working out in the fields just as much as if you were bent over a spinning machine in one of Lancashire's mills or scrubbing floors in a stately home. Open fires and unguarded machinery were common, and the air was filled with smoke, fumes and dusts of various degrees of harmfulness. Horses bolted, sending carts, carriages and machinery flying; poisons were in use everywhere; heavy and debilitating lifting was the norm; and protective hard hats were yet to be introduced into common practice. To James Brady, looking back on the untimely death of his Victorian father, it seemed that 'nobody cared in those days.'

Certainly, deaths and injuries at work were greeted, in the main, with fatalism. Accidents 'happened', and, while it was sad and often tragic for the individuals involved, most people just accepted them. Acknowledged dangerous work might carry a small financial premium, but if you accepted such work you also had to accept the heightened risks. Mining was a particularly treacherous vocation, and this was reflected in the average wage. The standard of living in mining communities, such as those in the valleys of South Wales, the coalfields of Nottinghamshire or in the villages of County Durham was noticeably higher than that of agricultural or factory-working communities – as long as there was work to be done. How much real choice there was for men, women or children between safer and more dangerous work often depended on family circumstances. An extra mouth to feed, a run of doctor's bills or a relative unable to find work were all situations that could force people's hands. Even with the more limited medical understanding of the day, a range of occupations was widely known to be more dangerous than others. On the railways, it was the shunters, who attached and unhooked the freight wagons of trains, who died most frequently. Pressure to increase the speed at which the work was done led to 'fly shunting', where men darted between moving wagons, lifting the heavy couplings on and off. Such work was not highly paid, but it was regular, unlike much of the sporadic and seasonal labouring that was the alternative for these men.

Dust was another killer. The cotton-spinning and weaving mills caused much respiratory misery as the machines pumped fine dust into the atmosphere. The correlation between this dust and the ill health of the workers was undeniable, and the more sympathetic and moral of factory owners did try to provide ventilation. Unfortunately, the cotton spun and weaved better in warm and damp environments, which meant that most owners kept the windows closed. In addition, fans and ventilation shafts were expensive to install and many firms could not afford such amenities, even if they had the will. Elizabeth Gaskell's novel *North and South*, published in 1855, portrayed one young woman struggling for her last breaths, lungs clogged with cotton dust. She and her family had tried to move her to a factory with better ventilation when she had first started to show symptoms. But by then it was too late and the damage was done. This was a well-known danger during the Victorian period, and widely discussed.

That work, especially that done by the poorest people, would take its toll on the body was almost assumed. Many of those who wrote about their lives mention such injury almost casually; it was lamented perhaps, but thought inevitable. James Brady's father, as a young man, worked in a foundry churning out the iron rims that were attached to the bottom of working people's clogs. His son, describing how he would watch his father's skill and dexterity at work, finishes with the final ritual of the working day: 'He would smear a veneer of healing ointment over his blistered arms and hands before rolling down his shirtsleeves ready to go.' For Kate Taylor, the burns and scalds came in a different way, when her mistress sought to harden her up for a lifetime of work. She was thirteen, and working as a general servant in the dairy of a farmhouse: 'If she saw me flinch when I was getting dairy utensils out of the boiling sterilizing water she would push my whole hand in saying that was the only way to get hardened.' Eyesight was ruined for many women by long hours of badly lit sewing and other small-scale work. Punching the eyes of needles was notorious for straining eyesight: each prepared length of wire had to be accurately lined up by hand; the punch had to strike in the exact centre of each length. Victorian sewing needles, in general, were about half the thickness of modern needles – 0.25mm was not considered especially fine. With my own near twenty-twenty vision I can barely see the eye of such needles, let alone line up a punch that will perfectly bisect such wires.

THE MANUFACTURE OF NEEDLES.

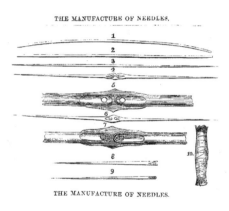

THE MANUFACTURE OF NEEDLES.

Fig. 64. Needle manufacture, 1853.

In Nottinghamshire, a young woman's eyesight was more likely to be ruined by the requirements of the lace trade. Machine-made lace needed hand-finishing, from repairing the tiny tears, holes and dropped stitches that occurred during manufacture, to adding elements of the pattern that the machines could not achieve. Twelve- to fourteen-hour days of such work in poorly lit conditions permanently altered vision. For those who tended machines, deafness was also a likely outcome. Weavers working the powered looms in the mills were almost invariably partially deaf by their mid-thirties. In towns where such work was common, a form of silent speech arose which exaggerated mouth movements, making it easier to lip-read. Foundries, forges, iron- and steelworks were other workplaces that deafened their workforces. A reputation for being loud in speech betokened the general level of impaired hearing.

Nor were working conditions in the countryside much better. For some people, working outdoors in all weathers could be just as debilitating as factory work, particularly young people. George Mockford recalled that his 'feet and hands became covered in chilblains, which soon broke out into open sores'. But work had to go on, and for George this meant lifting turnips from their winter storage beneath a great mound of earth and straw. It was common for pneumonia, bronchitis and arthritis to dog the lives of agricultural workers.

Accidents happened everywhere: dung carts turned over and trapped people beneath, axes slipped, loads shifted, and threshing machines used to separate grain from stalks and husks maimed and killed. Power hammers, kilns and foundries crushed, asphyxiated and burnt in the centres of industry. Men drowned entangled in fishing nets or cast overboard when boats foundered, while, underground, rockfalls and explosions killed. Victorian machinery was large and heavy, and its blades, intakes and hoppers were without guards. It tended to jam easily and usually needed close attention to operate, requiring people to dart in and out among the moving parts, oiling here, clearing dust and dirt there, adjusting screws and levers. Machines powered by water or steam were hard to shut down quickly, and those that relied on horsepower were subject to the panics and starts of the animals. None of course was intended to injure or kill and, if the human attrition rate was too high, they became uneconomical to run. But what counted as too high often changed according to economic necessity and greed.

Generally speaking, a fit, healthy adult with common sense can operate Victorian machinery with little incident. I have had the opportunity to work with a small range of Victorian machines, devices and methods, and they have all worked effectively, but there have been a few perilously close calls. I was once out with the horse-drawn tip cart, moving just over a ton of coal. As I was turning in the lane, a rabbit dashed out of the bank, and the horse – who shall remain nameless – jinked several feet to the right, causing the wheel of the cart to drop into a large pothole and throwing me off the cart and under the wheel. I just managed to roll clear before the cart with its ton of coal was pulled over me. About a year later, I watched as another horse bolted while ploughing a field of pasture. The plough was dragged from my colleague's hands and, as the horse turned away in its flight, the whole plough lifted from the ground, scything the air at head height. My colleague was able to jump out of the way and, fortunately, no one was injured, and the horse quickly calmed down. The out-of-control steamroller that I saw some years before was no less alarming, demolishing a series of barriers and crushing some picnic tables as people

Fig. 65. Agricultural machinery: an early reaper binder, 1857.

scattered out of its way before it came to a stop. In our recognition of the dangers of modern traffic, it is easy to forget that the vehicles and motive-power sources of the Victorian age were intrinsically much more hazardous than the infinitely more controllable equivalents of Britain today.

It is not just horses and steam engines that remind me of the vagaries of Victorian health and safety. Another colleague has found himself twice with splinters of metal in his eyeball from working at the forge. Added to this injury was the breakage of several fingers while catching sheep and manhandling equipment. Caustic and toxic substances were a daily part of the lives of many housewives; I have had cause on several occasions to be very glad of a plentiful supply of water to hand to rinse away any splashes and spills. I have also set myself on fire once, working in front of the kitchen range. The many layers of skirt and petticoats left me entirely unaware of the fact until someone else pointed out the flames. Some deft smothering with the rest of my skirts soon thwarted the situation with no further harm – other than a patching and darning job. But coroner's records show that such clothes fires caused the deaths of a substantial number of women.

However, what could make a difference between a few close calls and a tragedy was often what state a person was in at the time of such an accident. Most Victorians had a wealth of practical experience, but being fit, healthy and adult were not universal requirements for nineteenth-century workers. Long hours and an inadequate diet could undermine vigilance and slow anyone's responses. Reports of people falling asleep at their machines are common. Even today, accident rates rise towards the end of shifts. Victorian long hours could be very long indeed. One laundress interviewed in 1895 by one of the new female factory inspectors admitted that she had worked one unbroken stint of forty-two hours already that week. Legal limitations on the length of the working day had initially covered only children's hours of employment in specific industries, but, gradually, as the century progressed, new groups of workers were to be included. By 1850, the average working week was around 60–65 hours, then, in the 1870s, factory owner after factory owner agreed to cut hours. Unions and other labour organizations had long been arguing for a ten-hour day but, in the early 1870s, full employment strengthened their bargaining power and the 54–6-hour week became standard across a range of different industries. Most employers dealt with the shorter hours by stepping up pressure on their workers to work faster and more productively. The length of meal breaks was cut, machines were run at faster rates and increasing thought went into streamlining processes.

The extra hour in the evening and the free Saturday afternoon were a great boon to a swathe of working men and boys. Albert Goodwin's father certainly thought so, as he told his son: 'Of course, one had to find something to do in one's spare time because the factory hours were only 7 a.m. to 6 p.m. with half an hour for breakfast and one hour for dinner and 7 a.m. till 1 p.m. on Saturday.' Those extra hours of leisure were, however, mostly only for men and boys, legislation and powerful unions generally only being applied in industries and workplaces where male employment was the norm. Large numbers of people – mostly, but not exclusively, women – worked in unregulated businesses where working hours could vary dramatically in accordance with fluctuations in trade or season.

London dressmaking businesses notoriously demanded twenty-hour days for weeks on end from their employees during the social 'season', when fashionable wealthy women required a quick succession of new clothes in the very latest mode for an annual flurry of balls and social occasions. Domestic service, where the majority of working women continued to be employed, was entirely without limits; and outworkers who were paid per piece of clothing were similarly vulnerable to excessively long hours. This didn't just make people more vulnerable to accidents, it increased their exposure to unhealthy working environments. A person exposed to phosphorous during an eight-hour day at a match-making factory, while at significant risk, was none the less in a better position than one who was working eighteen hours a day in the same environment. There were also the health risks of simple overwork. Kate Taylor was in no doubt that the death of her thirteen-year-old sister Margery would not have happened 'if she hadn't had to work so hard for that stuck-up shop woman'. She records the circumstances of her exploitation with great bitterness. Overwork weakened people's immunity and left them with no reserves with which to fight illness. Victorians were typically adherents of the maxim 'hard work never killed anyone' – but many other Victorians knew that it most certainly did.

There were attempts to improve the health and safety of workers, and not just in the move to shorter hours. Some employers strove hard to improve the working conditions of their employees, ensuring that their premises were well lit and ventilated, installing water closets, providing bath facilities and, in some cases, setting up basic canteens. Very occasionally, there were even nurseries for workers' children, such as that at Blechynden Street, North Kensington, London, which cared for twenty-five babies from 8 a.m. to 10 p.m daily. Port Sunlight on the Wirral and Bourneville on the outskirts of Birmingham were purpose-built communities erected by industrialists for their workforces on the lines of the foremost health advice of the day. The rules and regulations of such workplaces, as well as their architecture, were formulated not just to ensure efficient and profitable production but also with the safety and health needs of the workforce in mind. At Bourneville, exercise sessions within the working day for under-eighteens coexisted with rules about cleaning the washrooms, bans on alcohol, strictures about keeping windows and ventilation shafts clear, and even limits on the amount of weight to be carried.

Fig. 66. Children being lowered down a coal mine, 1842.

Such conscientious employers were, sadly, in the minority. However, the same interest, zeal and concern could be found among many wealthy non-factory-owning Victorians, and pressure slowly built to introduce legislation that would force more employers to undertake at least a few basic health and safety measures. Before Victoria's reign began, legislation was already in place to mitigate some of the worst excesses of child labour in the textile mills. In 1838, freak flooding at the Huskar coal mine near Barnsley had killed twenty-six children trapped underground. One of Queen Victoria's first acts as Queen was to order an inquiry. The resulting report, with its accompanying line drawings of tiny children operating the trapdoors and slightly older children hauling the coal, caused an outcry which led not only to the legislation limiting the work done by children and women underground, but also began to impose wider safety measures for those whose underground work continued. Safety regulation would gradually spread out from the coal mines and textile mills to embrace more and more workplaces, and legislation slowly came to cover more and more hazards. The year 1844 saw the first legal requirement that certain machinery be fenced off; and these rules were tightened up in 1891. In 1862, a legal requirement was placed on many employers to ensure adequate ventilation to remove 'injurious gases dust and other impurities' generated by the manufacturing process. Meanwhile, mine safety was slowly improved, and 1855 saw a legal requirement that included fencing off all disused shafts, the installation of gauges and safety valves on all steam engines and the application of brakes and indicators on all lifting gear. Safety lamps became compulsory in 1872, reducing the risk of fire below ground. The very dangers of Victorian working life thus forced the invention of a health and safety culture.

Fig. 67. Funeral after a colliery accident, 1862.

Child Labour

Even at the end of the century, when education was both compulsory and free for all, most Victorian children spent far more of their childhood in work than in education. They worked in every branch of agriculture, mining, manufacture and domestic service, with very few sectors of the professions closed to them. Many worked in careers that were thought of as 'children's jobs', but others fulfilled adult roles too. If they were not in full-time employment, they could be part-time workers and part-time scholars: some had evening and early-morning jobs that fitted around schooling. Most also performed a large amount of domestic labour and childcare for their younger siblings at home.

Some children as young as five were recorded as being in full-time labour, and few Victorian children over the age of twelve had the luxury of not being a paid employee. The sons of many families that called themselves middle class might well be in full-time work shortly after their twelfth birthday, even if it was usually in an office of some sort rather than outdoor work. The office boy of Victoria's years really *was* a boy. He filled the inkwells, carried up the coals for the stove, fetched files and moved memos from clerk to clerk, as well as sweeping the floors and posting the letters.

At the beginning of the reign there was little in the way of either legislation or social pressure to restrict a child's access to a pay packet. The Factory Act of 1833 forbade the employment of anyone below the age of nine and restricted the hours worked by nine- to thirteen-year-olds to eight a day, and that of fourteen- to eighteen-year-olds to twelve. However, the act applied only to those working in textile mills, and inspections were scarce. Fines for employers who broke the law were also minuscule. The public at large had got used to child labour as a fact of life, and few Victorians had any major qualms about either employing youngsters or sending their own out to work. The first flush of the Industrial Revolution had created a new demand for child labour at a time when economic pressure made the extra few pence in the family budget the difference between survival and starvation.

The early machines that first took over from hand spinners and weavers were crude affairs that needed a host of small human assistances to work well. The work was extremely simple, but, without constant running back and forth tying snapped threads, feeding cards into appropriate places, brushing away fluff and reloading bobbins, the whole mighty machine would soon clog and stop. Adult labour was expensive and in short supply; children were not only cheap but were a scarcely tapped resource. As the northern mills got into their stride, they found that it paid to bring both boys and girls – mostly orphans and workhouse inmates – up from the south to tend the machines. The work may have been simple, but the hours were long and the dangers to their health were many. The dust-laden atmosphere in the mills was at its worst under the machines – the very areas where the youngest members of the workforce crouched, waiting for threads to snap and cleaning away the build-ups of waste. The small fingers and bodies of such workers allowed mill owners to pack more looms and other equipment into their mills, leaving only the tiniest of spaces between them for their workforce to move around as they carried out their tasks. The machines continued to run uninterrupted, giving many opportunities for youngsters who timed their actions wrongly to be pinched, caught or crushed.

The textile mills seemed to have an insatiable appetite for young labour, and it was here that the largest concentrations of working children were visible to the casual observer. From 1835 up to 1850, half of all of the workers in Britain's textile mills were under the age of eighteen. Such visibility attracted public attention in a way that no other employer did, so it was therefore no surprise that the first legislation to deal with child labour should be aimed at the cotton mills.

If, today, you want to get a feel for what life might have been like for the children of the early-nineteenth-century textile mills, make a visit to Quarry Bank Mill at Styal. It is run now by the National Trust, and it has made a good attempt at presenting it as it was in its working days. Of course, what you see will be cleaner, quieter and safer than the nineteenth-century reality – the National Trust, after all, has a duty of care for your health and safety – but the mill still offers one of the best working examples of what life working there may have been like. Styal was one of the most enlightened and benevolent mills of its day: the conditions and hours of work, the provision of schooling and the living conditions were all to a much higher standard than that required by the law. But, despite these improvements, the practical realities of dormitory nights and working days amid the cacophony of the machines were harsh.

It wasn't just that, with industrialization, there were more jobs suitable for smaller hands, but also that families were more in need of the money. For many traditional manufacturers, the new machines were driving down the wages of adult workers. The small army of handloom weavers, for example, was now competing with water- and steam-powered looms. As prices fell, families had to make up the deficit, and increasingly called upon their children to help out, at younger and younger ages. Pushed by hunger and pulled by the availability of work, child labour had boomed.

The highest concentration of very young workers in one place may well have been in the textile mills, but the majority of working children in early-Victorian Britain were engaged in agriculture. In 1801, 66 per cent of England's population was rural. By 1851, when the population had roughly doubled, 46 per cent still resided in rural communities. Even in 1911, when the population had once again roughly doubled, 21 per cent continued to make their homes outside the towns and cities. These families often worked on the land, and there were plenty of jobs for offspring of almost any age, either formally, as paid employees, or as helpers to their parents, boosting the pay of their mothers and fathers. Harvest time carried the biggest demand for child labour, a fact which the traditional British school-holiday timetable still reflects. Gathering the cut stems; tying them into sheaves; stooking the sheaves; gleaning the fields for fallen grain; and carrying in the harvest were all jobs for women, boys and girls. Other harvests also required such labour, whether it be pea-picking or digging potatoes, hop-picking or pulling flax. Weeding the fields was still done mostly by hand, and small hands were cheap and effective. Crow-scaring and woodcutting were generally jobs for boys, and so, too, was the cleaning of stables, yards and the building of dung heaps. Girls more commonly gathered up the cut stems, tied them into sheaves, helped with the milking and gleaned the fields of fallen grain. Each region of the country had its own agricultural jobs associated with children, from minding flocks of sheep to stripping osiers (twigs from the willow tree) for basket-making. As unwaged workers, helping their parents 'make ends meet', young boys and girls were also called upon to gather fuel, chop wood, fetch water, collect foodstuffs (for both people and animals) from the hedgerows and work the garden or allotment, and both sexes helped with housework and childcare.

Crow-scaring was frequently a rural boy's first job. William Arnold was six years and two months old when he was first sent to the fields. It was at the end of February or early March, 'and I do not think I shall ever forget those long and hungry days,' he wrote in his memoir. The job was a lonely one, standing all day in the open with a pile of small stones to throw at any birds that landed and tried to eat the seeds sown in the ploughed ground. The day had to begin before dawn and continued till past dusk, with no indoor break and no company out in the bitterly cold fields. As the season rolled on and the crop came up through the ground, bird-scaring gave way to minding a flock of sheep. At harvest, Arnold became an assistant to his parents, reaping the barley then leading the horse that pulled the carts back and forth to the barn. As the weather worsened once more, he was put in charge of forty pigs, and, in the depths of the winter, he joined the ploughing teams.

For Joseph Ashby, who was born in 1859, scaring crows was also his first job, but it did not begin until he was nine years of age, and then only part-time. Full-time farm work did not start until he was eleven. George Mallard, born in 1835, was full-time at nine years of age, scaring crows, chopping firewood and digging potatoes – work that continued throughout the rest of his childhood. None of these children, recording their lives years later, thought, at the time, that there was anything unusual in their work lives. For many rural lads, the part-time and piecemeal nature of their early work gave way to more regular employment at around twelve years of age, when they moved away from their family homes into the farmhouses of their masters for a year's agricultural labour. Such farm service, with its live-in lifestyle and year-long contracts, was disappearing in the south of England, but in the north of the country and in the lowlands of Scotland this formed the usual pattern for rural child workers. For some, it was a desperately lonely time, and casual abuse was common. Jesse Shervington, born in 1840, spoke of regular beatings in most of his positions: 'I am not speaking of this in any way irrespective and thinking I had unfortunate places, for cruel treatment, with ploughboys was merely a rule.' For Roger Langdon, the beatings came from the ploughman with whom he had to spend five years; pleas to the farmer and his parents for help brought nothing but reprisals from the same ploughman. Some, in contrast, found kindness and support from the families of fellow workers and employers. George Bickers, age unknown, was a pauper farm apprentice and orphan. The parish Overseers of the Poor paid a small sum to a local farmer to have him taught a trade and taken off their hands.

Such a child, friendless and alone, might have been expected to have encountered more cruelty and abuse than children with family to turn to, but Bickers was lucky, receiving not only a good training but emotional support from the farmer.

In the Midlands and much of the south of England, with farm service a job of the past, many children worked for gang-masters. These were middlemen who found work for and supervised groups of agricultural labourers. Moving their workers from farm to farm, they provided much of the unskilled labour to produce and harvest field crops. The children benefited from working together as a group and from going home most nights when the gang was within walking distance of home, but the life of the gang-worker was not without its hardships. Gang-masters set the pace of work. Joseph Bell recalled that the ganger walked behind the boys 'with a double rope bound with wax and woe betide the boy who made what was called a straight back before he reached the end of the field'.

Working outdoors in all weathers was tough on any child and, combined with inadequate clothing and a scanty diet, a lad working in the fields, rather than in a factory, had often taken the harder option.

While agricultural child labour continued, largely uncommented upon, and the children of the textile mills attracted the first protective legislation, it was the mines and miners that provoked the biggest Victorian outrage. The Royal Commission on Labour of Young Persons in Mines and Manufactures of 1841 exposed to the public gaze working practices which had worsened over the years. Miners were paid according to how much coal they brought to the surface. It made no sense for a grown man to break off from hewing the coal to carry it up, or for him to stop to remove unwanted rock or bring down the wooden pit props that held up the rock around him. To maximize his earnings, a man employed the help of his wife and children to move materials in and out of the mine while he concentrated on the business of digging it out of the rock. It was hot underground, and usually very wet, and there was little to be gained from ruining the few good clothes people owned, so most men, women and children worked in the dark, wearing only the scantiest of clothing. The mining people had no worry about this, but the general public, when they found out, were scandalized. Surely the women and girls would be molested, their morals corrupted! Alongside the affront to people's ideas of feminine modesty and delicacy came the heart-wrenching tales of the youngest mine-workers. Children as young as five were known to be left alone in the dark for twelve hours at a time, merely to open and close trapdoors for ventilation and access. Within the year, the Mines Act was passed: it banned all women and girls from working underground and all children under the age of nine from going down the pit.

It did not stop the practice immediately, of course. Organized inspection of mines began only in 1850, and the act related only to coal mines; other types of mining were not brought into line until the 1860 Act. But, in general, the child labourers in the Victorian mines from 1842 onwards were predominantly boys. One lad who started work underground at the age of nine in 1849 left an account of his early working life. We do not know his name, as he credited himself only as 'A Trade Union Solitary'. His first job was as the assistant or 'hurrier' to an older man whose rate of work was slower than most. As such hurriers had to work at the same pace as the miners, keeping the coalface and working area clear as the man hewed (or dug), a slower miner made the work of a hurrier more tolerable. The next year, working for a much stronger and faster man, the lad was pushing twenty-two loads a day five hundred yards up to the surface, then five hundred yards back. 'I had a rather rough time for a lad of ten,' he wryly remarks.

Edward Rymer also began work underground at the age of nine. He recalled crying his eyes out on his first shift sitting by a trapdoor, terrified in the pitch black. Fred Boughton described how 'they put an endless strap about six inches wide on me with an opening for me to put my head through, then they hooked it to a hod or box of coal, and my job was to drag it on my hands and toes. I could not stand up because the hole was only three foot six high in some places. The only light I had was a candle stuck on the side.' The physical toll of such work on young bodies was graphically described in parliament when Lord Shaftesbury quoted the words of the young Robert North: 'I went into the pit at seven years of age. When I drew by the girdle and chain, the skin was broken and the blood ran down ... If we said anything they beat us. I have sometimes pulled till my hips have hurt me so that I have not known what to do with myself.'

As the century progressed, minimum ages in regulated industries very slowly crept up. By 1872, ten was the minimum age for boys to work underground, and, until they were twelve, they were only permitted to work part-time, with compulsory schooling forming the other half of their day. In 1878, similar limitations were imposed upon a range of factories, with a minimum age of ten and a restriction to half-time working for all ten- to fourteen-year-olds. In 1891, the minimum age rose to eleven years of age. By the end of the century, children were not generally starting full-time work until they were eleven or twelve, just as things had been two hundred years before, at the start of the eighteenth century, before the early industrial expansion had dragged the very young into its employ. However, these were still the regulated industries, and there were plenty of children working in others to whom the legislation did not apply. If one employer turned you away as being too young, there were plenty of others who would take on a child.

Equally, many children and their parents felt that they needed the work, regardless of their age or the conditions (see Plate 16).

A boy could earn serious money. From about eleven years of age, most lads could be bringing home more than their mothers could earn; by sixteen or seventeen, many were out-earning their fathers. Women's work was consistently badly paid throughout the whole Victorian era. Even in jobs that were identical to those of men, women received around a half to two thirds of that which was paid to their fathers, husbands and brothers. Many jobs were so structured that the two sexes did slightly different tasks, which disguised the discrepancy, but even the most skilled and industrious girl or woman was at a major financial disadvantage. Married women needed to combine their paid jobs with the duties and responsibilities of housework, and mothers had the additional duty of childbearing and childcare. A boy's mother could not devote the same hours to earning that would allow her to bring in two thirds of her husband's wages. Her more sporadic work pattern trapped her in the worst paid of women's jobs, unable to compete with even her daughter's earning power.

These economic facts shaped the lives of children. Up to the age of eleven, wages for children were so low (two shillings a week was standard for much of the century) that it generally made more sense for boys to be employed, where possible, in part-time and ad hoc jobs, supplementing their work in the home by babysitting and helping with domestic tasks. Their help in the home freed up their mothers for some paid labour, which did at least pay better than that of a seven- or eight-year-old boy. But once a lad was eleven or twelve, then full-time employment for him was the best option. At a time when an adult male labourer was bringing home around fourteen to sixteen shillings a week, his eleven-year-old son could earn six shillings, if he was lucky; at fifteen, the lad could be bringing home ten to twelve shillings a week. His mother took over all the household responsibilities from him, relinquishing her own paid positions. This was a strategy that brought the family the maximum income possible. Many working-class families were as dependent on the earnings of children as they were on those of adults. Boys (so much better paid than girls of the same age) were the family's second-line workers, and a family with several sons in work could manage, if necessary, without an adult male breadwinner.

The money that boys earned was, almost without exception, handed over to their mother, who returned the odd, tiny sum as pocket money while employing the rest to the family's best advantage. A wage-earning son almost always improved the diet of the other children in the family, something that lads were only too well aware of. Almost all the men who wrote about their childhood lives mentioned the pride and satisfaction they gained when they were at last able to hand over a decent wage to their mothers. Boys felt like men. In putting food on the table and easing the hardship of life for their mothers and siblings, boys became respected figures within the family, and their own diet improved as they were treated to a taste of the preferential treatment their fathers got at meal times. In working families all over Britain, it was the breadwinner who was fed first and fullest. Any chance of a scrap of meat or fish went to him, and the largest portions and the greatest variety were his prerogative, as his health and fitness, above all, were paramount if the family was to continue to enjoy his wages.

Work thus brought lads status, more food and a small amount of pocket money. It also brought exhaustion and the risk of permanent damage to his body. In a vicious cycle of overwork and poverty, one of the main reasons a lad in his later teens could out-earn his father was that a man approaching forty was often too broken down physically to keep up, his own working life, begun at a similarly young age, having worn him out. The dangers of overstressing children's bodies were well known, and both legislators and individuals did try to protect children from overwork. Will Thorne's mother decided that his job at the brickfields was too hard; he was being 'slowly killed by such work', and 'it was making (him) humpbacked'. The job had been a well-paid one and the family was very much in need of the money, but the job itself consisted of nothing more than relentless heavy lifting. The young workers of the brickfields were employed to haul the clay to the brick-makers and to carry the bricks to and from the kilns. They moved it all in baskets and sacks upon their backs over uneven ground, braving the fumes and the heat of the kilns, water running out of the wet clay as they went. The Thorne family decided to endure a hungrier few years while a less taxing – and less lucrative – job was found for young Will.

8. Back at the House

Chamber Pots

Most women and girls in Victorian Britain began their day's work cleaning chamber pots and slop pails from the night before. Most men were blissfully able to walk away from this dirtiest of tasks.

Until the twenty-first century, chamber pots were a daily part of British life. While, today, we might find the very idea of them distasteful, they were a necessity of Victorian living until the advent of indoor WCs and electric lighting. Mostly made from earthenware, and glazed on the inside and out, they could be plain and functional in appearance or beautifully painted. There were even comedy pots that had an animal or person to aim the waste at painted on the inside. Medieval pots had come in a variety of shapes and sizes, some designed for men and some for women, but Victorian pots were remarkably standardized: a squat, round bowl with a wide rim and a handle on one side. For the sick, there was a range of bedpans, bottle-shaped or in the form of slipper pans if the invalid was bed-bound, and these were differentiated according to the sex of the person using them.

Chamber pots were one of the most basic household utensils; one would be among the possessions of those with even the very least. There might not have been a bed to put it under, but even those who were forced to sleep on a pile of rags had some form of chamber pot. Before electric lighting, to walk through a house in the pitch black and out into the yard or garden, picking your way by starlight to a darkened privy, was no easy task, and could be extremely hazardous. For children or the elderly and unwell, it was even more of a risk. Even towards the end of the century, when wealthier urban people had an indoor water closet, a chamber pot might well be a necessity. Everybody had grown up with chamber pots and knew how to make the best use of them.

A few practical experiments quickly make you aware of the importance of strict chamber-pot etiquette. Here are my tips:

- Always keep the pot in the same place, *underneath* a piece of furniture or right against the wall in the corner of your bedroom. You need to be able to find the pot reliably in the dark, even when you are disorientated or groggy from sleep. And more important than being able to find the pot is being able to avoid stepping on it or knocking it over – especially someone else's possibly full pot.
- Have your own pot. Sharing is hazardous. How do you know that a shared pot is empty? A shared pot is a potentially full pot, and not something that you want to discover in the dark when you are anxious to relieve yourself.
- Get a lid for your pot, and use it.

Someone, of course, had to empty the pots in the morning. They were emptied into the privy and washed out as soon as possible before being replaced in their allotted spot. Florence Nightingale was keen to have pots individually removed to the privy and washed outside, but most homes made use of the slop pail in order to reduce the amount of running back and forth. These were generally simply buckets that were assigned for the task, but the better sort came with a lid, convex, and sloping down towards a hole in the centre of about three inches in diameter. The design of the lid not only prevented splash-back, but also stopped the contents from slopping out when the pail was carried from room to room, or bed to bed, collecting up the waste. It was this aspect of their use that Miss Nightingale objected to: bringing the waste of one sick person to the bedside of another went against all her ideas about hygiene.

Mrs Beeton's instructions for housemaids in her influential book on household management included emptying the chamber pots in each bedroom daily, just after the housemaid had served breakfast and thrown open the bedroom windows. Emptying chamber pots was part of a routine that also involved cleaning all the jugs and basins used for the morning ablutions. For healthy people, the contents of an overnight chamber pot were, it should be remembered, unlikely to be anything other than urine. Mrs Beeton next, avoiding mention of the vulgar words 'chamber pot', politely instructed that the housemaid should empty the slops: 'In doing this, everything is emptied into the slop pail, leaving a little scalding-hot water for a minute in such vessels as require it; adding a drop of turpentine to the water, when that is not sufficient to cleanse them.' The ideal housemaid was then to empty, rinse and dry the bowl and jugs used for the morning wash before carrying the slop pail away, and emptying and cleaning it. I am well versed in doing this job. It is best to make sure that there is some water in the slop pail before the chamber pot's contents are emptied. This prevents anything from sticking to or soiling the pail. Once you have emptied the slops into the privy, you will then have a much easier job of washing out the pail in its turn.

In very grand homes and up-to-date institutions at the end of the century the slops were sent not to the privy but to a 'sluice room' with a good drain and plenty of clean water to be washed. There is a particularly fine sluice room at Lanhydrock House in Cornwall. Built in the late 1880s to the latest in Victorian design, the house does boast a few indoor WCs, but these were not considered suitable for nocturnal use, situated as they were at the ends of the bedroom corridors. Both family and guests continued to use chamber pots in their bedrooms for reasons of privacy and convenience. The sluice room is a marvel, containing several specially designed sinks with taps, and a flushing cistern. A slop pail could be brought into the room, the grate over the sluice lifted, the contents of the pail poured in and the chain to the cistern pulled to flush all the waste speedily away. If the grate was then lowered back over the sluice, the pail could be stood upon it, directly beneath the taps, for easy scrubbing.

With the breadwinners packed off to work and the chamber pots emptied, mothers, and any servants under their employ, could now attend to the needs of the younger members of the household.

Childcare

Long before it was common practice for adults to wash their whole body in water, a daily wash was recommended for toddlers. In his *Advice to Young Men and (Incidentally) to Young Women*, written on the eve of the Victorian period, William Cobbett insisted that this was part of a parent's duty. The bathwater, according to a later writer, should be 'about 90 degrees; but in the absence of a bath thermometer, the nurse may test the temperature by dipping her bare elbow in the bath, and taking care that the water is not hotter than she can bear with comfort . . . The child must be bathed at least once a day.'

THE ORDER OF THE BATH

Fig. 68. Bathing your baby, 1859.

As the infant grew, the daily bath was allowed to lower in temperature. Cobbett thought it promoted health and strength, and, while he admitted that babies and toddlers hated the procedure, he suggested that the parents should sing loudly throughout the bathing to drown out the cries and to teach the child to get used to it.

Bathing the baby was just as sensible in poor households as in the homes of the wealthy. Any basin would do, and not a lot of water was required, but a baby who was sluiced down daily was one who suffered and cried less. It did not have to be a fully immersive bath to be effective; placing the child in an inch or so of water for a minute or two was good enough in most cases.

Apart from its supposed benefits in toughening them up, water-washing was important for babies in order to avoid nappy rash. It took very little for this to develop, and it could make a baby's skin sore and its mood fractious. Neglect could turn this soreness into a serious health problem, with broken skin being exposed to faeces and infection. Scrupulous cleanliness was the best pre-emptive approach, and this meant frequent nappy changes, careful wiping, a daily wash and the use of barrier (or nappy) creams – the same methods we use to clean babies today, of course. But the nappies in use then were of cloth and had to be laundered. In 1837, they were diaper woven cotton or linen napkins – hence American 'diapers' and British 'nappies'. Diaper cloth was an especially absorbent weave that had a pattern of small diamonds on the surface and was used wherever a washable material was required to mop up spills and liquids of all kinds. Looped towelling did not become usual for either towels or nappies until the early twentieth century. The diaper napkins were large – about a yard square, and folded in a variety of ways to fit babies of different ages. One fold was used for newborns; another when the child reached three months or so; and a third as the infant got to nine months. Different folds were suitable for boys and girls, the thickest and therefore most absorbent parts of the nappies being positioned just where each sex was likely to make it wettest. The nappy was held in place with ordinary large pins carefully placed so as to keep the point as far away from the baby's skin as possible; the invention of safety pins in 1849 was, however, a boon to babykind. A sensible parent also had a series of nappy covers to prevent the nappy itself from leaking. These were made of materials it was hoped were water-resistant, if not actually waterproof. A tightly woven and glazed cotton served this purpose and was at least relatively soft. Some parents employed oilcloth, which was more waterproof, but also more uncomfortable for the baby.

Soiled nappies had to be washed, and the nappy bucket was a mainstay in most households, regardless of class. A dirty nappy was first tipped into a chamber pot so that any loose matter could be disposed of in the privy, then it was dropped in a bucket of cold water to soak. A handful of salt or – later in the century – disinfectant in the water helped this process. The lid was put back on the bucket to keep the smell in. When it came time to wash the nappies, the dirty water was poured away and the nappies were given a rinse. This combined soak and rinse removed about 95 per cent of the muck and made the nappy clean enough to wash in the usual way. Nappies were among the first garments to be boil-washed, as, even before germ theory, the link between faeces and disease became clear. Mrs Beeton, along with many other authorities, recommended a half-hour rolling boil.

For some of the very poorest, this was all just too much work. With no time (everyone over the age of about ten would have been working all hours) and few resources, they resorted to laying a piece of oilcloth in a cradle next to a handful of straw or another easily disposable absorbent. The bare-bottomed baby was then laid straight into the cradle. This cut down enormously on the amount of baby linens a parent needed, as well as on the amount of washing. If there was a decent layer of straw, the baby would mostly be lying clear of the mess and would be less likely to develop nappy rash. Middle-class visitors to such homes were often shocked by this practice, but desperately poor mothers had little choice. Who was going to buy them stocks of nappies when they could barely eat?

For most of the century, nappy cream, for both rich and poor babies, meant lard. A smear of lard over a clean, dry bottom kept the urine off the skin and prevented damage and soreness. A wealthy mother could make up, or buy, a scented version, just as she did for hand cream, but it was still, essentially, lard. Medicated creams usually meant the addition of zinc oxide, but they were not widely used for nappy rash. Drying powders after the bath were another refinement that wealthier nurseries some-times employed. Again, they resembled the toilet items of the woman of the house, being based upon either talcum or starch powder. But, for babies, they were usually used plain and unscented.

Baby Clothes

Once a mother had washed her child, she would begin the com-plex operation of dressing them. Even though the older practice of swaddling newborns had largely disappeared by the start of the nineteenth century, baby clothes were still, by today's stand-ards, multifarious and complicated.

One vestige of swaddling that hung on throughout society was the binder. It had several names, including bellyband, roller, swathe and sweather, but it was essentially a simple strip of cloth that was wound around the ribcage and abdomen, usually about a yard in length and four inches wide. Most Victorian advice advocated woollen flannel for this garment, but a number of the surviving examples today are made of cotton or linen, which suggests that cheaper varieties were available too. It was the very first item a baby was clothed in and one that remained their undermost layer for several months. Immediately after birth, when the baby had been washed and the umbilical cord tied, a small pad of cotton (or sometimes a coin) was placed over the cord and the binder wrapped around the child. The loose outer end could be pinned with a common dress pin or tacked with thread to hold it in place. Some mothers sewed tapes on to the binder so that it could be tied in place, rather than pinned, as they were worried about pricking the baby. In general, this binder was quite firmly wrapped around the child, as people still sought to provide warmth and structural support to the new-born child – the old belief that babies were born with soft bones still persisted. The firm binding was also intended to help the umbilical cord heal quickly and cleanly, shrinking back to create an indented belly button, which was thought to be much healthier, as well as more attractive.

Baby clothes were remarkably classless, as well as sexless. Miners and aristocrats alike began life wearing the same outfits. Admittedly, the fabrics they were made from varied in quality and price, but the shapes and styles were near-universal.

With the binder secure, a nappy could be put on, with its separate, semi-waterproof cover or 'pilche' over the top. Next came the shirt. Babies' shirts were generally of the softest cotton or linen that a mother could afford and their shape was kept deliberately simple, with no more than basic cap sleeves. The idea was to have as few seams as possible; these could rub a baby sore. Slightly older babies progressed, in an ideal situation, on to wearing warm flannel shirts; these were considered to be too harsh upon the skin of newborns. While most mothers made their own baby linens, by the 1880s there were ready-made sets for sale. However, the absence of advertising and marketing

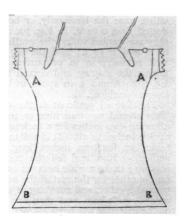

Fig. 69. Layer 1: a shirt for the newborn baby.

for such baby clothes compared to that for older children's underwear indicates that the market was small. Sewing for baby was part of the experience of pregnancy. Fortunately, such clothes lasted well and could serve an entire family of babies, one after another. Informally, many baby clothes were handed on from family to family when a woman felt that her childbearing days were over. This certainly helped to ease the sewing burden.

The need for frequent laundering of baby clothes meant that a mother needed a plentiful stock. *Cassell's Household Guide* considered twelve shirts to be appropriate for a newborn – six for daytime wear and six for nightwear – along with twenty-four nappies and four pilches. One of the reasons that newborns' clothes were so often sewn at home was a desire for them to be hand-stitched rather than machine-sewn. Many people felt that the machine-made seams were too rough and lumpy for babies, which was a real testament to the average Victorian mother's sewing skills: her hand-sewn seams were smaller, smoother and neater than the machine-made alternative.

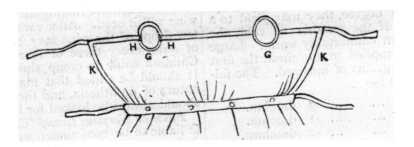

Fig. 70. Layer 2: the barracoat to wear over the shirt.

On top of the shirt went the flannel (or barracoat, barrow, or even whittle; the name varied across the country). This, as its name suggests, was made of flannel material, for warmth. The bodice was a simple band about five inches in depth, and to it was sewn a long skirt, which was pleated around the waist to give fullness. This was about six inches longer than the baby. Cotton tapes were sewn on to the top to form shoulder straps, and further tapes allowed the flannel to be tied around the baby. There were no sleeves on the garment and, at this stage of dressing, the baby still had entirely bare arms. The additional length of the skirt, however, did ensure that their legs and feet were warm. Just like shirts, there were day- and night-time varieties of barracoats so that babies did not stay in the same set of clothes for too long. The only difference between them was that barracoats worn in the day occasionally had more decoration. The simple shirt design allowed for a fold to be tucked down over the top edge of the bodice, ensuring that the baby did not have a hard or scratchy flannel edge around the neckline but only the smooth and soft cotton of their shirt.

A cap was tied on to keep the chill off the baby's head – especially important in the weeks before their hair had grown. These under-caps were worn indoors both night and day but were not

Fig. 71. Layer 3: the petticoat.

considered sufficient for outdoor wear. Catching a 'cold in the head' was common, particularly when Victorian homes could be so cold and draughty. Mothers who were worried about this turned to flannel for under-caps, usefully, a fabric that was also advised as a preventative for cradle cap (the greasy, waxy secretion which many babies develop on their scalps in the first few months of life).

With all these layers already in place, the baby was finally ready for their petticoat. These were typically cotton, white cotton being much preferred, although unbleached was cheaper. Like the barracoat, the petticoat was sleeveless with a long skirt gathered at the waist. Petticoats were more decorative than barracoats, because their hems were likely to show when the child was fully dressed. Scalloping, lace and rows of tiny sewn-down tucks were popular embellishments around the bottom edges, although the tops remained largely plain so that they would sit smoothly underneath the final layer of clothing.

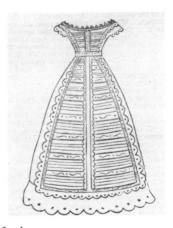

Fig. 72. Layer 4: the frock.

Lastly, over the top of the shirt, barracoat and petticoat came the frock. For new babies, this was also of white cotton, often a very fine and filmy variety, if the family could afford it. In shape, it was scarcely any different from the petticoat, but it usually carried a far greater level of adornment and pattern. A complex mix of tucks, embroidery and lace were often lavished upon a baby's frock. The frock, too, had no sleeves, and the neckline was low. Despite such complex layering, Victorian babies thus faced the world with bare arms and necks and often fewer warm clothes than their parents: only one of the layers was made of a woollen fabric – the barracoat; everything else was sewn in fine, thin cotton fabrics.

Concern about overdressing and over-restricting babies had replaced the conviction that swaddling was beneficial. As so often happens when a long-entrenched idea and pattern of behaviour is overturned, people swung heavily the other way. In their proselytizing fervour to persuade parents to leave off the swaddling bands, the pioneers of the eighteenth century promoted instead a theory of hardening and toughening up babies to help them fight off disease. Just as exercise was necessary to build up healthy muscle, exposure to the elements would enable children to endure the cold without taking a chill. The cold would, it was thought, stimulate and strengthen their general constitution.

By 1850, parental enthusiasm for these ideas was causing alarm among the medical profession. Dr Bull argued that 'unfortunately, an opinion is prevalent in society that the tender child has naturally a great power of generating heat and resisting cold; and from this popular error have arisen the most fatal results.' He labelled the baby fashions of the day, with their bare arms, shoulders and neck a 'fatal practice' that could lead to croup and inflammation of the lungs. But he also quickly distanced himself from the old swaddling practices and advised against over-coddling a child. Despite his concerns about underdressing, he also warned about too much warmth enfeebling the constitution. It was a confused message, but, despite many similar public 'rants', Victorian children continued to be left shivering.

Thankfully, when venturing outdoors, there was much more protection against the elements, in the form of a cape and bonnet. Capes were woollen, with one long layer reaching well below the feet and a second, shorter layer reaching to the knees. This provided two layers of warm, woollen fabric over the arms, as well as over the rest of the body. Some mothers removed the cape the instant they got indoors with their child, but many left it on when January's chill permeated the house. Colour also crept into a baby's wardrobe, as many capes were cream or grey or, very occasionally, red. Victorian baby boys were dressed in white, and so were Victorian baby girls. As well as being symbolic of purity and innocence, white was a suitable colour for babies because it showed up the dirt. This may seem the wrong way round to a twenty-first-century mind, but it was felt to help maintain standards of cleanliness, which, of course, were essential to a baby's health.

On a practical note, white clothes could be aggressively washed using soap, boiling water and vigorous scrubbing. The dyes of the Victorian period could only withstand so much laundry before they would run or fade. Coloured clothes on a baby would have been very quickly ruined, which could easily have made parents reluctant to do much washing. Red had, for centuries, been the colour of the blanket (or bearing cloth) a swaddled baby would be wrapped in. It therefore had a place in people's hearts as a suitable colour for a baby's outdoor garment, unlike pink or blue, which had not yet gained a cultural role in babywear. A red flannel cape looked dazzling against the whites of one's other clothes, which may have been another factor in its popularity. However, red was not the most common colour for Victorian baby capes; that honour went to cream-coloured wool. Many cream capes have survived into the twenty-first century, often with white cotton – or silk – ribbon outlining the edges.

After Nine Months

At about nine months old, a baby's clothes began to change. The main difference was the new length. Newborn or 'long' clothes stretched well below the child's feet – in 1840, they would be perhaps as much as a yard longer than the baby. (By the 1880s, they were rarely as much as a foot longer than the baby, but the feet and legs were still well buried beneath the layers of barracoat, petticoat and frock.) The change into 'short clothes' was intended roughly to coincide with a baby sitting unaided and beginning to crawl. Long draperies would have got in the way, so what was needed now was ankle-length clothes. Mothers were generally advised to resist the temptation of simply cutting off the bottom of the existing garments, because there was a realistic chance that, in a year's time, she would have another newborn to clothe. It would be much more economical in the long term to leave the long clothes and make a new, shorter set; besides, at this age, the first visible differences between male and female clothing became apparent.

Up until the nine-month watershed the only difference between the garb of boys and girls was in the folding of the nappy, but from this point on the two sexes gradually moved apart in sartorial matters. It was a long process, with many small, incremental changes, but it would eventually lead to an almost total separation of dress. To the modern eye, it is difficult to discern these differences. At nine months, they amount only to a slight flare of the skirt and a variation in the style of the trimmings, those on boyswear slightly bolder and more likely to consist of braids stitched on to the clothes than that of the girls, who were more likely to have their frocks trimmed with lace. Tucks and pleats were to be found on frocks worn by both sexes. Elsewhere, the gendering of clothes was subtle at this age.

Now that baby garments were ankle-length, the baby's feet and legs were much more exposed, so it was at this age that babies usually began to wear socks and stockings. Once again, both sexes wore both. It was possible to buy shoes for children this young, but most parents chose not to out of concern that the shoes would deform their growing feet (something that rightly still remains a concern in some quarters today).

The other main shift that occurred at this time was the leaving off of the binder, and its replacement with a stay band. Still largely home-produced, the stay band was much more reminiscent of a soft mini-corset and was worn by both sexes. Two layers of stout fabric, canvas or jean were cut into a strip five inches wide and twenty-two inches long. Along the top edge, two shallow crescents were cut out for the armholes. The two layers were stitched together, with a series of vertical rows forming long channels, which were then threaded with stout cord or string. These firmly fixed vertical rows of string stiffened the stays; they were the soft, infant version of whalebone in corsets. The garment was neatened with tapes sewn on to form shoulder straps and another set of tapes to fasten the stay band around the body. The resulting garment was not rigid or hard, and much less firm than, say, wrapping a piece of cardboard around yourself. There was no practical way of tightening it, and it could not be used to pull a child's waist in, but it was a much bulkier piece of clothing than twenty-first-century children are accustomed to wearing. To the Victorian mind, it provided a necessary form of support for the growing child.

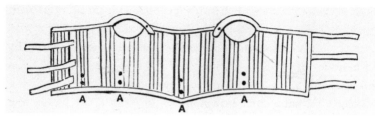

Fig. 73. The stay band for an older baby.

At the age of two, my own, very vocal, daughter demanded a corset of her own. She was already well used to me wearing one, and she wished to be like the grown-ups. Not, of course, wishing to put a two-year-old in a true corset, I made her one of these stay bands. She loved it. It certainly didn't stop her doing anything, and as an articulate toddler she was well able to say if she found it at all uncomfortable. She chose to wear it a lot, even to playgroup, although there were plenty of other garments she made a fuss about – anything with elastic around the waist, for example. The stay band never provoked any complaints from her.

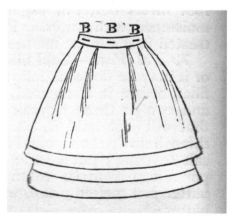

Fig. 74. A petticoat over the stay band.

As soon as a baby could pull themselves up on to their feet, quick alterations could be made by means of a series of horizontal tucks in the hems of all the ankle-length garments, bringing them up higher to prevent the child from tripping over. As the child became more confident and independent, the skirts were gradually raised again, eventually ending not much below the knees. A toddler dashing about the place need no longer be concerned by any additional fabric getting caught around their lower legs. It did, however, leave the child exposed, so, with the shortening of the skirts, a new garment was added – pantalettes. These were simple, thin cotton trousers, or long drawers, that reached down to the ankle. The nearest modern equivalent is pyjama bottoms. Pantalettes define the early- and mid-nineteenth-century toddler look: a short-sleeved dress ending below the knee with cotton pantalettes poking out beneath. Both sexes sported a head of curls, the caps having been abandoned at about the same time as a child learned to walk. Lots of curly hair was encouraged both for the warmth and insulation it provided and also, perhaps more importantly, for the look. To call a baby 'pretty' was a compliment, even for boys; babies and toddlers were supposed to be beautiful, to gladden their parents' eyes and hearts.

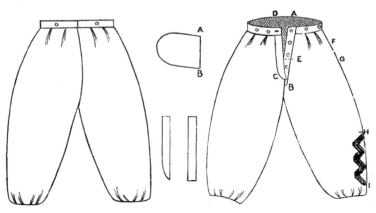

Fig. 75. Pantalettes to cover the legs.

Fig. 76. A dress to complete the outfit.

The list of baby clothes supplied to the few babies born within a prison environment was remarkably similar to that recommended to middle-class parents for their newborns. It included flannel binders, under-caps, shirts and nappies, covered with flannel petticoats, flannelette frocks and even flannelette and calico gowns and shawls. Flannelette was not a woollen fabric, but rather a thick, soft-brushed cotton. It was warmer than the plain cotton fabrics advised for middle-class frocks, but not as warm as real flannel. As a result, though, a prison-born baby may have actually been the most warmly dressed infant of all of the social classes (although one presumes that he or she was deprived of frills, tucks, embroidery and lace).

The working-class child outside of an institution was heavily reliant upon flannelette for their clothing; it retailed at less than half the price of flannel and was much easier to wash. Swansdown was another working-class option: again, a brushed cotton, although not as good quality. The real problem for mothers and their working-class babies was providing *enough*. This was true for clothing, as for everything else. Aside from the problem of warmth, the fewer changes of clothes a baby possessed, the dirtier and more unhygienic they would become, which would inevitably affect their health. At the very worst, a young baby could be kept simply wrapped in a shawl when out of the cradle, but as soon as they began to move about independently, some form of clothing had to be found for them. Private individuals and charitable foundations tried to fill this shortage with donations of baby clothes, but a large number of babies and toddlers ended up inadequately covered, or in ill-fitting and heavily worn garments, as a result. The lack of stretchability in the fabrics exacerbated the problem, and attaining a comfortable fit that neither cut into a baby nor swamped them so they were unable to move was troublesome, particularly when a mother was reliant on hand-me-downs and items picked up cheaply or second-hand. Most parents seem to have preferred to err on the side of caution and growing room, and to have chosen to bundle their children up as much as was possible to keep out the cold. It was a common sight to see small heads emerging from great balls of fabric, pinned immobile by their clothes.

Dressing Older Children

With the baby washed and dressed, a mother could turn her attention to the clothes of the older children, helping them to dress themselves as well as making a start upon sewing new outfits for them.

At the very end of the Victorian period, some working-class mothers recorded their daily working timetables for the research of social reformers. Mrs O. (the names were not given, in order to preserve people's privacy) had two small children. She dressed her young daughter at 7.30 a.m. when her husband left for work, and the baby was washed and dressed at 8.30 a.m. after she and her daughter had eaten breakfast. At 11 a.m., with some basic housework accomplished, she sat down to start making a frock for her daughter. She sewed for an hour before starting to prepare the meals for the day.

Getting a whole family of children up, washed and dressed could be a major daily chore. There were no zip fastenings and no Velcro (invented in 1948) to ease or speed the operation. Buttons had to be fastened and tapes tied into bows; all tasks that were much too fiddly for small fingers to manage by themselves. A two-year-old boy faced with a twenty-first-century wardrobe of elastic, pull-on clothes would probably make a reasonable attempt at dressing himself without too much assistance and be fully dressed in five minutes. A two-year-old of today faced with a Victorian wardrobe would be stumped. Even with adult help, the process was more likely to take fifteen minutes. The lack of stretchiness in the clothes made it much harder, for example, to get arms into armholes, and, besides the difficulties of buttons and tape ties, there were also several layers of clothing – as in babyhood – that were required in order to keep the cold out. Stay bands were covered by vests, shirts and drawers. These, in their turn, were covered by pantalettes, petticoats and pelisses (dresses or tunics), in addition to socks, shoes, coats and hats.

In Victorian times, the clothes of a two-year-old boy were similar to those worn by a two-year-old girl, but, as children grew older, their clothing gradually became more distinct. For girls, dresses lengthened and trimmings and shapes grew incrementally closer to the fashions of their mothers. Corsets replaced stay bands at seven or eight years of age. By puberty, girls were little women; only their hairstyles, shorter skirts and a preference for pale colours marked the difference in attire from their mother.

Fig. 77. The fashionable dress of young boys in 1850.

Boys' clothes, on the other hand, went through a number of distinct stages. Their pantalettes began to be made of heavier cloth, and the frills and lace gave way to pleats and braiding until they looked less like pyjama bottoms and more like a three-quarter-length trouser. The waists of the petticoats and pelisses remained looser than those of the girls, and skirt lengths inched above knee level. Throughout the 1840s and 1850s, the combination of the pelisse and pantalettes was worn until a lad was roughly six or seven years of age. Frederick Hobley was six years old in 1840, and, years later, writing an autobiography for his family, he remembered his new outfit, worn at the annual school treat. 'I had on a new pelisse, it was of a dark green colour, had a fitted body, and a full pleated skirt, this was before I wore trousers.' It would be more than a year before Frederick made the jump to full trousers. 'I well remember when I was first "breeched", that is, wore trousers for the first time – these were long enough to reach to the ankle – still they looked rather short.' By which time he was just shy of his eighth birthday.

Fig. 78. A knickerbocker suit, 1875.

From the early 1860s, a new intermediate style of clothing began to emerge: knickerbockers. At about three to four years old, a boy now left behind the skirts of his toddler days and was dressed in his first pair of short trousers. The skirts had been practical for nappies and toilet training, as they gave easy access. They had been useful, too, for those first years learning to walk, when the stiff and bulky fabric of Victorian trousers would have been uncomfortable and awkward. But once both these skills had been thoroughly mastered, it was time for a boy to move on to knickerbockers. These were easy to make at home, requiring only approximate fitting, and their bagginess allowed plenty of room for growth. The knickerbockers, usually belted at the waist, were fitted in a loose band below the knee, and the area in between the waistband and the knee bands was roomy and shaped much like the pair of drawers a lad would wear underneath them.

The knickerbockers formed one half of the knickerbocker suit. While they were definitely not the skirts of babies, toddlers and girls, they were also not the suits of grown men. The jackets were more like tunics: unshaped, collarless and thigh-length.

Most knickerbocker suits were made of sturdy wools or fustians, with tweed being especially popular, both for warmth and durability, among those who could afford it. Beneath the knickerbocker suit, a boy also experienced greater freedom of movement: the stay band was now left off and replaced simply by a flannel vest worn beneath his shirt. These were clothes for being a boy in, and lads like Frederick Hobley could climb trees and roll in ditches, play cricket and get into mischief. Boys from roughly four to ten years of age were dressed primarily for an active lifestyle, without the formality and restriction of clothing they could expect as they matured into adulthood.

Boys were some of the first people to be clothed by the ready-to-wear market. This may in part have been fuelled by middle-class mothers' disgust at tailors' prices but was also strongly influenced by the manufacturers. The knickerbocker suits that came into fashion in the middle of the century were eminently suitable for mass production. The shapes were simple, they were loose-fitting and few sizes were required. Trends in fashion could be expressed through the use of trimmings. A manufacturer could therefore have a basic shape cut in numerous fabrics, year after year, simply altering the trimmings and colours to stimulate sales. Mothers, aware of the need for 'growing room', were very happy with the approximate nature of the ready-to-wear fit, as they were with its low prices. Many were relieved to have found an alternative to making their son's clothes at home.

Ready-to-wear clothes also permitted an element of 'dressing up', with outfits inspired by regional costume, military uniforms and historical dress. In the 1880s and 1890s, a mother could go along to one of the ready-made-boyswear shops, or peruse their catalogues, and choose something for her son from the following: a sailor suit (white canvas with blue tapes sewn on to mimic naval uniforms), a Highland kilt suit, a Little Lord

Fauntleroy suit (inspired by a popular book character, it was a velvet knickerbocker suit with an elaborate, large, lace collar), a Tyrolean suit (mimicking lederhosen and complete with a small hat with a feather in it), a Norfolk suit (a tweed jacket and knicker-bockers, such as country gentlemen wore when grouse-shooting), a hussar suit (with lines of braid across the chest to suggest the military uniforms of the Prussian Empire), an American suit (a cowboy outfit) and many variations upon each of these themes. The Highland suits were generally worn by the youngest boys, while the sailor suit, which first appeared shortly after 1856, when a miniature naval officer's suit was made for Prince Edward, stretched to the middle age-range, up to around nine or ten years of age. Norfolk suits were particularly favoured for boys in their early teens.

Fig. 79. A boy's sailor suit, 1850.

The enormous popularity of ready-to-wear clothes for boys allowed this section of the market to flourish and experiment with more sophisticated manufacturing techniques. Makers of boyswear were industry leaders, and their innovations allowed them to lower their prices further as the century progressed. A perusal of Victorian clothing catalogues shows the prices of boys' suits falling. The cheapest suits advertised in the 1870s were 8s 6d, but, in the 1890s, most of the surviving catalogues include suits for around half that price. The advantages of home-sewing, even for the most willing and cash-strapped of mothers, were fading fast. In an age when adult-male wages for unskilled workers hovered around the 20s mark, these sorts of prices made the purchase of new ready-made boyswear a genuine possibility for working-class families in the later years of the century. Photographs of boys entering Dr Barnardo's institutions show an accurate cross section of the clothing of the poorest boys of the 1880s and 1890s. About a third of them wear sailor suits, while another third are dressed in lounge suits. Norfolk jackets are visible on about 10 per cent of the lads and 'Greenwich' suits on about 20 per cent. What is apparent is that, even among families who were in need of charitable assistance, there was a sustained and substantial effort put into ensuring that boys had at least some fashionable clothes, and that they wore the items that suited their age group, worn and ill-fitting though they often were.

Baby Food

Feeding the baby was a mother's next task. In 1830, William Cobbett issued a long and impassioned plea in *Advice to Young Men and (Incidentally) to Young Women* for mothers to breastfeed their own babies. In his opinion, only the biological mother of a child could provide the love and care a newly born babe required. Unlike today, when the debate is between breastfeeding and bottled 'formula' milk, at the beginning of Victoria's reign the argument was *which* woman should breastfeed a child. If a mother could not produce enough milk herself, then

1. Laundry was an unpopular job, wet underfoot, steamy and involving a lot of heavy lifting. Tempers often frayed on washday, and I can understand why.

2. Laid out on the washstand ready for use: a jug of warm water, a bowl to wash in, a bar of soap in a dish, a hairbrush, hair pins, a jar of bandoline, a clothes brush and a hand mirror. This was the most common experience of personal hygiene in the Victorian era.

3. Housework involved the home production of an array of 'products'. I have found that brick dust is highly effective as both a metal cleaner and a scouring agent for the toughest of jobs.

4. By the end of the century fully enclosed ranges were the dominant form of cooker. This single-oven model proved its worth during my year of Victorian farming.

5. Double-oven models such as this catered for the larger establishment, although many people preferred to have one oven plus a water boiler rather than a second oven.

6. Mary Ellen Best, *Our Dining Room at York* (1838). The table is laid for dining '*á la française*'. This was usual until the 1860s, when dining '*á la russe*' arrived.

7. Frederick Daniel Hardy, *Baby's Birthday* (1867).
A comfortable home to be enjoyed by the wealthier working classes or
the lower-middle classes. Note the early-style 'open range' on the far right
of the picture.

8. Robert Scott Tait, *A Chelsea Interior* (1857).
Jane and Thomas Carlyle in their characteristically middle-class home. The
Victorian love of colour and pattern is represented in both the furnishings
and in Thomas's warm and informal smoking jacket.

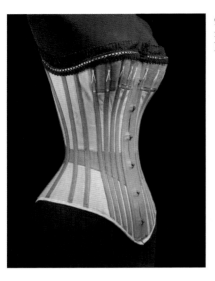

9. A cotton corset, 1890. Such models were affordable to the lower-middle classes.

10. A metal hoop crinoline *c.*1860. Unlike the crinolines of the 1850s, the front is flattened. A change of crinoline could update an old dress at comparatively low cost.

11. The newly invented chemical dyes exploded on to the fashion scene after 1856. For the next fifteen years it was not possible to be too brightly dressed. This example is from 1869.

12. A tartan velvet waistcoat, 1850. This was an area of dress where men could outshine women.

13. Worn in 1868 by six-year-old Edwin Hollis Perks, this dress was typical of the style worn by young boys over a pair of pantalettes resembling pyjama bottoms.

14. A man's frock coat of the 1830s. Its pale shade, fitted waist and flared skirt were in the latest fashion.

15. Garden Seat Omnibus, c.1890, in the later, improved style, with an extra-wide wheelbase, an external staircase rather than a ladder, and with proper seats on the top deck. Horse-drawn omnibuses of this type predominated in the 1870s and 1880s, before trams began to supersede them.

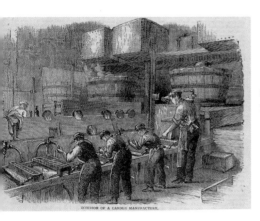

16. Boys working alongside men in a candle factory, 1889.

17. Mrs Winslow's Soothing Syrup was one of numerous brands containing opiates which were designed for babies.

18. The child monitor teaching a group of younger pupils, a system that radically decreased the cost of mass education.

19. A playing card depicting Benjamin Disraeli, 1826. At this stage of his life (twenty-two years old) he was well known as a novelist.

20. Instructions from *Cassell's Household Guide* on calisthenics. An excellent form of gentle exercise for those who spent too many hours hunched over their sewing – or over their keyboards, as my daughter can testify.

21. Lawn tennis in 1886 was played in full fashionable dress.

22. Archery was the first sport to be equally open to women and men, but was strongly associated with the very highest social classes.

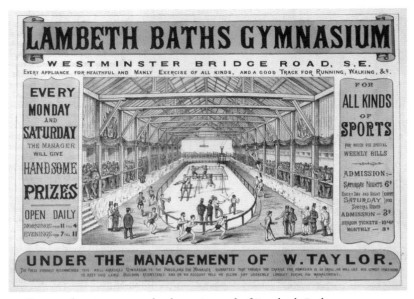

23. During the winter months the main pool of Lambeth Baths was drained and reopened as a venue for gymnastics. The low prices allowed respectable members of the working classes to participate.

24. Walter Richard Sickert, *The Music Hall* (1889). Music halls attracted large mixed crowds, including those seeking commercial sex.

employing another woman – a practice known as 'wet-nursing' –
was a baby's best chance of survival.

Among those who could afford to do so, hiring a wet nurse
had long been an established practice; sometimes even if a
mother had a plentiful supply of her own milk. With another
woman feeding the baby, a wealthy wife was in a position to
resume her role as head housekeeper and hostess more quickly
after the birth of each child. The tension between social pressure
to fulfil her duties towards her husband and household, and the
desire to do her best for her new child, had been played out in
wealthy families for hundreds of years.

For the poor, maternal breastfeeding had always been the
default position. But poor diet undermined many women's
ability to provide nourishing milk for their babies, and the
need to work caused further problems. When a woman
already had four or five hungry mouths to feed, the pressure
to earn financially could be extreme and compromises had to
be made. Family and friends who were willing and able to
breastfeed were pressed into service where possible, while
other mothers resorted to a mixture of breastfeeding themselves when they had the time and allowing the baby's minders
to hand-feed them (either from a spoon or from a bottle) in
between.

Many mothers had to rely entirely on hand-feeding. As Victoria's reign continued, it became more and more popular, as
wet-nursing declined. Baby food – when it was not breast milk
– was sometimes bread softened in water. Unsurprisingly, few
babies entirely fed upon the nutritionally poor bread and water
lived very long. But it was a viable option for those for whom it
was a stopgap between sparse breast-milk meals. If the change-
over to bread and water came after the first six weeks, then the
child's chances of survival rose significantly.

Fig. 80. Mother and baby, 1875.

If the family had more resources, it might be milk that the bread was soaked in, rather than water, and this was what most doctors prescribed. Ideally, it would be ass's milk, but few people could afford this. Sheep and goat's milk were the next-best options, but these were still difficult to procure. Cow's milk was by far the most common.

In the 1830s and 1840s, hand-feeding or 'bringing up by hand', a method by which Charles Dickens' Pip was fed in *Great Expectations*, meant the careful business of a parent or guardian pouring a few drops of milk into a teaspoon and holding it to the baby's lips, trying to dribble it in as the child tried to suck. The most successful of those who hand-fed children usually dipped their own finger into the milk to act as a bridge between the liquid in the spoon and the baby's mouth: young children found it much easier to suck on a round finger than the lip of a spoon.

In the first few weeks of a child's life, the milk was watered down to a consistency of half water and half milk, and sugar was added. Out in the countryside, the likelihood of having access to good-quality milk was reasonable, although tuberculosis was very prevalent even in well-kept herds. In towns, the chances of getting pure milk from healthy cows were much slimmer. Much of the milk sold in town had already been watered and coloured by people keen to enhance their meagre profits. Town milk could be more than 50 per cent water and was often lower in fat in the first place, due to the poor living conditions and fodder of the town-kept herds. Such second-rate milk and water mixes often took on a bluish tinge which those who sold it sought to counteract by colouring the milk with anything from chalk to alum to make it appear more like the healthy country equivalent.

Medical advice to boil the milk before giving it to babies stemmed from a belief that this made it more digestible. Many young children experienced difficulties digesting cow's milk (and even more so some of the adulterated mixtures). Today's advice is to avoid giving cow's milk to very young children; sheep and goat's milk is much more compatible with human digestion at such a young age. The Victorian suggestion that boiling cow's milk made it easier for a child to digest was erroneous, although such boiling would have helped kill off many of the bacteria. Unfortunately, in so doing, much of the nutritional value would have also been destroyed. While milk offered a baby a better chance of survival than just bread and water, it was still far from ideal.

Aimed at people with more money at their disposal, a host of commercially produced baby foods was beginning to appear upon the shelves, alongside glass feeding bottles. Most of these new foods were based upon wheat flour, water and sugar cooked up into crisp, hard biscuits and then ground to a powder. The mother was to mix this powder with water, boil it for about ten minutes and allow it to cool before straining and mixing it with cow's milk and a sprinkle more sugar. In practical terms, these powders were nutritionally very similar to the bread and water that poorer mothers resorted to. Mothers looking to make an artificial baby food at home were advised to try sago (a starchy grain) or arrowroot (another starchy plant substance, this time extracted from the root of the plant, and frequently found in Victorian desserts). The sago was boiled to a mush, strained and mixed with milk and sugar; the arrowroot much the same. In both cases, they provided starch and not much else, along with the milk and sugar added to them.

By the end of the century, enough scientific analysis had been done to see just how far these baby foods differed in composition from breast milk. The leading brands had evolved from the simple baked flour and water biscuit of the 1850s and 1860s, but even their improved formulas fell far short of the mark. The analysis undertaken was crude by modern standards, but breast milk was found to contain a ratio of one part 'nitrogenous' matter to three parts non-nitrogenous matter, or one part of nitrogen to every thirteen parts carbon. (In modern scientific parlance, this 'nitrogenous' matter would be described as fats and proteins.) Such figures are useful only in that similar analysis of the leading brands of baby food in the 1890s showed none of them to match those proportions, all being much too high in starch and much too low in fats. An understanding of what vitamins are and what role they play in health and nutrition was still to come, but these early attempts at analysis were already showing that artificial baby foods were not doing a sufficient job in replacing breast milk.

Babies fed on such foods could and did survive, and, if they were fed enough, they appeared to grow fat, but their health was an illusion. The starchy diet allowed babies to put on weight, but without the fatty acids, proteins, vitamins and minerals present in breast milk — and unlike the best of today's baby-milk formulas — bones did not form properly, nor brains develop as they should. Rickets was a major problem for these babies, as was scurvy. Most people could recognize an artificially fed baby by their pasty looks and lack of strength and energy. Despite being chubby, such children walked later and were much more prone to disease than breastfed babies.

From 1870, condensed milk became another option for baby food. Initially, it was hailed as a great step forward. It was a clean and reliable milk source, one that was free from the problems of watering and adulteration which plagued the fresh-milk market. It was also very reasonably priced, and many poorer people turned to it, and to evaporated milk, for their babies. Unfortunately, the cheaper brands were made from evaporated skimmed milk with large amounts of added sugar, therefore the basic fats, with their vital vitamins A and D, were once again missing from the baby's diet, leading to the same old problems with rickets.

A baby's food problems did not just involve the food itself, but also the method of delivery. Spoon-feeding was painfully slow and wasteful, with much more being spilt than consumed. Many a baby ended up severely underfed as a result of long and frustrating failed feeding sessions. Bottles with teats seemed a much better plan. The glass bottles that were newly available in the Victorian era were hailed as a significant advance, since it was possible to see whether they were clean inside, unlike the pottery bottles that had gone before. Up until 1856, the teats that were fitted on to the bottle for the baby to suck upon were made from a range of different substances, but most people agreed that those made from a calf's udder were the best. They were boiled so that they would soften, and were then tied on to the bottle with a fine string. People also resorted to a piece of soft chamois leather or a few folds of linen with a small cone of sponge inside. A couple of pinpricks in these materials allowed the milk to flow. The introduction of the rubber teat in the 1850s gradually replaced these methods, but the calf's teats were still being recommended in the 1860s.

The danger in all of these products lay in the lack of sterilization. That the bottle and teat should be clean was well understood, but for many years this was thought simply to mean that traces of sour milk would upset the baby's stomach and digestion and give them diarrhoea. This of course was true, and diarrhoea was still something that killed a lot of babies, but Victorians were unaware that a bottle or teat *looking* clean was not enough. In this sense, bottles were more dangerous than spoon-feeding. A spoon-fed child often swallowed far less food than a bottle-fed baby, but the bottles were much more likely to harbour reservoirs of bacteria. When germ theory came to be accepted in the 1860s, a range of disinfectants became available, along with the understanding that washing a baby's bottle meant not just hot or soapy water but boiling water. It is probable that such knowledge saved many babies' lives, although the disinfectants in use at the time were generally not suitable for ingesting, even in trace quantities.

For the breastfed majority, the perils of Victorian baby food were put off for several months. The length of time a baby was breastfed varied enormously. Teeth were taken to be the turning point. While a baby had no teeth, milk and milk alone was considered to be the best diet on which a baby could subsist, although many mothers, concerned that their child was not getting enough to eat, did supplement their milk with meals of bread pap, sago, arrowroot and the commercial starch-based foods at about four months of age. As the teeth appeared, beef tea and chicken broth thickened with boiled rice appeared on the menu for middle-class babies, followed after a month or two by soft-boiled eggs and the softer, plainer sorts of pudding. Milk puddings of all descriptions, from rice pudding to pannacotta, were much recommended as suitable for nine- to twelve-month-old children.

However, neither fruit nor vegetables were advised for babies.

The traditional fear that fruit would cause diarrhoea remained strong. This was based upon the observation that a sudden glut of fruit can cause a loosening of the bowels. There was little understanding of the difference between this and bacteria-induced diarrhoea. Diarrhoea was, admittedly, a child killer, claiming thousands of lives, so, understandably, few parents would risk anything they believed to be linked to the murderous disease, at least until the child was well past their vulnerable first few years. Fruit was therefore kept well away from the nursery. Vegetables, other than potatoes, were generally felt to be low in nutrients and were thus largely ignored in the diet of the young. Even such an enthusiastic proponent as Dr Allinson, a newspaper columnist and vegetarian, wrote that only 'after a child is two years old and if healthy and strong, he may be allowed vegetables and a little plain pudding at dinner.'

Parents instead concentrated on giving their babies what they considered to be the most sustaining and nourishing foods they could afford. The advice was always to stick to 'plain' food, which, aside from no fruit and vegetables, also meant scant meat, fish and fat – which left starch and carbohydrates with a sprinkle of sugar to enliven the diet. Between nine and twelve months of age, a large proportion of babies stopped being breastfed entirely and joined their less fortunate brethren upon the starch diet full-time. A blend of tradition, financial necessity and medical advice encouraged the rearing of small children from all backgrounds on a diet based almost entirely upon carbohydrates. Those who were breastfed at least started their toddler years with a full range of vitamins and minerals in their system, and so had months of healthy development behind them before they began the life of childhood stodginess. Those for whom the starch began earlier often had a harder battle for health ahead of them.

Medicine and Babies

Drug abuse was widespread among Victorian babies. A day's feed would often be accompanied by a dose of medicine, and while rural babies, far from pharmacies, were much less likely to become 'users', in towns and cities, where supply was much better, large numbers of newborns and toddlers were fed copious amounts of drugs purchased by their parents. Gripe waters, for babies with colic and stomach ailments, as well as other soothing syrups, were the most popular methods of drug-taking for the very young, although preparations to assist with teething also existed. Overuse left infants drowsy and addicted.

This was not a new problem. Dr Baker made a report to the Factory Commission in 1834 about a practice that was already well established in the textile mills. He concluded that many mothers, on account of needing to work, were in the habit of feeding opiates to their babies, such as Godfrey's Cordial (a well-respected medicine of long standing based on pure opium), as well as doses of straight laudanum (a potent mixture of alcohol and morphine), so that their infants would sleep while they were at work during the day (see Plate 17). Wages were so small that the whole family needed to be employed: a woman taking time out to care for a baby ran the risk of jeopardizing the lives of the rest; a typical family of four malnourished children could face far greater hunger with the arrival of a fifth. The need to sacrifice the welfare of one for the welfare of the whole family unit could therefore be extreme.

Such administration of drugs was an epidemic that had been building for some time, and one that was not to go away during the nineteenth century. Drugged babies slept more and cried less, but the opiates also suppressed their appetites, and it was the children eating less that most often led to their premature deaths. Adult addicts today can often be recognized by their half-starved appearance, but in babies such malnourishment could easily prove fatal. A drugged baby didn't suck when put to the breast. Thin and wizened, they slipped quietly away. One commentator at the time believed that as many as a third of all the deaths of infants in industrial Manchester were because of drugs. Malnutrition was rife: underfed and weak babies, their pupils dilated, with an appearance like that of an elderly person but long before their time, were a distressingly common sight. People were well used to seeing the children of the poor in this state. The malnutrition and starvation could arise from a simple lack of food, or from a loss of appetite due to opiates, or a combination of both.

Overdose was another danger for the drugged child. Preparations bought at the pharmacist's varied in strength. One sample of Godfrey's Cordial tested in Manchester proved to contain half a grain of opium, while another sample in an identical bottle contained four grains. The amount a mother administered also differed; also, the opiates had a habit of settling at the bottom of the bottle, making the last few doses – sometimes fatally – stronger.

Fig. 81. Infants Preservative, an opium-based 'tonic' for babies, 1872.

Godfrey's Cordial was by no means the only opiate-based baby product. Atkinson's Infants Preservative was another very popular brand, along with Dalby's Calmative, Mrs Winslow's Soothing Syrup and Street's Infant Quietness. The product names often gave a clear idea of their purpose and main selling point: the doping of babies to quieten them. Atkinson's Infants Preservative, an opiate mix like all the others, chose not to emphasize its ability to quieten a child but presented itself as a general health tonic and medicine; a baby dosed with this product would be sure to grow 'big and strong'. The advertising maintained that by not giving your child Atkinson's Infants Preservative you were in fact endangering their life. This approach certainly seems to have worked; many young, poor mothers reported to researchers that they used the product to 'bring the baby on' when it looked exhausted or unwell.

Opiates were present in most adult 'health tonics' recommended to cure an extensive range of ailments, including depression, lethargy and, ironically, loss of appetite. A sick and ailing child, it must have appeared to many a worried parent, would also benefit from such a revitalizing tonic. Atkinson's Infants Preservative, with its beautiful, cherubim images of fattened, happy babies on the label, must have seemed ideal. The ingredients, after all, were not listed on the bottle. Later in the century, when concerns about the effects of opiates were becoming more widespread and generally known, Atkinson's Infants Preservative altered its advertising to make the claim that it was purely herbal and natural, unlike its opiate-riddled rivals. In fact, it continued to be made from a mixture of chalk and laudanum.

While there were many loving, well-meaning and desperate parents trying to soothe and quieten their babies as they struggled financially, many other babies were being drugged by parents who, rather than trying to quiet their babies, were in fact attempting to make them stronger and healthier, and were sometimes even consciously trying to avoid such opiates. All were being wildly misled by the advertising.

Nor were wealthier babies safe from drug abuse and addiction. Upper-class homes often employed nursemaids for the day-to-day care of their offspring, and these were young girls drawn from the poorer end of society who shared the general belief in the efficacy of patent soothing syrups. Middle- and upper-class mothers were no more immune to the advertising campaigns of the drug companies than their poorer sisters, and were just as likely to introduce the products into the nursery, although they did have much more access to literature which warned about excessive use of such medicines. Yet there were surprising endorsements for the products. Mrs Beeton's *Book of Household Management* recommends Dalby's Calmative for cases of diarrhoea. Only a handful of years earlier, Dr Bull had published the very influential *Hints to Mothers* with an entire section upon the dangers of opiates in the nursery, listing case after case of infant death linked to the use of a range of preparations. Dalby's Calmative is mentioned as being only second in popularity to Godfrey's Cordial, 'and one of the most fatally destructive'. And yet, at the end of the chapter, Dr Bull is careful not to condemn any of these medicines out of hand. The problem, he said, was in their being administered by women at home, rather than by a qualified doctor. They were decent and useful medicines, he maintained, but women were simply not qualified to achieve the correct dosage. This was hardly the ringing accusation against the advertisers one might have hoped for.

In addition to opiates, most babies were also subject to a bewildering array of laxatives. Baby-care books never failed to have a large section devoted to purging babies' bowels. Doctors expressed concern that women were administering laxatives too often and in too harsh a form for the health of the child. Yet when one examines today the list of recommended ingredients as well as the times to administer them given by these same doctors, you are left wondering how any child survived the doctor's regime, let alone the supposedly harsher general maternal regime of purgatives. Any slight sickness was generally treated in the first instance with a laxative of some sort – even diarrhoea. Any slight change to the smell or appearance of the baby's faeces signalled a call for another dose. Stomach pains, or the suspicion of stomach pains, would lead to yet another. Teething itself was believed to require regular purging. Bad temper was sometimes interpreted as yet another sign that a child needed a purgative. Medical theory of the day assigned great importance to regular bowel movements; for adults as well, but in children and young children especially, it seems to have had a particular weight in the popular mind. One of the major underlying feelings about health in the Victorian era was that the body could heal itself only if the poisons, waste matter and noxious substances of disease could be quickly drawn away. Florence Nightingale's clarion call for water-washing and lighter, porous clothing to remove the poisons that were excreted (or so she believed) through the skin was another aspect of this. The curative power of fresh air, too, was believed to be a solution, flushing away any polluted air that may have hung around the body: air that may have formed the used and now tainted breath of you or others. Just as the skin and breath allowed the waste and poisonous gases to be expelled, laxatives and purgatives allowed solid waste and poisons to be removed speedily. All this formed the bedrock of a healthy, detoxified lifestyle.

Concerned parents had a wide array of laxative and purgative options available to them in their attempts to do their best for their children. At the simplest and more traditional end of the range, rhubarb, prunes and tea made from senna pods could form regular parts of the general diet. A spoonful of olive oil or linseed oil once a day were other long-established options, though these were largely superseded in the mid-nineteenth century by castor oil, which was both cheaper and more effective – and powdered jalap (the root of a Mexican vine) even more so. All these products could be bought freely from the pharmacist in their basic form or made up into mixtures by them, either to their or your own recipe. Patented laxative medicines were likely to be based upon calomel, a mercury preparation, and one with a much more violent action than any of the others above. Its violence, in many ways, was the reason for its popularity – one certainly knew that it was doing something! There was a general belief that the more unpleasant the medicine, the greater the good it was doing you. In the case of calomel, twenty-first-century science would be horrified. It could do irreparable damage to the stomach and lining of the intestines, yet was prescribed regularly by Victorian doctors for babies and was present in most of the purgative products intended for use in the nursery.

If the various powders, pills and concoctions did not work, there was always a form of colonic irrigation to consider. Warm water was the simplest purgative, but barley water, milk and even thin gruel were all recommended by doctors as being gentle enough for use on infants. A large syringe would be filled with the liquid and connected to a pipe, which would be smeared with lard for lubrication. The liquid would then be slowly injected a couple of inches into the anus. When the syringe was removed, the child was to lie quietly for a few moments while everything drained out. Appreciating the more delicate nature of infants, the pipe would be of rubber, rather than the more usual ivory which was used for adults. Such apparatus for home use was available in most pharmacist's and there were several well-known brands on the market. Many middle-class homes invested in such equipment, although it was much too expensive for working people to afford.

Such infant medicine and drug abuse may seem invasive to our sensibilities today, but we must not forget how much fear Victorian parents held for the health of their children. Most people lost some of their children in babyhood, and newborns were vulnerable to a plethora of infectious and fatal diseases which were a daily occurrence. It was no wonder parents were often over-anxious, leaping to the medicine chest at the slightest sign of trouble. And, once a small child was sick, the temptation to try anything that might help them was too great.

Ultimately, it seems likely that many babies died from the side effects of medicine, and that many others had their long-term health undermined, even as they survived individual crises. There was slim difference between the richer infant ministered to by a doctor and the poorer child whose parents would have settled for cheap patent medicines from the pharmacist. Both doctors and parents were administering the same drugs, and, while doctors claimed that they were better at determining a safe dose – which was probably true in general – even at the end of the century, medical knowledge in this domain was still highly questionable. And if richer babies were benefiting from more supervision over their dosage, their parents were also in the position financially to be tempted into using medicine more frequently and in greater quantities, which could be equally dangerous. The poor may well have been dependent on perilous patent medicines, but they may not have been able to afford a fatal cocktail of them.

The top end of the working class, in which the man of the house was a skilled, regularly employed artisan who was able to keep his wife at home, even if the children went out to work, and the bottom end of the middle class, where, once again, the woman was at home but there was precious little cash for medical intervention, may well have been the best places to have lived as a baby. In such households, opiate-laced soothing products were unlikely to be common; the range of medicines in the house would have been small and supplies eked out rather than used liberally. With Mother at home, there was less need to keep the baby in a drugged stupor, and it would be she, rather than a hired nursemaid, who was often not yet even in her teens, or siblings still too young themselves to go out to work, who would look after the baby. Whatever later life may have brought these children, this was not a bad place to start.

9. The Midday Meal

Taken at noon, the midday meal was known as 'lunch' or 'dinner'. The name largely depended upon social background, but it was also dictated by the function of the repast. In a working-class family, the meal was referred to as 'dinner' and, in cases where a man could return home from work at this hour, it was the family's main meal of the day, consisting mostly of suet pudding or potatoes, gravy and a small portion of meat (at least for the wage-earning man of the house). However, as the Victorian period continued, this scenario applied to an ever-shrinking number of the population.

Most men and boys found themselves working too far away from home to come back at noon, which meant that their meal usually consisted only of items they could carry with them to work. For the majority, this meant a piece of bread, but, when times were more prosperous, there was a range of traditional, local, packed meals. In Bedfordshire, farm labourers could expect their dinner to be delivered to them in the fields by their children. A 'clanger' was made of flour, suet and water formed into a roll and then filled with a few rashers of bacon in one end and a spread of jam in the other. According to family legend, my own great-grandfather would walk across the fields of Hertfordshire daily to reach the new development of Letchworth Garden City with his father's dinner in an enamel pail. Lined with insulative straw, the pail contained a pudding basin full of steak and kidney pudding, or stew and dumplings, and was covered by a tightly fixed cloth lid so that his bricklaying dad could have a hot meal in the middle of the day. Cornish tin-miners famously took pasties to work when they could afford to. Simply wrapped in a handkerchief, pasties, like clangers, could be easily transported and eaten without any call for crockery or cutlery. Such food was filling and nutritious, as well as practical.

With so many men eating away at work, a sit-down working-class dinner was increasingly taken only by women and children. Here, meat was in far less evidence, and dinner consisted of boiled potatoes or plain suet pastry served with a spare helping of sauce or gravy. From the middle of the century onwards, shop-bought sauces such as Worcestershire, HP and various mushroom ketchups provided some flavour to these stodgy dishes.

Sundays, of course, were the exception. For one day of the week, the whole family could eat together at the traditional, midday dinner time. The best provisions were bought and prepared, and centred, wherever possible, on a joint of meat. Mrs Widger's signature dish was 'baked dinner'. She mixed breadcrumbs, parsley and a chopped onion together with a slither of scraped fat from the frying pan. This went into a saucer that was laid in the centre of a large baking tin. Whole peeled potatoes were then placed around the saucer in a thick layer, and a small joint of meat (generally beef) was rested on top. The baking tray was then placed on top of the kitchener at its hottest point. Warm water from the kettle was carefully poured into the baking tin until it just began to run over the edge of the saucer and into the breadcrumb mixture. As soon as the water came up to a rolling boil, the whole dish was transferred to the oven and baked for several hours.

When the dinner was ready to be served, the joint was transferred to a plate to be carved. The rest of the food, including the potatoes, the stuffing and the gravy (which had been created by the breadcrumb mixture, the water and the juices of the meat), was simply placed on the table, ready for everyone to devour.

The only refinement was a folded newspaper beneath the pan to prevent it from soiling or scorching the table's surface; there were no tablecloths, napkins or centrepiece.

Among middle-class families, the midday meal was generally called 'lunch' – or 'luncheon', to give it its full title – but the same sex segregation was common. Men at the office did not return home, nor indeed did they take lunch breaks. They breakfasted heartily with the family, and subsisted on tea and biscuits during working hours until they came home in the evening. Francis Kilvert, despite being neither an office clerk nor a worker, followed this male middle-class pattern. As a curate in Clyro in Wales, he carried his luncheon with him whenever he was out visiting parishioners, a meal that consisted of a handful of biscuits, an apple and a flask of wine.

At home, the women and children sat down to a small meal of cold leftovers from the night before, accompanied by one or two quick and easy-to-cook dishes. According to Anne Bowman's 1867 cookery book, lunch could include 'cold meats of all kinds, game, fowls, ham, brawn, pates, broiled or hashed meats, soup, cutlets, mashed potatoes and even a pudding, with ale, porter or wine on the table.' If few middle-class homes regularly served the full array, they did at least enjoy a varied menu. Ragouts and hashes – being in the main reheated leftovers in a sauce of some kind – were considered archetypal lunch recipes. Eliza Acton's hashes are some of the tastiest. Her 1845 recipe for Norman Hash calls for two dozen small shallots to be peeled and fried whole in butter until lightly brown. A tablespoon of flour is stirred in and cooked through for several minutes before half a cup of red wine and a cup of beef stock are added to form a rich gravy. The sauce is then seasoned with salt and pepper and a splash of lemon juice (a clever touch that brings out the flavour). This simmers until the onions are cooked fully; meanwhile, cold, cooked beef is sliced and laid in a saucepan.

Once ready, the sauce is poured over the meat and the dish allowed to stand for half an hour for the flavour to infuse. It is then gently warmed on the kitchener (but not allowed to boil, as that can toughen the meat) and served.

Hannah Cullwick crossed the dinner–lunch divide. As a trusted servant, she ate more richly than most married working-class women. Meat was a common component of her dinners, and in a routine diary entry on 3 March 1863 she recorded 'mutton chop and beer' as her midday meal. Hannah, like all servants, worked punishing hours, but this diet gave her a major advantage over most of her peers. It was no surprise that she boasted in her diary that she weighed over eleven stone – this healthy weight could only have been achieved with the aid of the meat dinners.

Another unusual dining trait that Hannah exhibited was her plural naming of the different meals. While she always referred to her own midday repast as 'dinner', she recorded that of her employers and their guests as 'lunch'. However, this made sense, because she was responsible for cooking for both herself and her fellow servants and for the family: two separate meals, with two separate menus (as well as names). 'Two Ladies came to lunch. I got it ready, and our dinner' is a typical entry in her diary.

Upper-class 'lunches' during the period were more elegant affairs still, taken by both sexes as they waited for the increasingly late evening meal. An informal air, however, dominated lunchtime, even in the grandest of homes. The food at a shooting-party lunch, for example, could be hot, plentiful and elaborate, but was often served buffet-style. Game pies accompanied pâtés, tureens and potted meats. Cold, roasted meat was served alongside hot game hashes with cream- and wine-based sauces. Artichokes, asparagus or dishes of garden peas tossed in melted butter served as vegetables, while pickles and cheeses complemented seed cake, champagne, claret and sherry. But, unlike dining in the evening, which, as we shall see later in the book, involved ornate table decoration and serving rituals, lunch was simpler and did not require the ladies to withdraw at the end of the meal, nor did the seating need to be so formally arranged. One did not need to 'dress' for lunch, and invitations to lunch carried far less social significance and thus allowed for more fluid social mixing. The dinners hosted by Prince Edward at Sandringham House, Norfolk, for example, were twelve-course affairs that went on for hours, but a menu for a shooting-party luncheon could consist of only six dishes carried out from the kitchens in hay boxes and set up on trestles, outside if the weather was good, or in one of the numerous hunting lodges if wet. A December luncheon menu from the end of the era – written in French, as was the custom – listed a light game soup, a Scottish-style boiled mutton, roast partridge, cauliflower in hollandaise sauce, a chocolate soufflé and a dish of stewed fruit.

10. The Day's Work Resumes

Laundry

Perhaps the job most loathed by Victorian womanhood was doing the laundry. Anyone who could afford to pay someone else to do it for them did so. Laundry involved hard physical toil and enormous disruption to the usual routine (see Plate 1).

In 1837, a built-in copper to heat one's water was still something of a luxury. Most people heated their laundry water on the fire or range, in kettles or pans. Naturally, this impeded their cooking for the day, but it also promoted economical use of resources. Doing the laundry was a vast operation, one that consumed much of the energy from the fire, required a large amount of working space and an even greater amount of time. Planning was therefore crucial to ensure that everybody ate, that cleaning areas and utensils were available and that all other jobs could be put on hold.

A woman began by checking over the laundry for holes and rips in the fabric. Washing clothes was such a vigorous process that any small tear would quickly become a major one, and anything that needed a stitch was immediately repaired. Fabrics were then sorted into different grades of dirtiness and fibre. Woollen clothes required more delicate care than cottons and linens, and some grades of cotton could withstand more agitation and wringing than others. Mistakes at this stage could prove costly.

Once sorted and mended, most items were put to soak. Well-soaked clothes required substantially less vigour and work to get clean; mud and similar types of dirt dissolved in water, while other stains were softened by a long soak which enabled the fibres of the fabric to absorb the water and swell, further dislodging much of the dirt. For many people, soaking was a Saturday job. The washtubs were taken down and wiped clean, parked in a corner of the kitchen – or scullery, if you had one – out of the way and filled with water, which was fetched by bucket from the pump, well or local stream. A small scattering of washing soda might be stirred in before the laundry was immersed.

Fig. 82. Mending and marking the linens at the model commercial laundry, 1884.

By Monday morning, everything had soaked for long enough and the washing proper could occur. Cold leftovers from the Sunday meal would have to suffice as the family food for the day, as the range would be in use for heating the water. The day itself began early and, with so much work to be done, most women woke up several hours earlier than usual (another reason it was such an unpopular job). The fire would be lit and all available pans and kettles filled with water and then laboriously carried into the kitchen. All the pre-soaked clothes were drained and squeezed out. The water they had been soaking in now had to be disposed of. For most families, this meant once again transferring it into buckets and carrying it out to the soakaway (an area of soil, usually covered by loose rubble or a grating, where water could be poured away and allowed to soak into the ground without creating a muddy patch), or ditch; the number of people with any form of indoor drainage was minute. By this time, the smallest of the kettles would have risen to a warm temperature, if not boiling point, and this water could be used to lather up the soap (soap was ineffective in cold water). Using a sparing amount of soap and warm water, collars, cuffs and other areas prone to concentrations of grease and sweat were scrubbed. If there was a pan big enough, clothes were boiled on the range for approximately half an hour after this initial scrubbing. Usually, however, this was not practical – certainly not for bigger items such as sheets – so large items would be laid in a washing tub and submerged in hot water.

Next came the dollying, or possering. Just as with a modern washing machine, the clothes were cleaned by being churned forcefully in water. A modern washing machine achieves this by tumbling the garments around so that they continually bash against each other, as well as against the sides of the drum, which forces the water through the fibres of the materials. This dislodges the dirt and stops it clinging to the clothes. In medieval Britain, a similar result was accomplished by beating the wet laundry with a big stick, which was, in form, much like a cricket bat. In Victorian Britain, the clothes were stirred around and bashed in the tub with a dolly, which looked like a small three-legged stool on a long handle, or a posser, which resembled a large copper plunger. Both the dolly and the posser allowed a woman to beat and swirl the clothes around vigorously while standing, so without having to bend down to the tub. From my own experience, I can attest that this is hard work, but far easier than getting down on your knees to a floor already soaking wet from splashed water and scrubbing the clothes by hand.

Normally, half an hour of strenuous 'washing' in this manner would drive out the dirt. Each item would then be wrung out. An ordinary housewife would do this by hand, and would then painstakingly empty and replace the dirty water to rinse the clothes. A second 'wring out' would follow, and yet another tub of water would be fetched. This time, a small amount of blue dye would be added to the water as a brightener (a similar colouring can be found in twenty-first-century laundry detergent). Victorian laundry was in particular need of the blue dye to counteract the yellowish stain left behind by the soap. However, if the dye was not thoroughly stirred into the water, blue streaks would appear.

The wringing process was simplified if a family could afford a machine wringer. This was intended to compress the water out of wet laundry as it moved from soak to wash, from wash to rinse, from rinse to blue dye and from blue dye to the washing line. The machine consisted of two wooden rollers set together with a spring that allowed the rollers to move apart as laundry was fed between them. As it was sprung, the rollers could accommodate different thicknesses of fabric. Wringers certainly helped with the basic laundry process, as garments could be wrung much dryer by machine than by hand, and they cut down on the amount of water spillage and thus waste as garments were moved from one tub to another. They were also much gentler on the hands than hand-wringing, and often reduced the number of rinses necessary, because most of the soapy water would be removed.

At the start of the century, the wringer was a separate piece of equipment to the mangle, which had a different purpose: to press and give a shine to dry or mildly damp laundry. The mangle was initially an enormous wooden machine the size of a double bed. It was useful because it reduced the need for ironing. In the laundries of large country houses, maids would crank the handle of a mangle, and a huge wooden box weighted with stone would descend upon the carefully folded sheets and tablecloths, smoothing out creases and adding a shine to the surface of the linen. By the end of the century, rather than the mangle being a vast wooden press, it, too, had become an iron frame with two rollers, but, unlike the wringer, it was built with rollers of rubber that had far less spring adjustment; many were unsprung, and the gap between the rollers was adjusted by a screw. In general, mangles were set at a much higher pressure than wringers, and any fingers that got caught between the rollers were in peril.

Fig. 83. A mangle.

Just as 1839 saw very few people equipped with a built-in copper, so, too, were wringers and mangles scarce at the start of the reign. By the 1860s and 1870s, wringers became very similar in form to mangles, and combined models were available at the end of the century. As these became more common, they took on a status as an instrument of self-help. A working-class woman who acquired a wringer or mangle – especially a mangle – could charge her neighbours for its use, or increase her efficiency and begin to take in washing for others. Countless women were handed a mangle in lieu of any other form of aid in hard times. A cartoon in *Punch* concerning the despicable safety records of the railway companies drew upon this tradition. It pictured two men who worked in the goods yards 'shunting' wagons discussing the recent death at work of their former colleague; with irony, they describe the generosity of the company to his widow, making her a present of a mangle instead of any insurance payout.

The records of private charities and Overseers of the Poor show that such gifts were common. A woman from Norfolk recalled, in her childhood, assisting her mother at just such a mangle: 'We helped mother in her efforts to get us a living. It was hard work. At first we couldn't reach the handle at the top of the stroke and we used to tie a scarf to help us pull the handle round. But as we grew taller we were able to turn the wheel without it.' She and her sister worked the mangle every evening after they came home from school in the 1890s and delivered the clean laundry in the morning before class began. The *Pall Mall Gazette* in 1894 noted that 'widows and washing, misery and mangles seem, somehow, indissolubly connected'.

Returning to the washing routine, once the batch of laundry had been put through the wringer and mangle, it was virtually finished and needed only to be hung out to dry. Unfortunately, few households had just one batch of laundry to do; most had four or five. It paid to begin with the finest and cleanest load and work towards the coarser and dirtiest. This allowed one to reuse the water rather than having to carry four new tubs for each batch. Women's caps, doilies and other fanciful or delicate items – if you were fortunate enough to own them – formed the first load, whereas shirts, drawers and nightclothes made up the second. Tablecloths, sheets and pillowcases followed (normally in a number of batches), and last came aprons, kitchen cloths, nappies and sanitary towels.

If you possessed woollens – and most people did, in the form of flannel vests and petticoats – washing them required a different process, because hot water and friction could damage the material and cause it to shrink alarmingly. A Victorian piece of flannel could more than halve in size if incorrectly washed, as I have learned to my cost. Woollens were generally not pre-soaked but placed into clean cold water in a pan on the fire. Soap was grated into the water and the pan gently brought up to a hand-hot heat. Once lifted off the fire, the water was allowed to cool, and the woollens were gently swished around in the warm, soapy water; using a dolly or posser would have been too violent. When the water had cooled to lukewarm, it was possible to drain the woollens and place them in another bowl of water to be rinsed, where again they were gently stirred around and squeezed out (mangles and wringers were too coarse and physical to be used).

Fig. 84. Laundry in a working-class household, 1887.

To both my pleasure and discomfort, I have had much experience of Victorian laundry in my career and can vouch for just how much hard work it is. A day thus spent is exhausting, and it is no surprise that so many women from the period mentioned in their diaries tempers fraying on wash day. It is difficult to say what was more tiring, the dollying or the carrying of all the water back and forth, but together these tasks left a woman fit to drop. In my own encounters, I did not mind the steam that filled the kitchen like a fog, but the constant change of temperature, from working inside with the hot pans to being outside in the cold moving water around, was almost unbearable. (It was also considered to be unhealthy even in Victorian thinking.) The sheer weight of the tubs, as well as the substantial extra weight of the wet clothes, meant that one had to be physically strong. In Kate Mary Edwards' words: 'You had to be as strong as a man to lift the great wooden washtubs . . . even without the weight o' the wet clothes.'

It is hard to imagine the whole commotion being attempted in a spacious modern kitchen, let alone in a one-roomed Victorian family home. Steaming pans and kettles were boiling all day, tubs and bowls perched on every surface, dripping laundry was moved from here to there and back again, and trying to keep the floor clean as you traipsed in and out with buckets of clean and dirty water, as well as coal for the fire, was often futile.

The public-baths movement began when one woman offered the use of her copper for laundry to the other women in Liverpool Street during an outbreak of cholera. Hers was the only copper in the street and, without such a facility, her neighbours struggled to maintain the cleanliness that was the only preventative measure against the disease within their reach. Having a built-in copper to heat water was a major advantage in several ways. Firstly, it kept the laundry out of the cooking space; such a copper was usually sited in an outhouse or cellar, away from the kitchen, which not only freed up the fire or range from its role as water heater but usually allowed the wet and disruptive routine to occur away from the family's main living space. Coppers were also relatively cheap to run, as their small fireboxes could burn most waste materials and cheaper fuels: they did not require the better-quality 'house coal' needed to fire ranges. They were also vastly bigger in size than any pan or kettle could be, allowing much larger quantities of water to be brought up to heat at once. But, most importantly, a built-in copper was ideal for boiling laundry. In 1836, in the midst of the cholera outbreak, people did not know or understand the science behind why boiling one's laundry rendered it safe and no longer a carrier of infection, but they were at least aware that it worked. Germ theory was later to explain the importance of sterilizing anything that had been in contact with infection. In an age at war, with not only cholera, but typhoid, typhus and a host of other highly infectious diseases, boiling your sheets, tea towels and underwear provided you with a chance of protecting your health. By 1900, coppers were standard equipment even in housing built for the poorest. In the 1850s and 1860s, the public baths offered such laundry facilities for those who did not possess their own, but, by the end of the century, such public facilities were in decline, as most people had coppers fitted in their homes.

In wealthier homes, laundry was carried out not by the mistress of the house but by her servants. In the lower-income bracket, this meant that a woman came in especially to do the job, or at least a portion of the work. Such daily washerwomen usually undertook only the washing enterprise, leaving ironing and starching to other hands. Those who had enough money to employ several servants could have specialist staff, particularly households that were likely to have more complicated laundry requirements. The higher up the social ladder a person climbed, the more expensive and elaborate their clothes and household furnishings became. Frills and lace adorned underwear and bed-linen; simple cottons and wools gave way to silks, velvets and furs; embroidery and trimmings proliferated; and social position required that the most elaborate items of laundry were prepared to a higher standard: starched, stiffened, goffered (ironed into frills and pleats) and set.

Upper-class establishments boasted whole suites of rooms devoted to laundry and whole departments of staff with their own carefully preserved hierarchies. One of the best preserved of these upper-class laundries is at Erddig in North Wales, a house now managed by the National Trust. Much of the original equipment is intact. In addition to coppers, sinks and tubs, the laundry boasts one of the oversize wooden box mangles, an ironing room and a drying closet, in which large racks run on castors and can be pushed in and out of the heated drying room. The maids in such houses were skilled and knowledgeable enough to be able to tell at a glance whether a lady's petticoat was satin or sateen, whether that particular dye would change colour under the heat of an iron – and several of them did irrevocably – whether a dash of ammonia would prevent a garment from fading when wetted or whether it needed vinegar in the rinse. It must be remembered that Victorian fabrics and dyes were emphatically different to their modern equivalents and were proportionately much more expensive. Some violet and mauve dyes faded if you used washing soda along with soap, but other violet dyes were actually improved by soda in the final rinse. Black and navy-blue linens turned an unsightly grey if you used soap, but a mixture of grated potato and ammonia cleaned them perfectly, without any discoloration. Fabrics with a range of special finishes could easily be ruined or, at least, altered by laundering, and many garments had to be protected and treated differently in the wash.

Crape, the quintessential fabric for mourning, became nothing more than silk gauze if you washed it in water. Instead, it needed steaming to revitalize its raised texture and, if dirty, it could be brushed, sprinkled with alcohol and carefully rolled in newspaper while the alcohol evaporated away. Velvets, too, could be cleaned only by steaming and skilled brushing with deft flicks of the wrist which drew the dirt out of the fabric. Lace had to be carefully laid on a white washing cloth, the two fabrics being folded up as one into a parcel and then tied with white cotton tape before being gently washed. This protected the lace from being pulled or distorted during the process, as well as preventing rips or tears.

Some of the ingredients used in the more sophisticated laundries were highly toxic or dangerous: chloroform was brought in to brighten colours, sugars of lead worked as a fixative for fugitive dyes, and sulphuric acid was introduced to achieve similar results. A range of solvents was employed as home dry-cleaning agents, the safest of which was alcohol, gin being widely recommended, as it was both clear and cheap. Dry cleaning could also be done with a brush. Very few people nowadays know how to clean a garment by brushing, but, for any fabric with a pile and for fabrics made of wool, it is one of the most effective and thorough methods. Firstly, you must select the right brush for the job, one whose bristles match the strength and bounce of the material to be cleaned. The broadcloth of a high-quality overcoat is best brushed with a brush of short and rigid bristles. Velvet requires a brush with very soft but springy bristles that will not wear the velvet down but will be able to penetrate the fabric to dispel the dirt. Technique also varies depending on the cloth, the type of dirt to be removed and the overall shape of the garment. Much of the dry brushing was done in the great houses not by laundry maids but by lady's maids and valets. In lesser households, it was often the owners of the garments themselves who did it. Brushing his own jacket and trousers was one of the very few household tasks most middle-class men would take upon themselves.

Whether a man was looking after his own jacket, or a valet was doing the same for his master, the garment would first be hung over a wooden horse and beaten gently with a small switch or cane. A lady's whip was thought to be the best 'dusting' tool. It was advisable not to strike too hard, in case the buttons broke. Two clothes brushes were required to do the job well, one hard, one soft. The former was to be used only to remove dried-on mud, while the soft brush was best used wherever possible to remove hair, lint and dust, due to the fact that it did not wear down the nap of the jacket in the same way as its harder equivalent. After 'dusting' or beating, the jacket would be spread out on a table, with the collar towards your left (if you were right-handed), so that your brushstrokes would always move down the length of the garment towards the hem. First, the inside of the collar would be brushed, then the back and sleeves. Each stroke of the brush would follow the nap of the cloth, usually down from the shoulders to the hem. The two lapels would be done next, and, lastly, the outside of the collar, before it was folded over and brushed on the inside in the same manner. Such treatment can totally transform a tired and dishevelled garment.

A colleague of mine undertook a similar operation but rubbed pipe clay into the jacket first. He was following period instructions for use upon a jacket that had been worn throughout nine months of hard farming. I know that he was sceptical before he started and utterly amazed afterwards. I have used such methods on a range of garments for years, and a good brush, combined with airing the garment outdoors in the sunshine (hung inside out), leaves coats and woollen jackets cleaner and sweeter-smelling than would treatment by most twenty-first-century dry cleaners.

For the middle and working classes, laundry was often a

once-a-week operation, though the actual washday was normally followed by further labour over several days to starch and iron the clean clothes. In grander houses, the routine could be much less regular. In the seventeenth and eighteenth centuries, it had become a matter of snobbery to have very infrequent and, as a result, mammoth laundry sessions rather than small, recurrent ones – not because people did less laundry, but because they had more clothes. If a person owned only three sets of underwear, obviously they had to wash them often if they were to have a clean supply. If, however, you had a vast stock of clothes, laundry sessions could be much further apart. Boasting that you did the laundry only four times a year told everyone that your entire household had sufficient changes of clothes for three months. Some items of dress, such as nappies and sanitary towels, did of course have to be washed soon after use, but sheets, towels and shirts could be allowed to accumulate. Some aristocratic families, upon this principle, installed laundry facilities at only one of their several properties. They sent all their laundry back to this one house, no matter where they were living at the time, confident in the knowledge that they had plenty of clean linens on hand to last until the laundry was returned. At the other end of the social spectrum, those surviving on the least resources were unlikely to have more than one set of clothes and, for them, laundry was possible only if the family wash was done overnight while they lay in bed naked, changing back into their damp garments in the morning.

According to the 1861 census, 167,607 people were then employed as professional laundry workers. Of these, 99 per cent were women. By 1901, the total figure had risen to 205,015. Unlike almost any other form of work, married women outnumbered single women. Most worked in small laundries, many of them in their own homes. London had the largest number (around fifty thousand), although port cities were well provided for, as were

Oxford and Cambridge and the larger seaside resorts. Anywhere with large institutions or seasonal inhabitants generated extra business for commercial laundries. Glasgow, for example, was home to over 3,500 laundresses and, in the village of Headington, on the outskirts of Oxford, almost every adult woman was recorded as a laundress. Hours were long and the pay was low, but the work was easy to come by and required little in the way of capital investment or training. It was also a profession that lent itself well to the necessity of combining work with family responsibilities. Those working within their own homes were able to combine domestic duties with childcare and often employed their children to help with their work. Kate Mary Edwards, quoted above, and her sister, were not the only children to turn the mangle handle, nor to deliver the laundry. Peter Arnold recalled in his autobiography collecting and delivering parcels of washing with his sisters. The parcels had to be tied on to their bodies with string, as they were too large for the children to carry in their arms. Older children often helped fetch water and coal, and girls especially were pressed into long and punishing ironing sessions.

Women who went out to work in the larger laundries still found a degree of flexibility in the work, which allowed them to balance it with their family life. Still, the strong prejudice towards Monday as washday meant that most laundries received the vast majority of their work on a Monday morning and customers wanted it back by Saturday. This led to a pattern of long hours for a few days and then little or no work the other days of the week. Exactly when in the week a laundress was busy depended on whether she worked mainly in the washing department or in the 'getting up' department, whereby the laundry was starched, ironed and packed. For most laundry employees, the hours generally consisted of four to four and a half long days of work, which left them with some time to do their own weekly wash, shopping and housework.

Fig. 85. Ironing at the commercial laundry, 1884.

Ironing was the best paid of the laundry work, particularly for garments with delicate frills and ruffles that had to be pressed into shape with a range of alternately shaped irons after careful starching. It was hot work, as the different irons had to be kept warm on the stove, but the process still required less physical stamina than actual washing. The irons themselves were simply shaped lumps of metal. The whole appliance, including the handle, became hot, and the person using the iron required a pad of dry folded cloth to pick it up from the stove. Gauging the heat of the iron came with practice. A dry hand tapped against the surface could give an indication, as could the sizzle a drop of spittle would make as it skittered and dried on the surface. Cotton and linen generally responded best to a very hot iron, but if it got too hot, the fabric would scorch.

By 1901, technology and machinery had begun to make inroads into the larger commercial laundries. Steam-powered washing machines were the most labour-saving of devices. Hand-powered washing machines had been available from the beginning of Victoria's reign, but they were hardly any less work than the dolly or posser, simply replacing a plunging and twisting motion with hand-cranking a handle. Many maids presented with such a machine by their employers simply refused to use them. Steam-powered washing drums, however, which began to appear in the 1880s, were a completely novel invention. The modern domestic washing machine has much in common with these early steam versions. The clothes were put into large drums, water and soap added and the drum sealed. The steam engine provided the power to rotate the drums. Unlike today's equivalent, however, they were unable to spin the water out of the clothes. Nonetheless, these machines really did remove a significant amount of labour from the process of doing the laundry. They were, unfortunately, used only on an industrial scale and affordable only by the largest enterprises.

My own historical laundry experiences have led me to see the powered washing machine as one of the great bulwarks of women's liberation, an invention that can sit alongside contraception and the vote in the direct impact it has had on changing women's lives.

Family Medicine

Sickness in the twenty-first century is unrecognizable from the Victorian experience. Measles, diphtheria, whooping cough, tuberculosis, cholera and typhoid were a major and incessant threat in every nineteenth-century household. There were no antibiotics and far fewer forms of pain relief. Hospitals were small and few in number and dealt mostly with the poor; their coverage of the population was sparse at best. Doctors' fees could be financially crippling, even for the wealthier families, and most of those who fell sick stayed at home and were nursed by female relatives. With such high rates of mortality and infection there can have been few women, as mothers, wives, sisters and daughters, who did not have to nurse someone in their family through serious illness. Basic home medicine involved administering a worrying array of drugs and performing countless nursing tasks. Professional (almost exclusively) male doctors, supported by professional (mostly) male pharmacists concocted the drugs, but ordinary, medically uneducated women were expected to put their instructions into practice and administer the dosages.

Cholera was a disease that had been endemic on the Indian subcontinent and the cause of a large number of deaths among the colonists. In 1831, it arrived in Britain, initially in Sunderland. It spread north along the coastal shipping lines, first to lowland Scotland and then down to London, sending its tendrils out from these two areas to the rest of the country. It is highly infectious and is spread, we now know, by faecal matter passing into the water supply. A person who contracts cholera can be dead within two days of showing the first symptoms and, during those two days, they themselves are extremely contagious.

In 1832, the disease reached the community of Bilston, near Wolverhampton. William Millward was twenty-six years old and living in Duck Lane. As an engineer, he was one of the up-and-coming middle-class professionals able to call on the services of medical professionals, and was provided with a comfortable, well-equipped home. Sometime around 20 August, he began to vomit. It was likely that, within the hour, severe diarrhoea would have set in. He would have been unable to control his bodily functions, and everything he was wearing would have been fouled, along with the bed sheets – he would already lack the strength to use a chamber pot. If a doctor was called that evening, he would have been able to prescribe little other than an opium-based medicine to ease the pain, but the best hope of recovery lay within a person's own strength and with attentive nursing care. A victim would be badly dehydrated, yet any liquid, including water, would pass through their system without effect. By the following evening, most invalids would have blue lips and their faces would be sunken, their skin yellow. On 24 August, William died.

In 1832, what caused cholera to spread was not known, but most thought that it was connected to smell. A family's greatest chance of survival was to clean up the vomit and diarrhoea as thoroughly as possible. Everything would be boil-washed, if they had the time and facilities, and sulphur would be burnt to fumigate the rooms. (Laundry maids, as a result, were often the most susceptible to infection. If they, too, succumbed to the disease, they were sometimes rushed to a fever hospital in the hope of preventing the rest of the family contracting the illness, although the dismal survival rates in such charitably funded hospitals offered little hope to the girl herself.) Despite all the Millward family's efforts, two-year-old Catherine followed William to the grave three days later.

If the experience of cholera was desperate in the well-provided-for middle-class home, it was inevitably worse for those with fewer resources. In practical terms of mortality rates, being unable to afford a doctor made minimal difference, but cramped and squalid living quarters meant that a sick person could not be separated from the healthy. With insufficient clothing and bedding, a patient could not be kept clean, and the rest of the family were even more exposed.

The Baileys formed three, probably related, mining families living in the same community as William. John and Elizabeth lived in Ettingshall Lane, and both were forty years old. After contracting the illness, Elizabeth died on 15 August, and John followed a day later. Their seven-year-old daughter survived another fortnight, while their four-month-old baby, Anne, lived into the middle of September, presumably looked after by neighbours or relatives. It may well have been the other Bailey family also living in Ettingshall Lane, William and Elizabeth, who initially took Anne in. William was thirty, his wife two years younger, and they had a five-month-old daughter of their own. All were dead by the end of August. The third Bailey family were living just around the corner in Lester Street. Thomas, Elizabeth and three of their children, John, Henry and Ann, all died within eight days of each other.

Some people did survive: a strong constitution saved the fortunate patient, but compassionate and persistent hand-feeding also helped. Two effective drinks, when administered in frequent doses, were weak beef tea, which contained natural salts, and barley water, which contained small amounts of sugar. No one knew at the time, but a sparing mixture of salt and sugar in water could provide the essential rehydration a body needed after severe diarrhoea. Unfortunately, many people died for lack of this knowledge. Sometimes there was a chance that an invalid could be unwittingly provided with these simple restoratives through other foods and liquids. Forcing someone with cholera to absorb enough liquid to make the critical difference, however, took dedication and selfless courage. Nursing care in such fearful conditions was an act of bravery.

Most women learned their nursing informally, from other family members or from having been nursed themselves through childhood illnesses. As such, there was great variety in home-nursing practice, and many traditional techniques ignored the more progressive ideas promoted by the medical profession. Doctors were often scathing, both in voice and in print, about the standards of the sickroom. Specifically, they deplored the practice observed by many women of keeping a patient's room very warm by building up fires, blocking out draughts and piling up extra bedding on him or her, a custom which the medical profession had come to believe would surround the patient with infected air and hold toxins next to the skin, from where they were likely to be reabsorbed by the patient. The professionals also fulminated against women's insistence on unprescribed laxatives, despite the fact that they regularly prescribed them for patients themselves. The food that women served to the sick also came in for frequent criticism: it was too rich and too indigestible, they thought.

For the poor or working-class woman, who had less access to professional medical advice, such nursing practices went largely untouched throughout the reign. This also caused great consternation among the charitable health workers who attempted to aid the poor at the end of the century. The perceived ignorance of safe practice appalled them, but much of their shock was provoked by the terrible living conditions. The lack of ventilation, in particular, continued to be an enduring concern. The poor desperately tried to shut the cold air out of their homes, and in the absence of sufficient resources to heat their rooms fully, they wrapped the sick up as tightly as they could in clothes. Body heat was another working-class solution, which utilized the bodies of family members as living hot-water bottles. Wet-nursing was another. A weak, sickly adult was sometimes fed by a woman direct from her breast. It was an old and accepted nursing technique, prescribed in the Old Testament, where it was extolled as an act of great charity. However, late-Victorian philanthropists and medical staff often found it difficult to accept, and many were disgusted by the practice.

When breast milk was not used to feed the sick, the poor, whether they lived in a damp and dilapidated cottage in the country or a filthy eight-to-a-room slum, sought to provide the 'best'-quality food they could to strengthen the ailing. As opposed to the usual subsistence diet of bread and jam, they prepared treats such as soft-boiled eggs. A dish of calf's foot jelly was another traditional health-bringing meal, believed to contain the meat's concentrated goodness. Earlier in the eighteenth century, charitable women had often provided the dish to the sick of their own neighbourhoods and parishes. The poor of the nineteenth century clung to this tradition as yielding a healing and life-giving food.

Meanwhile, the medical profession advocated a style of care which was most fully outlined by Florence Nightingale in her highly influential *Notes on Nursing*. Published in 1859, the book was to dominate both professional and middle-class home nursing for the rest of the century. Her thesis was based upon the principles of the 'sanitary' movement, which was first outlined in the 1830s and 1840s. 'Sanitary' and 'sanitation' were words that encompassed the whole gamut of healthcare, in particular the role of the environment and fresh air. Sickroom windows were to be kept open, and the patients themselves were to be well spaced out so that clean air could circulate between them. Chamber pots were to be removed immediately to prevent noxious airs, and bedclothes were to be light and porous so that poisonous gases exhaled by the body could disperse. The diet was intended to be basic and plain so that digestion was eased, and a quiet, peaceful atmosphere would allow mental rest. Every detail was designed to rid the sick of infected waste and airs, and

Fig. 86. The sick room.

to provide the body with time and relaxation in order to heal itself; too much excitement and over-stimulation was strictly prohibited.

However, even though doctors were only too happy to endorse *Notes on Nursing* (it bolstered their authority with its strict insistence upon following doctor's orders), by the time the book was published it was already out of date medically. Most notably, it contained nothing of the new and controversial practice of germ theory, which promoted the use of disinfectants. As a book written by a woman, it also reinforced traditional gender roles: nursing was a female profession and it offered no therapeutic techniques or medicine at all; this was the realm of men. Yet because the book was so fully supported by mainstream medical opinion, it came to dominate almost all future Victorian writings on the subject. Whenever the topic of nursing arose, readers were directed back to Florence Nightingale, from Mrs Beeton's *Household Management* of 1861 to McGregor-Robertson's *Household Physician* of 1890.

Mrs Beeton's book recommended that every housewife should invest in a stock of drugs to be kept at home, ready for use. The list contained twenty-six different drugs, some of them brands and some of them raw ingredients. None were expensive, and all were widely available, without prescription, over the counter at a pharmacy. The list included 'blue pills', one of the miracle 'cure-alls' of the day. This was a lucrative brand, made according to a secret recipe that claimed to treat a vast range of complaints and diseases, from cholera to liver disease, influenza to rheumatism and syphilis. Later analysis of blue pills showed them to contain a number of strong laxative ingredients and a dose of mercury. This would certainly have had a noticeable effect upon the body, but would not have contributed to wellness in the least. In addition to branded drugs, Mrs Beeton's list also contained powdered opium and laudanum (a preparation of opiates in alcohol). Both were recommended for all forms of pain relief and fever control, as well as for 'nervous' complaints. Some of the other recommended drugs were less dangerous for home use, such as senna leaves (yet another laxative) and Epsom salts (for upset stomachs).

As well as drugs, she also recommended a number of tools for the home medicine chest, including a lancet (for lancing boils, cutting off moles, removing splinters, and other minor surgical operations), a probe (like tweezers, for removing foreign material), forceps (to help with difficult births) and curved needles (to stitch up wounds). Ultimately, it is a list that provides a graphic illustration of just how much home medical practice was expected of a woman at this time. Health professionals were called as a last resort, and the average woman, with no medical training, was often administering opiates and performing minor surgical operations. There were, of course, a range of advice books she could turn to if she had the financial and educational wherewithal. But, in the main, she was reliant on the knowledge she could glean from the women around her, on the sensational promises of adverts, and on the items she could afford to purchase from the pharmacist.

Advertisements were powerfully influential and dictated most people's experience of Victorian medicine. Early pharmaceutical companies were able to manipulate people's purchasing behaviour effortlessly, frequently modifying their pitch to exploit a recent breakthrough, real or imagined. The advertising industry itself was entirely unregulated in the early and mid-nineteenth century, leaving manufacturers and retailers free to make any claim they wanted for their products, no matter how far-fetched or bold the lie. In 1908, shortly after the Victorian period, the British Medical Association, concerned at just how misleading and dishonest the advertising was, and had been, conducted a series of tests to analyse the most popular branded medicines. They published the results in a book, *Secret Remedies*. Beecham's Pills, for example, which were made and marketed by Thomas Beecham, who had begun business in St Helens in the 1850s, claimed in their advertising that the ingredients consisted entirely of medicinal herbs. The label also listed twenty-nine conditions the pills would cure, from 'bad legs' to 'liver complaints' and 'headaches'. Yet chemical analysis revealed that the pills were made solely from aloes, ginger and soap. Even then the medical profession knew that such a mix was highly unlikely to cure anything at all, let alone the range of conditions promised by the advert. At best, it was a placebo. However, Thomas Beecham was extremely adept at advertising and continued to spend vast amounts of money marketing his products. In 1891 alone, his company spent £120,000 on these services, enough money to purchase a small estate.

Another wildly mis-sold drug was Tuberculozyne, an American product that claimed to be a cure for tuberculosis. It consisted of two separate bottles of liquid, one to be taken after the other. The first, when analysed, proved to consist of potassium bromide, several colourings and flavourings, caustic soda and water. The second liquid was glycerine, almond flavouring, water and caramel colouring. Neither liquid possessed a single therapeutic effect; they were, in essence, coloured and flavoured water being sold as medicine. Unfortunately, however, because there was no requirement that the ingredients appear on the packaging, the only information most people received about the products was from the false claims of the advertising.

In the cases of both Beecham's Pills and Tuberculozyne, some comfort can today be taken from the fact that neither of these cures was likely to do a person any real harm. However, in 1837, some of the most popular medicines on the market contained calomel – a preparation of mercury – and laudanum. These highly dangerous drugs were available in a number of forms and under a number of different brand names. Large volumes of sales meant they brought great profits to their manufacturers. However, with absolutely no restrictions upon who could buy or sell them, the women of the first few years of Victoria's reign could purchase and use anything to which a professional doctor had access. This freedom was welcome to most people, who could not afford a doctor's fees. Once you had diagnosed what was wrong with you, why spend money on a doctor, when the very same medicine could be bought from the pharmacist or, even more cheaply, if the ingredients could be bought and the medicine prepared at home?

For several hundred years previously, women had generally been in charge of producing home medicine. Wealthier women led the way in dedicated 'still rooms' (the name is a reference to the process of distillation), but most women still possessed enough knowledge to prepare roughly two dozen basic herbal remedies. Women typically concentrated on simple herbal medications – more complicated chemical preparations were prepared by male professionals who had the capital and equipment – but such knowledge was still a part of ordinary womanhood, much like bread-making. By 1837, this traditional skill set had endured nearly a century of scorn from doctors, who were keen for the new advances of science to rid the industry of the remnants of 'superstition'. However, a change began when women started to move from the countryside to the towns for work and lost access to many of the plants that had once formed their basic stock. By the start of the Victorian era, the traditional role of woman as home medic had largely transformed from being a maker of medicine to being a purchaser. Still, the decisions about what drugs to use and when to administer them remained firmly under the woman's control.

It was not until the 1868 Pharmacy Act that women faced any

restrictions upon their right to buy medicines. After a series of scandals about poisonings, both accidental and premeditated, legislation was introduced to control who could sell certain substances. From that moment onwards, anyone wishing to purchase one of a small number of poisons – principally, arsenic and cyanide – had to sign for them. They could still be purchased, but the pharmacist – and it did have to be a qualified pharmacist – would ask the customer a few questions about the use it was to be put to before motioning them to sign his book and pay the money.

Since the majority of over-the-counter medicines were dispensed in the home by women, most of the pharmaceutical companies targeted their products to play upon traditional female responsibilities and fears. Overt emotional blackmail was a favoured technique. Eno's Fruit Salts adverts, which featured images of cherubic children with wings ascending to heaven, were labelled with guilt-laden straplines such as 'the jeopardy of life is immensely increased without such a simple precaution as Eno's Fruit Salts.' Regular clearing of the bowels and 'blood-cleansing tonics' filled the void that had been left behind by the old herbal practices, and became a recognized part of a family's routine, taken in much the same way as many people in the twenty-first century take vitamin supplements. Throughout history, there has in fact been a tradition of family-based preventative dosing that runs unbroken from tansy omelettes, whereby the juice of the tansy herb was squeezed into springtime omelettes in the sixteenth and seventeenth centuries to 'clean the blood', through syrup of figs and castor oil in the Victorian period, to vitamin tablets and 'friendly'-bacteria yogurts today. Each took advantage of the health worries of its age. The Epsom salts and senna leaves on Mrs Beeton's list of medicines fell firmly within this tradition. Her readers, like most Victorian women, from all classes, would have considered it nothing less than their duty to see that all their family had regular bowel movements and underwent a periodic 'detox'. Medicines and preparations that offered these services were, as a result, enormously popular.

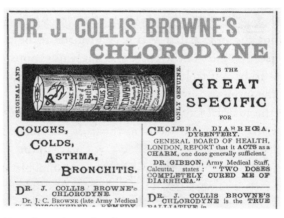

Fig. 87. Chlorodyne, formulated in 1848.

Pain relief in 1837 was largely dependent upon laudanum but, as the century progressed, new methods of preparing opiates became widespread and better pain-relief drugs were developed. Chlorodyne was a concoction thought to have been compounded in 1848 by Dr Collis Browne while he was serving in India as an army doctor. In 1854, when home on leave, he was asked to assist during a cholera outbreak in a village near where he was staying. Two years later, he set up in business, manufacturing and selling the compound, which had brought relief to sufferers in Britain and the colonies. Unlike many other medicines, it was not a heavy advertising campaign that made the drug popular but, rather, word of mouth. In contrast to so many other mixtures available in the 1840s and 1850s, it really did make people feel better. However, when one learns that it was made from a mixture of morphia (a form of morphine) and chloroform, this comes as no surprise. The mixture was extremely potent: a single 1oz bottle contained thirty-six doses of chloroform and another twelve of morphia. It was highly addictive, and later formulations of Chlorodyne even contained traces of cannabis extract. And Chlorodyne was not the only form of chloroform. Popularly administered to relieve the pain of childbirth, chloroform itself could also be found in cough medicines and cholera treatments.

Fig. 88. Coca wine, fortified with cocaine.

Another popular drug was cocaine, which was first isolated from coca leaves in 1860. However, it was not in widespread use until the 1880s, when it became particularly favoured for use in tonic wines, recommended as giving a general 'lift' to those who were feeling tired, lethargic, nervous or depressed. Heroin came later still, in the mid-1890s, at about the same time as aspirin made its first appearance. Morphine, opium, cocaine, laudanum, heroin, chloroform, ether, aspirin and cannabis were all purchasable, without any form of medical supervision, and for a very few pence, at any pharmacist's shop by the end of the century. Many people might not even have known that they were buying them, as they could also form part of the undisclosed ingredients in a huge range of patent medicines and 'tonics'.

Addiction, therefore, became a staple of the Victorian experience. Florence Nightingale was thought to have become addicted to laudanum, as was Elizabeth Barrett Browning, the poet, and Elizabeth Siddall, the wife and model of the painter and poet Rossetti. Even Sir Arthur Conan Doyle's detective, Sherlock Holmes, was a man of his time in his dependency upon opium and heroin. Any bout of serious sickness could easily leave a patient with an addiction, even after they had recovered from the initial illness, due to the fact that both doctors and home nurses made liberal use of opiates. It was a danger that did not go unnoticed. Dr Pye Chevasse's *Advice to a Wife* is a text that is largely based upon the fear of drug dependency. His recommendation of a regime of cold baths and long walks was accompanied by long and impassioned pleas for young women to refuse the medicinal opiates they were offered. Much of the popularity of the water cures of the nineteenth century was due to their providing an alternative to taking these drugs. Unfortunately, water cures were expensive, and laudanum was far cheaper, costing about a penny an ounce, the same as a loaf of bread.

Quite how many people became addicted is difficult to say. There were no records of registered addicts; there were no sales figures for the drugs themselves. Addiction and overdose rarely appeared as cause on death certificates but were hidden behind phrases such as 'wasted away', 'pneumonia' and 'died in his sleep'. Also, the symptoms of addiction could be hard to separate from the symptoms of poverty and lifelong deprivation. The hollow-cheeked, sunken-eyed faces of those brought up in the workhouse could have been the effects of hunger and overwork, without the added danger of morphine addiction. Even in the homes and lives of the wealthy, it was hard to know what part addiction played, for with so many chronic diseases, and without effective treatment, many of these men and women were lifelong invalids.

In the Victorian period it was often commented that women were more prone to dependency on 'physic' (another word for medicine) than men. This may have been the result of misogyny, but, because women generally had more responsibility for drugs in the home than men, it may well have been true that they were more likely to have used the opiates themselves. They were certainly easily available, and advertisers were only too keen to promote their addictive 'tonics' as pick-me-ups for the overworked, the overtired or the hysterical woman.

Hysteria was a common diagnosis for a range of symptoms. Later, at the beginning of the twentieth century, these symptoms would be referred to as 'nervous complaints'; in the 1930s and 1940s, they would come together to be known as a 'mental breakdown'; and in the twenty-first century, they would likely be termed 'depression'. Nineteenth-century wisdom held that only women suffered from hysteria. Both the term and the understanding of the illness derived from Ancient Greek medical thought. A woman's womb, according to this tradition, was mobile within the torso, and as it rose and fell it interfered with the proper workings of the rest of the body, and the 'mind', in particular. Anatomical studies notwithstanding, Victorian medicine maintained that there was a link between a woman's reproductive functions and her mental balance (remnants of this belief survive today in popular thought with the vestigial bias about 'hormonal' women). Treatment for the hysterical woman was extremely varied, from opiate-filled tonics, to cold-water bathing to electric-shock treatment in the 1880s and 1890s. Small, hand-powered electrostatic machines were widely advertised for home use, and many pharmacists kept one on the premises to offer treatment sessions for small fees. Both doctors and medical institutions invested in larger, more powerful sets of apparatus. Once the unit was charged, a pair of contacts was applied to various parts of the body – such as the temples for cases of migraine, or the chest when treating asthma – which completed the circuit and allowed a current to flow through the patient. It was indicative of the widespread use of this apparatus for female hysteria, and of the Victorian understanding of the 'illness' in general, that most of these sets of apparatus came with a 'vaginal attachment'.

11. Meanwhile, for the Young, There was School

The interest in schooling, and a belief in its usefulness, grew throughout the Victorian period. Education was soon desired not only to push an individual towards personal success in life, but for the economic development of the nation. Many of those involved in the political fight to extend the vote to ordinary working men – the Chartist movement – felt that education was an essential tool, one that would ensure that people used their vote wisely; for others, an educated workforce was seen as a means of increasing productivity and innovation; while, for some, it was a moral crusade, one that could widely disperse advice on health, hygiene and the messages of religion.

The biggest obstacle in broadening education was money. Who was to pay for the teachers, the books and the buildings? Private philanthropy could only stretch so far, and parents only afford so much. At the very beginning of the nineteenth century, two men, Joseph Lancaster and Andrew Bell, brought to Britain a scheme that claimed drastically to reduce these costs and still provide more children with a basic grounding in reading and writing. It was known as the monitor system, and in it one teacher could instruct a number of older students in the day's lesson, and they in turn could instruct a group of younger children. Joseph Lancaster claimed that a single master could govern an entire school, no matter how large, and that a single book could teach a whole school to spell, another to read and a third to do sums. He considered that five hundred boys or girls could be taught by one educated man, and all for the cost of between four and seven shillings per child per year.

Such schools were built as a single large hall containing a central row of desks where the boys (there were some girls' schools and mixed schools at the start of the century, but the vast majority were only for boys) would sit to write. Along the walls of the room was a series of chalk boards, divided into areas called 'drafts'. In these drafts, small groups of boys would be gathered, standing, for reading exercises and instruction.

The school day began early (six o'clock in some establishments), when the monitors, most of whom were twelve to fifteen years of age, gathered around the master, who took them through the day's lesson. When the rest of the pupils arrived an hour later, each group would be supervised by its own monitor, who would ensure silence and attention. The main lesson could be given by the teacher to the whole, crowded room, while the monitors ensured that the younger children behaved. At intervals throughout the day, the monitors would lead their groups to one of the teaching stations. They would put the reading text up on the wall and hear each boy read aloud, either individually or as a group. It wasn't necessary for the monitors to be more than one lesson ahead of the pupils in their charge: much of their role was disciplinary rather than tutorial, and most carried a stick with which to beat their charges. As child workers, monitors were cheap labour, providing the main source of cost-cutting in the new schooling system. In the 1840s, Frederick Hobley was a child monitor. 'For this we were paid a half penny a day, that is 2½d a week, and this gave us some pocket money.' He recalled few details of the actual work or teaching that he was required to perform but, several years later, when he was sixteen years old, he went to Oxford to sit the entrance exam for a teacher training college. For Frederick, the monitor system had at least offered him a route to a higher education (see Plate 18).

James Bonwick began his education at the Borough Road School in Southwark, London, at the age of six. When he started, he sat in the row of 'sand desks' at the very front of the room. Each child had a sand tray in front of them, along with a stick to write in it, and a 'smoother' of wood or stiff leather to wipe away their marks and create a clean surface. A large copy of the alphabet was hung at the front of the room so that all the children could see it. 'My little teacher pointed to a letter and shouted its name, which we repeated aloud. He then told us to smooth the sand in front of us, and try and make the letter by marking the sand. After this was done, we again shouted the letter.' James's teacher was only around ten to twelve years of age. Once he had mastered the alphabet, James and his classmates moved back a row of desks, where they worked upon slates rather than sand trays. They were taken at intervals to the first 'draft', where they gathered around a printed card stuck upon a wooden board and learned to recognize a series of monosyllables such as 'ab' and 'ad' and sound them out. When a monitor was happy that a child had understood the set lessons of his class, they moved up to the next class, sitting further back in the schoolroom and attending the next 'draft' up the hall. These schools normally accommodated pupils from five to ten or eleven years of age.

In 1803, Joseph Lancaster published a book outlining the workings of the monitor system. Five years later, he and a group of influential friends formed the Royal Lancastrian Society to encourage the further building and development of such monitor schools. The idea was popular, but Lancaster himself was not: most members of the society soon deserted him. However, two rival networks of schools were soon established, each of which used Lancaster's model. One was known as the 'British' schools (supported by a group of religious nonconformists); the other, the 'National' schools (supported by the Church of England).

Each sought to bring affordable education to the working classes and, while it was hoped that wealthy patrons would provide the money to construct the buildings, it was thought that the fees paid by the parents alone would be enough to cover the basic running costs.

The only major development of this model came with a move to provide better education for the child monitors themselves. The qualified teachers in charge of schools were offered an additional fee if they would give extra, after-hours tuition to the pupil-teachers. The youngsters were encouraged to follow a formal course of study in their own time and work towards passing a national teacher's qualification. Such instruction, it was hoped, would help them to become qualified teachers in their own right.

Becoming a pupil-teacher could provide a route to social mobility for a bright working-class child. Not only were there no teaching fees to be paid, but a child could earn a small wage during their training. This money was crucial: many families were reliant upon child wages for survival and, while pupil-teachers were not the best paid among child-workers, all but the most desperate of families could allow a child this chance in life. The determined and hard-working among them could gain an education and qualify for a profession that transported them into the middle class. To move from labourer to professional in one generation was a vast social upheaval, but one that opened up for significant numbers of youngsters of both sexes as the need for teachers continued to grow.

Beyond the world of the British and National schools, a patchwork of other educational opportunities existed. Ancient grammar schools flourished, serving a largely middle-class clientele, as did old and new public schools, serving the wealthier middle and upper classes. Small private schools also sprang up to serve the needs of the school-fee-paying members of society.

Daughters of the clergy were often sent to charity schools, which could resemble the cold rooms, poor meals and oppressive conditions of Lowood School for Girls in Charlotte Brontë's *Jane Eyre*. Back rooms and cottages throughout the country also housed tiny 'Dame' schools, in which a combination of child-minding and rudimentary lessons in reading and writing were offered alongside, in many cases, teaching in handicraft. The fees for these establishments were minute, and their proprietors were generally very poor themselves. Often they were run by an elderly man or woman with no other means of earning a living. Parents valued these places as much for the child-minding they offered as for the education, but they did provide useful skills. The handicraft tuition, for example, could often deliver far more practical and lasting results to a child, and their parents, than could literacy. Lace-making schools, straw-plaiting schools and knitting schools all offered a genuine trade that could enable a child to earn a living, both in the short term, and for life. Schools and parents varied considerably in how much emphasis

Fig. 89. A ragged school of 1846, set up to offer free education to those who were too poor to wear respectable dress.

they placed upon the craft and how much on the book work. The nature of the local economy and the finances of the family could tip the balance either way. Of course, the teachers of these schools were also strongly aware of their own needs in terms of keeping the parents happy and paying their fees.

Just as upper- and middle-class parents saw the advantages in literacy for their children, many working-class families tried to offer their sons and daughters such skills and, where affordable education was available, few parents declined it. When education became compulsory, from 1870 to 1880 (it varied regionally), there was very minor resistance. That the Dame schools remained so popular in the age of British and National schools was testament not to working-class reluctance to educate their children but to a combination of economic necessity and a preference for schooling that was responsive and sensitive to family needs and opinions. Children attending Dame schools were spared the heavy religious moralizing many working-class people found objectionable in the British, National and, later, Board schools of the formal sector. Timekeeping, too, was a contentious issue. Dame schools were understanding about the occasional need for a child to help out at home or to take a few weeks off for a lucrative harvest job; they were willing to adjust the times and length of the school day to fit in with the parents' work commitments.

Despite providing a more informal education, Dame schools often produced well-rounded students. While some remembered their desultory attempts at learning the ABC, others left as confident readers. Thomas Cooper recalled his time under the tutelage of Gertrude Aram, or 'Old Gatty', with particular warmth and gratitude. Her schoolroom 'was always full; and she was an expert and laborious teacher of the art of reading and spelling. Her knitting too – for she taught girls as well as boys – was the wonder of the town.' Under her instruction, Thomas became a fluent and self-assured reader, capable of understanding even 'the tenth chapter of Nehemiah with all its hard names "like the parson in the church"'. Similarly, the anonymous writer of an article in the School Board Chronicle of 1872 was adamant that the education he had received at his Dame school had been both more pleasant and more efficacious than the schooling he later encountered at the formal 'National', which he bemoaned for having only crushed his spirit and interest in learning. However, experiences did vary, and for Frederick Hobley, his time at a Dame school was quite the opposite and no more than a childcare exercise, one that he barely remembered, or, if he did, only as a place to be avoided whenever possible.

Corporal punishment was universal throughout the Victorian educational experience, from the public schools attended by the wealthy to the institutions of the destitute. Dame schools were sometimes tamer environments, which may have been a reason some parents favoured them over other schools; but, generally, most adults felt that it was almost impossible to teach a child without some form of physical discipline: from the sixteenth century onward, it had been popularly thought that a boy 'learned' best through his backside. The more humane approach of engaging a child's interest and expressing disapproval at their poor behaviour verbally was a minority attitude. The large class sizes encouraged corporal punishment, as did the youth and poor education of many of the teachers. How else was a lad of sixteen to control a room full of sixty or seventy ten-year-olds?

In addition to bolstering authority, corporal punishment was employed to ensure concentration and attention. Many teachers firmly believed that an error in a child's work was the result of 'not trying', of the child not having listened properly to their instruction. Child after child was beaten for their spelling mistakes, grammatical errors, incorrect sums and messy handwriting.

Beatings, especially in public settings, were thought to ensure silence and to make certain that children looked in the right direction, and sat or stood when they were told to. They encouraged a child to pay close attention to a teacher's every word.

Punctuality and obedience were highly desired and valued traits, partly because the ability to follow instructions accurately and the self-control to handle boredom and repetitive exercises were thought to produce good factory workers. If many schools felt like a factory, especially towards the end of the century, it was deliberate. School was meant to be a training ground for life: a rigid hierarchy with strict rules and regulations. Instant submission to those in authority was required of everyone, from maidservant to office worker. The direct and physical lessons that corporal punishment in schools taught those who strayed even an iota from the rules was thought to be valuable preparation for the real world.

When corporal punishment was not resorted to, a range of humiliating public rituals was frequently employed. Dunce caps were common, as was the practice of making a child stand in the corner, or up on a chair in front of the whole school, often with a board hanging around their neck with their supposed offence written in chalk upon it. Some teachers employed even crueller tactics. In one school, the guilty party had to stand while the rest of the class sang a song, 'Look at the foolish one, who didn't learn his lesson.' Other teachers adopted a series of what we would now refer to as 'stress positions', requiring children to stand holding a book or other object at arm's length for long periods of time. Canings, employing a variety of sticks, leather straps and wooden rulers, also often took on the form of public humiliation and were surrounded by ritualistic behaviours, such as requirements for the victim to kiss the rod used to beat them, both to increase the dread of the punishment and to give it a deeper significance.

In 1862, the Education Committee, which had been established partly to monitor the grants which the government was now investing in schools, began a regime of payment by results. Robert Lowe, who headed up the reform, promised that his system would provide either low-cost education or effective education, though not both at the same time. For the first time, schools which did not bring their pupils up to the desired levels of learning would receive less government money (the low-cost option), and those who did would be rewarded with their support (the effective option). Every year, each grant-receiving school would be inspected and each child examined in reading, writing and arithmetic. A series of standards was set for different ages of children, and these would apply across the country. It gave an entirely new focus to formal education. Previously, there had been a temptation for a teacher to concentrate his or her efforts upon the few motivated pupils who attended regularly and responded well to the school environment. Reluctant pupils with poor attendance, and those who struggled to adapt to the rigid regime, could be allowed to slip by the wayside. But, with the school finances so tightly pinned to results, teachers were under heavy pressure to ignore the brighter and compliant members of the class and concentrate instead upon producing the basic levels of attainment required by the inspections. Rudimentary literacy results were raised at the expense of more inspirational teaching.

Despite the enormous expansion of Dame, National and British schools in the middle years of the nineteenth century, they didn't cater for all children. All charged fees, albeit small, which put them out of the reach of poorer members of the population. Workhouse schools filled one of the gaps, providing simple literacy for child inmates, alongside an attempt at teaching them a trade. However, such schools were notorious for their poor academic standards, and for the violence that was often endemic in their institutions. In 1868, one inspector reported that he had found one workhouse school being run by the thirteen-year-old daughter of the governor. In another school, he discovered that not a single child could read; instead, they had been trained to recite a few sentences while holding their books up. The fact that many of the books were, unwittingly, held upside down gave the game away. Worse still, a teacher sent to take up his post at Deptford workhouse discovered that he was replacing two illiterate seamen who had held the position for many years, and had merely endeavoured to keep the children quiet. A similar story emanated from Walcott workhouse in the 1830s, when a visiting clergyman reported being taken into a room where thirty small children stood, a man holding a whip in their midst. There were no slates and no books. 'Are you the schoolmaster?' he asked. 'Yes,' came the reply. 'What do you teach the children?' 'Nothing.' 'How then are they employed?' 'They do nothing.' 'What then do you do?' 'I keep them quiet.'

Stories of brutal floggings in workhouse schools abound. All schools had their darker faults, but workhouse schools were often particularly violent. In 1858, Mrs Emma Sheppard detailed the condition of a girl beaten so excessively for an incorrect spelling that 'the skin of her back came off on her linen when it was removed.' Another child found crying claimed that the 'missus ha[d] roped me'. Her back and arms were red and covered with great weals. The newspaper reporter Sir Henry Morton Stanley (who, famously, is reputed to have met the great African explorer of the age with the words 'Dr Livingstone, I presume?') received his boyhood education from a workhouse school at St Asaph. Over fifty years later, he recalled two terrible floggings among the constant barrage of slaps; one was for mispronouncing the word 'Joseph'; another was for eating blackberries. He also described finding the bruised and cut body of one of his classmates in the mortuary. However, in between the violence and misery, he was able to obtain enough knowledge to make a career for himself as a journalist.

Alongside their traditional religious role, Sunday schools were also involved in the wider effort to promote literacy, and their numbers grew at an exceptional rate in the period. In Middlesex, in 1833, there were 329 Sunday schools; by 1858, there were 916. These institutions could make an especial difference to rural children. Formal school provision in the countryside was still extremely uneven, and many villages had no more to offer their poorer inhabitants in the way of education than that provided on a Sunday by the wives and daughters of the wealthier inhabitants. Just as with Dame schools, such education could vary significantly in character. Some Sunday schools offered very little instruction besides hymn-singing and reciting the creed, but others were able to provide children with literacy

Fig. 90. Free state-run schooling, the Board school, 1894.

skills to rival those taught in the best formal schools. Small class sizes and dedicated teachers could, in some cases, achieve more with one day a week of tuition than huge halls full of rote learning could achieve in five days. William Chadwick was working a thirteen-hour day at the cotton mill from the age of eight. He learned to read and write at Sunday school and evening classes sufficiently well for him to rise, in time, to the rank of Chief Constable of the Metropolitan Police. Sunday schools provided a stable and continued education for many children who had joined the world of work at a young age.

As in William's case, such 'top-up' learning was also available from a range of evening schools and boys' and girls' clubs, which became popular for children whose lives were dominated by work. This piecemeal schooling was often all they could manage to fit in. As a result, many youngsters received a nomadic education. Joseph Burgess learned his alphabet at a local Dame school before attending a National school further afield for about a year. However, with a family financial crisis looming, he was withdrawn before his seventh birthday and put to work punching cards for jacquard looms for sixty hours a week. A year later, at the age of almost eight, he got a part-time job at a spinning mill as a piecer. Spinning mills were subject to new legislation governing children's work which enforced compulsory schooling in the afternoons. Therefore, Joseph, after a long and tiring morning in the mill, would head to the classroom. Unfortunately, this experience was also short-lived, and on his twelfth birthday he moved to another job in a different part of the textile industry. Here, the Factory Act did not apply, and so his schooling promptly ended.

School for All

By 1880, schooling finally became compulsory for all children between the ages of five and ten. In communities where there was a shortage of school places for this surge in pupil numbers, 'Board' schools were established and run by the local government. In practice, they were virtually indistinguishable from the British and National schools, but, in 1891, when education became not only compulsory but free in these schools, they became the near-universal experience of education in Britain, largely replacing all the other institutions, except the public schools of the wealthy.

In late-Victorian Britain, the vast majority of children began school at around four years of age, although in rural districts teachers would sometimes take children as young as two to help families who desperately needed the mother to work. They took their place in the infants' class until they were old enough to begin a more formal education, at around six years old. From then on, the classes were arranged in 'standards', from I to VII. Each year's tuition ended with an exam: if you passed, you moved up a standard; if you did not, you had to repeat the year. A bright child might well be able to pass a higher standard and gain entry to a higher class. The opposite was also true. In 1894, the British school at Bath, for example, still had two ten-year-olds and one twelve-year-old in their Standard I class, while the Standard IV class encompassed everyone from two eight-year-olds to one fifteen-year-old, although the majority of the pupils were ten or eleven.

A child with a school-leaving certificate could reach the level of attainment that is currently expected of a child of eight within the modern British education system. The reading test generally took the form of a randomly selected paragraph from the class's reading book. As the students had been using the same book all year, a degree of familiarity with the text was to be expected, and many children could rely on their memory if their reading skills were not sufficient for the task. Writing was tested both by the children copying out a passage, in order that their handwriting ability be assessed, and by dictation. To gain a pass at Standard V, a child needed to be able to write down a short paragraph from one slow read-through. The text, once again, was taken from their school reading book. Spelling was assessed from an approved list of words, which could be drummed into the children with endless repetition. Arithmetic was more challenging. A Standard V pass required simple multiplication and division, fractions, decimal places and sums using money.

Charles Cooper was a pupil at Walton National school from 1876. He was an academically gifted child, passing through all seven standards by the time he was twelve, before becoming a pupil-teacher. To write, he used a copybook and, with the ever-present threat of the cane for ink blots, he was required to hold the pen in an approved style: 'thumb on the left side of the pen, first finger on top, second finger on [the] right side, little finger resting on the paper, wrist flat and end of pen pointing towards the right ear'. No deviation was allowed, even if he was left-handed. For arithmetic, his master taught the four senior standards together. All their work was written on slates, and the children were stationed around the room alternately so that no two in the same standard were sitting next to each other. One standard after another would be called to the front of the room, given a set of sums to work on and then sent back to their place. Shortly afterwards, each group was called in turn back to the front of the room for their slates to be marked. The sums would be worked out on the blackboard with a full explanation, and then the teacher 'would invariably punish any child guilty of carelessness with the cane'. Spellings, multiplication tables and geography (they studied only lists of rivers, capes, bays, mountain ranges and principal regional trade goods) were learned by rote. All Daisy Cowper had to recall about her experience at a similar school in Liverpool was that 'nothing nice seemed to happen there.'

Ideally, all children were to reach Standard VII before they left school, at the age of twelve. However, each local school board was permitted to set the attainment level for their catchment area's school leavers. Unsurprisingly, the areas of the country that continued to have a high demand for child labour generally chose a much lower minimum level of attainment than those who were not under the same pressures from employers. Standard V was the most commonly employed leaving certificate, but some areas were willing to accept a Standard IV, while others required a Standard VI. Rural schools were generally those with the lowest levels set for the leaving certificate, as well as being those where magistrates were most likely to turn a blind eye to children absenting themselves for periods of work at busy agricultural times. Magistrates and school governors were frequently the same men who employed such children, and the education of a district could easily come to reflect closely the district's labour needs.

Those who stayed on at school, however, to obtain the final Standard VII class, or who showed potential as future pupil-teachers, frequently discovered that the quality of their school life improved drastically in this final phase. There was more scope for exploring their individual interests, for questioning, for enjoyment and learning for its own sake. The academic achievements of these pupils who were destined to progress, perhaps via scholarship, to secondary education or to become pupil-teachers, were a major advancement on those required for the conventional leaving certificate.

Public Exams

The public written examination is an institution that is almost entirely Victorian in its origin, form and ethos. Earlier in the century, around the 1830s, very few people even knew what an exam was, and it was only the tiniest number of students who had any experience of them at all. However, by the end of the century, every child of the working classes, along with most middle-class boys and a smaller group of middle-class girls, knew all about exams. Life chances and opportunities now came to be influenced and seen through the lens of their results, much as they are in our own times. For the middle classes, exams came to be the way an employer judged a prospective employee, looking for proof that the – almost exclusively – male applicant had actually learned his lessons. For the working classes, exams were the method by which their teachers were judged and paid, as well as the manner in which the child transitioned from school to full-time work.

Before the introduction of exams, a teacher's report was the only form of feedback available to either parents or prospective employers, and there was no way of accurately knowing how the 'good' pupil of one school measured up to the 'good' pupil of another (apart from the reputations of the institutions – which were, of course, often wildly prejudiced). Nor, for the most part, did this really matter to anyone. The good jobs at all levels of society were generally acquired through personal connections and recommendations. When a great house wanted a new chambermaid, the position was generally advertised among the existing staff, one of whom would often have a suitable young female relative to suggest. When a new seam was opened up at the colliery, miners brought in their sons and brothers. Clerical positions were no different: staff could be found amongst the relatives and friends of long-standing workers and employers. For most ambitious young men, the path to preferment was through connection and patronage. Education was a way of maximizing one's opportunities when they came, but it was not a passport to finding them in the first place.

Nationally recognized written examinations began not with schools but with the Navy in the eighteenth century. They were a resounding success, and the superiority in performance of captains and lieutenants who sat the tests compared to those who had previously progressed in their careers by purchasing commissions was stark. Reforms were made, and the exams for would-be officers eventually adapted for other professions. The examination model went on to improve the administration of the whole empire.

The universities followed suit. For centuries, assessment had been based on the student giving a lecture, in Latin, and answering questions upon it from the assembled professors. The new system enabled more students to be examined at once – a crucial development as universities expanded. It also allowed for a more objective form of testing and a clearer grading of a student's abilities.

Meanwhile, the professional world in general was becoming more meritocratic. The Indian civil service in 1853 became the first area of government to insist upon its recruits passing an entrance exam; and the home civil service followed in 1858. The Army finally abolished the purchase of officers' commissions in 1871, replacing that entry route with a new competitive entrance exam. In basic Darwinian terms, a difficult examination served to keep down the numbers of competitors, to raise the social status of those who achieved membership of the profession and to justify their exclusivity in the eyes of society. It also offered hope to the hard-working and intelligent, regardless of their family connections. In 1839, for example, anyone could have opened a pharmacy to dispense medicine, so long as they could find the start-up capital to do so. By the end of the century, however, a similar pursuit required years of study and the completion of countless exams. One had to become a qualified pharmacist to enter the profession, and legislation was passed so that no one but those qualified professionals could distribute medical drugs.

Schooling for Girls

In the 1860s, small groups of anxious, wealthy parents could often be found hovering outside the headmistress's offices of the newly conceived 'high schools' for girls. As with all areas of education, serious female schooling was expanding, and, for families with enough money, there was an abundance of choice. The education of privileged daughters had long been in the hands of governesses within their own family homes, but, increasingly, schools offered a broader curriculum with better facilities. Earlier in the period, the middle-class girls' schools of the 1830s and 1840s focused on promoting social graces and the acquirement of female 'accomplishments' – activities such as piano playing, drawing and French language. By the 1860s, there was a move to include studies closer to those taught to boys. However, many parents were worried. Would their daughters be permanently damaged, physically and mentally, by the new curriculum? Worse still, would the schools try to enter their daughters into the new exams, the precursors of today's GCSEs and A levels?

The problem was not one of seemliness, or of 'correct' feminine behaviour, but of health – specifically, menstruation. Deeply engrained within the Victorian psyche, and common to both the layperson and the medical expert, was the notion that the male body was the perfect 'pattern'. Most female traits, therefore, were an aberration of this ideal. Menstruation, though well known to be an essential part of the reproductive cycle, was unconsciously accepted as a weakness. It was referred to in terms of illness and was often considered to be an unpredictable and hazardous period. Puberty was generally felt to be a developmental stage of particular vulnerability, one that would tax a girl of her strength and energy reserves. Accordingly, anything untoward that could upset or unbalance a girl was feared to have long-term repercussions. The intellect, the emotions and the physical care of the body all required careful and gentle restraint if the girl was to become a healthy, happy woman.

How, then, were affluent parents to guide their daughters through this delicate and confused period? Rest, in all its physical, emotional and intellectual capacities, was the most generally approved strategy. Exercise was to be carefully monitored, and absolutely forbidden during menstruation; a day in bed each month was widely recommended. Teenage girls were advised never to run up or down stairs, or to undertake any activity that could upset their wombs. Many girls were taught to bandage their lower abdomens during menstruation to support the additional weight of a womb engorged with blood. Bathing was another troublesome area for menstruating girls. While some experts advocated washing (but not submersion), others were adamant that water be avoided entirely. Nor was the changing of underwear always permitted. Menstruation was a time to wrap up warmly, to avoid anything that could give a girl a sudden shock of cold – stepping out of a warm bed on to an icy floor was frequently mentioned as an unnecessary risk – and to eat plainly and enthusiastically.

Emotional rest was to be ensured by restricting social occasions to a minimum, far away from periods of menstruation. Stimulants of any kind were to be avoided: tea-drinking, for example, was frequently singled out as unsuitable for young girls. Parents were also required to be vigilant about a girl's reading material. Sensationalist or romantic literature, such as Emily Brontë's *Wuthering Heights*, was likely to cause emotional turmoil and overstimulation of sexual feelings. Even the novels of Jane Austen worried some parents. Girls who read novels were widely believed to reach physical maturity more quickly than their less adventurous reading sisters. An early or rapid passage through puberty was thought to be detrimental to one's health and a stain on one's morals. Suitable reading matter for teenage girls was therefore widely discussed and the cause of heated debate in many homes. Mrs Child, in her work *The Mother's Book*, wrote that 'girls should not read anything without a mother's knowledge and sanction; this is particularly necessary between the ages of twelve and sixteen, when the feelings are all fervent and enthusiastic.' She went on to condemn all the works of the poet Byron and the bestselling novels of Mrs Radcliffe, recommending instead a list of acceptable reading matter. For thirteen- and fourteen-year-olds, this included the biography of Bishop Heber, Nichols' *Catechism of Natural Theology* and the *Tales of a Grandfather* by Walter Scott (which was recommended as it contained 'the history of France').

Intellectual 'rest' was most directly under threat from the rise of education for girls. Educating a prepubescent girl alongside her brothers posed no risk to her health; however, from the age of twelve or so, a girl's education was treated very differently. While boys of the same age and social class progressed intellectually and entered national exams, girls were academically reined in, trained for the next few years of their lives in gentle, unchallenging pursuits that would allow them to emerge into adulthood healthy and mentally unperturbed, fit to be the mothers of the future. One correspondent to *The Times* in 1872 asserted that no female could 'follow a course of higher education without running the risk of becoming sterile'. For, as Dr

Henry Maudsley (the eminent physician after whom Maudsley psychiatric hospital is named) opined, 'When nature expends in one direction, she must economise in another.'

As the century progressed, some of these worries began to ease. By the 1890s, there was a series of studies and nearly thirty years of serious female schooling practice to draw from to demonstrate the effects of intellectual pursuits on girls. Mrs Henry Sidgwick, speaking of her experiences at Newnham and Girton College at Cambridge University, was able creditably to assert that the health of the young women who had attended the colleges was much the same as that of girls of their own class who had not. Furthermore, she maintained that even a 'delicate woman may go through the course of training for an honorary examination without any injury to her health', although she did qualify the statement by saying that it was only true if the girl in question worked steadily at her own pace, and not excessively. A number of widely publicized investigations into the health of American high-school girls and college women showed much the same results. Girls, even during puberty, could handle intellectual effort, as long as they were allowed some flexibility in their study patterns. A general consensus emerged that girls needed rest during menstruation but could quickly resume their study afterwards and still go on to achieve just as much as boys. The important point was to allow them a rhythm of study that suited the female body rather than forcing them to mimic the male pattern. For this purpose, separate schools and colleges would be needed for the two sexes.

However, much of this anxiety and concern was centred upon the girls of the wealthier classes: such considerations rarely touched the vast majority of girls' lives. Most girls of twelve, even at the end of the century, were never given an opportunity to pursue an intellectual life, nor to play sport. Most of them were working full-time in jobs that demanded heavy physical labour. No factory owner considered giving his female teenage workers a day off every month to rest during their period, although, just occasionally, some understanding was shown to a working-class girl. Mary Halliday, in her guide to *Marriage on £200 a Year*, included a chapter on mistress–servant relations which showed a far more humane approach than did most writers of the period. She called on mistresses to be aware that 'some days of slovenly and half-hearted work may have a reason other than that of idleness or carelessness, and [the mistress] ought when needful to lighten the burden of work to her servant accordingly.' As the majority of servants were girls between twelve and twenty years of age, such consideration would have been greatly appreciated by countless young women.

Girls and Sewing

If you were to count up all the hours of tuition of all Victorian girls throughout all the years that Victoria was on the throne,

Fig. 91. Traditional female education, *The Workwoman's Guide*, 1838.

you would find that they received more tuition in sewing than in any other subject. The compulsory free education of the last few decades of Victoria's reign may have seen a preference for reading and writing, but mathematics, certainly, would have finished a poor fourth at any time in the century.

Sewing was almost like breathing: one of the most ubiquitous and necessary of skills. It was taught at all levels of society: at home, by family members and governesses; and, at schools and colleges, by professors and tutors. An aristocratic girl may not have needed to sew her own underwear, but she was often proficient. She would also have been required to be adept at some of the more decorative and sophisticated branches of needlework. To be unable to sew was unthinkable – comparable to being unable to use a phone in the twenty-first century. Sewing skills formed a basis for earning a living, for saving money within the family budget, for many recreational pursuits such as embroidery or making toys, for social occasions, for following fashion, for expressing love and for teaching one's own children. Many men and boys had a basic grasp of sewing if they had to do some, but it was essentially a female skill. Male tailors naturally made their living with a needle, and men in the armed forces – especially sailors – were well accustomed to tending to their own repairs. Other men largely contented themselves with being able to replace a button if they could not find a woman to do it for them, but most sought female assistance in these matters.

The level of skill considered 'normal' and wholly unremarkable was higher than that of many twenty-first-century textile professionals. Take, for example, the instructions to be found in magazines aimed at middle-class girls. These were not girls who had received any professional training; few had attended school and still fewer had ever expected to have a career in needlework. The magazines were concerned with leisure and sewing as a pastime; the items they provide instructions for are largely superfluous: decorative outfits or garments made for one's own amusement. But they require astonishing skill to make. The casual language of the patterns belies their young readers' proficiency in a range of needlework techniques; the instructions do not waste any time in explaining technical phrases, as these are all presumed to be understood. A girl wishing to make one of the doilies featured in *The Young Ladies' Journal* was simply told that 'the star in the centre is ribbed pique, worked with black silk in point Russe' and that the 'outer scallops are buttonhole stitch and the remainder of the work satin stitch'. This, along with a small engraved picture of the design, was considered sufficient instruction. The magazine

Fig. 92. An elaborate needlework project from *The Young Ladies' Journal*, 1866.

would assume that a girl would know before she started to wash, iron and stretch the fabric. Next she would know to mark out the design, scaling it up from the two-inch-square image to an eight- or ten-inch-square item. Meanwhile, she would know exactly what equipment she needed, what thicknesses and qualities of thread and fabric would work best together, and she would also be skilful enough to execute a complicated and intricate design, requiring somewhere in the region of thirty hours' work.

When Mr and Mrs Beeton launched their first magazine for women in 1853, they wanted the publication to appeal to a practical, married audience: a middle-class but frugal demographic. The inclusion of dressmaking patterns in the magazine was a revolutionary idea. The hand-drawn patterns were several inches high on the page, and no scale was given. Other garments were not even drawn to the same scale but were instead roughly shaped outlines which a woman was supposed to enlarge and adjust to fit. Normally, about fifty words of text accompanied the illustration, which crudely described the garment but often did not include any instructions on how to make it. Once again, it was taken for granted that a woman would be able to hem and to seam. It was presumed that she was accustomed to planning and cutting out fabric. No mention was ever made of linings or stiffenings, facings or fastenings; these were all assumed to be common knowledge. These so-called 'patterns' were ultimately no more than suggested designs for competent and practised dressmakers. In later years, full-sized paper patterns appeared in the magazine, rather than the small line drawings that preceded them, but there were still no instructions.

If married women were expected to have known these skills, it was in girlhood that they would have acquired them. For most girls, sewing lessons began at three or four years of age. Scraps of fabric and brightly coloured threads, used to make simple rag dolls, kept the youngest girls amused while simultaneously teaching them the crucial dexterity required to handle textiles. In most households, the practice of sewing skills was regular and focused. Exquisite samplers sewn by eight- and nine-year-old girls were testament to breathtaking precision and patience and hours of practice among middle-class families. Poorer girls could not be indulged with attractive coloured silks or extravagant sewing projects in quite the same way, but they were not practising any less than their richer compatriots. Girls might be given simple and practical sewing jobs from a very early stage in their needlework education. Even a five-year-old could tack up a hem in preparation for her mother to sew it.

This opportunity to be useful, and the intense personal one-to-one tuition and time spent with a mother or sister, could be a source of enormous pleasure for many young girls. Sewing was not an enforced or oppressive regime but often quite the opposite: a quiet and intimate break in an otherwise busy day when a mother could bestow all her attention upon her daughter and the two of them could tell stories and talk as they worked. An hour a day of such attention and tuition could produce remarkable results. Producing a tangible, finished product was also a source of self-esteem and great pride for any child, and the better they became at the craft, the more likely they were to seek out the activity for its own sake. There were therefore genuine emotional rewards that came with learning to sew.

When education for the working classes became more common in formal institutions, from the 1870s onward, sewing took its place on the official curriculum. In classes for the youngest students, both boys and girls were taught the basics but, later, when boys and girls were separated from each other (even if this was in terms of seating within a classroom rather than separate classrooms), the boys mostly left sewing behind, and were taught additional mathematics instead. Sewing classes became so large that a new method of teaching had to be implemented. Just as reading and writing were taught through rote learning and copying in order to manage classes of up to a hundred children at a time, a system of drills and large-scale demonstration aids began to emerge. Several handbooks for teachers were published in the last thirty years of the century which set out these systems. They usually began by outlining the 'proper' method of putting on a thimble, threading a needle and then holding the 'work'. These drills, which were led by the teacher, were obeyed and repeated in military-style unison by the children. They were thought to ensure that certain actions would become second nature, providing a foundation for good posture and technique. Here are the commands that one author of a manual for teachers, Miss James, recommended for the 'stitch drill' form – shorthand for the efficient and complex movement of sewing using a thimble: 'Needle held ready, needle to work, take up the stitch, push with thimble, take hold of point, and pull through.' Along with the carefully drawn pictures of the hand in each position in the book, the drill meant that even the youngest children from a class could master the method, which was one of the quickest and most accurate of sewing techniques. Someone who could use a thimble and carry out the movements described in the drill could generally sew at about twice the speed of the most practised non-thimble user. In my own career, I hand-sew, for both contemporary and historical garments, and I also teach the thimble method. Undoing the bad habits of the non-thimble user is one of the hardest challenges as an instructor. Students will resist the technique, claiming that the very precise approach makes them clumsier. However, as soon as they relinquish their doubts and succumb to the technique fully, they are often converts within hours. Their sewing becomes tidier, more exact and much faster. Miss James and her ilk were master craftswomen.

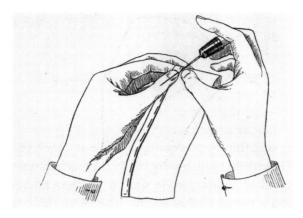

Fig. 93. A 'stitch drill'.

Building on these drills, Victorian schoolchildren were taught
to sew a variety of stitches, including four different types of
hemming stitch for use on cotton material and another two for
use on woollen flannel, as well as learning to darn and knit.
They learned how to make buttonholes and plackets (the re-
inforcing of slits or openings), as well as how to set in a sleeve
(making it fit into the main garment) and knit a sock. By the
time they left school, at around ten or eleven years of age, girls
were required to be able to cut out and sew all the essential
undergarments and nightwear usually worn by an adult woman,
a baby and a child. This may seem like a tremendous challenge
for a ten-year-old, but most managed it successfully. These were
skills that they would use in later life, and they were probably
already practising them at home.

Most children left school hoping that they would have access
to a sewing machine to help them with their daily chores (instead
of having to do everything by hand, as they would have had to
in class) but, nonetheless, they could appreciate the value of
their sewing lessons. It should be pointed out that many manu-

facturing bosses also valued this training of working-class girls, and not just in the garment industries. The supreme manual dexterity that sewing bestowed on them made girls extremely useful in a range of industrial processes, especially where small components had to be finished and assembled, as happened in watch-making workshops and sewing-machine factories. It wasn't just the cheaper wages that convinced many employers to hire girl workers; for many types of work, they were simply better employees than boys or men, being neater, more precise and much faster at light hand-work such as that required in the straw-hat industry.

Middle-class girls did not attend the same educational establishments as the girls of the working class, nor was their experience of sewing replete with drills and exams. The same level of competency was achieved mostly through aiding their mothers with the household linens and through sewing play. *The Home Book for Pleasure and Instruction* of 1868 sought to teach through the making of doll's clothes. It was quite explicit in its aims: 'in dressing dolly, the young girl acquires a skill with her needle and in the art of cutting out, which will be invaluable to her in future years.' The instructions that followed were detailed and fulsome with patterns, fabric and trimming types, orders of work and types of stitch required for a complete and elaborate mini-wardrobe. Here were all the instructions that patterns aimed at older girls and women would later exclude.

12. A Few Snatched Hours of Leisure

The early-Victorian working week offered few idle hours. There were not many people who enjoyed a day that was less than twelve hours long, and many endured considerably longer stints. Sundays were generally kept free, as a day of rest, though rural members of the population who tended livestock and horses had a range of Sabbath chores to get through. Sundays also entailed cooking and housework for most women. Mondays, however, were a leisurely workday for the masses, even if on an unofficial basis. Monday mornings saw factory hands, farmers and even office clerks arriving late at the workplace. Once at their job, the average Victorian employee refused to work hard on the first day of the week, preferring to work longer hours on a Thursday or Friday to make up for the more relaxed start. And, as we shall see later, working-class sport was frequently a Monday phenomenon.

As the century progressed, employers applied increasing pressure on workers to give up this ancient slack Monday, introducing draconian fines and threats of sackings. A culture that favoured business was in the ascendancy. In 1825, the Bank of England closed for forty holidays; in 1834, this had fallen to just four days. Meanwhile, employees campaigned for shorter overall hours. Initially, it was the bosses who held the whip hand, but, in the early 1870s, a sea change occurred.

Aided by a dip in the economy, which meant that many establishments were already offering shorter shifts, company after company across the industrial spectrum agreed to ten-hour working days with a half-day on Saturdays. The 1847 Factory

Act, which had previously permitted only women and children these more favourable conditions (and only in specific industries such as cotton mills and coal mines), was living proof that no great economic harm had occurred, despite the fears of industrialists. On the contrary, from 1874 onwards, employers discovered, much to their amazement, that shorter hours failed to dent their profits. Workers became more efficient, machines were run at faster speeds, meal breaks were shortened and processes were streamlined. Mondays became true work days. The factory hand had, in effect, traded a slow Monday, with time for play and chat, for a free Saturday afternoon to do with as he or she pleased, not to mention an extra hour or two every weekday evening.

In 1837, a 7 a.m. start at the mill had meant an 8 p.m. finish six days a week. From 1874 onwards, a mill worker could begin his shift at 7 a.m., as his father and grandfather had done, but finish at 6 p.m. from Monday to Friday and at 2 p.m. on a Saturday. Perhaps speaking on behalf of this whole new generation of workers, Albert Goodwin's father articulated the feeling that he 'had to find something to do' with the spare time that the new working practices granted him. He was certainly not the only one. Whether it was sport, drinking, gardening or holidaying, a new industry was born – leisure – and an array of activities was available.

Leisure time did, admittedly, remain unregulated for some Victorians. Hannah Cullwick worked from six in the morning to eleven at night. Her diary did not record a regular allotted period that was set aside for herself. However, she still occasionally took advantage of snatched hours in the day and a few evenings off. 'A walk along the pier with Ellen', for example, was built into one weekday when she was working at a household in Brighton. Another time, she spent several hours away from her home with the servants of a neighbouring household.

When she was granted the evening off, she washed up after tea and laid out a cold dinner for the family before leaving the house at around 7 p.m., returning after 10 p.m. Yet even for those like Hannah, who had the least free time during the period, it was undeniable that 'leisure' was fast becoming a universal experience. The next decision was what one would choose to do during these precious breaks.

Sport for Men

Sport and exercise were perhaps the biggest pastimes for men in the nineteenth century. At the advent of the era, it was horse racing that regularly drew the largest crowds. Turnouts of ten thousand spectators were considered ordinary at one-day meets close to large towns, while the arrival of a railway line in the vicinity caused the numbers regularly to top thirty thousand. The headline fixtures of the day, such as the Grand National or Ascot, could pull in numbers in excess of sixty thousand. Temporary or permanent grandstands and enclosures allowed the wealthy to pay for a degree of exclusivity and social protection from the working-class masses who swarmed around the course for free (until fully enclosed courses became the norm towards the end of the 1870s). They could be rumbustious places, with a huge range of stalls and sideshows dotted around the ground. The song 'Blaydon Races', which was written in 1862, describes the scene: 'There wes spice stalls an' monkey shows an' aud wives selling ciders.' Gambling was a large part of the attraction for many; it is estimated that at the 1851 Chester Cup around £1 million changed hands. Meanwhile, as the alcohol flowed freely, race meetings often erupted into violence. Usually, it took the form of common brawling, but, according to the *Birmingham Mercury*, in 1855 the day at Aston Park ended with eleven thousand ruffians dividing into two gangs of 'British' and 'Russians' to re-enact the battles of the Crimea, with many of the participants ripping up the fence posts around the race course to use as weapons. The action spread into the neighbouring town, and sixteen people were hospitalized.

Fig. 94. A day at the races, 1850.

However, for all its headline-grabbing antics, horse racing was not the only popular sport. Boxing had a tremendous following and was already well-established by the mid-eighteenth century. Bare-knuckle fights could be found outside inns and pubs, in barns and on village greens. When people moved into towns and cities, the boxing went with them. Primarily a working man's sport, such fights also enjoyed an enthusiastic following among gentlemen and aristocrats. There were both informal and organized bouts, regional established circuits with nationally known fighters, gentlemen's sparring matches and working-class prizefights.

Men practised for exercise, for strength, for fun and for money at different social levels. Only the middle-class man seemed to be immune to the allure of the boxing ring. When Henry Lemoine published his short book *Modern Manhood; or the Art and Practice of English Boxing* in the late 1780s, he described a raucous, often illegal world of prizefighting and heavy gambling. Famous boxers competed for modest prizes, while young aristocratic men betted far more upon the outcomes. When the illustrious Tom Cribb defeated the equally celebrated black American Tom Molineaux, he was able to retire with enough money to buy a pub in Panton Street, just off Leicester Square in London. (Tom Cribb eventually squandered the property betting on horse races, but the pub is still there today.) Twenty thousand people watched that fight between Cribb and Molyneaux in rural Leicestershire, and Tom Cribb's wealthy backer, Captain Barclay, won £10,000 on the fight (a sum that would have bought not just a pub but a sizeable country estate).

Schools of boxing, often run by ex-fighters such as the phenomenally popular 'Mendoza the Jew', rose and fell in popularity during the period. They provided an income for old professionals and places of exercise for many who never intended to fight publicly as well as training grounds for those who did. The rich rubbed shoulders with the poor, championship bouts were long and bloody, and behaviour outside the ring could be just as violent. To Henry Lemoine, boxing was a martial art, one that promoted skill, strength and courage; one that perfectly equipped the Englishman for war. Donald Walker, more than a generation later, recycled much of Lemoine's technical advice. He praised the 'manly art' for its character-forming traits, claiming that it was boxing that had developed the British sense of fair play. He recorded the sport's continued popularity, as did the newspapers of the mid-century, which reported large turnouts all over the country.

Fig. 95. A boxing match between Mr Mace and Mr Goss, 1863.

It is the Marquis of Queensbury's rules of boxing that we are all familiar with today. Written by John Graham Chambers, they were promoted under the name of the most enthusiastic aristocratic supporter of boxing of the day. Before their general acceptance, a round could last any length of time, ending only when one or both of the contestants fell to the floor. At that point, they had a count of thirty seconds to get to their feet and come up to the scratch marked in the dirt ready to fight again. (The phrase 'come up to scratch' originated here.) Matches ended only when a contestant was unconscious or conceded defeat, and could go on for hours at a time. There was a range of banned 'moves', such as headbutting or kicking your opponent when he was down, but a large number of wrestling moves were still allowed. From 1867, the Marquis of Queensbury's rules stipulated three-minute rounds with a single minute's rest between them. Effectively, they banned all wrestling moves and also advised that gloves be worn at all times. Gloves – or 'mufflers' – had been worn for most of the century, but usually only for practice or exhibition bouts. They were made of leather and padded with rag; more rag was wound around the boxers' hands. At first, it was only the amateurs who followed the marquis's rules, but, in time, professional prizefighters also obliged. In 1892, John L. Sullivan decided that he would defend his world-championship title only in a gloved fight under the Marquis of Queensbury's rules. The fight took place in a well-lit arena in front of ten thousand people, many of them wearing formal evening dress.

As the century progressed, and as boxing became a more ordered and controlled sport, it also became a more urban one. In 1837, rural boxing was widespread and vigorous. Though the championships were mostly held in London, countrymen were avid followers of the numerous smaller, local meets, and many took part in fights themselves. The same held true in the 1850s. By 1900, the tradition had largely declined in villages. It still, however, remained a powerful force in the poor districts of large cities. In London, in particular, the sport was promoted by religious leaders keen to engage working-class men and boys. Men such as Father Jay in Bethnal Green set up boxing venues and clubs to draw men into the life of the Church. Christians – presumably of the muscled variety – saw the sport as a point of communality, a distraction from the world of the pub (which we will shortly examine), and a road to redemption for the working-class, slum-dwelling man. Such outfits fed off the enduring popularity of boxing and the social standing of fighters but also helped to bolster the sport against middle-class disapproval. Informal fisticuffs and brawling were still part of everyday life; the pub punch-up is a long-standing British tradition.

If you preferred a less violent form of exercise and a more

genteel sport, cricket was a nineteenth-century favourite. By 1860, it was the most popular sport in the country. Both town-and countrymen would play – there were plenty of working-class cricketers and spectators – but, typically, it attracted a more middle-class crowd than boxing. In the countryside, gentleman farmers and the clergy usually led the village team, while in sub-urban towns the sport was normally run by office workers and shop owners. Cricket in more urban environments was less common, but it did thrive in some areas, especially in the north-ern towns. One journalist in Sheffield noted that 'on a Monday afternoon', among the large manufacturing companies, 'when little or no work is done, the men of one establishment chal-lenge those of another to a game of cricket.' The workers of Messrs R. Timmins & Sons in Birmingham owned a range of sports equipment in common, including bats, wickets and balls.

Fig. 96. Cricket, bowled underarm, 1850.

At the start of the period, matches were normally local events; the emphasis was on playing the game rather than watching it.

Dress codes were relaxed and the rules could be adaptable. The cricketer of the 1830s generally wore trousers (not always white), though a few wore the more old-fashioned breeches. Tall black hats were common, though some players preferred a straw hat; ordinary shirts were usually topped with a flannel jacket, though occasionally these were exchanged for military-style jackets. Leg pads were introduced in 1836, after a widely publicized injury occurred during a county game when a batsman's shins were not just broken, but smashed. As shin guards became more widely worn, in 1845 a cartoon in *Punch* showed the model cricketer in a military jacket, a peaked cap and large, padded tubes over his trousers which made his shins and ankles look like two heavily insulated drainpipes. There were many different designs of shin pads; others were constructed with vertical canes held together by lines of woven tape. In 1850, shin guards began to be advertised as being stuffed with horsehair and fastened on to the leg with straps and buckles, thus resembling something close to the twenty-first-century form. Gloves also began to be common in the 1850s, by which time tall hats had largely given way to flannel caps and cricket 'whites' had become de rigueur. By 1860, when cricket was rising to the peak of its popularity, the cricketer was wearing clothes and using equipment that is immediately recognizable to players of the modern game.

The rules of cricket had first been published in 1744, but revisions and updates were required regularly. Bowling, especially, changed from underarm, to round-arm (reminiscent of a baseball player's pitch), to overarm. For many years, overarm bowling was deemed too dangerous; the ban on it was lifted only in 1864. While these technical changes were occurring, the sport continued to grow, and travelling teams, making full use of the railway network, spread interest across the country from its southern, rural birthplace.

It was in 1864 that W. G. Grace made his entrance into 'first-class cricket', playing for some of the best teams in Britain.

Grace was cricket's first and greatest – arguably, still to this day – superstar. So vast was his fame and popularity that admission prices to matches were often doubled if his name was on the team sheet. He was the second of three brothers to play cricket at the highest level, and all three had long and illustrious careers. They had been taught by their cricket-obsessed father from an early age: he would make all five of his boys practise on their lawn with bat, ball and stumps, while his daughters would be pressed into service as fielders (they weren't allowed to bat or bowl). The Grace family were staunchly middle class, and W. G. was put through medical school to provide him with a profession. This maintained his 'amateur' status out on the field, despite the money that the game brought him through personal appearances and sponsorship deals. (He did practise as a GP, though presumably with a very limited roster of patients.)

Up until this point, cricket was still primarily a game to be played rather than watched. This created problems in itself. Liverpool, for example, had over sixty clubs, all of which needed pitches and space to play. Accordingly, teams complained regularly to the local newspapers about the lack of suitable playing facilities. Cardiff, too, struggled to find grounds for its ninety-three clubs, many of which belonged to distinctive communities such as the Caledonian Cricket Club, all of whose members claimed a Scottish heritage. By the 1860s and 1870s, however, this mass participation evolved into mass spectatorship. The performances of W. G. Grace were partly responsible. Here was a man, easily recognizable, good-looking and flamboyant in his play, who dominated the game. These few lines from *Bailey's* sports magazine were typical, both about his sporting prowess and the esteem in which he was held: 'Yet such is the strength of the North that their eleven was quite formidable enough to take care of any team that did not include Mr W. G. Grace . . . the great batman's revenge for his discomfiture on the first day was signally overpowering. Out of 300 runs he made 200, and out of a total of 436 he contributed 268.' In a cricketing career that lasted well into the next century, Grace was a celebrity who drew huge attention to the sport. One did not need to attend a cricket match to have heard of him. His heroic image and superstar status inspired thousands to take up the sport, or at least to buy tickets to the matches.

Fig. 97. W. G. Grace, 1875. Arguably the most famous cricketer of all time.

The trajectory and development of cricket into a spectator sport prefigured the course that would be run in the history of football, the men's sport that came to dominate the end of the nineteenth century. The disciplines which we now refer to as football and rugby had existed in various guises for centuries. Each group of players possessed their own traditional rules; games ranged from battles royal that pitched all the menfolk from one community against another in a free-for-all – only with a ball somewhere in the middle of it – to six-a-side matches outside pubs. The annual football match between St Peter's and All Saints parishes in Derby was famous for its bewildering array of tactics, which included swimming down the river with the ball, as well as removing the ball's stuffing and hiding it under someone's shirt. Simple kick-about matches, however, were much more common. The sporting paper *Bell's Life* covered football fixtures between pub teams as early as the 1830s. Other clubs were supported by churches and chapels: football had a reputation as a more innocuous sport, one that was removed from the culture of heavy drinking and gambling associated with boxing and horse racing (which had long been a vice in Britain in the eyes of the Church). Employers, too, were early advocates of football. Many of today's major British football clubs can trace their origins back to this era of local, free-form football. Manchester United was once called Oldham Road and was based at the Three Crowns pub, with its players recruited from the men who regularly drank there. Everton began life at the Queen's Head pub in the village of Everton in much the same way. But Queens Park Rangers started not as a pub team but a school team – the Droop Street Board School in Kentish Town. Bolton Wanderers embarked on their sporting career as the Christ Church Football Club, established by the Revd J. F. Wright (four years later, they relocated to the Gladstone Hotel). West Ham was founded at the A. F. Hills shipyard and went by the name of Thames Ironworks; and of course Arsenal was a club set up by the workers at the Woolwich Arsenal factory complex. The surprising thing was that none of these clubs had in common the rules of the game. Could you pick up the ball and run with it? How big was the goal? How many players should there be to a side? These were all questions that had to be settled, or argued about, before the start of a game. A report of a match played between men of the F Troop and the D Troop of the 13th Light Dragoons written up in *Bell's Life* in 1844 mentioned that there were twelve men on each side, but at the rematch a few weeks later, fifteen men played for each team.

In 1845, three senior pupils at Rugby School were asked to write down the rules of the game as it was played at the school. Once published, these rules became a standard that many clubs turned to when settling pre-match disputes with their opponents. In 1863, a second influential agreement of rules was published – that formulated by the Football Association. These two sets of guidelines, which had different visions for the game, separated to form what we now recognize as rugby and football (soccer). In 1895, rugby split again into two distinct forms: Rugby Union and Rugby League.

The two forms of rugby had strong regional followings, but the popularity of football dwarfed them both. As cricket evolved to become more about watching than 'doing', the energy for participating seemed to pour into people playing football. However, it must be said that those who were taking up the sport were far more likely to be working class than the cricketers a generation before them. As discussed at the start of this chapter, this was, in great part, due to working practices. In the 1850s and 1860s, when cricket playing boomed, large numbers of white-collar workers had found themselves with leisure time at their disposal. The job market of the middle years created many similar positions, and a substantial new demographic of men had free time to expend. Office hours had become much more standardized than previously, and most shifts were shorter than before. By the 1870s and 1880s, restrictions upon factory working hours meant that a large proportion of working-class men could also have a small amount of leisure time. The 56-hour working week provided relief for these men on Saturday afternoons, which they had off, and also on weekdays in the evenings. The white-collar workers of the 1850s had hit upon the emerging game of cricket to provide them with some exercise, and to entertain themselves. By the 1870s, when the working classes were looking for the same pleasures, cricket had already become associated with the upper class, so they turned instead to football, which was still class-neutral. The surge in popularity of playing football can be glimpsed in the rise of Birmingham's football teams. In 1870, Birmingham was almost football-free. By 1880, over eight hundred clubs had been formed. The same meteoric rise was visible in nearly every industrial town and city in Britain. Space, once again, proved difficult to find, and many of these early clubs shared facilities with rugby and cricket players. Many more were obliged to use the public parks, before they could afford to rent or buy premises of their own.

As football became a more unified game, the clothes that people wore to play it became more defined. In the 1840s and 1850s, players typically wore a motley assortment of ordinary daywear, with moleskin trousers and waistcoats as common as knitted vests or even tweed suits. However, by the 1870s, a generic kit had emerged. Most wore collarless jerseys, below-the-knee breeches and long socks. On their heads perched a variety of peaked caps or soft pill-box-shaped hats. Feet, in these early sporting days, were booted in several different styles of working boots, though none of them were specifically designed for football. Team colours, on the other hand, had just been introduced but quickly became ubiquitous, although they frequently only extended to the jerseys; socks could still be very individual. In 1867, *Routledge's Handbook of Football* suggested that 'if it can be arranged . . . one side (should wear) striped jerseys of one colour, say red; and the other . . . another, say blue. This prevents confusion.' Finally, to complete the outfit, boots became more specialized as the century drew to a close. Individuals could choose between lace-ups and elasticated boots, with and without various types of stud. Walking out on to the pitch, the footballer was now instantly recognizable.

Even with the acceptance of the Football Association's rule-book, however, the game was still changing. Up until around 1870, for example, the referee controlled the game with a flag; whistles became common only around 1880, after Joseph Hudson's cylindrical Airfast whistle had made its mark among the constabulary. Tests showed that the new whistle, with its 'pea', could be heard over a mile away – a fact that proved to be of great benefit to policemen in hot pursuit and to referees struggling to be heard over roaring crowds. According to the 1863 rules, what we would now refer to as 'goalposts' consisted of two upright posts eight feet apart (the height of the poles was never specified). In order to count as a goal, the ball had to pass between the posts, 'or over the space between the posts'. Disputes were common, and pitch invasions and fights occurred periodically as rivals argued whether the ball really had travelled between the posts or not. With a hard or high shot, it could be almost impossible to tell. Within two years, there was a rule change; now, a tape was to be stretched between the posts at a height of eight feet, and any ball sailing over the top would not be a goal scored. Crossbars fitted above the two posts were the next development, but goals acquired their nets only when John Brodie, a Liverpool City engineer, persuaded the FA to try out his new invention, patented in 1889.

It was not just the goalposts that were moving. The pitch markings took on their modern form only in 1902; the penalty area did not come until 1937. That first set of rules included no markings on the pitch at all, just four flags at the corners of the field. The pitch itself could be any size the players wanted, up to 220 x 100 yards (football pitches today are recommended to be 110 x 70 yards by the FA – approximately half the size). In 1891, all these specifications were formalized. From this point onwards, goal lines, touch lines, a centre circle and the goalkeeper's areas were all stipulated. Groundsmen had to procure the use of a line-painting machine – frequently borrowed from the tennis fraternity. Although the rules, the pitch markings, the goalposts and the nets all gradually changed, the core experience of kicking and chasing a ball around a muddy field remained the working man's most popular form of non-work-related exercise for the rest of the Victorian period.

Like cricket, football was also quickly to morph into a spectator sport. By 1901, many more people were watching than playing. The first English Cup Final in 1872 was watched by just two thousand people. In 1888, interest was growing, and the final was witnessed by seventeen thousand. By 1895, a grand total of 110,000 people flocked to the Crystal Palace arena. Football had taken on a whole new role in British life. As the Victorian age ended and the Edwardian began, football became less to do with kicking the ball, and more about standing on the terraces with your friends.

Sport for Boys

Fig. 98. Street football, as played by lads in 1888.

As a boy in the 1890s, Fred Boughton was larking about on stilts and playing Cat in the Forest of Dean, Gloucestershire. The 'cat' was a stick about nine inches long, sharpened at both ends and stuck into the ground. The boys took turns to use a second stick to hit one end and send the cat flying great distances. The winner was whoever made it fly the furthest. Around the same time, Walter Southgate, in Bethnal Green in the East End of London, was out in the street playing football and cricket: 'We had no apparatus except what we improvised ourselves – coats down in the road for goalposts; the lamp post for a cricket stump; a rough piece of wood shaped for a cricket bat . . . balls of pressed paper and string.' Across the whole of Britain, and across the century, boys played team games on wasteland, in streets and in yards. Exact rules were often not recorded, but, as with the sports of their fathers and elders, there seem to have been numerous variations of football, rugby, handball, tennis, squash, baseball, rounders and cricket. Each area had its own style, and often its own unique pitches or markings. On the Tyne and Wear, the Buddle Board School had a wall that divided the playground in two, boys on one side and girls on the other. Here, on their side of the wall, the boys took to playing handball. It became so popular that the enlightened school governors heightened the wall to its present nineteen feet and added buttresses to strengthen it. An unexpected outcome was that the buttresses from then onwards served as the dividing line between one game and the next, spread out along its sixty-foot length. A cluster of handball sites is also recorded in the south-west of England, usually found against the walls of churches or pubs. The ball was struck with the palm of the hand against the wall and allowed to bounce once on the ground before the other player struck it in turn. If you missed the ball on your turn, or if the ball missed the agreed section of wall after you had struck it, you lost a point. At Eton, the boys called the game Fives. They wore gloves and played it against the chapel wall. The idiosyncrasies of the chapel architecture, with its thick base and thinner, higher wall, as well as its ecclesiastical buttresses, dictated how the ball would spin and ricochet.

Fig. 99. A game of Fives, 1868.

It is widely reported that sports such as rugby were developed in the public schools of England. Rugby itself is, famously, said to have been invented at Rugby School, and, as we saw in the section on men's sports, its rules were widely adopted by others. On a larger point, it seems to be true that it was ex-public-schoolboys who spread the rules beyond the school yard. English public schools at the beginning of the Victorian era were remarkably unsupervised places. Apart from the actual lessons, the boys were mostly self-governing and had very little adult input. They had their own unsupervised traditions of games and pastimes, passed from generation to generation of youngsters, each with its own slowly changing set of rituals, rules, locations and timings. As a tradition of boys within a school culture, these games naturally all had slightly different rules and forms from those played in other places. Like species of fish isolated in remote caves, the schools formed isolated communities developing along their own idiosyncratic lines.

These public-school boys grew up to be powerful and influential men within Victorian society, so it should come as no surprise that it is the games of this group of boys that have been most thoroughly recorded for posterity. There is very much less information about the games that other boys played.

The games themselves often contained rigorously enforced rules. Boys were clear in their own minds about exactly who could play and who could not. Girls, for example, were often allowed to take part in some sort of fielding capacity, but not in any batting or goal-scoring role. Outside the public-school system, most Victorian boys were working in full-time employment, which meant that, even after the introduction of compulsory education in 1880, when the average school-leaving age still hovered around ten, eleven or twelve years old, the majority of kick-arounds were independently organized by working-class boys. These matches occurred at times when they could all take breaks from their shifts. Factory yards probably saw as much play as schoolyards.

The crucial factor that eventually differentiated public-school games from the matches of their poorer cousins was the involvement of adults. From the early 1860s onwards, a new interest in athleticism pervaded Victorian society and teachers suddenly took note of the boys' games. Their entirely novel involvement in organizing and participating in their pupils' games came to be used by the headmasters of public schools as a tool to engender and instil a more community feel and, particularly, to break down some of the class barriers that had formed between the mostly upper-class boys and their generally middle-class teachers. The early part of the century had seen frequent and violent rebellions at public schools. At Winchester in 1818, the situation had got so bad that the boys stormed part of the school, barricaded themselves in for twenty-four hours and ignored a summons by a magistrate who was accompanied by several constables. Only when the local militia was called out did the boys surrender. As a result, organized, teacher-led games sessions became common in these schools in the 1860s and 1870s as part of a general plan to improve discipline. By the 1880s, they had become a compulsory part of the curriculum. The adults tidied up and codified the games the boys had been playing, and made them more appealing to other adults.

Vigorous outdoor activity was now being prescribed by Victorian doctors. Medical understanding was particularly in favour of male muscular development: 'The youth who has never had sufficient exercise never attains to fullness of growth and development,' one Dr Brown asserted. Strong, healthy men could best be produced by plenty of boyhood exercise, preferably outdoors, where they could also gain the benefits of fresh air. In exercising the body, it was believed that a boy would also stimulate his brain – so long as he didn't go too far and develop the body to the detriment of the mind. Outdoor team games seemed to be ideal. The running around promoted comprehensive fitness, rather than overdeveloping one set of muscles while neglecting another, and the activity was good for exercising the lungs and for stimulating the blood circulation. Meanwhile, the knocks and bumps, along with the cold, would all serve to help toughen a lad up.

In addition to the physical benefits of organized games, many influential thinkers began to see these team games as having a moral and social benefit as well. Charles Kingsley, a clergyman and bestselling author, summed up the benefits of such activities as promoting 'not merely daring and endurance, but, better still, temper, self-restraint, fairness, unenvious approbation of another's success, and all that "give and take" of life which stand a man in good stead when he goes forth into the world, and without which . . . his success is always maimed and partial.' Team games fostered team spirit; they encouraged boys to merge their individual interests in those of the whole. They rewarded courage and endurance and were fiercely competitive: all values much admired and looked for in Victorian manhood.

Very few working-class schools enjoyed the benefits of such attitudes as those of the Buddle Board of governors towards sporting provision for their pupils. Charles Cooper's experiences were much more common: 'The playground was small, and the pupils [were] forced out on the roads for most of their games . . . No games at all were taught at school and no articles for games were supplied – not even a bat or cricket ball or football or hockey stick.' The onset of the Boer War was finally to provide an impetus to the provision of physical education in schools with working-class pupils. The nation was shocked by the appalling levels of unfitness in the young men who volunteered in 1899, with only two out of every nine being judged fit for combat. Military-style drill in the playground was quickly incorporated into the regular school curriculum, and many schools hired retired military men to run the sessions.

The 1880s saw further practical attempts to extend the benefits of organized sport to working-class boys. Lads' and boys' clubs were established as an antidote to the difficulties of young working life. They usually included sporting facilities, as well as libraries, and ran a range of evening classes. Many had 'homely' spaces for boys to relax in, away from the influence of alcohol. The Gordon Institute in Liverpool, founded in 1886, opened a large gymnasium in 1887 and organized clubs for cricket, rounders, football, swimming and boxing, in addition to gymnastics and athletics. At about the same time, the Hulme lads' club opened in that district of Manchester, offering a similar range of facilities. By 1907, in the Edwardian period, ten thousand boys were attending such clubs in Manchester, another ten thousand were doing so in London, and similarly large numbers in many other towns and cities too. Regardless of the educative hopes of their founders, it was the sporting facilities that proved the main draw to most boys.

Besides team games, there were two other basic sporting traditions among Victorian boys: swimming and fighting. According to Alfred Ireson, who was growing up in the 1860s, 'the free open country provides fun and mischief for boys and girls alike. It was here where I learned to swim and fight. These things formed a great part of a boy's life.' Lads had been stripping off and launching themselves into ponds, streams, lakes and rivers for centuries; it was a long-established summer tradition. Over most stretches of water there was a rope tied to a branch of an auspicious tree that allowed one to swing out over the water and drop with a satisfying splash into a pool that swarmed with small, naked boys on warm afternoons. Alfred records that, for him, school lunch hours 'during the summer were spent bathing in the river Nene [Northamptonshire].'

Industrial towns were no less provided for than rural villages.

Fig. 100. Fighting was a common experience of boyhood.

Early photographs of docks and canals often included skinny-dipping lads. The Burlington Street Bridge over the Leeds and Liverpool canal was a very favoured spot, as the outflow from the Tate and Lyle factory heated the water. A photograph taken around 1890 shows a posed crowd of about thirty naked boys, with another dozen or so in clothes, congregating there. Death by drowning was, sadly, common for young boys, as coroners' records too painfully show. As the plunge pools of the public baths (which we shall examine in a later chapter) became more and more popular and in response were enlarged, many lads transferred their swimming games to heated indoor pools. But on hot, sunny days, the lure of the riverbank and the canal continued to be felt by those whom puberty had yet to embarrass.

Finally, fighting, brawling, boxing and general scrapping formed a big part of most boys' experience of boyhood, from the highest gentry to the lowest paupers in the land. It was an activity which adults and parents subversively encouraged. Being able to stand up for yourself was a trait much admired in boys and men, whereas running from a fight was not. Although 'picking' a fight was generally frowned upon, standing your ground was expected. A number of subterfuges could be employed in order to cover, or at least make more socially acceptable, any challenge to a fight. Complicated rules of 'respect' allowed a lot of leeway for engaging in a contest; actions such as knocking someone's hat off were universally acknowledged invitations to a brawl. Few fights were totally without rules. Such rules were usually informal ones; nonetheless, they were generally known among the boys. Any sort of knife or weapon was perceived to be 'unfair', 'unacceptable' and cowardly, as was initiating a fight with someone much smaller than yourself. Staying down when knocked down signalled the end of a fight. Punching was by far the most admired technique of fighting, while scratching was too feminine a trait for most boys to use in front of their peers. Fights, after all, were generally meant to be witnessed, preferably, and for maximum prestige – as far as the victor was concerned – by a large group of one's peers. An evenly matched fight between two boys who both stuck to the 'honourable' style of approved fighting techniques could bring greater stature for both parties. A one-on-one bout surrounded by a circle of other boys was, of course, the ideal, and one very close to the adult form of boxing. Fred Boughton recalled making his way down to Bernard Parker's tin shack, where, along with quieter games such as dominoes, 'some used to play boxing and you would see chalked up on the shed, "Big Contest on Tonight. Bill Wet v. Jack Frost, 10 Rounds. Don't be late."'

Sport for Girls and Young Women

In addition to walking and calisthenics, archery and croquet were the first socially acceptable sports for girls among the upper echelons of society. Neither sport involved too much movement of the body; neither required a woman to wear clothing that was too 'unbecoming'; both could be practised in large, safe groups. Nonetheless, married women rarely took part. Pressure to maintain decorum was heavier upon them than upon single women, and the ever-present possibility of pregnancy made them more cautious about engaging in activities which continued to be seen as provoking miscarriage.

Archery as a sport took on a new lease of life in the eighteenth century when aristocrats such as Sir Ashton Lever and Sir Thomas Egerton, following the enthusiastic lead of Sir Lever's secretary, Thomas Waring, set up a series of gentleman's clubs. Almost from the outset, women were included both at the butts, and as members of the clubs. They competed alongside men, sometimes in their own separate competitions but often directly against them. By the middle of the century, female archers could outnumber male participants at tournaments (see Plate 22).

Straw targets were placed upon easels at a variety of distances, and competitors loosed an agreed number of arrows from a long bow that would not have looked too out of place on the fields of Agincourt. Points were scored for hitting the target, with higher scores for those arrows which landed closest to the centre.

Archery was very much the preserve of the aristocracy; it was a high-fashion activity and went with special high-fashion clothes. Several archery bodices survive in different clothing collections; the Platt Hall Gallery of English Costume near Manchester has a particularly early example. Made from fine worsted wool and silk, it is in the bright-green club colours of the Royal British Bowmen (which granted women full membership as early as 1787). It is in a wraparound style that would have given the wearer ample movement across the shoulders while still maintaining the fashionable silhouette over her corset. Hats with a single perky feather (reminiscent of the headwear that Errol Flynn would later wear in *The Adventures of Robin Hood*; 1938) were a common sight at archery meets.

An article in *Bailey's* magazine in 1874 described the scene of an archery meet at Powderham Castle in Devon. It marvelled at 'the rainbow colours of the dresses of the lady archers, flashing in brilliancy of hue' as they 'wend[ed] their way between the targets'. The *Bailey's* report, largely sardonic in tone, devoted a whole page to the women's high fashion on display but only three lines to the actual shooting results.

If a woman was fortunate enough to be invited to one of the exalted archery meets, she would need to invest in the equipment, which, at between £2 and £5 for a lady's set (according to the *Home Book* of 1868), was well beyond the purse of most middle-class girls. Lady's bows were generally smaller and easier to draw than those of the gentlemen, although women such as

Queenie Newall, who went on to win gold at the 1908 Olympics, used bows with equal draw weights to those used by men. In addition to a wooden (usually yew) bow, a lady required a set of her own arrows, a quiver to carry them in, a leather arm brace to keep the fabric of sleeves tidily out of the way and to protect her wrist from the bow string or feathers of the arrow, and a small leather finger tab to protect the fingers of her draw hand.

Anthony Trollope's 1875 novel *The Prime Minister* has the prime minister's wife, Lady Glencora, order that an earthen bank be raised upon three sides of a half-acre area of lawn to accommodate the archery at the house party the pair hosts. With the grassed-over bank providing a backstop to prevent stray arrows from injuring wandering guests, the straw targets are set up. The ladies and gentlemen practise together, flirt and compete in a series of friendly matches over the ensuing days.

Fig. 101. A game of croquet played in 1866.

By 1875, archery was not quite so at the forefront of fashionable behaviour as it had been, but, nonetheless, the novel-reading public still expected aristocratic ladies to be toxophilites.

Croquet was a less exclusive pastime. It grew in popularity rapidly, from being a virtually unheard-of sport in 1862 to become a 'fashionable and almost indispensable' game by 1868, according to *The Young Ladies' Journal*. All you needed was a lawn and a croquet set, which could be had for about two shillings. It was the lawn, of course, that was the limiting factor. The invention of the lawnmower had made it possible for a middle-class villa home to have a lawn, but it was impossible for the working classes. Conceived as a family game, suitable for both sexes and every age, it was especially seized upon by girls, as they had so few other physical opportunities. You don't run or jump in croquet, but walk. This was a game that could be played in corset and crinoline outdoors in the healthy fresh air with no worries about overtaxing the girls' reproductive workings. The curate Francis Kilvert thoroughly enjoyed the mixed-sex croquet parties he attended at Clifford Priory: 'Great fun on the lawn, 6 cross games of croquet and balls flying everywhere.' He picks out Miss Allen, Mrs and Miss Bridges and Miss Oswald as looking particularly lovely among the sporting party. Within fifteen years, croquet's popularity had passed. It had, however, demonstrated that no harm need be caused by a woman engaging in sporting activities, and the fear of female injury from overexertion was beginning to pass.

Lawn tennis developed in the mid-1870s at around the same time that croquet finally faded. Within twenty years, it had lured most of the upper middle classes back out on to their lawns; a tennis court marked out in one's garden became a potent symbol of respectability and wealth. Girls were enthusiastic players from the start. The sport, of course, did not appear out of nowhere. Real tennis had arrived in Britain from France in the fifteenth century. Henry VIII was known to have been an enthusiastic player, running up sizeable accounts – the documentation for which still exists – for replacement tennis shoes. From the seventeenth century onwards, the courts were all, architecturally, based upon the one built in 1625 at Hampton Court Palace, but this requirement proved detrimental to the spread of the game. Courts were expensive to build; there needed to be high walls around them that the ball could ricochet off in a way similar to that in a modern game of squash. However, this meant that the spectators were limited to one small, galleried area, which could only accommodate around thirty people. Real tennis had evolved as a game for courtiers within an elite environment; it did not lend itself to mass sporting involvement. The game needed to move outdoors, and to lose some of its arcane ritual.

There are two independent claimants to the title 'inventor of lawn tennis'. In 1874, Major Walton Clopton Wingfield patented a new game and began to sell boxed sets. Harry Gem, a Liverpool merchant, claimed to have invented the game some fifteen years earlier with his Portuguese friend Augurio Perera. Using ordinary real-tennis rackets (wooden with gut strings) on Harry Gem's underused croquet lawns, they used a new air-filled rubber ball which would – unlike the old, solid cork and string balls used in croquet – bounce upon the turf. Along with the rackets, they borrowed the net, many of the court markings (though reduced in size) and much of the scoring system from real tennis. And of course the new game would not have been possible without Charles Goodyear, the American who discovered the 'vulcanization' of rubber in 1839, which let the ball bounce, or indeed Edwin Budding, who invented the lawnmower in 1827.

Lawns were crucial to the near-instant popularity of the sport. Many were left unused from croquet's heyday, and minimal effort was required to convert them into tennis courts. A few lines of white paint, a net, a couple of rackets and a ball or two were all you needed to engage in the fashionable new pastime. Tennis was undeniably more energetic than croquet, involving running and sharp changes in direction (which obviously led to heavy breathing and perspiration), but having such a close association with the older sport made the game acceptable to those concerned with the 'delicate' health of the women playing. The first girls to take up tennis were encouraged to do so only in a gentle manner, but as the century drew to a close real athleticism came to the fore. Francis Kilvert, the former croquet-loving curate, played his first game of lawn tennis in July 1874, weeks after the boxed game set first went on sale. 'A capital game, but rather too hot for a summer's day' was his comment.

The first girls to play the newly devised game wore their full fashionable day dress – not crinolines, which had gone out of fashion, but tightly waisted corsets and long, draped skirts looped up at the back into bustles. By 1879, it had become common to wear an apron when playing tennis, to protect the fashionable, expensive dress beneath, and hats became de rigueur. The 1890s saw the Swiss-belt-style corset emerge on the tennis court. Still cinched just as tightly around the waist, it was cut very high over the hips to allow freer movement of the legs, and cut very low under the bust (actually under the bust, providing no support or control) to allow vigorous arm movements. It allowed a young woman to take part in significantly more energetic activity than a full corset without sacrificing society's desire for her to display a petite waist. Over the top of such a corset it became common to wear white for playing tennis, with fewer of the frills and trimmings of a girl's usual daywear. Fashion plates in magazines began, by 1890, to depict specific tennis dresses, normally with full, loose bodices and crisp, tight cuffs and collars (see Plate 21).

Lottie Dod was a five-time ladies' tennis champion at the Wimbledon All England Lawn Tennis and Croquet Club. She gave up the sport at the age of twenty-one, and went on to become a ladies' golf champion in 1904; she was later awarded the silver medal for archery at the 1908 Olympics. In addition, during her astonishing sporting career, she was a notable ice skater, show jumper, rower and yachtswoman. However, her sporting career began with lawn tennis, and it was in this discipline that her athleticism and talent was first publicly recognized. By the end of the century, lawn tennis had become the sport most widely played by girls, forging acceptance for other female sports, such as lacrosse and hockey, which many new girls' schools began to adopt. By 1900, there were around three hundred clubs affiliated to the Lawn Tennis Association, including Wimbledon, which had begun life as a croquet club, in 1868.

By the last decade of Victoria's reign, much of the earlier fear regarding female exercise had diminished. However, most medical, educational and parental advice still advocated a girl or woman taking a break from physical activity when she had her period.

Parks and Gardens

Those looking for outdoor leisure activities beyond sport increasingly turned to gardening. At the start of the century, gardens were enjoyed by the wealthy but were nurtured by the working class, who also tended their own small plots. When these working men gardened of their own accord, it was mostly to put food on the table, but there was room for pleasure too. The 1830s to 1850s were the heyday of florist's societies: groups of mainly urban working-class men who grew competition-quality blooms. For many of these men, whose working lives were spent in small, home-based workshops as weavers or frame knitters, carpenters or nail makers, flowers became their passion. They raised new varieties, selected the strongest seeds and perfected their chosen flowers over years of patient, careful propagation and superb horticultural skill. The plants they grew were cultivated on tiny patches of ground around their homes and workshops, and in pots and containers which stood in yards and on windowsills. Hyacinths, auricula, tulips, polyanthus, ranunculi, anemones, carnations and pinks had been the traditional florist's interest, but pelargoniums and dahlias, fuchsias, flocks and chrysanthemums soon joined them in a riot of colour. Cash prizes were awarded to those with winning blooms and money could be made by the most successful florists by selling the seeds or bulbs of their creations to other gardeners. The flower show at Dawdon, in Durham, was held on the first weekend of August throughout the 1840s and on into the 1890s. The floral society that organized the event comprised almost entirely miners. Thomas Cooper, the son of one such man, recalled 'the most beautiful flowerbeds in great profusion: the colours had to be seen to be believed. Every little hole and corner was decorated with boxes or barrels.'

In the countryside, some cottages were bordered with small plots of land, but for the rural folk without such gardens, allotments could be hired. These plots were primarily dedicated to potatoes and cabbages to supplement a family's diet, but the sense of ownership they bestowed on these working-class men, who could garden on their own land after a full day in their master's fields, was a source of great pride and satisfaction. Flora Thompson, in her recollections of life in 1880s Oxfordshire, remembered fondly that 'most of the men sang or whistled as they dug or hoed.' Growing purely for pleasure became more popular: flowers were planted around the edges of paths and against cottage walls, and a much wider array of fruit and vegetables was grown by the men than the philanthropic middle-class observers thought suitable. Cottage gardeners were advised, for example, to limit their fruit crop to rhubarb by their

well-meaning wealthy neighbours, yet gooseberries and straw-
berries found their way on to many allotments, with wallflowers,
sweet williams and pinks, as Flora Thompson recorded.

By the 1850s, the middle and upper classes were also discovering the joys of gardening. Women and clergymen especially
became keenly involved for the first time. A gamut of books and
magazines was published to aid them, taking full advantage of
the new market. One could spend hours flicking through beautifully illustrated pages of garden designs, flowers, tasteful
arrangements for window boxes and adverts for lawnmowers
and garden tools.

Fig. 102. Gardening, 1868: 'the glory of the English girl'.

Flower arranging had long been a desirable feminine activity, calling for aesthetic skill in the domestic sphere. Botany,
too, had a tradition as the acceptable front of science for girls,
women and clergymen. Gardening called on all these skills and
pleasures, and nourished them. According to the *Home Book* of
1868, 'the flower garden, in all its various forms, can scarcely
fail to be the delight, the occupation, the pride, the glory of the
English girl.' Gardening was rapidly seen as an expression of

nurturing, domestic virtues, embodying a love of order and neatness alongside visual taste and botanical expertise. Complete ranges of garden tools were redesigned for 'lady gardeners' – lighter and smaller than those used by the male professionals. And for those who were not blessed with large gardens, there was plenty of published advice at hand for creating window boxes and indoor herbariums. The royal family were keen early adopters of the gardening craze. Prince Albert insisted that all his children should have their own patches to cultivate in the palace grounds.

At the same time that the middle classes discovered that there was a pleasure to be had in digging, weeding and deadheading, the public park movement got into its stride. Liverpool proved to be a leader in this area. Birkenhead Park was conceived as a way of mitigating the worst effects of urban life and housing on the working-class family. As the Merseyside docks boomed and people poured into the area for work, the tightly packed terrace houses accommodating them became grossly overcrowded. Buildings that had begun as modest two-up-two-downs, or which had been built with just one room on the ground floor and one above to serve a single family, were now occupied by multiple households. Rows and rows of streets were without a tree or a patch of grass and pubs pervaded everywhere. A park, it was hoped, would give the people somewhere to go where the air was cleaner, where there would be room for 'rational' entertainment and leisure, far away from alcohol. Birkenhead Park was unique: it was the first to be set up by a public body with public money, unlike the royal parks of London, which had come as gifts to the nation, often in lieu of settling royal debts. Laid out in curving walks, and sweeping around landscaped vistas of trees and lakes, Birkenhead was modelled upon the very best in aristocratic-garden design. It was hoped that the soothing influence of nature and the calm orderliness of the layout would act as a moral and social compass for those who lived nearby. Still to this day, having had the opportunity to stroll along its paths myself, I can say that it is a beautiful place. For once, the people who established these grounds for the poorer members of society did not stint or try to pass off something second-rate.

Birkenhead Park was built to be large and to facilitate myriad strands of park life. There were wide, open spaces for sport, including a cricket ground; wilder areas of foliage and shrubbery for those who wanted a memory of their countryside childhoods; formal planting and bedding for flower lovers; a rockery; lakes with bridges and summerhouses; wide boulevards for promenading and narrow, winding paths for private walks and quiet moments of reflection. Birkenhead inspired the creation of a number of new parks across the country and beyond (it was a model for Central Park in New York). In Liverpool, and elsewhere, these parks proved to be hugely popular. Birkenhead itself had forty thousand visitors in its first week alone. Early Victorian film footage of several urban parks shows them crowded with people, all dressed in their best clothes and enjoying themselves in these new social spaces. A walk in the park was free, the area was beautiful after the drab and dirty life of the town, and humming with people. Parks also often had a bandstand. Free concerts were common, as were sporting opportunities, and parks proved to be places where the classes could mix for a change, sharing their leisure.

However, for all the popularity of parks, gardening and sporting activities, the leisure pursuit most common among Victorian men, and some women and boys, was drinking.

The Pub

If you were to walk into any Victorian pub, the first thing to strike you would be the warmth. However economical with fuel the Victorians were required to be in their homes or work-place, there was always a bountiful fireplace at the pub. Warmth, masculine company and beer were the main attractions. In the countryside, the village pub – and most villages had several – was indistinguishable on the outside from any of the other houses. Only the sign hanging above the door marked it apart. Inside, too, there was little difference. One room, usually the largest, at the front of the house, served as the public area, but there was no sign of a bar.

There are several Victorian village pubs that survive today in their original form dotted about the British countryside. The one I know best is the Drew Arms in Devon. The house is thatched and lies close to the church. If you enter the front door, the public room is on the left, a small space, about twelve foot by eight. The fireplace is on the far wall and quickly brings the room up to a warm fug. The walls that border the stone-flagged floor are wood-panelled to a height of around six feet and are painted white. Around the edge of the room runs a built-in wooden bench, fronted by a couple of basic wooden tables and chairs, which can accommodate no more than a dozen people in com-fort. Just to one side of the door by which you enter the room is a small hatch, and it is from here that the beer is served. It was a rugged space, intended to withstand the wet and muddy agricul-tural labourers at the end of a long working day stamping the mud off their boots as they came in and collapsed on to the benches. Men chose the village pubs they patronized largely according to who else drank at them regularly, each pub forming, in essence, a small club whose members knew each other well.

Many urban pubs were similar: situated in the front room of someone's house and simply furnished with a thriving fire. They served beer, and perhaps gin, from a hatch, or across a half-door from the storage room behind. Like the village pub, such establish-ments were small and numerous. One pub for every thirty houses was not unusual in working-class districts. The desperately cramped conditions at home made the pub a welcome relief from crying or boisterous children, from the cold of an unheated room – and provided a way of escaping housework. Another Devon pub, the Welcome Inn, in the city of Exeter, survives largely unchanged from its Victorian days. Built in the working-class quarters, the original gas lighting and a scattering of oil lamps still provide the only illumination. The walls are painted dark brown to hide the dirt, so that no one returning from the factory needed to feel uncomfortable about their grimy dress. A fireplace continues to heat the room.

However, not all Victorian pubs were like this: some were very grand, veritable palaces of the people. The 1840s to 1860s saw the height of the sparkling, exquisitely tiled and lavishly fitted urban pub. Breweries with money to invest did their utmost to make their public houses as appealing as possible to potential customers. Inside and out, the pubs shone with brilliantly coloured tiling, large windows, bright, hospitable lights, gleaming metal trim and highly polished woodwork. Pubs were often the first buildings to adopt gas lighting – and, later, electric light – in the district. I think that the finest example of such a pub I have ever patronized is the Stork Hotel in Birkenhead – not far from the park that sought to entice people away from such a drinking culture. The wooden bar stands in the centre of the building and a series of small rooms radiates outwards, each with a large, convivial fireplace. The bar itself is an enclosed space with a succession of small hatches through which drinks are served. Exuberant decoration runs everywhere: in the frosted glass, the patterned tiling on the floor and walls, the wallpaper and even the plaster on the ceiling. Such pubs were a major investment and appeared most frequently in newly built districts in order to capitalize on the expanding market, where informal, house-based pubs had not yet had time to become established.

Pubs had a number of social functions beyond pure drinking: they served as club houses for sporting groups, premises for debating societies, meeting rooms for floral societies; and many ran savings schemes of one sort or another. In the Sherlock Holmes story 'The Adventure of the Blue Carbuncle', a goose club was run by the landlord for his regular customers, who paid a small sum weekly in exchange for a goose at Christmas. At Berkeley in Gloucestershire, several of the pubs hosted friendly societies, whose members saved to provide sick pay and other benefits for members. Once a year, these societies shared out any profits. The first Wednesday in May was 'march out' day, and the members of the clubs based at the Berkeley Arms, the White Hart and the Mariner's Arms, headed by a brass band and silk banners, would march around the town to the houses of the wealthier citizens, who would put on cider and beer to greet them.

Fig. 103. Unscrupulous brewers adulterating the beer with treacle and blocks of salt, 1850.

There were, however, dark sides to Victorian drinking culture. Landlords and brewers were notorious for adulterating the drink with a huge range of substances, from plain water to foxglove, henbane, nux vomica (all poisonous in quite small doses, and used to increase the intoxicating effects of watered beer) and Indian berry, a kidney-shaped berry from the Malabar region of the subcontinent – the most common adulterant, and used alongside molasses and water. Of course, with pubs, too, along came alcoholism, poverty and violence. Many of those whom we have heard describing their Victorian lives in this book also record the influence of alcohol on their families. Alice Foley's hungry childhood was punctuated by her father's bouts of heavy drinking and savage drunken outbursts: 'I recall his following mother persistently round the kitchen whining monotonously, "lend us a penny, Meg, lend us a penny; I'm choking." At length in a fit of desperation, a penny was flung on to the table.' Alice then had to fetch a gill of beer in a jug from the pub and the cycle started all over again, eating up the family's food money. Albert Goodwin's grandmother suffered a similar addiction in the 1870s: anything of slight value that entered the house was pawned, the ticket sold, and an orgy of drinking would follow. Clothes, blankets, pans and kettles all went the same way.

The wealthy Victorian man generally drank at least as much – often more – than his poorer brethren, but he did so at home and in clubs; the all-male clientele and comfortable surroundings of such clubs made them, essentially, private pubs. Male social space came with alcohol. It was a blight which the Temperance Movement fought to banish from British life, but, while the Band of Hope and other temperance organizations attracted enormous membership among women and children, adult men were much more susceptible to the allure of the warmth and comradeship the drinking premises offered.

Play

Children's leisure had to fit around work and school. Visit any playground in Britain today, and you will witness Victorian games in action. Various forms of Tag, British Bulldog, Grandma's Footsteps and What's the Time, Mr Wolf? still form much of the charging about when children gather. Games of marbles can be found in quieter corners, Five Stones and Jacks are still popular, and many girls are still highly skilled with a skipping rope. Some Victorian toys have faded away, such as hoops and whipping tops. Both were games that required a child to keep a set of toys in motion. The hoops were bowled down the street and tapped with a stick to keep them rolling; the most skilled player could attempt to duck through the hoop as it travelled along. Whipping tops were simpler. The wooden cone was set spinning by winding a length of cord around it and pulling it sharply. The top could be kept in motion by whipping it with the string in the direction of the spin.

Fig. 104. Playing with a hoop and stick, 1868.

A Victorian child would have little trouble joining in with most activities taking place in a modern school playground. Schoolyard football resembles the disorganized kick-abouts of the early Victorian period much more closely than the official game of football taught today in PE lessons. Many walls are still pounded with tennis-sized balls to the accompaniment of rhymes. Even regional rules which vary from school to school tie twenty-first-century children directly to the games played in the Victorian period, before many pastimes we now regard as sports were codified and standardized.

The description of the game Oranges and Lemons that appears in the 1868 edition of *Home Life* is identical to the way I played it as a child. A line of children take turns to duck underneath an arch made by two of their friends while a rhyme is chanted that ends with the words: 'Here comes a chopper to chop off your head.' At this point, the two children making the arch attempt to catch whoever is passing beneath them. Only recently, I heard the game being played on a playground next to a friend's home, the children using the same rhyme and rules, but I have also witnessed the game being played with a song based on pop stars' names. Children seem to have a preternatural gift for modifying playground games but simultaneously clinging to their original foundations. In 1877, the Mill Hill School magazine recorded a counting rhyme the children had been heard chanting in the yard: 'Eaver weaver, chimney sweeper, had a wife, and couldn't keep her, had another, didn't love her, up the chimney he did shove her.' An eleven-year-old girl in Welshpool was recorded using the same line nearly one hundred years later. Another rhyme, 'Queen, Queen Caroline, dipped her head in turpentine. Why did she look so fine? Because she wore a crinoline,' was sung in Edinburgh in 1888 and noted in Flora Thompson's *Lark Rise to Candleford*, a work based upon the author's rural childhood near Banbury in Oxfordshire. Queen

Caroline actually predates the Victorian period entirely, and crinolines were a garment of the 1850s and 1860s, but the lyrics persisted, as they do today in a variety of twentieth- and twenty-first-century versions. In yet another example, I am again reminded of my own childhood by the Victorian skipping rhyme 'Mother, mother, I feel sick, Send for the doctor, quick, quick, quick. Doctor, doctor, shall I die? Yes, my dear, and so shall I. How many carriages shall I have? One, two, three, four . . .' This was recorded in 1864 in the December issue of *Notes and Queries*, but I still skipped to this ditty in the early 1970s in Nottingham.

At the end of the Victorian age, when improved photography allowed for informal action shots to be taken, photographer after photographer recorded impromptu children's games in the streets. From the East End of London to Yorkshire villages, cricket wickets were chalked on to walls, and packing-case slats or crudely carved sticks were pressed into action as bats. Bundles of rags, bound together with string, served as balls, which were kicked, struck or thrown against walls. Games that could be scratched in the dirt of the countryside transferred easily to the paved city streets, marked out instead with chalk or lumps of charcoal from the fire. Hopscotch appeared in photos all over the country – one of the few games that was dominated by girls rather than boys, though a spiral version of the game was captured being played in Glasgow by a group of young lads. Two of the youngsters are lying down on their bellies, trying to ascertain whether a thrown stone was inside or outside the line, while another is in mid-hop.

Formal skittles and bowls equipment were beyond the reach of many children, but both remained popular games in a more makeshift format: throwing stones at a variety of targets was a game easy to set up and popular among mischievous boys. All manner of objects were balanced on fence rails or on the tops of walls, from rotten apples to beer bottles. The latter, when they could be sourced – most possessed a small return value so were rarely left lying around – were, of course, perfect for a game of skittles. Many Victorian photographs of large groups of children usually include sheepish-looking boys, often with stones clutched in their hands, waiting for the camera and its operator to move on before resuming their game.

Large balls for games of bowls were very hard to come by, as were most of the obvious substitutes: apples, cabbages and other fruits were much more likely to be eaten than pressed into service for children's play. However, equipment for the miniature version of bowls – marbles – was much easier to find. Discovering suitably sized stones or conkers could be half the fun, although from the 1850s onwards fizzy-drink bottles offered excellent glass marbles for urban children. The huge surge of interest in carbonated non-alcoholic drinks fuelled by the Temperance Movement led to much commercial innovation, not only in the drinks themselves, the labels and their advertising, but also in bottle design. By far the most successful one used a glass ball in the neck as a stopper, forced up and creating a seal as the fizz tried to escape. To drink the contents, one administered a sudden, sharp, downward pressure on the marble with the finger, breaking the seal. The bottles could be washed and reused, and the drinks companies were happy to offer a return fee on them in order to lower manufacturing costs. Such an initiative was environmentally friendly and an early example of Victorian recycling, but those glass balls in the neck of the bottle could be quite irresistible to a marble-playing lad. Smash the bottle and you had a perfectly round, strong and eye-catching marble, the envy of all your friends.

A shared trait among these children at play was their age. It was rare to find a Victorian child of more than eleven or twelve years of age involved in a frivolous game; most were much younger than that. Six- and seven-year-olds had playtime, but such freedom was quickly taken away as they grew older. Moments of release could still be snatched, but work and schooling filled most youngsters' days from end to end. Work was necessary for family survival and, in some cases, even preferred by the children themselves. One girl, interviewed by Henry Mayhew in the 1860s, talked of her working life as a street-seller as being much more enjoyable than staying at home and being bored. At home, she was without toys or companions. At least out in the street, working, this girl could see some life, talk to people and occasionally join in with a game if she saw others playing in the street. For her, work was the framework of her play. She was seven years old.

Indoor play was traditionally much more of a middle-class phenomenon. Working-class children usually spilled outside in search of light, companions and space to move. Their homes were tiny and full of people. In the majority of homes, sitting under the table playing make-believe with a doll or a toy soldier was often the only option for a child in search of amusement.

Fig. 105. A fortunate child with a range of simple toys, 1887.

On the other hand, for middle-class children, and especially girls, the street was not a possibility. Boys might make use of the garden to charge around with their brothers or cousins, but, for girls, even this outdoor space was carefully curtailed by concerned parents.

Toys were both more necessary for these children and far more widely available. Today, along with dolls, indoor skittles are among the best-represented surviving Victorian children's toys. They were generally very simple. Lengths of stick varying from two to six inches high were cut, the bark stripped. Some basic woodturning was used to shape some of them, while others were merely smoothed off before paint was applied. Many rural working-class children may well have possessed similar sets, without the paint or shaping, merely simple lengths of stick which may have gone unrecognized by anyone but their owners as toys and ended their life on the fire. Most of the surviving dolls follow much the same pattern: a length of stick would be smoothed off, crudely shaped, sometimes only with a deep groove to separate the head from the body, and then painted. Toy soldiers could be sawn from the feet upwards to form two crude legs, rather like a clothes peg (such dolls are usually referred to as 'peg dolls'). Both skittles and dolls of this type had a habit of falling between floorboards, only to be found many years later, when they became heirlooms and museum pieces.

Wooden spinning tops and basic carved models of animals, and later trains, served many children well. These were toys within the reach of most families, with painted versions for the wealthier working-class or lower-middle-class child. Tin toys were much more expensive, and, while the son or daughter of a wheelwright or a small shopkeeper might be able to play with a painted wooden toy cow, only families that could call upon the services of two or more servants were likely to be able to give a child the gift of a tin train. Lead soldiers, rather than wooden-peg soldiers, were another indicator of wealthier families, as were wax- or porcelain-headed dolls.

The mass manufacture of goods made producing toys cheaper and thus made them accessible to a wider group of children; new technologies allowed toys to do more, to be more luminously coloured, to bounce higher and to stretch more. The discovery of 'vulcanizing' rubber in 1839 made all kinds of toys more enjoyable for children, especially balls, which could now have a greater bounce to them. Catapults were another major beneficiary of the harnessing of rubber, as were a host of wind-up toys. Powered by an elastic band, small boats could be sailed across ponds and bathtubs; miniature roundabouts could be made to turn; windmill-style helicopters could float slowly down through the air. From the 1860s, new inks and dyes were brightening up many areas of Victorian life, and, combined with leaps forward in printing technologies, these colours could be relatively cheaply applied to picture books and to printed labels and papers that were pasted on to toys. Plain wooden or even cardboard toys were enlivened by such pasted-on designs. The very first jigsaws were one result of this series of technical innovations; toy theatres, another. More traditional toys also benefited from a bright, cheap overhaul. A crudely cut-out wooden ship, for example, was a much more attractive toy as a result of a decent printed ship design pasted on both sides.

Scrapbooks also began to flourish with the colour-printing revolution. Children, and especially girls, had long been encouraged to keep newspaper and magazine cuttings, as well as odd assortments of items to be used to decorate objects, or to be put in books to be looked at as mementoes. The availability of colourful printed matter made this a much more appealing pastime, which, in its turn, prompted printers to create sheets of brightly coloured designs expressly for the purpose. Just as, today, many young children enjoy collecting stickers and putting them into sticker books, Victorian children carefully cut out and glued images into books, on to boxes, or even on to fire screens.

In the last few years of the Victorian era, precision engineering advanced sufficiently for clockwork toys to be available in the shops at prices that a doctor or lawyer could afford. In 1838, an animatronics figure would have been an adult amusement for the very wealthy, being both delicate and prone to wearing out if overused. By 1901, a careful child could be given a clockwork train and play with it for years without mishap.

Seaside Holidays

One final aspect of leisure, one that could be enjoyed by the whole family by the end of the century, and which developed during the Victorian period thanks to changes in working practices, was holiday time.

It was a very different story at the beginning of the period, when a few weeks by the sea at the outset of the century would have been a health holiday for the wealthy. Many towns around the coast of Britain, from Brighton to Scarborough, packaged themselves as elegant resorts, with an array of leisure facilities. Their customers were well-heeled and well-dressed. Light-coloured cotton dresses, often in bold, striped patterns, formed the usual seaside fashion for women, whereas elements of naval dress crept into the outfits of men.

Initially, it was the sea itself that drew such people to the coast. The wealthy went to the seaside to breathe the healthy, ozone-laden air and to take gentle walks for exercise along the seafront. For the more robust traveller, bathing in the sea was considered to be a tonic that would stimulate and invigorate the circulation, and assist in clearing toxins out of the body. Sea bathing simply meant standing in waist-deep water and dunking oneself under the surface two or three times before climbing out, drying off and getting changed back into normal daywear. Men usually performed this operation naked, but for women there was a special garment to preserve their modesty: the bathing suit. Normally worn for no more than ten to fifteen minutes, it almost completely restricted one's movement, so swimming was impossible. Ideally, no one of importance would see you wearing it either, and bathing costumes of the 1850s were therefore meant to be cheap and simple; it should cover your body, but not matter if the seawater spoiled it. In essence, bathing suits were woollen sacks with a drawstring neck and simple slits at the side to put one's arms through. They were voluminous and long so as to cover as much of the body as possible and were usually made of dark-coloured flannel.

The railways democratized the holiday market by reducing the cost of travel. First, it was the middle-class families who were to join the wealthy, taking a house for a few weeks in the summer. Then, as train-ticket prices fell even further, the working classes began to enjoy their first daytrips to the beach.

By the mid-nineteenth century, beaches up and down the coastline were sprouting bathing huts. These were small wooden sheds on wheels, fitted with a set of steps at the front. During the first thirty or so years of Victoria's reign, it was customary for the bather to enter the hut fully dressed at the top of the beach. The hut was then hauled down the sand, usually by donkeys, into waist-deep water, while the bather got changed. When suitably attired, he or she would emerge upon the steps of the hut and walk down into the water. The 'dipping women' – the working-class owners of the huts – stood in the sea fully clothed and assisted the bathers as they submerged them for a few minutes at a time (dipping them) before the bather retreated back to the hut to dry themselves and change. The hut was then dragged back up to the top of the beach, where the bathers came out, cleansed and fully dressed. A flowing tide was recommended as the healthiest option, as this was thought to contain purer water, unmixed with the refuse of the beach or other bathers.

Fig. 106. Bathing huts. Women in the water wore old, sack-like garments, while the ladies on the steps sported new two-piece outfits,1873.

At the start of the 1870s, many men and women were swimming in the sea, for exercise and fun, and this gradually ousted bathing as a medical practice. Most popular beaches had become sexually segregated, with resorts publishing maps to assist holidaymakers in finding the 'men only' and 'women only' stretches of shore. Francis Kilvert, the Welsh curate, recorded with delight the pleasure he gained from stripping naked and running into the sea on his holiday at Weston-super-Mare in 1872: 'There was a delicious feeling of freedom in stripping in the open air and running down naked to the sea, where the waves were curling white foam and the red morning sunshine glowing upon the naked limbs of the bathers.'

However, naked bathing was not to last, and quickly became socially deplorable. Men were forced to cover up on the beach, and, as they did so, mixed bathing began slowly to take hold over the coastline. By 1873, only one year after his carefree exploits,

Francis Kilvert was in trouble for his nudity and required to wear a pair of red-and-white striped drawers. In his diary, he recalled the unsavoury interest of some small boys, who referred to him as a 'rude naked man', but he did point out that 'the young ladies who were strolling near seemed to have no objection.'

Higher up the beach, fully clothed fun was developing at a rapid rate. New promenades, gardens and seating areas were laid out by forward-thinking town councils. New businesses sprang up to serve food and drink to the growing numbers of holiday-makers, while theatres, concert halls and bandstands provided entertainment into the evening.

Fig. 107. The beach was generally enjoyed while fully clothed, 1876.

Even though it was still a very new idea, the concept of going away for a holiday was becoming established in the Victorian mind. Pleasure and leisure in previous centuries had rarely involved more than a day's excursion, to the fair or to the races. The upper classes had traditionally moved seasonally from London to their country seats, and back again. But the idea of setting aside a fixed time and place, apart from business or other social obligations, and purely for reasons of enjoyment, was new. As a place 'apart', life at the seaside was generally felt to demand different rules of conduct. Clothing could be brighter, lighter and less formal. Behaviour could be more frivolous, perhaps even flirtatious.

Paddling in the water was now playful and, by the 1870s, dipping women were disappearing from the water's edge. As the shoreline became increasingly liberal, men were, typically, bolder than women, having fewer concerns about their modesty. They remained in their bathing costumes for longer, not feeling the need to change so swiftly, but enjoying the freedom of movement. Sea air and sunlight for their skin was another benefit, which men had few qualms about; they, after all, did not need to worry about freckles or tanning, which were considered unsightly only for women. A number of younger men seem to have relished showing off their bodies in more revealing bathing costumes. These often echoed the styling of various male athletic and sporting outfits, resembling a short-sleeved, thigh-length wetsuit in its figure-hugging nature. A young, fit man at the end of the century could feel confident and masculine striding about the beach, or in and out of the waves, in full view of the watching young (fully clothed) women.

Bathing costumes for women were also changing. Instead of a loose sack, these now consisted of a knee-length tunic and a pair of below-the-knee drawers in matching fabric, trimmed with a contrasting coloured braid and a belt at the waist. Serge took over from flannel as the material of choice. Still a woollen fabric, serge was a much tighter-spun yarn and a much tighter weave, both of which technical differences meant that it absorbed far less water. However, the loose, unstructured nature of these costumes obviously unsettled many women who had spent the rest of their lives corseted. As a result, in 1868, *The Englishwoman's Domestic Magazine* had an article about a newly invented bathing corset: it was 'very small, and made with whalebones but no steel, on purpose to wear when bathing'. By 1877, the fashion magazine *The Queen* was answering queries about the 'new bathing stays'. Some women clearly preferred the familiar feel of corsetry even when swathed in a loose bathing costume. For the vast majority, however, bathing outfits consisted either of the two-piece tunic and drawers, or a pair of 'combinations' with a detachable skirt. These covered the figure down to just below the knees, but left the arms bare. The garment was caught in at the waist to provide some shape and, importantly, to hold the fabric firmly in place to stop it getting in the way in the water.

I have worn a two-piece Victorian bathing suit, as described in many of the fashion articles from the period, and it was a fantastic experience. I enjoyed not having to bare my midriff, and, while the costume was slightly heavier when wet than a modern swimsuit, it was not so heavy as to be a nuisance or to hinder my movement. It did take longer to dry, which is why I, and perhaps many Victorian women, chose to change out of it relatively quickly. But, as a dry garment, worn before entering the water, it was much more comfortable for the beach, offering protection from the vagaries of the British weather. Made from woven fabric, the costume was easy and comfortable to wear, pleasant to swim in, and it kept its shape, wet or dry. It was, of course, not designed for those who were interested in getting an even tan. The Victorian woman was generally horrified at the idea of any tanning at all. White skin was what a woman aimed for in order to help differentiate her from those who had to work outdoors for a living. And with no such thing as sunblock to protect a person from sunburn, covering up was doubly sensible.

By the 1890s, bathing huts, too, were well in decline. Instead, lines of changing huts or tents were now strung out along the promenade edge. People, once they had changed their clothes, simply walked down to the water themselves. And there were many more people doing so, as even members of the working classes, albeit the wealthier ones, could enjoy a seaside holiday. Resorts were booming, each rival town catering to a different audience to maximize its business. Blackpool, for example, invested in fun fairs to attract factory workers, whereas, a few miles up the coast, in Southport, the town invested instead in golf courses and elegant shopping parades, hoping to attract the factory owners rather than their employees. Punch and Judy shows, travelling groups of 'Pierrot' entertainers dressed as white-faced clowns, donkey rides and 'penny lick' ice-cream salesmen characterized the beaches of working-class customers. Those with a middle-class clientele generally kept the commerce off the sands and confined it to more expensive outlets along the front. Tram lines, formal and botanical gardens, ice rinks, ballrooms and sporting facilities lured the holidaymakers back from the shoreline into towns, whose foremost business had become tourism. It is believed that, by 1900, half the British population was able to take an occasional short holiday by the sea.

13. The Evening Meal

It is impossible to describe an 'average' Victorian evening meal with any degree of accuracy. Geography and wealth each played a vital role in determining what a British family could eat, and, over the course of Victoria's reign, the ingredients themselves were to alter radically. However, if we examine a sample of homes from the beginning, middle and end of the period, we can get a better idea of the enormous range of food and drink that was available, even if it was not always available to everyone.

The Start of the Reign

On a typical weekday in 1837, an agricultural labourer's wife living in the south-east of England, such as the mother of Frederick Hobley in Thame, Oxfordshire, would have offered her family a simple serving of a few slices of bread for the evening meal, which was known as 'supper'. The family did not always sit down together for the meal, sometimes preferring to eat their bread alone; they each returned home at different times from their long working days. The bread would have been baked at the local shop from locally grown and ground flour. The mother would not have possessed the facilities to bake her own bread; home bread-baking was the preserve of wealthier farmers, who owned better ovens and could afford the fuel. Working-class people, from both town and country, had long turned to professional bakers to fulfil their daily needs.

The bread itself would have been made not from pure wheat, which was expensive, but from a mixture of wheat and barley grain, which would have given the wife and mother nearly twice as much volume for the same amount of money as wheat alone. In more prosperous times, she might have been able to welcome her family home in the evenings with a home-made pudding. This would have consisted of flour, water and a tiny scrape of fat mixed together into balls and dropped into boiling water along with a handful of herbs. Once ready, this was served with a glass of beer.

On the same day in 1837, the wife of a factory hand in Lancashire, such as Alice Foley's grandmother, would have prepared a pot of boiled potatoes with a pinch of salt for her family. Occasionally, the budget would have stretched to a piece of bacon, which would be fried, chopped and stirred into the meal. The family would have washed the meal down with beer brought home in a jug from the local pub. For the sake of variety, they might also have sometimes eaten a bowl of porridge made from oatmeal and water, flavoured, once again, with salt.

In 1837, northern and southern Britain would have eaten very differently. Those in the south were still dependent on the ancient diet of bread and beer, while those in the North usually replaced wheat with oats and potatoes, the potatoes having been adopted from America. Though their meals were simple, the factory workers in the north undeniably ate better than the farm labourers in the south. They dined vastly better, too, than those living in parts of Ireland. In the same year, a family living in a cottage in County Cork may not have eaten or prepared anything at all, such was the extent of the crop failure. In all families, the working man, as the family breadwinner, would be allotted the largest portion and the best-quality food the family could afford.

Meals improved dramatically as one ascended the social ladder. In the home of a skilled tradesman such as a carpenter or blacksmith in almost any market town of England or lowland Scotland, the main meal of the day would have already been taken at midday. The evening meal, whether it was called 'tea' or 'supper', was based upon bread and butter, usually with a cold cut of meat, a small amount of pickle and a cup of hot cocoa. Some days there was a piece of cake too.

This was markedly different again from the evening fare of a family of a London clerk, the sort of family that Hannah Cullwick was to work for a generation later. They would have dined in the evening when Papa arrived home from work, on tripe, stewed onions and a large slice of bread followed by a roly-poly pudding. The clerk's wife, assisted by their one servant girl, would have begun preparing the meal about three hours earlier. The dessert would take the most time to prepare and was normally put together first. A large pot of water would be placed on the hottest part of the range, directly over the open fire in the centre, to bring it up to the boil (fortunately, the range would have been kept on all day and would already be warm, so there would be no difficulty in attaining the required cooking temperature). A lump of suet would be carefully picked clean of all its membranes and veins then shredded; an essential but slow and tedious job. Two measures of flour and one measure of suet would then be mixed together in a clean bowl and cold water poured in and stirred to make the dough. This would be rolled out upon the table to a thickness of about half an inch, jam generously spread over it and the whole rolled up into a sausage shape. Next, a cloth would be soaked in water, wrung out, sprinkled with flour and wrapped around the jam-smothered dough (it would be removed when the pudding was served). As soon as the water in the saucepan was at a rolling boil, the pudding would be immersed in it; the flour on the cloth would react on contact with the boiling water to create a watertight seal. For it to cook through, the pudding would be kept at a boil for the next two hours.

The wife or servant now had only to check, every quarter of an hour or so, that the fire was hot enough and that the pan did not run dry (a kettle at one side of the fire aided this task, allowing the pot to be topped up with hot water at a moment's notice), and so had time to prepare the tripe and onions. The tripe would have been bought that morning by the servant girl and required only a rinse in cold water. The onions would be peeled, chopped and dropped into a pan of milk placed on the coolest part of the range to come up to a simmer; it would take half an hour to do so. The tripe would be cut into two-inch squares and added to the milk and onions to cook slowly while the table was laid and the bread sliced. When the husband finally returned, his meal would be waiting for him: it had been only three hours in the making. With it, tea and cocoa were just as likely to be served as beer.

As one rose again through the social classes, the meals became more extravagant. The fashionable middle and upper classes sat down to dine at five o'clock in the evening. They may have partaken of lunch, or tea and cakes, earlier in the day, but this was their primary mealtime, and they called it 'dinner'. The kitchen staff in a successful barrister's town house – a household similar to that in which Jane Carlyle lived – would have prepared a menu, if the family were alone, of, for example, mulligatawny soup, a roast rib of beef, Yorkshire pudding, marrow and potatoes, followed by a damson (plum) pudding. For a family dinner such as this, all the food (with the exception of the damson pudding) would be put upon the table as a single course; this style of serving was known as '*à la française*' (see Plate 6). The soup was kept at the top of the table, where the woman of the family would sit. The soup plates would be stacked to one side of her and the ladle laid on the tablecloth beside the tureen. At the bottom end of the table would sit the man of the house and, in front of him, beneath a cover, the beef joint. The vegetables and

Yorkshire pudding, in covered tureens, would occupy the centre portion of the table and at the very centre would stand a small vase of fresh flowers. Candlesticks would be placed on the centre line towards the two ends and cruets of salt, pepper and other sauces would rest somewhere near the flowers. Each diner would have, laid out in front of them, a folded napkin with a small bread roll; to its left, a soup spoon, to the right, a knife. A wine glass would have been placed near the tip of the knife. Dinner would begin with the woman of the house serving the soup and the attendant servant passing the filled soup plates (wide-rimmed, shallow bowls) to the rest of the family. As soon as everyone had their soup plate, the servant would remove the soup tureen and ladle and leave the room. If there were guests, another dish of food would replace the soup upon the table, but, in an everyday family meal, the space would remain empty.

By the time the servant had returned from the kitchen, the soup would have been eaten and the soup plates and cutlery could be removed. The man of the house could now commence carving the joint. A fresh stack of plates would be brought from the sideboard, along with new cutlery. As the meat was carved, the servant would hand around the plates, also helping the diners to pass around the tureens of vegetables. The servant would then ensure that everyone was served with wine, and again leave the room.

When everyone had finished, a ring on the bell would bring the servant back to clear the table. Fresh plates and cutlery would be laid in front of the diners before the pudding was placed at the head of the table for the woman to serve.

'*À la française*' is a form of service that still lingers on in many twenty-first-century houses, for one day of the year at least – Christmas Day – when many still like to carve the bird at the table and pass around the vegetables. Of course, if our Victorian barrister's family had been entertaining, there would have been more food, and it would have been arranged not in one main course with a dessert to follow, but in two courses. After the soup, its 'remove' (the dish brought in to fill the empty space left by the departed soup tureen) and the first course of dishes were finished, the table would be cleared and a second array of food would arrive. In its turn, that would be replaced with a cheese and a salad spread, before, eventually, the table was cleared and set for dessert. All the plates, cutlery and glasses required for this would have been ready on the sideboard; used crockery and cutlery would quickly be whisked away.

The Middle of the Reign

If we were to visit our families a generation later, in 1865, we would see a number of changes.

Frederick Hobley's life would have changed completely. His education had seen him rise to the rank of schoolmaster, so he had left his working-class roots behind him. His childhood neighbours, however, still lived the routine of the farm labourer and, by the mid-Victorian era, would have been persuaded to give up their beer, despite its usefulness as a source of calories and vitamins, because of its danger of incitement to drunkenness. They would now drink tea, when they could afford it, although it contains none of the nutritional benefits. Their reliance on bread would remain the same, but about once a week they could enjoy some bacon, which would join the pudding and the herbs boiling in their pot: a small change, but one that would have an immense effect on both the flavour of the food and the morale of the diner.

The Lancashire family would be doing less well. As Alice Foley's mother recalled, their trade was undergoing a crisis, wages had fallen and unemployment was rife. They would no longer be able to afford the small ration of bacon they used to enjoy, and water would now be all they were drinking. Porridge and boiled potatoes would form their only daytime food. While the history of the nineteenth century is generally one of improving diets, it was by no means a steady or uninterrupted progression. Lancashire weavers were only one group who saw their living standards fall significantly at various points during Victoria's reign.

A new Irish family would have moved to the cottage – our first family is likely to have starved – and would be faring better than their predecessors. With a million people dead, another million fled, and with the worst of the potato blight over, life would have begun to thrive once again. Land holdings were bigger now, and the new tenants would have been able to plant more diverse crops. Potatoes were still important to their diet, but they were, crucially, also eating bread and butter, so as not to be totally dependent on tubers.

Skilled artisans, so long as their trade was stable, would have been eating more plentifully than ever, with one meat meal per day. The pudding that followed would now often be accompanied with custard, as custard powder had become a common product in shops. Custard, which required eggs and milk, would have been out of the family's financial reach before, but now, with extra money in her pocket, the upper-working-class wife could afford the milk which Mr Bird's very reasonably priced custard powder called for. Convenience foods, too, were making a substantial difference to a woman's workload – no more shredding suet; it was available in pre-prepared bags.

Our London clerk whose cooking was administered by Hannah Cullwick was now one of a rapidly growing band. Lower-middle-class jobs were abundant, as new industries and businesses proliferated. The family diet remained based upon carbohydrates and cheaper cuts of meat. Fresh produce was becoming even harder to come by as the city expanded, and fruit and vegetable prices were rising faster than lower-middle-class wages, despite the improved transport links in from the countryside. However, a whole range of new processed foods at reasonable prices could be used instead. Both condensed and evaporated milk could be bought, and were more reliable than the dubious 'fresh' milk sold in the city. Macaroni pudding made with watered-down evaporated milk offered an excellent dessert to follow boiled mutton and potatoes.

The barrister's family had more good fortune, with fresh vegetables, dairy, parcels of game and garden produce from wealthy estate-owning friends and clients in the country enlivening the table at frequent intervals. For the novelist Anthony Trollope, the son of a failed barrister, the success of his writing revived his family's fortunes. By the 1860s, he was able to live and eat in a style that suited his new wealth and station in life. His family could afford to pay the high prices for the finest-quality food that arrived in town. Asparagus, when in season, was on their table the very day it was picked, courtesy of the highly efficient coordination of growers, railways and retailers. The family also bowed to the latest fashion, which drove their hours of dining later into the evenings. As Mrs Beeton recorded, the evening meal would now commence at 6 p.m., instead of the 5 p.m. start common at the beginning of the period.

The End of the Reign

Onwards again to another generation and, in 1901, there would be significant deviations.

Kate Taylor was the fourteenth child of an agricultural labourer in Pakenham, Suffolk. The meals that she recalled were typical of the families who were still working on the land. Jam had been added to their regular diet, but the bread they were spreading it on had changed irrevocably. Roller mills had replaced the old stone mills. These were much faster, which made the process significantly cheaper, but they could also produce far whiter-looking flour, which was selling well: the whiteness of the flour had long been seen by the British public as a sign of its quality. However, the nutritional effect was not a positive one. When flour is stone-ground the wheatgerm is ground along with the starch and mixed around; when it is milled by rollers, it is crushed into a small, separate flake which can be sifted out. Millers and retailers had two strong reasons for sifting it out: firstly, as we have already mentioned, it made the flour whiter and more attractive to the consumer, and, secondly, the wheatgerm releases its oils when broken open by milling, which means the flour goes rancid in a shorter time. This did not matter when you were regularly milling and selling the flour locally, in small batches, but the new large-scale firms wanted to store and transport ready-milled flour from their highly efficient roller mills all over the country. The wheatgerm thus had to be removed. Unfortunately, no one at the time realized that much of the nutritional content was located in the wheatgerm. The new, whiter flour, and the new, whiter bread that it produced was therefore lacking in vital minerals and vitamins − and in vitamin B most of all. This would not have mattered much to people who were eating a varied and plentiful diet, but to those for whom bread was such a major element, this deficiency could cause serious long-term health problems. The labourer's diet was now made up of white, roller-milled bread with jam, tea and pudding, and a cheap cut of meat, such as brisket or scrag end of lamb, once or twice a week. This food was also now supplemented by potatoes, which had finally become as popular in the south as they were in the north.

Alice Foley's Lancashire factory family, by the end of the

period, would also be back on a healthy track. White bread and jam had made inroads against the porridge, and tea was also becoming more common. The availability of baking powder and the new margarine, which was so much cheaper than butter, enabled simple baking to enter a home cook's repertoire. Rock cakes were particularly popular. Potatoes remained a staple, sometimes now in the form of chips from the chip shop, along with battered fish, as a treat. Meat, too, made an occasional appearance.

The clerk in his London home (aided by Hannah's successor) would be making full use of the new range of processed foods. Frozen New Zealand lamb was a favourite among his peers, its low price allowing them often to share a joint, along with the cheaper tripe, trotters, liver, oxtail and similar cuts. A variety of table sauces, such as Worcestershire and mushroom ketchup, livened up his diet, and all could be purchased from the corner shop. Factory-made biscuits were also popular. They were relatively cheap and offered a light snack without the need to cook.

The Trollope family and their barrister's family peers would not have noticed much difference in what they were eating; the new, processed foods made an indiscernible impact upon their diet, although changes in dining fashions certainly would have been observed. Back in 1865, when formal dining '*á la française*' was still socially acceptable, Mrs Beeton included several formal dinner plans for this older method, but, by 1901, it was utterly forgotten. Dining '*á la russe*' was now how all formal occasions were organized. Dining '*á la russe*' divided dinner into a long series of different courses, each with its own crockery and cutlery, each dish carved, plated and served by waiting staff. It is a pattern we still recognize as formal dining. No food was laid upon the table except for the cruet, with its salt, pepper and other condiments, and bread rolls. The centre of the table was reserved for displays of fruit, flowers and candlesticks; tableware, too, became more decorative. In the '*á la française*' style, all the spare cutlery and glasses had been laid out on the sideboard, but this became the new preserve of the food; cutlery and glasses were instead placed upon the table at each diner's place.

The system was essentially simple: a complete set of cutlery for each course was set out, the outermost to be used first and the diner gradually working their way inwards during the meal. Glasses, however, were laid outwards from the diner. The first to be used was placed closest to him or her, and the diner would move through them diagonally as the meal progressed. Dining '*á la russe*' showcased the quality of a host's tableware, their polished silver cutlery, immaculate porcelain and glasses which glittered in the candlelight and reflected the artistic displays at the centre of the table. The food was divided into as many separate courses as could be managed, the diners taking no part in carving, passing around or serving the food. More servants were required to serve dinner in this manner, as well as more tableware, but it did mean that the carving was all done by a professional and that food could be kept in the kitchen until the moment it was needed at the table.

Another set of changes over the period which concerned the etiquette for eating with various cutlery and food implements was more subtle and ensured that wealthy gourmands developed a stranglehold over the constantly evolving set of table manners. Whether one ate their peas from the front or the back of the fork, whether one used a knife or a spoon to eat a grapefruit, whether parfait should be eaten with a dessert fork or a spoon, whether one should break a bread roll in half by hand or with a knife – all these trivial details were debated. Only those who dined regularly at the most exclusive establishments could hope to keep up with these – often unspoken – rules. Such constant change allowed ample room for some to sneer at those left behind in the great table-manners race.

By the end of the reign, the upper classes did not dine until eight o'clock in the evening. This was a shift that would not have been possible without a technological dawn in home lighting – most critically, in illuminating the kitchen. An eight o'clock dinner hour required cooks to be working long after dark in the winter, and for the washing-up to take place in fading light, even at the height of summer. Washing up by candlelight was simply not practical, and, while oil lamps were an improvement, it was not until the widespread adoption of gaslight in the 1860s, and electric light from the 1880s, that a late dining hour became possible.

Learning to Cook

Most of those who were cooking the 'dinner' or 'tea' learned how to do so from lower-middle-class women – either their own mothers, or their mistresses while they were in domestic service. Working-class mothers could not risk spoiling precious ingredients in an attempt to teach a ten-year-old, and many such women had extremely limited cookery knowledge themselves. A lifetime of bread and potatoes and a repertoire of three or four simple recipes had given them scant opportunity to develop their skills.

However, in the last twenty years of the century, a concerted effort was made to train working-class girls for their future lives, both as servants and as wives, through cookery lessons at school. Board schools devised a curriculum and printed textbooks. I own one of these textbooks; it is inscribed in the front with the name Mabel Lewis, the date 1889 and the words 'Age 11'. The hundred or so recipes are simple and clearly explained. They range from the very simplest – boiled potatoes – to such familiar British favourites as toad in the hole and steak and kidney pudding. The assortment of recipes would have been just within financial reach of the family of a skilled artisan in full employment, and eminently suitable for the family of a clerk, or similar worker, who could employ a girl to help his wife. This was therefore a cookery book and cookery course that fitted a girl for service, rather than to cook in her own home. Irish stew, with its 1lb mutton, 2lbs potato, ½lb onions, water, salt and pepper was unrealistic for the majority of working-class families; it was food for high days and holidays only – if they were fortunate.

The success of the teaching inevitably came back to the vexed question of money. For cookery lessons to be in any way meaningful, the school had to invest in cooking equipment and the girls' families had to be able to afford the ingredients. In an attempt to reach a wider audience, many schools offered evening cookery courses for girls already in employment, encouraging mistresses to pay the requisite fee. However, Mary Halliday's *Marriage on £200 a Year*, written in 1893, sums up the more usual situation: 'The mistress – as she usually does in such households – attends to the cooking herself . . . and by watching her mistress, any girl who is bright can soon gain some knowledge of cookery.' If the mistress was a good cook, with the time and patience to teach, a girl could acquire an invaluable set of skills. But for many of the young, middle-class mistresses, cooking could be a tremendous burden. If they were not wealthy enough to afford the minimum of two servants, which allow a cook to be employed, they were required to make the meals for the family themselves, alongside the added job of teaching a young girl.

The literature of the period was full of diatribes about the poor education of middle-class girls. Many felt that girls were wasting their time on fashionable 'accomplishments' such as drawing and piano playing when they should have been learning household management and cookery. Political commentators (mostly male) worried that girls on the upper rungs of society would be unable to supervise their servants if they had insufficient knowledge of the kitchen; those lower down the ladder might grow up to be terrible cooks and drive their husbands out to the chophouse (cheap restaurants of the day) or the club in search of a decent meal. In reality, most young brides felt extremely nervous and under-prepared when it came time for them to take charge in their own homes. Perhaps this was less to do with an inadequate cookery education and more to do with the daunting nature of having such responsibility at the age of twenty or so.

Cookery books filled an important role not only in reminding a young woman of all that she had ever been taught and expanding her repertoire of recipes but also in giving her reassurance that she was not entirely alone; a cookery writer was always there to help. One of the reasons Mrs Beeton's recipe collection proved so popular over so many years may well have been her willingness to provide richly detailed instructions about the very simplest of recipes. For example, there are three recipes for boiling potatoes: 'to boil potatoes', 'to boil potatoes in their jackets' and 'to boil new potatoes'. Each one gives as fulsome an explanation as that given for a soufflé or a game pie. In addition, there was nothing in the language that made one feel embarrassed at needing assistance. If you needed to know how to boil an egg or toast a slice of bread, Mrs Beeton had the answer available in simple, clear, practical terms. She and her fellow cookery writers could help a young woman to plan and cook that all-important dinner party but also to equip a twelve-year-old maid with a foundation of basic culinary knowledge.

By 1901, almost everyone who was in work was eating better than at the start of the reign. Even the sustenance of most Irish families was improving. Along with potatoes, butter and bread, a good-quality ration of bacon could occasionally feature in their diet. However, now that hunger was less of a concern, at least in most quarters, there were other considerations for families to make about food.

Food Science and Dieting

In August 1862, a 66-year-old London tradesman, William Banting, found himself struggling to climb the stairs. He had gained weight steadily since his forties and was now discovering that, at over fourteen stone, his health and quality of life were fast deteriorating. He was a short man, only five foot five, so fourteen stone was indeed large by Victorian standards. Keen to lose some of this weight, he devised a diet for himself. When he had successfully shed two and a half stone in only nine months, he published his diet and methods for others to use. William Banting turned out to be blessed with a touch of flair when it came to publicity, and to have touched a nerve in Victorian society. Before long, his name had been adapted to form a verb: 'to bant', or to diet.

Many reducing diets had been published before this, and there were any number of supposed slimming drugs on the market, but William Banting's diet proved to be much more enduring than any of them. It was based upon the simple precept of eating less starch, fat and sugar. For breakfast, his regime permitted the following: four or five ounces of beef, mutton, kidneys, broiled fish, bacon, or any kind of cold meat except pork; a large cup (or two) of tea without milk or sugar; and a small amount of biscuit or dry toast. At midday, the main meal of the day, a person was allowed five or six ounces of any fish except salmon, any meat except pork, any vegetables except potatoes; one ounce of dry toast; cooked, puréed fruit; any kind of poultry or game; and two or three glasses of claret or sherry.

Port, champagne or beer was forbidden at any time while diet-ing. A daytime snack, if eaten, was to comprise only two or three ounces of fruit; several rusks; and a cup of tea, without milk or sugar. Finally, at the evening meal, he permitted three or four ounces of meat or fish with a glass of claret.

Banting's meat, fish and fruit diet was informed by the new Victorian understanding of food and nutrition, which excited much public as well as scientific interest in the subject. Justus Frei-herr von Liebig, a German chemist, made the biggest breakthrough in the late 1830s and early 1840s not only with the most accurate chemical analysis of food in his time but by showing that foods were chemically reorganized within the body. In one experiment, he examined how a goose fed upon maize had put on fat, although the maize itself contained a negligible amount of fat. The fats were manufactured in the body of the goose, he correctly theor-ized, as the food and its constituent parts were broken apart and reassembled in new forms. He divided foods into two main groups: nitrogenous foods, which he believed were body-building nourishments (today, we would refer to these as proteins) and non-nitrogenous foods, which he believed to be the chief source of animal heat and energy (carbohydrates and fats).

Meanwhile, in America, one Dr Beaumont was researching the workings of the stomach by undertaking a direct experi-ment upon a patient who, after an accident with a gun, healed in such a way that his stomach was permanently open to view. Dr Beaumont was able to introduce foods into the living stomach and watch as the stomach digested them – not by fermentation or maceration or even putrefaction, as had previously been sug-gested, but by the action of the stomach juices. Liebig's work is heavily referenced in Mrs Beeton's *Book of Household Management* as she tries to apply the new ideas to the practice of cookery. She, like many people, saw this new information as highly rele-vant to daily life. If one had an understanding of the chemical make-up and role of foodstuffs, she felt, more economical and nutritious food could be provided. Waste could be reduced as the regime of provisioning and cooking could be more accurately targeted.

Recipes were themselves influenced by ideas of nutritive value and also of digestibility. Already, by 1845, Eliza Acton was calling on cooks to utilize Baron Liebig's advice when preparing broths by slow heating. Putting the meat into cold water and bringing it gently up to the boil could extract the maximum juices and nutrients. She discussed the need to overhaul all old soup and broth recipes in light of this new scientific information. When, later in her book, she reached the subject of boiled meats, she again returned to Liebig's work. When the meat was to be eaten, the recommendation was to drop it into rapidly boiling water so that the meat was sealed and all the goodness remained within it. Mrs Beeton, in this, as in so many things, followed Eliza Acton. And where these two giants of the food world led, the rest followed.

Manufacturers were not far behind, in rhetoric if not much else. A range of products appeared on the market claiming to be based upon the results of the work of Liebig and others. Liebig himself attempted several times to produce health foods. His meat-extract products were manufactured in Fray Bentos, in Uruguay, where ranchers had huge cattle surpluses that they were having trouble selling on the world market. The claims on the packaging stated that 1lb of the meat extract contained the goodness of 38lb of beef. His beliefs that such extracts could replace the full nutritive content of the meat itself were ill-founded, and reports to that effect were received by him with great bitterness. Yet, as an additional, supplementary food, these meat extracts did have a nutritional value and continued to sell.

Food science also turned its attention to the problem of adulteration. The attempt to pass off inferior-quality food as premium goods was not new: unscrupulous sellers and dealers had long utilized an armoury of tricks for increasing the resale value of stale, rotten or substandard goods and for padding out their wares with other, cheaper substances. In 1820, Friedrich Christian Accum published his treatise on the Adulteration of Food and Culinary Poisons, which used scientific analysis to expose the numerous substances common in this underhand trade. His book was a sensation, as much because it named and shamed the culprits as for its advances in analytical discoveries. However, frankly, it did not lead to any tangible results. Other chemists refined the techniques and again tried to bring their results to the public's attention. Laws were belatedly introduced (the first Food and Drugs Act in 1860), but had minimal effect; there was no funding for carrying out further analysis, and no will to prosecute among the authorities. The scale of fines and prosecutions did rise after the 1872 amended act, and this did at least make the adulterating practices less blatant, even if it did not succeed in stamping them out altogether.

The range of substances that were added to food during this period was astonishing, as was the near-complacency of both the authorities and the public. It was discovered that chalk and the mineral alum were almost ubiquitously present in flour and bread. Chalk was also added to milk as a whitener if it was too watery; cider and wine were sweetened with lead; and brick dust was often used to thicken cocoa. Tea leaves often contained nominal or no actual tea leaves but rather the dried leaves of a variety of hedgerow plants dyed with red lead. Most people were aware of such sharp practices, and an intelligent, informed woman was supposed to be able to circumvent the worst abuses through careful shopping; most cookery books aimed at the middle class included a section upon good marketing and best practice for grocery shopping for these very reasons. Women were also instructed in a number of simple home tests to determine the quality of the produce they bought. However, although some of the cheats were relatively easy to spot – a lot of chalk and alum in bread left it sticky and gluey – others required a degree of chemical analysis that was well beyond what even the most dedicated and knowledgeable woman could manage domestically.

Common advice to women on the subject usually petered out in a general exhortation to buy only from reputable retailers. The majority of the population, though, without the money for shopping around and seeking out quality suppliers, had no choice but to accept what they could afford. The most adulterated foods were naturally the cheapest, with bread, flour and tea suffering the largest substitution of non-edible adulterants. The poorest families, already short of nutrients, were further starved by the chalk, pipe clay and alum that replaced a portion of their bread and flour. Most knew it, too, but there was nothing they could do.

The growing popular interest in dieting during the period was unsurprising, due to the many scientific discoveries that equated food quality with health. William Banting's diet plan was merely the most famous of the 'reducing' diets; many others made it into print, as, too, did a range of more specific health diets and dietary cures. In the 1890s, a 'grape cure' had a brief phase of popularity, with two-week courses of bread and grapes – mostly grapes – being the only permitted food, and grape juice and water providing the only drink. Others, such as Dr Oetker's regime, involved exercise as well as diet, combining two strenuous bouts of what we might recognize as step aerobics a day alongside an intake of meat, fish and fruit – much like Banting's diet, although it did not allow the claret and sherry that he condoned. The vegetarian and near-vegetarian diets promulgated by Dr Allinson, who wrote in the 1880s and 1890s, offered a more balanced approach than many. He recommended these for citizens who wanted 'better health than ordinary people', and suggested pasta, vegetables and pulses for dinner, instead of meat and two veg. His ordinary diet for those who wanted to maintain good health without appearing 'odd' (and therefore still including meat) was also very different to Banting's regime. Breakfast was to be brown bread, butter and a cup of cocoa, or, for a change, porridge, eaten with brown bread and stewed fruit. For dinner at midday, it was to be four ounces of lean meat or fish with two different vegetables, as well as a milk pudding, stewed fruit or a fruit pie to follow. The last meal of the day was to be tea, which he recommended as comprising more brown bread and butter, along with some cooked vegetables or stewed fruit with a weak cup of tea.

Most modern dieticians would recommend Dr Allinson over William Banting, but both were drawing heavily upon the food science of their day. Whereas Banting called upon the work of Liebig, Allinson utilized the scientific analysis of the white, roller-milled bread of the period and its lack of both wheatgerm and bran. So concerned was Allinson that the new roller-milled bread was lacking in the essentials of life that he eventually purchased a flour mill and started his own bread company, producing a loaf that retained both wheatgerm and bran.

By the end of Victoria's reign, food was understood in Britain in a totally novel way, yet, comparing this understanding and the usual practice with today's standards is a complex matter. The vast changes in lifestyle alter much of what we believe we 'know' about food and diet. The high temperatures we maintain with central heating in our homes, schools, offices and other indoor spaces make very different demands upon our bodies than the ambient living and working temperatures of Victorian life. The level of physical activity in our daily lives is also markedly dissimilar to the Victorian norm.

At a very basic level, I have experienced these differences myself. Living in a barely heated Victorian house through a whole winter and engaging in the daily physical routine of Victorian domestic and farming life, I found that my appetite and tastes temporarily changed. Foods that I would simply dismiss in my twenty-first-century lifestyle became delicious. I was able to eat with enthusiasm the bread and dripping, the pig's trotters and the plain suet pastry with a scrape of jam. The notion of Mediterranean food seemed laughable and utterly unappealing. When I thought of more exotic foods, the tastes I imagined seemed thin and insubstantial in the taste buds of my mind; when I thought of roly-poly pudding or a dish of brawn (jellied pig's head), my mouth watered. My body was telling me in no uncertain terms that it needed plenty of carbohydrates and animal fats to sustain the Victorian lifestyle.

I also began to understand the Victorian aversion to strong flavours. Blandness is an insult often applied to nineteenth-century cookery and, undoubtedly, the use of herbs, spices and even simple flavourings like onions was sparse. I was quite amazed at how soon I adjusted to this lower level of flavouring, how quickly and how completely my palate changed. I am unsure whether this was just a matter of getting used to a different way of eating, a re-sensitizing of my taste buds, or whether it, too, was a function of the lifestyle. I became acutely aware of the subtle inflections of taste in different varieties of potatoes; gravy became an explosion of flavour; and a single clove of garlic rubbed around the bowl and then discarded could season enough mashed potato for a whole family. As for my weight, did I put on pounds as a result of the additional carbohydrates and fat? No. Did I lose any weight with all the additional exercise and hard work? No. It seems that, given the opportunity, my body regulated my food intake to fit with what was required of it.

14. A Bath before Bed

A hot bath had to wait until the end of the day, when the range or copper was free from other tasks and had reached a suitable temperature to heat the water. Bathing involved a vast amount of preparation, particularly when few people had dedicated bathrooms, plumbing of any kind or even bathtubs. When people did go to such lengths, the purposes that bathing served were often quite different from those of our own time. For most of Victoria's reign, baths were not related to cleanliness; they would travel a long way before they became the relaxing soak before bed many people in the twenty-first century think of them as.

Baths for Health

The early-Victorian bath was taken for health reasons and came in a variety of temperatures, sizes, shapes and even substances. Hot, warm or cold, there was seawater bathing, freshwater bathing, mud, air and even sunbathing, which, as the name suggests, was simply exposing the skin outdoors in good weather. There were baths for the feet, baths for the bottom and baths in which to immerse the whole body. One could take a plunge to soothe and calm your nerves, or to stimulate and invigorate your circulation. There were baths for skin problems, baths for liver and digestion difficulties, baths for rheumatism, and any number of bathing regimes for nervous disorders.

During the 1850s, when medical bathing was at its height, the

Portable Bath Company was one of the retailers to profit from
the boom. They advertised widely in newspapers and magazines
and offered a range of bathing tubs which could be purchased or
hired by the week, month or year. The company would also
supply hot water, carried in by men wearing slippers, so as not
to disturb the invalid. It made its money from the fact that most
people, including the wealthy, did not own a permanent bathtub of any sort. When physicians began to prescribe the new
regimes, it was far cheaper to buy or rent the equipment than to
visit private medical clinics for the purpose.

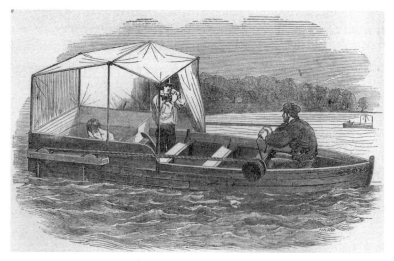

Fig. 108. The floating bath of 1850 allowed gentlemen to bath safely and
without mud in local rivers.

Bathing became known as 'hydrotherapy', and was a departure
from the long-established European practice of 'taking the
waters'. This had involved travelling to renowned springs to
drink from the waters, which were thought to possess minerals
that could cure certain ailments and conditions. However, many
commentators of the period were likely correct in their asser-

tion that the fresh air and exercise that accompanied these trips contributed significantly to their efficacy. Many health resorts actively promoted this aspect of the 'cure' by providing promenades for their patrons.

At the beginning of the nineteenth century, new uses for spring water were being developed on the continent. The most influential practitioner was Vincent Priessnitz, who was based in Silesia. His cure involved drinking the water in the traditional way, but accompanied by pouring large quantities of it over the body, too, in a variety of ways, from standing underneath waterfalls, through sitting on rising jets of water to wrapping people up in soaking bed sheets. Cold-water bathing had already begun to make an appearance by this point, particularly for men. It was believed to act as a tonic that enervated the body, the shock forcing the blood to circulate more vehemently. Acclimatizing oneself to cold temperatures was also thought to offer the body a hardening benefit, making frequent users sturdier and more resilient to common illness and disease.

The wrapping of a patient in wet sheets was entirely Priessnitz's own invention. Swathed in layer upon layer of sodden linen, the body gradually began to behave as if in a twenty-first-century wetsuit, warming the water held next to the skin. This ensuing warmth, while the body was swaddled and unmoving in the sheets, was reported as being soothing and relaxing, and received rapturous reviews in the press. The periodical *Simple Questions and Sanitary Facts* claimed that 'the wet pack [was] a simple and almost certain way of preserving health, and curing disease, where human agency is available ... It reduces fever and inflammation in a surprisingly short time.' It went on to note that the therapy was 'most deliciously soothing when the mind or body [was] over tasked and excited, and may be believed, on the authority of those whose every nerve sometimes quivers in undue excitement, to be inexpressible peace'.

The therapy arrived in Britain through the person of Dr James Wilson, who had travelled to Silesia to undergo the revolutionary new treatment himself. Having convinced his friend and colleague Dr James Gully, the two of them set about offering the treatment at the Malvern Springs in Worcestershire, long a location of medicinal water-taking. The pair were commercially astute as well as innovative, and their water cure, provided at a fee, became popular. Yet their attempts at explaining the therapeutic effects were hampered by the science of the time. Without today's knowledge of the immune system, the two doctors thought that the answers lay within the expunging of congested liquids from the body. Excess blood, in particular, was thought to collect in the tissues of a sick person, but if they could bring about a 'crisis' in the patient's body by stimulating circulation with their water cure, then the body could purge this matter in the form of urine, faeces, vomit, or through the pores of the skin. Bringing about this 'crisis' was one of the main aims of early-Victorian medicine. Drs Wilson and Gully thought that their cure offered a safer and more natural alternative to the frequently poisonous substances that were used elsewhere by doctors.

I once underwent my own brief taster treatment of the Malvern wet-sheet wrapping cure, followed by a dip in a cold sitz bath. GP Dr John Harcup, an expert in traditional Malvern water therapy, administered the treatment. He described how, in a series of experiments conducted some years ago, he had found that the white-blood-cell count of people who took a daily five-minute cold bath rose significantly. It would appear that the immune system is stimulated in much the same way as was originally claimed, although Drs Wilson and Gully could not have known about the role that white blood cells play in the fighting of disease. Dr Harcup assured me that I would find the wet-sheet packing extremely relaxing, predicting that I would fall asleep. My experience was not quite so satisfactory. I did begin to warm up eventually in the wet sheets, but it took far longer than I had expected and, though I closed my eyes, I stayed resolutely awake, and shivering. Of course, the proponents of the wet-sheet system would say that my experience merely proved how much I would benefit from a sustained course of therapy. If I were to use it daily, it could be argued that my circulation would soon improve and I would benefit not only from warming up the sheets much more quickly but I could be warmer the rest of the time too.

Next followed the cold sitz bath. The sitz can best be described as a bath that you sit in, but many people also know it as a 'hip bath', due to the height of the water level. Most Victorians would sit with their feet out over the edge, and the bath would be filled with only four or five inches of water. This would only cover a person's bottom, upper thighs and lower abdomen. Among the many benefits claimed for the sitz bath was its alleged ability to 'draw down bad humours from the head'. It was recommended for a host of stomach problems, especially for indigestion and bowel troubles. It was also commonly used for back pain. Pye Chevasse in *Advice to a Wife* seems to champion the sitz bath as a remedy to virtually all 'women's complaints'. Period pains, pain in labour and miscarriages are just some of the ailments, according to him, that can be improved by a sitz bath.

My own experience was less miraculous. I lowered myself into approximately five inches of near-freezing water, at which point more buckets of cold water were poured over me. How much this achieved for my immune system, I am unsure; I was, admittedly, tired, run down and suffering from a slight sore throat at the time. But the next day I lost my voice, and it did not return for six weeks. Ever since, I have had some reservations about the water cure.

By the end of the Victorian century, the science behind cold-water bathing had greatly improved. It was still believed to stimulate blood flow, but the wilder claims about preventing congestion were finally discredited. It was given less prominence by doctors and recommended to far fewer people, only the strongest and fittest. Instead, a range of warm and hot baths were introduced to improve one's health.

The sitz bath and the foot bath were perhaps the most widely used outside of health spas. Both were cheap and simple and came with widespread medical endorsement. The foot bath was even easier to organize at home than the sitz bath, being nothing more than a basin of warm water in which you could soak your feet for ten minutes or so. This was the first bath to be within the reach of even the working classes. Everybody had a basin of one form or another, and you only needed a kettleful of warm water. Recommended as a remedy for the common cold, it was also a bath for which many people could see a tangible use. Images abound of men sitting on chairs with their trouser legs rolled up, their feet in a bowl of steaming water and a blanket around their shoulders. It became a standardized image, visual shorthand for flu.

The warm or tepid bath was meant to soothe and relax, and it was also recommended in cases of fever, whereby gentle sponging with lukewarm water was believed to ease the condition. Teething in young children was another opportunity for the tepid bath, while skin complaints of any variety called for warmer water.

Hotter still, at the very top of the thermometer came the vapour and Turkish baths. The vapour bath was a close relative of the modern sauna. These were usually installed at specialist premises but could also be rigged up in the home if necessary. A shallow pan of boiling water was set on the floor and a chair placed over it. The undressed patient sat down on the chair, and a large blanket that reached to the ground was then thrown over them. The space inside this makeshift tent filled with steam, and the patient was encouraged to breathe deeply and bathe in the vapour. Sulphur, spirit and herbal baths could be home-produced in the same way, by simply adding the required ingredient to the boiling water.

The Turkish bath, on the other hand, was an exotic luxury for most, and mysterious to many. It was available only at exclusive bathhouses, and those that existed (Charles Dickens in his *Dictionary of London* of 1888 lists ten, only four of which catered for ladies) were expensive and out of reach to all but the upper classes. The description given in *Simple Questions and Sanitary Facts* magazine would have been enlightening to most readers. It reported that the bather would first undress then enter and stay in a hot room 'for five or ten minutes' before moving on to several 'successively cooler rooms for ten minutes'. Next they would journey to the 'warm room', where an attendant would work on their whole body, rubbing them down to remove 'all loose effete skin', and 'grasping and kneading' their muscles to keep them supple. The bather was then 'soaped and scrubbed down' before being rinsed with 'warm, then tepid and finally cold water'. They were plunged through one more cold bath and then re-entered the dressing room, where they would be dried down with warm towels. Such complexity required a huge amount of spare time and resources that most people simply did not have.

Another form of bathing that was not readily available at home was the douche bath. These operated via 'a single jet of water, varying in thickness from the size of a quill pen to the thickness of a man's forearm'. This was 'projected with great force, either from above, below, or one side, upon a particular part of the body'. At Malvern Springs, the falling douche was a huge weight of water released all at once upon the standing figure. One person who experienced the bath recalled that the water struck him 'straight on the shoulder' and 'knocked [him] clean over like a ninepin'. But, depending on personal preference, there were variations of the douche, from jets of water squirting upwards while the patient was seated to contraptions that mimicked rain.

By 1900, medical baths had become a side issue. People's fears had been assuaged by new understandings of bacteria and viruses, and water was no longer something to be looked on with caution. If the medical efficacy of bathing was slipping away, however, it had left an enduring mark upon people's habits. People now wanted to bathe to get clean.

Baths for Cleanliness

A galvanized tin bath hanging on the back of a door was not a typical Victorian sight. Not until the beginning of the twentieth century did it become common in poorer homes. Such an item represented a considerable expense for someone living on a working wage, and retailed at around twice the price of a set of children's clothing. Mining families appear to have been the first to invest in them. They did, admittedly, have the most pressing need for a thorough clean, but they also had significantly more disposable income than most working-class families; while we may think of the hardships of the miner's life, their filthy, hard and dangerous work was lucrative and made them some of the best-paid among Britain's workers.

Once a tub was purchased, the first problem was how to heat enough water to fill it. If you possessed a copper, the task was much easier. This was a large pan supported by a brick plinth with a coal firebox at the bottom (a chimney would dispense with the unwanted smoke). Stored in a scullery, away from the main cooking range or fire, its sole purpose was to act as a fixed pan for boiling water. To operate, the copper first needed to be filled. If you were living in a town and were fortunate, you may have had access to a tap or a pump on the premises. You were more likely, though, to share a pump with several other households on the street. Conversely, if you lived in the countryside, you would use the local stream or well. To have a decent-sized bath, you would need something in the region of five buckets of water. Depending on how far you were located away from your water source, filling the copper could take anywhere from ten minutes to an hour.

The next task was to light the copper fire. Fuel was, of course, expensive, but a copper fire was conveniently designed to burn cheaper materials and did not require the best-quality house coal. Many people saved lumps sifted from the cinders of the range to light their copper, and, once it was burning, anything could be used to keep the copper fire alight. Five buckets of water would take approximately an hour to come up to heat from a cold start; if the copper was already warm, it would take half the time. The final stage was to scoop the hot water out of the copper and carry it to the bath.

Not all households owned a copper; some premium kitchen ranges did, however, include a built-in water tank at one side of the fire. This provided a supply of water that could be kept permanently topped up, and hot water could be drawn from the tap at any time. These ranges usually held a gallon, or sometimes two. Obviously, such a small volume was not going to fill a bath on its own, and cold water was normally mixed in to make up the remainder. If this was still not enough, heating a kettle on the range would provide the rest. This was also the method used if you had access only to a simpler, cheaper cooking range. You would need a number of large pans and kettles to heat the water, and in order to bring all the pans up to temperature at the same time (some parts of your range would be hotter than others, depending on the concentration of the fire), you needed to rotate the pans as they heated. Careful preparation was thus essential for heating water, regardless of whether you had a copper boiler or not.

The location of your bathtub in the home was equally important. Generally, it was put in the warmest part of the house, usually the kitchen, as it was often the only room with a fire. Not only would taking your bath be much more pleasant in a warm room, but the bathwater also kept its temperature for longer. Many people tried to insulate their bathtub from the cold of the floor by laying rugs, towels or newspaper underneath it.

Having gone to these great lengths, it made sense for the whole family to use the same bathwater. It would have been unthinkable for one person to have a bath, when a simple jugful of warm water and a bowl could provide a perfectly adequate wash. Most mothers and wives also found other uses for the used bathwater, and would often soak laundry in the tub in preparation for wash day. From my own washing experiences of filling and emptying a Victorian bathtub, I can state that I was very reluctant to go through the ordeal too often, particularly when the weather was cold and the days were short.

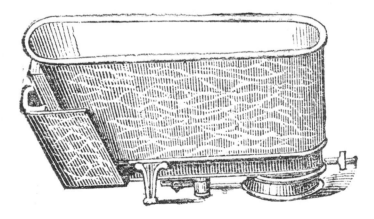

Fig. 109. A bathtub, 1880.

Towards the end of the century, upper-middle-class homes were installing baths for washing in. At first, servants were required to fill them by hand. Water was heated on the kitchen range and carried upstairs in a metal can to the dressing room. Several trips were required and, of course, the water had to be carried down the stairs afterwards to be disposed of. So much labour was costly and impractical for most households. However, bathing became much easier from the 1870s onwards, when indoor plumbing became a realistic option and the first dedicated bathrooms began to appear. Gas-fired geysers were especially helpful in providing hot water to a separate bathroom. Lord Ernest Hamilton was one of those whose family had made the investment, but still recalled the bath of his aristocratic childhood in the late 1860s and early 1870s as less than satisfactory:

> A call on the hot water supply . . . did not meet with an effusive or even a warm response. A succession of sepulchral rumblings was succeeded by the appearance of a small geyser of rust coloured water, heavily charged with dead earwigs and bluebottles. This continued for a couple of minutes or so and then entirely ceased. The only perceptible difference between the hot water and the cold lay in its colour and the cargo of defunct life which the former bore on its bosom. Both were stone cold.

Today, we are so familiar with washing ourselves regularly in clean, tiled bathrooms that we might be tempted to imagine that, as soon as the Victorians were given the opportunity to have a bath, they never looked back. Surely a hot bath would have been a necessity worth investing in? Surely everyone who could afford one would have bought one immediately?

The Victorians thought differently. There were the practicalities to consider. Even among the wealthy, home ownership was not always common. Wealthy tenants might want a bathroom, but the landlord would only install one if he could raise the rental value. Plumbing a property involved a substantial amount of upheaval as well as expense, and only structurally sound buildings and buildings that were large enough for the piping were suitable. There was also another popular alternative to bathing at home. It was known as the Public Bath Movement.

Public Bath Movement

In the twenty-first century, when we think of public baths, we think of swimming pools, but this was not their original purpose. The first public baths to be introduced in the Victorian period were just that: baths for the public to use. They were conceived as a way of offering the latest advances in personal hygiene to those who had no access to a bathroom and possibly not even piped water in their home. The earliest public-bath buildings were often connected to a laundry room, so that people could also make use of the running water and large sinks to do their weekly wash, rather than trying to manage in their own cramped and ill-equipped lodgings.

The idea first seems to have aroused interest with an article in the newspapers about a woman in Liverpool. In 1832, five years before Victoria became queen, a cholera epidemic killed hundreds of thousands, especially in the great port cities. Mrs Kitty Wilkinson was living in a very poor street in Liverpool with her husband, Tom. They were, however, in the fortunate position of owning a fitted water 'copper' which they could use to boil water relatively easily. Their house was the only building in the street to possess such a convenience. As the epidemic raged, Kitty and Tom took the initiative of opening up their superior facilities to their neighbours, converting their yard into a drying area and allowing people to do their washing in their basement and, later, in their kitchen. All they asked for in return was a contribution of 1d per family per week towards the costs of coal and water. In 1832, no one really knew how cholera spread, but it was widely believed that boiling clothes and bedding offered some protection from infection. The Wilkinsons' generosity and altruism at this moment of crisis were all the more admirable, because most of the working class was reliant upon second-hand clothing and bed-sharing. Kitty and her husband were running an increased personal risk in opening up their home to potential cholera infection, but were offering practical help to a host of frightened families. When the newspapers heard of the story, they quickly hailed Kitty Wilkinson – laundry was a female domain, so it was she, rather than Tom, who was celebrated – as the 'saint of the slums'. What made the story even more newsworthy was that she was a working-class philanthropist and, moreover, a labourer's wife who had been born in Ireland and emigrated in her youth. Of all of the Victorian social groups of the time, the Irish immigrant labourer was seen as the lowest of the pile, and here she was, dispensing the charity and applied self-help that the middle classes uneasily acknowledged as their own duty.

Spurred into action, a public wash- and bathhouse movement began. The District Provident Society and the wealthy philanthropist William Rathbone stepped in to offer their own assistance. There were various political manoeuvrings, which eventually led to the opening of the very first public baths and wash houses in Britain. It took nearly ten years but, in May 1842, the Frederick Street Baths opened in Liverpool, with Tom and Kitty Wilkinson as the superintendents. Initially, of course, it had been laundry that was the main focus, but baths to allow the working classes to wash themselves, as well as their clothes, were soon installed. Within four years, lobbying had succeeded in passing the Baths and Wash Houses Act through parliament and, from 1846, local authorities were empowered to build such facilities in their own communities, paid for out of taxes.

Fig. 110. A private bathing establishment, 1844, just before the Public Bath Movement got into its stride.

In 1846, Liverpool opened the second of its bathhouses, in Paul Street, which had six times the capacity of the Frederick Street Baths. A year later, London finally opened a public wash house in Glass House Yard, shortly followed by the Goulston Square wash house and baths in Whitechapel, deep among some of the poorest of London's housing. Within ten years, Liverpool had added a third set of baths and refurbished the original Frederick Street establishment, while, in London, they had added another seven bathhouses: two in Westminster, one at Marylebone, one in Bloomsbury, one in Hanover Square, another in St-Martin-in-the-Fields, and Poplar Baths in the East End.

The baths themselves were divided into different sections. There were male and female areas, but these were often subdivided by price or class. The best and most expensive of the baths provided spacious, richly furnished cubicles with bathtubs, plentiful supplies of hot water and space to change. Towels and soap were also available. The cheaper baths were in much more cramped and basic cubicles, but they still usually provided enough water to bathe comfortably. The cheapest option was a dip in the public plunge pool. These were seen as a place where, having changed in one of the cubicles around the edge of the pool, you just jumped in and washed alongside everyone else.

The plunge pools initially cost just ½d, rising to 1d, a time. This was the sort of fee that an earning lad of eleven or twelve could afford – indeed, the pricing had been set for that specific reason. The early plunge pools were not large, but they were mildly heated. No soap was provided – indeed, you weren't allowed to use it – but it was thought that a dip and a brisk rub-down would still provide an effective, if basic, bath. The boys would be naked – swimwear was not compulsory in most public pools until the early twentieth century – one of the main reasons pools were strictly single sex. The water, unfiltered, was changed once a week, and in many early establishments was simply river water piped in. Silt and general waste accumulated during the week, but the dipped and rubbed bodies would still be generally cleaner when they climbed out than when they jumped in. That, of course, was the thinking behind and the original purpose of the plunge pools, but they rapidly developed into something far less po-faced. The lads had fun. They larked about in the water and spent time with their friends: the plunge pools became social spaces for working-class boys. In addition to this, they were pleasantly warm environments, which must have provided great comfort and attraction to those who rarely spent much time in heated rooms of any kind. Immersing themselves in balmy water would provide a rare opportunity for the boys to drive out the deep cold from their bodies. Cleanliness was simply a by-product of the fun for many of them. People reported that small gaggles of boys often congregated outside the public baths begging for the 1d that would buy them entry. The popularity of the plunge pools led to new and even bigger pools being constructed, and these were carefully divided by class to avoid the boys' frolics interfering with the finer sensibilities of the wealthier clients. It may seem unpleasant that these lads were segregated into second- or even third-class pools, but it did offer them, perhaps for the first time, a public freedom and a place where they would not be constantly disapproved of.

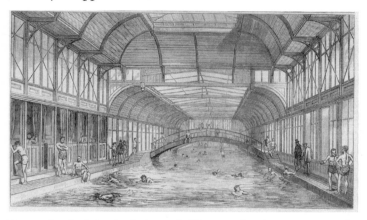

Fig. 111. London's floating baths on the Thames enjoyed great commercial success in the 1870s. Other cities, such as Chester, boasted their own floating baths.

The initial proposal for the St James's Baths in Westminster, London, which were built in 1852, was for sixty-four bath cubicles, divided into men's first- and second-class and women's first- and second-class areas. A warm bath in the first-class area was 6d, and only 2d in the second-class. A cold bath would be available for half price in both classes. Two large plunge pools, one first and one second class, would finish off the bathing facilities. The laundry department got equal billing with the bathing department. There were to be sixty cubicles for clothes washing, sixty separate drying chambers and sixteen ironing compartments – with irons and the necessary equipment provided. Use of the laundry facilities was charged at 1d per hour.

It is apparent when one looks at the provision for the two sexes that public baths, whether intended for a middle- or working-class clientele, were primarily intended for male usage – although the laundries were used exclusively by women doing the family wash. Women's baths were fewer in number, open for fewer days and, while there were several establishments which were male only, there were none that catered exclusively for women.

The laundry facilities were the first to go from the public baths too. Even fifteen years after the first one opened, the word 'wash house' had largely been dropped from the title. After that first enthusiastic flush of building was over, newer establishments rarely included any laundry facilities at all. The next amenities to suffer were the baths. However, the one increasingly popular element was the 'plunge' or 'swimming pools'. The first few had been relatively small, envisaged as washing facilities rather than recreational or sporting facilities, but, as their popularity grew, the newer bathhouses catered for the demand by building larger and larger swimming pools. Hints of this future can be seen within a decade of the first public bath opening. The description of St George's Baths – one of the original wave of complementary wash- and bathhouses – contains as its opening line the information: 'Swimming bath, 66ft by 30ft.' This was obviously considered to be the main selling point, the lead attraction; availability of the bath and prices came next; laundry facilities were at the bottom of the list. In the same section, Albany Baths, one of the more expensive establishments, saw fit to advertise swimming lessons 'taught by Prof. Parker'.

A not-insubstantial number of Victorian bath cubicles survive into the twenty-first century across Britain at public bathhouses. I used one myself as a student, and was only too glad of its prolific provision of hot water.

15. Behind the Bedroom Door

Bedtime for the curate Francis Kilvert was normally soon after eleven o'clock in the evening. Occasionally, when he had guests, he would retire later for the night, sometimes returning home from dinner parties as late as midnight. On Tuesday, 5 April 1870, he stayed up later still, talking and enjoying the convivial company of his close friend Morrell until half past twelve. But this was unusual. Working people in the period usually turned in for the night much earlier, exhausted from a day's labour and unable to afford the prolonged glow of artificial lighting. During winter, in particular, the cold and the dark encouraged people to burrow deep under their covers at the earliest opportunity. As night fell on an agricultural labourer and his family, it made scant sense to stay awake in an icy, gloomy cottage, as they would not be able to afford the expense of candles or oil for a lamp, and the extra hours awake would only intensify the hunger pangs born of their short food rations. By seven o'clock, most families were bundled up in their bed sheets, even if they were not asleep.

Warmer summer evenings could tempt people into staying up later, as Jack Wood, the son of a navvy from Oldham, recorded in his early-nineteenth-century diary: 'If it was a pleasant evening people would be sat on their doorsteps until eleven or twelve o'clock, and then go quietly inside to bed.' Only at the very end of the period, as fuel prices dropped and it became cheaper to light and heat one's home, did the hour of slumber retreat. Ellen Calvert, a young mill worker in the 1890s, was 'in bed at 10pm as work started each day at 6am'. Ten o'clock suited many people, an hour that provided ample time for an evening meal, an hour spent together with the family and enough rest for the day's work ahead. However, during every stage of the period, before men and women could enjoy the gentle release of sleep, they first had to navigate the complex world of sex.

Ideas about Male Sexuality

It was an established Victorian truth – nay, a fact, and one endorsed by the medical profession, the Church and by the population at large – that all men were possessed of a naturally strong sexual appetite. How a man should behave and how he should lead his sexual life was, however, less clear. Two schools of thought ran in parallel throughout the century. The first position, which was stated in no uncertain terms, advised that a man should be allowed an outlet for his sexual appetites, one that could be healthily achieved through a combination of wife, mistresses and prostitutes, according to one's circumstances or station in life. The other stance, much to the contrary, argued that a man should rein in his appetites and curb his lust for the sake of his morals, as well as for the sake of his physical health.

Marriage proved to be the primary battleground. Men were believed to have the fundamental right, as bestowed by the Word of God, to call on their wife at any time; it was a woman's duty to comply. Yet there also existed a strong cultural belief that a 'good' man should exercise restraint in some instances. Sex with a heavily pregnant woman, or a woman still recovering from childbirth, was not condoned; neither was sex during a woman's period, when she was ill or on the Lord's Day. If a man broke these unspoken rules, he was held to be a 'brute' and his behaviour was cast as 'beastly' by men and women alike. Sexual appetite coupled with control was therefore the ideal.

Yet a man of large sexual appetite was still admired by both sexes for his masculinity. Women expected a strong sexual appetite in their husbands, whether they welcomed it or not; a man without libido could not be resolutely called a 'man'. Medically, too, there was a conflict of ideas. It had long been held that if a man did not regularly ejaculate, his sperm could become 'stale' and lead to health problems. 'Wet' dreams were believed to be a natural and cleansing action, proper for young boys and the celibate, although some moral authorities argued that such emissions could be prevented if a man were able to banish lascivious thoughts from his waking hours. The same thinking led many men, including doctors and, occasionally, even churchmen, to recognize the need for men to have regular sex for the sake of their medical wellbeing. Masturbation was not considered to be a wholesome alternative; Dr Howe noted in 1884 that 'the occurrence of seminal ejaculations three or four times a week from legitimate sexual congress will not be felt very much by a healthy man, while the same number of losses from masturbation or nocturnal pollutions will soon super induce mental and physical debility.'

Sex with a woman was held to be the perfect cure for a range of male health problems. Men who suffered from depression, restlessness, apathy, great fatigue and headaches were all at times diagnosed as suffering from a lack of intercourse. There is no knowing how many doctors prescribed marriage, a mistress, or even a visit to a prostitute to their male patients. There are, however, several complaints in print from doctors who were angered at regularly examining male patients who had consulted them only to seek permission for promiscuity. Dr Acton, a leading physician and author in all matters pertaining to sexual health, was of the opinion that 'most people, especially the young, [were] often only too glad ... to find an excuse for indulging their animal propensities.' He considered that the symptoms complained of were 'often much exaggerated' and, accordingly, prescribed a 'low diet' and the exercise of gymnastics for such sex-starved young men. However, had you been a patient of Dr Howe, the outcome might have been different. If marriage was not an option, he wrote, 'it [was] the physician's unpleasant duty to accept the fact and to regulate [a man's] illicit intercourse.'

Such medical opinion was a widely accepted excuse for the sexual double standard regarding men and women: women were required to remain strictly chaste, while men could be permitted infidelities. Such beliefs were held, too, by women, some of whom fretted about the health of their husbands if they were personally unable, or unwilling, to meet his 'needs' themselves. Such worries continued after the period, in the 1920s, when many wives wrote letters to the Marie Stopes clinics asking for help with contraceptive matters. Despite very real fears about additional pregnancies, the guilt of refusing one's husband could be overruling.

However, if some medical opinion prescribed a routine of regular sex, there was an equally strong scientific contingent who believed that too much sex was just as dangerous. Too much sex was thought to cause general weakness and debility, leaving a man languid and depressed. In the popular imagination, something of a man's life force was spent along with his sperm, and overindulgence robbed him of his vitality and his machismo; it could actually make a man effeminate. Quite how much sex was too much sex was harder to establish. Most experts were willing to admit that it could vary from man to man, with some able to sustain three or four times a week with no loss of vigour, while, for other men, once a week was too much. Doctors usually recommended that a man regulate his sexual activity to approximately once a week, although if they experienced any feelings of fatigue immediately after sex, the interval was to be lengthened.

Impotence was generally understood as the result of previous overindulgence in sex. A long interval between the wedding day and the first pregnancy was therefore interpreted as the result of too much sex in the first, passionate phase of marriage, which overstretched the man's ability to produce high-quality sperm. Pregnancy, it was believed, would often be delayed until the first enthusiasms of love had faded into a more controlled and infrequent rhythm. In this way, sexual restraint was promoted.

Most Victorian men steered a veering course of periods of self-control and periods of self-indulgence throughout their sex lives. Even for those who maintained a strict technical chastity, confining their sexual behaviour to intercourse with their wives, their activities could oscillate. Many couples embarked upon married sex with enthusiasm, only to choose periods of abstinence in order to space out births, or to address their own health problems.

Among the middle classes, the popularity of later marriages for men caused concern. Prevailing medical opinion asserted that male desire and sexual energy rose steadily from puberty, reaching a peak at around twenty-seven years of age, before slowly subsiding. However, as middle-class men began to delay getting married until they were in their thirties, by which time they would have accumulated sufficient wealth to support a wife and a family, an enormous strain was thought to be exerted on their ability to remain chaste; this would also undermine their facility to father children, as they had missed the most fertile period of their lives. Campaigners who strove to rid sexuality of its double standards, to move male continence into line with feminine chastity, were also keen to promote early marriage for men as a means of removing temptation and providing greater health, emotional happiness and sexual fulfilment. A marriage, however, should not take place too early either; sex could undermine a growing boy's health as well as his mental development. Most doctors and parents recommended that the earliest age for a young middle-class man to be wed was around twenty years of age. Somewhere between twenty-two and twenty-four years of age was considered perfect. This ensured that a young man had sufficient time to have finished growing, but no time for dissipation or sexual frustration to have set in.

The extremely fragmentary evidence that has survived of prostitute's clients (rather than of the prostitutes themselves) seems to indicate a strong bias towards the single man. Police records only named the clients when a wrong-doing had occurred, such as a fight or a theft. In such cases, aliases were often employed, but 'bachelor' was still the most frequent moniker. Private investigations conducted by concerned doctors, such as Dr Acton, and clergymen and journalists, such as Henry Mayhew, compounded the evidence. Soldiers, of whom only 10 per cent were given permission to marry, were a particularly well-represented demographic. (The rank and file were required to gain the permission of their commanding officer before they could marry, and the army insisted that no more than one in ten of its men should have that privilege at any one time.) A pattern of prostitute use during bachelorhood, which was later renounced in marriage, was commonly expected among Victorian men. Much discussion between partners about venereal disease fell into an acknowledgement of this pattern; couples feared that the sins of the man's youth would be brought into the marriage bed and corrupt their virtuous adulthood. Many fictional discourses gave credence to these attitudes, and the characters who seduced innocent girls were rarely portrayed as married men. The character of the 'rake', such as Mr Bellingham in Elizabeth Gaskell's ground-breaking 1853 novel *Ruth*, was thought to be a dissolute single man who had never been married. The 'reformed rake', however, another stock Victorian character, would be rescued by the love of a virtuous young woman and renounce his wicked past before they were married.

Masturbation

In the last half of the nineteenth century, masturbation, or, rather, a fear of masturbation, became close to a national obsession. Boys were considered to be most at risk from this 'evil' and in need of education and protection. Fathers, mothers, doctors, religious leaders and schoolmasters were all pressed into service to teach adolescents the inherent dangers of the vice and to instruct them in how to develop the necessary defences of self-control to resist its temptations. The new medical advances of the nineteenth century seemed to corroborate the older worries about a man expending his life force. Couched in clinical language, by the 1850s, doctors were linking masturbation with softening of the brain, insanity, epilepsy, dementia, asthma, nervousness, depression, hysteria and suicide. The basic argument stated that since a man's semen was the carrier of new life, its production must require a prodigious amount of energy. This was easily demonstrated by the fact that after ejaculation the testicles took longer to produce more semen and that a second ejaculation soon after the first resulted in an inferior 'yield'.

Moral fears compounded the medical concerns. Masturbation was perceived as a gateway activity, one that could lead to a life of immoral habits. Boys who abused themselves would easily fall prey to using prostitutes and taking mistresses. Such lewd behaviour would make them unfit husbands with no respect for women. In short, masturbation destroyed a boy's moral fibre.

Later in the century, from the 1880s onwards, the anxieties surrounding masturbation were joined by the perceived threat of homosexuality (which we will explore at the end of this chapter). As soon as homosexuality entered the public consciousness fully, it, too, was added to the growing list of consequences of masturbation.

Public schools were at the forefront of the autoeroticism epidemic. In 1866, Dr E. B. Pusey wrote to *The Times* about the perils of self-satisfaction in such institutions. He claimed that the despicable practice had been almost unknown fifty years before but had now become 'the besetting sin of our boys; it is sapping the constitutions and injuring in many the fineness of intellect.' It is difficult to imagine any other sexual issue being discussed in so public a forum. While a veil was drawn over so much of the Victorian experience of sex, masturbation was firmly in the spotlight.

One of the main criticisms of public schools was that boys caught the bad habit from each other. In this way, one 'corrupt' boy could lead a whole school into sin. Those who fulminated against the practice believed that it began with lewd language and furtive demonstrations. Schools responded by separating boys into their own beds (bed-sharing had previously been common, for reasons of economy and warmth) and moving these beds into separate cubicles, rather than their being in long, open dormitories. The rise of organized athletics and sport on the curriculum was in part another response to the fear of masturbation; most medical men and teachers believed that physical exercise was a preventative measure: 'send the boys to bed tired, and you'll have no trouble,' remarked one master. Food was also a consideration; large, hot meals were held to stimulate sexual appetite. To prevent this, supper was required to be a light, cold meal taken early, several hours before bed. Fewer bedclothes were another measure, recommended by Dr Dukes in his book

Health at School in 1894. A cooler bed would ensure that passions were kept cool, as would cold baths; there were stern warnings about the dangers of warm baths in the evening.

However, despite all these practical measures, as well as regular forthright sermons in public schools on Sundays, the onus remained on parents to teach their sons to exert self-control and to exhort them to chastity. American advice literature (also published in Britain) at the end of the century was strident in demanding that parents have these conversations with their sons. This was sometimes a father's area of responsibility, and some men in later life recalled such conversations with their agonizingly embarrassed fathers. Lord Lyttelton, a father of twelve and a respected Conservative politician during the period, sent his sons off to public school with a letter 'fine and robust in tone' about the moral dangers they might face, closing it with the words, 'I do not wish you to acknowledge this letter or ever to say anything to me about having received it.' Yet some advice books made it clear that the subject should already have been broached much earlier in a boy's life by his mother. According to Jane Ellice Hopkins, who founded the White Cross Army for 'social purity', a boy's mother should explain to him at an early age (at four or five, according to one book) that all impure thoughts and any action that stimulates impure feelings must be avoided. Dr Elizabeth Blackwell endorsed such training of children: 'The mother should caution the child plainly not to touch or meddle with himself more than is necessary; that his body is a wonderful and sacred thing, intended for important and noble ends, that it must not be played or trifled with, or in any way injured.'

Unlike almost any other form of perceived moral lapse, masturbation was believed to be more of a problem among the middle classes and their sons than among the poor. Admittedly, working-class boys lived under the constant eye of their mothers, were engaged in heavy outdoor work from an early age and were unlikely to be eating large, hot meals late at night or, for that matter, sleeping in sultry, feathered beds after luxuriating in warm baths. Due to their pitiful diets, cold living quarters and lack of exercise, the poor, at least in the eyes of society, were in much less moral danger from the 'solitary vice' than middle-class boys at school. Only in institutions would large numbers of boys be gathered at night and bad habits transmitted.

Female Sexuality

It is a popular misconception in the twenty-first century that the respectable Victorian woman was prudish and uninterested in sex. During the period, the oft-repeated statement made by the prominent doctor William Acton in 1857 that 'the majority of women (happily for them) are not very much troubled with sexual feelings of any kind' was, however, but one voice among many. Much literature disagreed and openly acknowledged that young married women took great pleasure in having sex with their husbands. William Cobbett in 1838 wrote that 'Nature has so ordered it, that men shall become less ardent in their passion after the wedding day, and that women shall not. Their ardour increases . . . and they are surprisingly quick sighted and inquisitive on this score.'

Common medical opinion professed that women were divided into three distinct groups when it came to sexual feelings. The first set had minimal or no sexual desire, the second set (the most numerous of the three) had a moderate sexual appetite, and the third group, though fewer in number, were subject to fierce passions. Even authors such as Dr Howe, who was suspicious of female sexuality in general, occasionally noted a propensity for feminine pleasure and conceded that orgasms did exist, at least for some women. He recounted the existence of sex toys manufactured for female use, noting that they were 'sold by means of unscrupulous female agents to school girls and others who [would] not take the risks incurred in ordinary sexual intercourse.' Wooden and leather toys were replaced with the modern rubber dildo by the middle of the century, which was a more comfortable and hygienic device that enjoyed a quiet surge in popularity. Accordingly, female self-pleasure was a major subject of discussion during the period, but not on the same scale as male masturbation. Auto-eroticism for women was considered to be less common and less damaging to the body than male 'abuse', for, while a girl might be degrading herself morally and, as several male commentators pointed out, spoiling her future enjoyment in 'real' sexual intercourse, she was not wasting her vital essence in the same way as was a man.

Dr Allbutt, writing in *The Wife's Handbook*, was insistent that both husband and wife should maintain a happy state of mind during sex. This followed a long-held, wildly contradictory set of beliefs that the mental well-being of both parents at the moment of conception could determine the characteristics of a child. Drunken sex, for instance, was believed to produce coarse, stupid children, whereas violent sex made them brutish. Unloving sex made for children who would be cold and cruel in later life, and a mother who was passionless produced children who were languid. However, lustful intercourse made for impetuous offspring who lacked self-control. The perfect conception, it was believed, occurred when both parents came together with love, consideration, control and pleasure.

This was but one in a range of traditional theories about sex. As Victoria's reign began, many people still held to the ancient belief that a woman's sexuality was latent in girlhood and only 'awakened' on her wedding night by her husband. From that moment onwards, her sexual appetite was thought to be lascivious, and greater than that of men. It was in need of firm male control, and it was up to husbands to ensure the carnal discipline of their wife. William Cobbett's comments in 1838, quoted above, about the wedding night were a reiteration of these lasting beliefs. The ideal bride was modest, naive, virginal and seeking an emotional rather than a physical connection with her bridegroom. Intense cultural pressure called upon women to suppress and hide their interest in sex prior to marriage. Once in union, when such pleasures were culturally accepted, desires were unshackled and, thenceforth, many women could be sexually liberated. Famously, Queen Victoria enjoyed an active and mutually pleasing sex life with Prince Albert. In a note to Lord Melbourne, she described her wedding night as 'most gratifying and bewildering' and in her journal recorded that they 'did not sleep much'. Elsewhere, although the language was generally discreet, many other married women documented an enjoyment of sex. In the 1840s, despite ten children and twenty years of marriage, Henrietta Maria, wife of Lord Stanley of Alderley, still bemoaned her 'cold bed' when her husband was away in letters to her friends. Ten years later, Isaac Holden and his second wife, Sarah (née Sugden), had to endure similarly long separations due to Isaac's business. She wrote to her absent husband that she was missing him and longed for them to be 'entwined in each other's embrace'.

Science was to challenge an altogether more serious set of traditional beliefs about sex. Previously, it had been widely thought that a woman needed to experience pleasure in order for her egg to be fertilized. This thinking stemmed from the 'evidence' that the male orgasm was irrevocably connected to the ejaculation of sperm. In his 1814 manual for the legal profession, Samuel Farr wrote that 'without an excitation of lust, or the enjoyment of pleasure in the venereal act, no conception can probably take place.' By the 1850s, however, doctors had largely come to accept that a woman could conceive without an orgasm, or indeed without 'enjoying' the act on any level. A woman, it was discovered, could become pregnant following an act of rape. While the new understanding afforded a few women justice and some sympathy in their plight, the most widespread and pervasive effect of the research was to exert pressure on women to maintain a sexless nature from spinsterhood into marriage.

However, the attitude towards passion had begun to change. Dr George Naphey, in his work *The Physical Life of Women* (1869), reported that some women came openly to pride themselves upon their distaste for sex and boasted of their indifference to passion. Elsewhere, even within marriage, passion was deemed a sign of degeneracy, to such an extent that it became a source of unhappiness and confusion for many couples. Mary Sidgwick, who married the Revd Benson in 1859, conceded that her own self-image as a 'pure' and 'good' woman, combined with her new husband's belief in her 'simple purity' contributed to the difficulties of their honeymoon: 'how I cried at Paris! . . . the nights!'

The prevalence of the sexless ideal can also be observed in the novelist Charles Kingsley's words prior to meeting, and marrying, Fanny Grenfell in 1844. He demanded that any future wife of his must be 'subject to like passions with myself!' and not an 'angel, passionless, unsympathetic'. From the middle of the century, as the desire for the 'purity' of women became a more established attitude, a shift occurred from the need for men to control the exuberant sexuality of married women to a position in which women were called upon to restrain and curb the sexual behaviour of their husbands. In later life, Mary Benson realized that one of her husband Edward's motives in choosing her as a wife had been 'to preserve himself from errant feelings in love'. He had, after all, known her since she was seven years old and married her when she was eighteen (he was thirty at the time). He believed that her 'simple purity' would act as a brake upon his powerful libido.

Another major influence on the habits of female sexuality, however, was inevitably the frequency of pregnancy and childbirth. The fear of pregnancy after a string of difficult births and the struggle to feed more hungry mouths made many women approach sex with trepidation. Working-class women could be particularly affected by this fear. At the end of the century, Maggie Fryett, a mother of three children, was keen to avoid the fate of her mother, who had given birth to a family of fourteen. Of her mother's experience, she wrote, 'I didn't want that. So I stayed up mending [clothes] . . . my husband would be asleep when I came to bed.'

Contraception

The vulcanization of rubber in 1843 offered a major improvement to the technical performance of contraceptive devices. Prior to the 1820s, condoms had enjoyed a long history, not so much as contraceptive devices, but as a means to improved male health. Wearing a condom during sex could prevent the transmission of sexual diseases and, in particular, syphilis, the disease that most men feared. The late eighteenth century saw the establishment of two shops in London dedicated entirely to the sale of condoms. Made out of sheep's guts, these condoms were carefully soaked for a couple of hours before use, to soften them and make them pliable and easy to put on. A ribbon was tied around the base to fasten them securely, and once they had been used they were carefully washed out, allowed to dry and stored in a small box until they were wanted again. Such sheaths were convenient for the wealthy man who had an established mistress or attended a regular brothel and whose visits could be planned and leisurely. More casual encounters rarely benefited from the protection of a condom.

I have attempted to make such condoms, but the handwork required is remarkably precise and complex. The sheep's gut has to be thoroughly cleaned, soaked in an alkali solution and stripped of all its adjoining tissue to leave only the gut wall. Such washing needs to be administered with care if the sheath is not to have holes in it. The cleansed gut is then cut into lengths and put over a wooden former, where a ribbon is rolled into one end and the other end firmly tied with a length of fine thread. When mostly dry, the condom is removed from the former and allowed to dry completely before being boxed up. Once made, these condoms would have sold for between 2d and 6d, but they were not so inexpensive as to encourage much working-class use.

Condoms made from vulcanized rubber, however, were a much more pleasant and reliable option. They enjoyed a surge in popularity in their rubber guise, as did the cervical cap, which was transformed, making it cheaper, easier to use, and more durable and comfortable to wear. The cap had an additional advantage in that it could be used by a woman discreetly, without the knowledge of the man. A description of the cap in Dr Allbutt's *The Wife's Handbook* draws parallels with the twenty-first-century equivalent: 'The pessary is in shape something like a round dish cover, the dome portion of which is made of thin, smooth India rubber which will collapse at a touch, the rim surrounding the cover portion is made of a ring of thick rubber which can be squeezed to any shape. The hollow portion of the pessary is intended to cover the neck and mouth of the womb during intercourse, so that no semen may penetrate into the womb.'

These two devices, however, were not the only options available to Victorians. In 1823, Francis Place published a series of pamphlets and handbills expressly intended to inform the British working class about the benefits of the sponge for contraceptive purposes. The sponge was a method that had been in use on the continent and was well known among elements of the well-travelled upper classes. It was another method of birth control that was in the hands of the woman, rather than the man. A small segment of sponge was attached to a length of ribbon, soaked in a spermicidal solution such as alum and water, and then inserted into a woman before sex. Afterwards, it could be retrieved by means of the ribbon and washed out.

Richard Carlisle was an author and activist who promoted the popular use of contraception. In his publication *Every Woman's Book*, which sold over ten thousand copies, he recommended condoms, coitus interruptus and the sponge method. Like Francis Place, Carlisle's writing came in for public condemnation and prosecution due to the scandalous nature of its subject, but the authorities could not stop the information that was now in the public domain.

In 1834, yet another method of contraception was introduced into the market. First described in Charles Knowleton's book *Fruits of Philosophy*, the vaginal douche worked by squirting a solution from a syringe into a woman's vagina two or three times shortly after intercourse (normally within five minutes). The logic was that this would sluice the sperm out of the vagina before it had a chance to begin its journey into the womb. Plain water could be used in the syringe, or a woman could make up a spermicidal solution for greater efficacy. Alum and water was recommended, as was sulphate of zinc with water, vinegar and water, saleratus (sodium bicarbonate) or liquid chloride of soda with water. The syringe was loaded with the solution and the woman squatted over a bowl, squirting the mixture into her vagina and allowing it to run out.

The work of Place and Carlisle was deeply radical for the period; they proposed a variety of contraceptive measures and argued for their use as tools for the health and well-being of women. Place was primarily concerned with sparing women from pregnancy when their health was in danger either from weakness and debility, or from deformations of the pelvis, which could bring about miscarriages and stillbirths. Carlisle was more rebellious still, claiming that contraception should free women to enjoy sex without the worry of possible pregnancy and should allow a more equitable and happily married life. Such forward-thinking ideas would resonate fully a century later, but at the time were still rejected by large swathes of society, particularly among the religious.

However, thanks in part to their teaching, the overall birth rate in England began to fall in 1876, and it was to continue to fall year on year until the 1920s. Among urban middle-class families, the fall could be traced back to the 1850s. The change spoke more of a shift in attitude, which was in time to pervade all levels of society, than of the impact of the new contraceptive devices themselves (there is no definitive evidence of exactly how many products were sold). Large families began to be seen as an active choice, and not an altogether responsible one. Having a smaller family became desirable, removing the strain on financial resources, and allowing families to concentrate on the welfare and education of their existing children. Fewer pregnancies typically left wives with more robust health, enabling them to play a full and active role in running their households and caring for their children and husbands. There had, of course, always been individuals who had restricted their fertility for various reasons before, but this was a new, society-wide response: a new cultural goal, a new way of defining oneself as virtuous and modern. For the last twenty years of the nineteenth century, the typical middle-class home was likely to contain no more than four or five children. According to the census, English couples who married between 1861 and 1869 had an average of 6.9 children, a figure which had remained steady since the start of Victoria's reign. However, those who married in the years between 1890 and 1899 had, on average, 4.3 children.

How to account for this decrease exactly is unclear. Certainly there were more contraceptive options than there had ever been before. But several of the contraceptive methods also had a range of uses unrelated to contraception. Vaginal douches were employed for a host of perceived medical purposes. Most doctors and midwives, for example, employed them to clean out the vagina after a birth, hoping thereby to reduce the chances of infection. To some people, they were simply part of a general cleanliness regime, akin to the use of a bidet. The cervical cap, too, is hard to differentiate from other vaginal pessaries which were employed medically for all manner of female complaints. Most families could have achieved the reduction in the number of pregnancies without recourse to any purchased item. Self-control was the prevailing sexual virtue for both men and women. As we have noted, both male and female health was considered to suffer if too much sex was indulged in, even within marriage. Such pressure came from medical authorities, religious authorities, popular advice literature, fiction, educational writers and schoolmasters. Couples wishing to limit the size of their family turned to abstinence much more readily than they turned to contraceptive devices. The withdrawal method (coitus interruptus) was likely to be an extension of this self-control. The euphemism 'being careful' came to represent the practice shortly after the Victorian period ended.

Abortion

Abortion, too, was perhaps a reason for the drop in birth rates at the end of the century. The full horror and extent of back-street abortion will never be known, but the disposal of life took on a number of forms. Dr Pye Chevasse, in *Advice to a Wife*, took great pains to point out that a foetus was alive before 'quickening' and that getting rid of a pre-quickening foetus was still abortion. 'Quickening' was the moment when a woman first felt her child move inside her. Traditionally, this had been taken as the moment when the baby became a living being; the very word 'quick' was an old one meaning 'life'. This had led to a firm belief that disposing of a foetus before it had quickened was not a sin, since it was not yet a living creature. Dr Pye Chevasse roundly condemned the large numbers of couples whom he imagined committed such abortions, and recommended with venom that for such parents, 'Transportation if not hanging ought to be their doom.'

For others, abortifacients induced a self-deception, whereby people could perceive abortion and 'bringing on a period' as two distinct and unrelated actions. Marketed widely as 'female pills', well known abortifacients were sold over the counter under the pretext of keeping a woman's periods regular and preventing a range of illnesses associated with menstrual difficulties. There were multiple brands of 'female pills' available at most pharmacies, or you could make your own; recipes were featured in popular magazines and advice books. They were advertised as general health tonics, as well as helping to stimulate the menstrual flow. The 1883 edition of *Consult Me*, a family advice book aimed at the respectable middle-class wife, contained two recipes, both including aloes, turpentine (which can cause kidney failure when ingested), lobelia (a purgative similar to nicotine that is particularly dangerous to pregnant women) and black cohosh (a relative of the buttercup, currently used in herbal preparations treating menopause), among other ingredients, to 'remove female obstructions, for headaches, lowness of spirit, nervousness and sallowness of the skin'.

Many women seem to have self-administered these toxic substances as a matter of course every month, either as a form of contraception or as a perceived health tonic, although the outcome would have been the same in both cases for a newly pregnant woman. One Victorian woman was fully aware of the use of abortifacients as a method to control the size of her family. Faith Dorothy Osgerby was born in 1890, an event that her mother admitted to having tried to prevent. Faith recalls her mother telling her that 'she even took gunpowder to get rid of me, mixing it to a paste in a soap dish on her wash stand every night.'

Sex outside Marriage

Estimates varied wildly for how many women made their living from prostitution during the period. The Bishop of Exeter thought it was as much as eighty thousand in London alone in 1839. However, as an anonymous writer in the *London City Mission Magazine* correctly objected, this would have meant that one in five of the entire female population aged between fifteen and fifty in London were prostitutes, a figure that was unquestionably bogus. The *Mission Magazine* suggested, along with others, that such exaggerated figures were based upon a desire to scaremonger and to drum up support for a range of 'moral missions' rather than on accurate data. Far more realistic, and likely to be the best estimates, were the figures given by the police, since their numbers were compiled at local level by officers on the watch and included all the women they knew of, not just those who were prosecuted. Such figures were still underestimated, due to the fact that 'kept women' and mistresses were largely invisible to the police, but they were at least based upon the observations of people who knew the areas well. In 1857, police figures for the whole of the Metropolitan Police District were declared as 8,600, around a tenth of the Bishop of Exeter's rather histrionic estimate. This gives a ratio of somewhere in the region of one woman in fifty. It is still an astonishingly high number, which goes some way towards explaining why prostitution was a perennial talking point during the period.

Period literature was rife with stories about 'fallen women'. The religious press carried more column inches than their more secular counterparts, including morality tales about the perils of succumbing to temptation, which constituted a major thematic thread in magazines such as *The Quiver*, which was aimed at Baptist readers, or *Sunday at Home*, which was aimed at a Church of England audience. Elizabeth Gaskell's *Ruth* is not only, to my mind, the best-written account of prostitution, but also the bravest and most sympathetic of stories in this tradition. The book charts the life of the eponymous heroine from abject poverty, working in a dressmaker's sweatshop, to seduction by Henry Bellingham, a young aristocrat who offers her help when she is sick and desperate. Once she is pregnant with his child, he abandons her. Even the courageous Mrs Gaskell could not allow her heroine to find complete peace and forgiveness from society (Ruth later dies), but Ruth still achieves a form of redemption through her love and care for her child, who is granted hope and a future. The novel caused a storm of protest at its boldness in addressing the subject matter with such warmth and understanding, but it also aided further discussion. Newspapers and sermons alike were also heavily involved in the public debate.

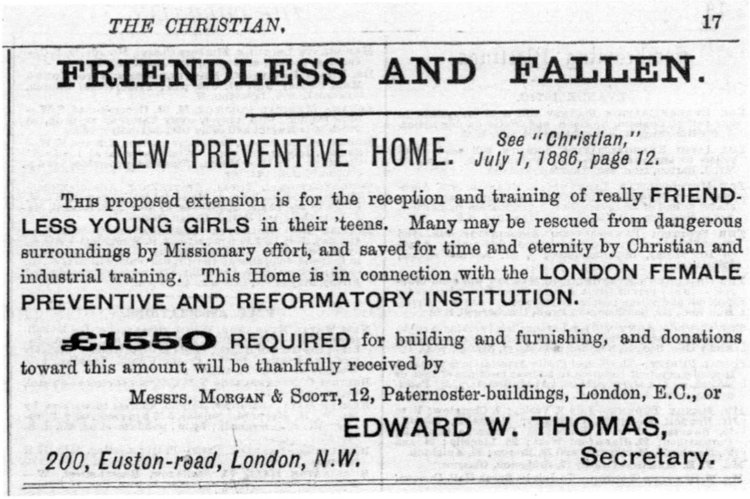

THE CHRISTIAN. 17

FRIENDLESS AND FALLEN.

NEW PREVENTIVE HOME. *See "Christian," July 1, 1886, page 12.*

This proposed extension is for the reception and training of really **FRIENDLESS YOUNG GIRLS** in their 'teens. Many may be rescued from dangerous surroundings by Missionary effort, and saved for time and eternity by Christian and industrial training. This Home is in connection with the **LONDON FEMALE PREVENTIVE AND REFORMATORY INSTITUTION.**

£1550 REQUIRED for building and furnishing, and donations toward this amount will be thankfully received by

Messrs. Morgan & Scott, 12, Paternoster-buildings, London, E.C., or

EDWARD W. THOMAS,

200, Euston-road, London, N.W. **Secretary.**

Fig. 112. Fallen women were widely discussed in all forms of the Victorian media. This charity appeal comes from *The Christian* magazine, 1886.

Homes and reformatories for fallen women were a popular charitable activity involving large numbers of middle-class people, especially women, in fund-raising and personal visits. Charles Dickens founded his own such institution, Urania House, while the poet Christina Rossetti devoted much of her time to working with young women in another halfway home. Meanwhile, as we shall examine shortly, in the political world two major pieces of legislation were about to be passed amid flurries of protest and discussion: one seeking to confront venereal disease and the other to raise the age of consent. This was not a subject that was ignored or suppressed. In many ways, it was more openly talked about, and more regularly debated, than it is in the twenty-first century.

In the early years of the reign, the main debate centred around sexual health and control of the commercial sex industry. Inspired by the continental practice of government-controlled and licensed brothels, it was proposed that Britain should impose health checks and treatment for prostitutes to prevent the spread of disease. One of the most influential advocates was the doctor William Acton. His 1857 book on the nature of British prostitution is the fullest description we have of the Victorian industry in London. He describes a world not of organized brothels but of individual women largely working for themselves, taking clients back to lodging houses and renting rooms by the hour. He depicted women who, for the most part, were elegantly and neatly dressed, with very few sporting make-up, quite unlike the popular cartoons of the day, which regularly characterized prostitutes with garishly painted faces and vulgar dresses. Men, it seemed, were repulsed by such displays, just as eager to see their illicit sexual partners conforming to the wider Victorian view of womanly beauty as they were for their sisters, wives and daughters to do so.

Acton described music halls (see Plate 24), theatres, dance halls and restaurants as the main areas of solicitation; very few respectable women – i.e. women who were not prostitutes – were present in the throng. In London in the 1850s, one such well-known area was the West End. Parks and pleasure gardens that were thoroughly respectable places by day changed their character as the evening wore on. By ten o'clock at night, the women at Cremorne Gardens by the River Thames, and those, too, at the gardens at North Woolwich, Highbury Barn and Rosherville were all available for hire, although such hire was quietly negotiated, and the men approached the women rather than the other way around. The Argyll Rooms and the Holborn casinos were favourite places for finding a prosperous, well-dressed prostitute, as well as being places to gamble and smoke. The Alhambra Music Hall was known for its especially alluring corps de ballet. As the night drew to a close and the music halls and theatres shut, the bars, cafés and clubs around

Haymarket became the focus of attention, and the mood more raucous. While the West End was the predominant soliciting area of London, in the East End, cheaper forms of sex could be sought around certain public houses and most music halls. The London Music Hall, usually known as the Shoreditch Empire, the Royal Cambridge Music Hall on Commercial Street and the Hoxton Hall were the largest premises, each attracting mixed and often rowdy crowds. Further north, Wilton's Music Hall enjoyed a vigorous life between 1859 and 1888, before it was converted into a Methodist mission. However, of all the Victorian music halls, this is the one that has survived largely unscathed. A visit today will still give you an indication of the exuberant appeal of such places. There was a much greater degree of social integration in these less prosperous areas; estimable women conversed happily with 'dubious' acquaintances, even late at night. This made it more common for prostitutes to solicit their clients; men feared to make the approaches themselves because it was probable that the 'prostitute' could actually be the respectable wife of the burly dockworker beside her. Such behaviour would not have been tolerated in the West End; a gentleman who was merely there to enjoy a night out at the theatre and a quiet smoke in a convivial atmosphere would have been gravely offended by such solicitation.

According to William Acton, prostitution in other towns operated similarly, although both Oxford and Cambridge seemed to him to be short of prostitutes for the size of their populations. One of his most thorough investigations outside the metropolis was in the garrison town of Aldershot, due to the large numbers of unmarried servicemen. Here he recorded a relatively small number of women: 243 recognized prostitutes, alongside 12,000 troops in the town. In his estimation, the women were accepting eight to ten clients each night. The 'trade' was centred on a small number of public houses such as the Army and Navy on King's Road and the Royal Military Hotel on the high street. The women who lived and worked in these areas were in financial bondage to the landlords, who rented them rooms and allowed them to solicit in their pubs only if both they and their clients purchased drinks.

However, the reports that Acton penned led not to the regulated brothels of France but to a number of controversial statutes, including the Contagious Diseases Acts of 1864, 1866 and 1869, which allowed the forcible medical examination of any woman believed to be a common prostitute, and her detention in special isolation hospitals. Such legislation was introduced to protect men, particularly soldiers and sailors, from contracting sexual diseases. It had generally been thought that more than one in four prostitutes was suffering from venereal disease, most frequently gonorrhoea. This was based on scant evidence, although figures did suggest that a third of all men on the army sick list were suffering in this way. The only way to curb this problem, it was thought, and to prevent a nationwide epidemic, was to have the prostitutes 'committed'; no restriction was put upon male clients. By 1869, any woman in a garrison town could be arrested on mere suspicion of being a prostitute and subjected to a vaginal examination against her will. Those with an infection could then be incarcerated in a 'lock hospital'. Once inside, the women were stripped, bathed and issued with institutional clothing before they were subjected to a regime of two internal inspections a week with a speculum and required to flush out their vaginas with a medicated solution using a 'vaginal douche' four times a day. Most were incarcerated for a six-week period, although some found themselves locked up for six months.

Protest was immediate and became a cause célèbre of the newly emerging women's rights movement; the Contagious Diseases Acts legislation is often cited as one of the founding moments of modern feminism. Fears that young and respectable working-class women were being subjected to what amounted to sexual assault, and even rape, in the name of the law, became an outrage that united women across society to stand up for their human rights. The gross inequality of the acts, which condoned male sexual behaviour while penalizing and imprisoning working-class women, led to a more general campaign for fairness and for greater female representation in all seats of power, both professional and political. Their suffragist battle and society's fight against vice became inextricably entwined for the rest of the Victorian period.

The Contagious Diseases Acts were, thankfully, repealed in 1884. However, at around the same time, a new scandal erupted into the news: white slavery and child prostitution. In 1884, the journalist Alfred Dyer reported on the trade of young British girls to brothels in Belgium, followed in 1885 by an investigation by another journalist, William Stead, published under the title 'Maiden Tribute of Modern Babylon', which recounted the abduction, incarceration and rape of girls, many of whom were not yet in their teens. A brothel keeper on the Mile End Road related to him how 'I once sold a girl twelve years old for £20 to a clergyman, who used to come to my house professedly to distribute tracts.' These stories make lurid reading, with tales of children enticed into houses with promises of treats. Older girls were either sought out from agencies who found work for servant girls, befriended at the workhouse door or deceived by the offer of honest work. Once inside, the children would be drugged, subjected to beatings and tied to bedsteads. Men would then pay large amounts of money to abuse them. Perhaps even more horrifying are the stories of children sold into the life by their parents. 'Mrs. N—, of B—street, Dalston, required little persuasion, but her price was higher. She would not part with her daughter under £5 or £10, as she was pretty and attractive, and a virgin, aged thirteen, who would probably fetch more in the open market.' To illustrate his argument even more graphically – and of course to sell papers – Stead actually purchased twelve-year-old Eliza Armstrong from her mother in the East End of London to show how easily and cheaply such a thing could be organized. The newspaper articles aroused widespread disgust and anger, and a rapid parliamentary response. By 1885, the age of consent had been raised from thirteen to sixteen years of age, which began to offer at least younger girls some protection.

However, despite the political campaigning and public outrage, most of the women who worked in the sex industry had to continue with the practicalities of their lives. In the poorest districts of the largest industrial cities, sex workers could be as young as twelve years of age, but most were in their mid- to late teens; very few women over thirty worked as prostitutes. They largely lived alone in lodgings and paid much higher rent than 'respectable' tenants. While most worked in more prosperous, entertainment-rich areas, taking their customers back to rooms that they hired by the hour, their lodgings were situated in the lowliest streets. A London girl might meet her clients at a café in the Haymarket and work from an 'accommodation house' in Oxendon. But she might maintain a room for herself back in Whitechapel. Some women did take clients to their own lodgings, though only if they were near enough to their place of trade. Sex outdoors, often in one of the public parks, was a cheaper option, but was far more dangerous, incurring the risk of prosecution and imprisonment, alongside a much greater exposure to casual violence.

The money for a successful sex worker was good, at least in comparison to the wages a working-class girl could earn. A prostitute could make in two or three nights what a servant girl could make in a week of drudgery. Even including the high rent such women were charged, they were more financially secure than most female factory workers and servants, their work was generally less physically taxing, their hours were much shorter, and most were able to keep their own independence, away from the supervision and interference of masters, mistresses and parents.

The stories of the lives of two individuals serve to show the realities of those who traded in extramarital sex. Mary Davies (née Kelly) was just nineteen years old when her husband was killed at work in a coal mine in South Wales. Estranged from the local branch of her family, she moved to Cardiff to live with a cousin who worked as a prostitute around Tiger Bay. In 1884, she moved to London, working in the West End before leaving for Paris for several months. Soon back in London, she lived for a spell at a brothel on the Ratcliffe Highway before her life was socially transformed in 1887. While they did not formally marry, Mary and Joseph Barnett set up home together. He was a dock-worker and porter at the Smithfield Market and for a time they lived as a respectable working-class couple. The union, however, underwent serious strain when bouts of unemployment sent them to the pawn shop, unable to pay their rent. The couple argued when Mary offered overnight shelter on cold nights to friends who still worked as prostitutes. Eventually, Joe left her and Mary had to return to sex work. We only know about the life of Mary from a later investigation that was prompted by her murder; she was the last of the victims of 'The Ripper'. The arc of her career, however, seems to have been a common one, oscillating between 'respectable' domestic life and sex work according to precarious circumstances in a world of grinding poverty.

The second story comes from Henry Mayhew, a journalist and social researcher who interviewed working-class people in London. Published initially in the *Morning Chronicle* before being collated into book form, his interviews provide a rare glimpse of the women themselves and how they viewed their own lives. One young woman (he never recorded the name or address of those he spoke to) was by profession a 'slop maker', a job that supported herself, and her aged mother, and involved sewing up 'slops', or trousers, for a large ready-made-clothes manufacturer. When the work was constant, she made just enough money in a six-day week working eighteen hours a day to pay the rent on their one-room home and to afford two meals a day. However, when the work was sparse, the factory might only send her enough clothes for four days of employment. Rather than face starvation or the need to send her mother to the workhouse, she entered into a casual relationship with a man who paid her for sexual favours. 'I was virtuous when I first went to work, and I remained so until this last twelvemonth. I struggled very hard to keep myself chaste, but I found that I couldn't get food and clothing for myself and mother.' Common with the moral attitudes of the middle-class, she assured Mayhew that she had only done so out of necessity, and that she would have much rather have remained 'honest', no matter how hard the work. However, she also accepted the working-class pragmatism that viewed her behaviour as sensible and was confident enough with her own decision to be willing to have it recorded, knowing that her neighbours would not condemn her. 'Many young girls at the shop advised me to go wrong. They told me how comfortable they was off [sic]; they said they could get plenty to eat and drink, and good clothes.'

In the most deprived constituencies in large cities, prostitution could be more of a conscious choice among young women, who believed that it was their only realistic chance of having any youthful independence or pleasure. In such areas, especially in London, many young women began their sexual lives in impulsive relationships with young men of their own age when they were about fifteen. These romances were often brief and serial, in a pattern that we might be more familiar with today than most Victorians were. Many of these young women went on to have conventional married lives, but a proportion had a transitional period working as prostitutes. For this group of women, commercial sex seems to have had very different cultural connotations than for the more prosperous members of society. Among their peers, it was a stage of a woman's life cycle, rather than an abandonment of hopes and morals.

Of course, not all sex outside marriage involved commercial transactions. For many members of the urban working population, the definition of marriage was more fluid than the Church or the morally minded would have liked. In the first instance, it was often hard to work out who was married and who was not. If a new couple arrived in a neighbourhood and claimed to be married, they were very likely to be believed; proving otherwise was extremely difficult. In their own minds, they believed that they were married, and such a union was enough for them. For other couples, an informal proceeding of divorce and remarriage was practised by the simple expediency of moving house. Many friends, family and neighbours were happy to turn a blind eye to the legality of serial partnerships, as long as the children were still supported and the ordinary, day-to-day behaviour of the couple conformed to social rules.

Further up the social ladder, there were a number of famous unmarried couples. Marian Evans, the novelist who wrote under the name George Eliot, and George Lewes, the philosopher and critic, were perhaps the most well-known partnership, living openly as man and wife (he was unable to obtain a divorce from his first wife, Agnes). The difficulty in obtaining a divorce, or the complexities of the incest laws, where a man could marry his own first cousin but not his dead wife's sister or even his wife's aunt, forced a number of otherwise respectable couples into unions unsanctioned by law. The Victorian incest law was based upon biblical affinity rather than genetic considerations. Genetics was still an unknown science; Charles Darwin himself married his cousin. Meanwhile, the Church held that, upon marriage, a man and wife became, literally, one flesh. Thus, a wife's sister was viewed to be the same as one's own sister. For many Victorian families who had to contend with the death of a young wife, marriage of the widower to her sister seemed an ideal solution; she would be naturally inclined to love her dead sister's children and would not be a stranger entering the family home. Ethel Gladys Huxley, for example, accompanied by her father, travelled to Norway to marry her late sister's husband, John Collier, the portrait painter. Some wives actually made this their deathbed wish to their husbands. However, because the law was unequivocal, many families, including the Colliers and the Huxleys, married abroad in an attempt to circumvent the legislation.

The law was also abundantly clear on homosexual relationships. The act of sodomy had been illegal since 1535, and the law was re-enacted and strengthened in 1828. Yet attitudes towards same-sex relationships were to change as Victoria's reign progressed. Male homosexual behaviour simultaneously became more visible, as policing became more widespread and effective, and as the national press grew and became more salacious. In short, more cases were tried and more people heard about them. There remained, however, for most of the century, a degree of room for manoeuvre. Take the case of Boulton and Parke, two young men who liked to cross-dress and publicly flirt with men at the theatre and in the shopping arcades of the West End. For over two years they lived a flamboyantly camp lifestyle, sometimes in full 'drag', often in male clothing, with feminine make-up and scent. They were reported at their trial as attending the Oxford and Cambridge boat race, the Strand and Alhambra theatres, the casino in Holborn and several balls at West End hotels. By 1870, they had pushed their luck a little bit too far and found themselves in the dock. However, since no one could be found to come forward to say on oath that they had had sex with either of them, and coupled with a judge who proved lenient, they were acquitted. The case was eagerly followed by the press, but the general tone was one of amusement and tolerance rather than the abusive mobs that greeted the arrests of other men. Boulton and Parke took the pragmatic decision to lead more discreet lives after the case and the question of whether they were a couple, or not, was never publicly aired.

It was the commercial aspect of male homosexuality that dominated the growing public awareness and unease. The London-based national press (there were no regional correspondents) ensured that it was London's vice and Londoners' behaviour that dominated the ordinary Victorian's awareness of news. The West End had a reputation for all manner of sexual transactions, and Piccadilly Circus became the acknowledged centre for male 'cruising'. As public concerns escalated in the 1880s, homosexual behaviour was viewed as primarily a moral failing; a degrading and obscene act from a person or persons with no self-control. The notion that a person might be born homosexual was largely absent from the British psyche (although such ideas were being discussed on the continent). Homosexuality itself was primarily perceived as a trait of the wealthy classes. Working-class boys and men were often involved in homosexual behaviour, but people understood their motivation to be one of money. The general understanding was that the louche and dissolute wealthy man was preying on, or corrupting, working-class men, who would not have sought out such encounters otherwise. Soldiers were believed to be especially vulnerable. Their smart uniforms attracted attention and their low pay led them into temptation. Living away from the moral compasses of their families and often stationed in areas where they would be exposed to the company of wealthy men on the prowl, the soldier – and espe-cially the guardsman – became almost a stereotype of the working-class homosexual. Several of the most prominent prosecutions of the era involved young guardsmen.

There were generally believed to be a number of outward signs by which a man involved in homosexual behaviour could

Fig. 113. Guardsmen, the stereotype of the working-class homosexual.

be recognized. Some were quite deliberate: a man looking for a male sexual partner in the 1830s would tap the back of his hand or stick his thumbs into the armpit of his waistcoat and drum his fingers on his chest. Effeminate behaviour was generally perceived to be related to same-sex desires, but not exclusively; it could also be a sign that a man was overindulging in heterosexual sex. The effeminate man was advertising himself as sexually uncontrolled rather than as a lover of men. Shaving was more explicit. The clean-shaven man was not necessarily in the market for male sex, but most of those who were looking for masculine sexual part-ners were clean-shaven. One description of a group of young men who seemed unnaturally keen on amateur theatricals and dressing up as women delineated them as 'terribly clean-shaven'. If, however, you wanted to advertise your complete disinterest in male sexual partners, you whistled. The French writer upon sexual matters Charles Féré was quite categorical in his state-ment that those with homosexual desires were unable to whistle.

This 'fact' soon passed into common knowledge in Britain too.

The infamous trial of Oscar Wilde in 1895 (Wilde was sentenced to two years' hard labour for his sexual relationships) both expressed a heightened public intolerance for alternative male sexuality and fuelled the hostility. From this point onwards, men were extremely wary of touching one another in public, save for the handshake. The trial marked a turning point. The mainstream response to male physical attraction was more violent than ever, but a reaction was also setting in; the first stirrings of a different understanding about same-sex love were beginning.

In 1898, Havelock Ellis and John Symonds published a book, *Sexual Inversion*, which addressed the new ideas that were circulating on the continent about the nature of both male and female same-sex relationships. It included a number of British case studies for the first time. The book was effectively banned when the bookseller was fined £100 for putting it on sale, but it did mark the beginning of a new dawn in sexual thought. It also shone a weak light on the realm of female homosexuality. Ellis's wife, Edith (née Lees), was a lesbian and continued throughout their marriage to have relationships with women – with Havelock's knowledge. She and her friends provided much of the evidence in his book. Lesbian relationships had never been illegal and attracted little attention in the press. The world that she and her friends described was one of schoolgirl crushes, bed-sharing, heavy petting and oral sex, in descending order of frequency. Few women in this small survey of middle-class womanhood went as far as oral sex, but manual stimulation was described as reasonably common and no barrier to an idea of chastity or marriage with men. Outside of this group of researchers, Havelock Ellis reported on famous cases of women masquerading as men and his opinion that many prostitutes turned to female sexual partners for pleasure and comfort as a reaction against the experience of being paid for sex by men. In the main, though, there was silence.

Epilogue

As the Victorian world slips away at the end of our day, I am more aware than ever of how much remains hidden from our eyes, and of how brief and transitory any such exploration as this can be. Despite all the wonderful glimpses left behind to us from people such as Frederick Hobley and Alice Foley, their thoughts and recollections remain but a part of the story. The surviving objects, too, are but a selection, an ill-representative sample, of what once existed as testament to a way of life.

In part, this is the allure of history; the desire to piece together the evidence, to hunt down the clues and to measure the facts and opinions. I have enjoyed the search enormously: climbing over a surviving horse-drawn omnibus, trawling through the letters pages of newspapers and magazines for complaints about the transport system, tracing the routes on maps and calculating the structures of fares. Areas of life that had never appealed to me before I set out to write this book have taken me by surprise. Take sport, for instance, which ambushed me with its exuberance and playfulness. From Francis Kilvert enjoying croquet on the lawn, and admiring the ladies as he did so, to stories about footballers negotiating the rules before each match; from swimming as a sport that was propelled by a desire to provide laundry facilities for the poor, to tennis, which led the way in corset design. These were all revelations to me, and have made me look upon twenty-first-century sporting occasions with a more favourable eye than ever before.

The search has also taken me down harrowing avenues of hunger, disease, overwork and abuse. The Victorian era was a catastrophic time to be poor. People's skeletal remains provide the most graphic and incontrovertible evidence of lifelong hardship, with effects upon the body as bad as at any other point in our national history. Life expectancy slowly rose throughout the era and was considerably higher than the late-fourteenth-century low point after the Bubonic Plague first struck, but the chances of long-term malnutrition and of body-deforming dietary deficiencies in Victorian Britain were as bad as any we have ever known. Such a fact can be easily forgotten among the huge leaps forward that this era can boast, but it is one that any investigation into the ordinary is permeated with.

My research has given me tremendous sympathy and admiration for those who somehow, despite dire circumstances, battled through. People such as Tony Widger, who quietly worked away in his kitchen in his underwear at dawn, carefully preparing a cup of tea and a biscuit for him and his wife to have in bed before they embarked upon their exhausting day's industry of fishing and housework respectively. Or Hannah Cullwick, who was required to complete two hours of work before preparing her employer's breakfast, and then her own. And not to forget six-year-old William Arnold, who stood alone in a field in January from dawn until dusk scaring crows, without even a bite to eat until he walked home after dark. All these people, ordinary in so many ways, seem to me heroic in their endurance, fortitude, love and commitment to their families.

If I could speak to any of them back down the years, I would like to say 'thank you'. I cannot imagine that any of the great improvements that have made my life so much more comfortable and healthy could have happened without their efforts. It is not just the revolutionary ideas or the actions of the powerful that make the world, it is the cumulative work of everyone. Victorian Britons — we owe you.

Acknowledgements

This book would not have been possible without the help, and work, of a great many people. In particular, I should like to thank all those people who have shared with me, and made possible, the practical experiments into Victorian living that have so expanded my interest and understanding. To Peter , Alex, Stuart, Naomi, Felicia, Chris, Guilia, Tim, David, Nick and Tom, thank you for all the support and encouragement when we were stood in the freezing rain, for sympathy when the parsnip allergy raised those terrible blisters, for rescuing me when I set myself on fire, and in all those other moments of doubt. Thanks also to my parents, Geoff and Claire, and to Joan and Shona, who gave me the basic grounding in the practical matters of life, the skills that make Victorian living possible.

The biggest debt, of course, is to those Victorian people who left behind their opinions, thoughts, instructions and memories in written form, whose work left us the objects that help us to untangle something about their lives. Whatever their varied motives were in recording contemporary life, I am deeply grateful to the diarists Hannah Cullwick, Francis Kilvert, John Castle; those who wrote and kept their letters, such as Jane Carlyle; people such as Stephen Reynolds, who documented family life at the Widger household; to autobiographers such as Frederick Hobley, Alice Foley, Joseph Bell, Jack Lannigan, John Finney, William Arnold, Joseph Arch, Alfred Ireson, James Bonwick, Albert Goodwin, Kate Taylor, Fred Boughton, Faith Osgerby, Joseph Asby, George Bickers, Joseph Terry, James Carter, Mary Marshall, Thomas Cooper, Daniel Chater, Joseph

Burgess, James Hopkinson, Marianne Farningham, Charles Shaw, Robert Blincoe, James Saunders, Israel Roberts, John Bezer, Ernest Shotton, William Wright, Roger Langdon, Ben Brierley, Louise Jermy, William Chadwick, Robert Collyer, George Mockford and Francis Crittall.

While the journalist Henry Mayhew stands out in his description of real Victorian lives among his professional peers, the writers of a host of newspapers, journals and magazines have proved invaluable, and I have been able to mine the vast resources of publications including: *Illustrated London News*, *Illustrated News*, *The Times*, *Daily Telegraph*, *The Morning Chronicle*, *The Family Herald*, *The Quiver*, *The Boy's Own Paper*, *The Girl's Own Paper*, *The Christian*, *Household Words*, *The Englishwoman's Domestic Magazine*, *The Young Ladies' Journal*, *Bailey's Magazine*, *Gardening Magazine*, *The Windsor Magazine*, *Cassell's Household Magazine*, *The Ladies' Cabinet*, *Bell's Life*, *Athletic News*, *Manchester Guardian*, *Good Words*, *Sunday at Home*, *The Woman at Home*, *Macmillan Magazine* and *Sports Argus*.

I have much reason to be thankful to the Victorian writers of advice books and manuals for their help in unpicking the prevailing ideas, etiquette and practical know-how of the period. *Enquire Within* was the blockbuster that outsold all others; first published in 1856, over half a million copies had been sold by 1878. It spawned a host of spin-offs and copycat publications, all of which I have found as useful as the original. The medical works of Drs Pye Chevasse, William Acton, Thomas Ball, Archibald Donald, Mary Wood Allen, Sylvanus Stall, John McGregory Robertson, George Naphys, Elizabeth Blacklock, all primarily aimed at a lay audience, were packed with useful information, while writers such as William Cobbett, Edith Barnett, Donald Walker, Florence Nightingale, George Frederick Pardon, Harvey Newcomb, Mary Halliday, Eliza Acton, Mrs Rundell and Mrs Beeton offered insights into other areas of life.

In the twenty-first century, I am indebted to a host of historians, such as Helen Rogers, Pamela Horn, Patricia Branca, Jane Humphries, Wally Seccombe, Matt Cook, K. D. M. Snell, Paul Ell, John Tosh, Dennis Brailsford, Simon Inglis, Barry Reay, Patricia Malcolmson, Neil Storey, Peter Hodge, Sue Wilkes, Norman Longmate, Iona and Peter Opie, Kathryn Gleadle, Adam Kuper, Julia Laite, John Burnett, Anne Brogden, Ginger Frost, Fergus Linnane, Clare Rose, Christina Walkley, Vanda Foster, Hugh McLeod, C. Anne Wilson, John Harcup, Deborah Lutz, Janet Arnold, Rachel Worth, Deirdre Murphy, J. Honey and Valerie Saunders, for their enlightening and inspirational works, and to the team at Penguin, especially Ben, who have had such an important role to play in shaping this book.

Lastly, but most personally, to Mark and Eve, without whom I could simply not breathe.

Picture Credits

Black and White Images

1. © Bacup Natural History Society, *c.*1900. 2. *Illustrated London News*, 1850. 3. *Illustrated London News*, 1895. 4. *Illustrated London News*, 1886. 5. *The Times*, 1897. 6. *Needlework Magazine*, 1898. 7. *New York Journal and Advertiser*, 1898. 8. *Cassell's Household Guide*, 1869. 9. *Health Culture*, 1911. 10. *Health Culture*, 1911. 11. *Good Words Magazine*, 1876. 12. *Illustrated London News*, 1850. 13. *Illustrated London News*, 1850. 14. *Good Words Magazine*, 1876. 15. *Cassell's Family Magazine*, 1884. 16. *Wisbech Prison Particular Book* © Wisbech & Fenland Museum. 17. *Illustrated London News*, 1850 18. *Cassell's Family Magazine*, 1884. 19. *Cassell's Family Magazine*, 1884. 20. *Cassell's Family Magazine*, 1884. 21. *The Sunlight Yearbook*, 1897. 22. *Good Words Magazine*, 1880. 23. *Women's Penny Paper*, 1874. 24. *Common Sense Clothing*, 1869. 25. *The Englishwoman's Domestic Magazine*, 1863. 26. *Common Sense Clothing*, 1869. 27–8. *Common Sense Clothing*, 1869. 29. *New York Journal and Advertiser*, 1891. 30. *Punch*, 1856. 31. *The Graphic*, 1895. 32. *Cassell's Family Magazine*, 1889. 33. *The Ladies' Cabinet*, 1839. 34. *The Englishwoman's Domestic Magazine*, 1862. 35. *Punch*, 1857. 36. *Good Words Magazine*, 1875. 37. *The Englishwoman's Domestic Magazine*, 1863. 38. *London Labour and the London Poor*, 1861. 39. *Punch*, 1858. 40. *Daily Telegraph*, 1876. 41. *The Times*, 1873. 42. *The Sunlight Yearbook*, 1897. 43. *The Ladies' Cabinet Magazine*, 1839. 44. *Illustrated London News*, 1850. 45. *The Young Ladies' Journal*, 1863. 46. *Quiver Magazine*, 1875. 47. *Woman at Home*, 1902. 48. *The Women's Penny*

Paper, 1892. 49. *New York Journal and Advertiser*, 1898. 50. *The Young Ladies' Journal*, 1866. 51. *Illustrated London News*, 1850. 52. *Illustrated London News*, 1850. 53. *The Christian Magazine*, 1870. 54. *The Windsor Magazine*, 1900. 55. *The Penny Illustrated Paper*, 1870. 56. *The Christian Magazine*, 1886. 57. *Illustrated London News*, 1847. 58. *Illustrated London News*, 1862. 59. *Illustrated London News*, 1887. 60. *Sunday at Home Magazine*, 1866. 61. *Illustrated London News*, 1850. 62–3. *Good Words Magazine*, 1884. 64. *The Englishwoman's Domestic Magazine*, 1853. 65. *Illustrated London News*, 1857. 66. *Royal Commission Report*, 1842. 67. *Illustrated London News*, 1862. 68. *The Graphic*, 1889. 69. *Cassell's Household Guide*, 1869. 70. *Cassell's Household Guide*, 1869. 71–6. *Cassell's Household Guide*, 1869. 77. *Illustrated London News*, 1850. 78. *Good Words Magazine*, 1875. 79. *The Child's Companion Magazine*, 1850. 80. *Quiver Magazine*, 1875. 81. *The Graphic*, 1872. 82. *Cassell's Family Magazine*, 1884. 83. *Cassell's Household Guide*, 1869. 84. *The Sunlight Yearbook*, 1887. 85. *Cassell's Family Magazine*, 1884. 86. *Quiver Magazine*, 1875. 87. *Good Things*, 1848. 88. *The Housewife's Friend*, 1899. 89. *Illustrated London News*, 1846. 90. *The Graphic*, 1894. 91. *The Workwoman's Guide*, 1838. 92. *The Young Ladies' Journal*, 1866. 93. *Longman's Complete Course of Needlework*, 1904. 94. *Illustrated Times*, 1858. 95. *Illustrated London News*, 1863. 96. *Illustrated London News*, 1850. 97. *The Sunlight Yearbook*, 1875. 98. *Illustrated London News*, 1888. 99. *The Home Book*, 1868. 100. *The Child's Companion Magazine*, 1868. 101. *The Young Ladies' Journal*, 1866. 102. *The Home Book*, 1868. 103. *Illustrated London News*, 1850. 104. *The Home Book*, 1868. 105. *The Sunlight Yearbook*, 1887. 106. *Punch*, 1873. 107. *Good Words Magazine*, 1876. 108. *Illustrated London News*, 1850. 109. *Cassell's Household Guide*, 1880. 110. *Pictorial Times*, 1844. 111. *Illustrated London News*, 1875. 112. *The Christian Magazine*, 1886. 113. *Punch*, 1873.

Colour Images

1. © Lion Television Limited. Photographer: Felicia Gold. 2. © Lion Television Limited. Photographer: Laura Rawlinson. 3. © Lion Television Limited. Photographer: Laura Rawlinson. 4. © Lion Television Limited. Photographer: Laura Rawlinson. 5. *Cassell's Household Guide*, 1869. 6. *Our Dining Room at York*, 1838, Best, Mary Ellen (1809–91)/Private Collection/The Bridgeman Art Library. 7. *Baby's Birthday*, 1867 (oil on canvas), Hardy, Frederick Daniel (1826–1911)/© Wolverhampton Art Gallery, West Midlands, UK/The Bridgeman Art Library. 8. *A Chelsea Interior*, 1857 (oil on canvas), Tait, Robert Scott (fl.1845–75)/Carlyle's House, London, UK/National Trust Photographic Library/John Hammond/The Bridgeman Art Library. 9. 2010EE8072-01 © Victoria and Albert Museum, London. 10. 2006BB1093-01 © Victoria and Albert Museum, London. 11. 2006AG4301-01 © Victoria and Albert Museum, London. 12. 2006AM0993-01 © Victoria and Albert Museum, London. 13. 2008BU0053-01 © Victoria and Albert Museum, London. 14. 1000LM0575-01 © Victoria and Albert Museum, London. 15. 1991-1-1 Garden Seat Omnibus 7061 © Wardown Park Museum. 16. *Cassell's Household Magazine*, 1889. 17. *Mrs Winslow's Soothing Syrup* advert, 1870. 18. *The Child's Companion*, 1879. 19. Benjamin Disraeli, 1826. Illustration for John Player Dandies cigarette card series. © Look and Learn History Picture Library. 20. *Cassell's Household Guide*, 1869. 21. *The Girl's Own Paper*, 1886. 22. *Cassell's Household Guide*, 1880. 23. *Lambeth Baths Gymnasium* advert, 1881. 24. *The Music Hall*, 1889 (oil on canvas), Sickert, Walter Richard (1860–1942)/Musée des Beaux-Arts, Rouen, France/Giraudon/The Bridgeman Art Library.

Index

Page references in *italic* indicate Figures.